THIS BIRTH PLACE OF SOULS

e are told we must leave the ground, a gener
der has been given. Mrs. F. was determined t
oss the river, although Col. Chamberlain wrot
 note discouraging it. We left us and took
mbulance while a   the Smith hou
 had no sooner   than I receiv
 note that a   a then on th
ay who neve   Husband h
me and was   Mrs. Mc Kay
on made her   across the ri
e. I procured a del   them broth over a camp
We fed the men,   as another tra
rning Mrs. Fogg dete   to remain and get
pper for them, while I went on with the team.
on after we started a tremendous thunder a
il storm commenced the ambulance leaked
 sever and notwithstanding I had two quilts
was drenched to my skin. I met the 6th Mai
d Capt's Furlong and Busford assured me
ugh's safety. He was with the Colonel.
Wednesday, May 6th.   Well, last night I had a
                  The streams were so swollen the

This Birth Place of Souls

THE CIVIL WAR NURSING DIARY OF HARRIET EATON

EDITED WITH

AN INTRODUCTION BY

Jane E. Schultz

OXFORD
UNIVERSITY PRESS

OXFORD
UNIVERSITY PRESS

Oxford University Press, Inc., publishes works that further
Oxford University's objective of excellence
in research, scholarship, and education.

Oxford   New York
Auckland   Cape Town   Dar es Salaam   Hong Kong   Karachi
Kuala Lumpur   Madrid   Melbourne   Mexico City   Nairobi
New Delhi   Shanghai   Taipei   Toronto

With offices in
Argentina   Austria   Brazil   Chile   Czech Republic   France   Greece
Guatemala   Hungary   Italy   Japan   Poland   Portugal   Singapore
South Korea   Switzerland   Thailand   Turkey   Ukraine   Vietnam

Copyright © 2011 by Oxford University Press, Inc.

Published by Oxford University Press, Inc.
198 Madison Avenue, New York, NY 10016

www.oup.com

First published as an Oxford University Press paperback, 2012.
The 2011 hardcover edition includes a comprehensive biographical dictionary.

Oxford is a registered trademark of Oxford University Press.

All rights reserved. No part of this publication may be reproduced,
stored in a retrieval system, or transmitted, in any form or by any means,
electronic, mechanical, photocopying, recording, or otherwise,
without the prior permission of Oxford University Press.

Library of Congress Cataloging-in-Publication Data
Eaton, Harriet, 1818–1884.
This birth place of souls : the Civil War nursing diary of Harriet
Eaton / by Harriet Eaton ; edited with an introduction by Jane E.
Schultz.
p. cm.
Includes bibliographical references and index.
ISBN 978-0-19-539268-5 (hardcover : alk. paper); 978-0-19-989954-8 (paperback: alk. paper)
1. Eaton, Harriet, 1818–1884—Diaries. 2. Eaton, Harriet,
1818–1884—Correspondence. 3. Nurses—United States—Diaries.
4. Nurses—United States—Correspondence. 5. Women—Maine—Diaries.
6. United States—History—Civil War, 1861–1865—Personal narratives.
7. Maine—History—Civil War, 1861–1865—Personal narratives. 8. Military
nursing—United States—History—19th century. 9. United
States—History—Civil War, 1861–1865—Medical care. 10. United
States—History—Civil War, 1861–1865—Women. I. Schultz, Jane E. II. Title.
E621.E24 2010
973.7'75—dc22   2010010270

Printed in the United States of America
on acid-free paper

FOR MY DAUGHTER, MIRANDA JUNE HOEGBERG

CONTENTS

Introduction   *1*

THE DIARY
53

1862 | October 6 to December 31
55

1863 | January 1 to May 12
101

1864 | October 12 to December 24
151

Notes   *185*

APPENDIXES
197

Letters, Newspaper Accounts, and Official Correspondence
Concerning Harriet Eaton
199

Biographical Dictionary
229

Bibliography   251

Index   267

ACKNOWLEDGMENTS

The labors large and small of an army of historians, archivists, friends, and strangers are represented in this book. Few people are aware of how complex and detailed the historical work of archivists is and how centrally important they are to those of us who want to understand the past. To that end, my first thanks go to the staff of the Maine Historical Society at the historic site of the William Wadsworth Longfellow House on Congress Street in Portland: to Jamie Kingman Rice, Nick Noyes, and Dani Fazio for answering my persistent questions, and to archivists extraordinaire William Barry and Stephanie Philbrick, both of whom went above and beyond the call of duty to help me track down elusive references with poise and patience. Anthony Douin, Jeff Brown, and Stephen Dean of the Maine State Archives in Augusta helped me with manuscripts in the Maine Relief Agencies Collection and with the rich trove of photographs among the state's Civil War holdings. Anthony in particular was tireless in answering my many questions. I also extend heartfelt thanks to Lynda Sudlow, author of *A Vast Army Of Women* (2000), for graciously sharing her expertise and documents relating both to Harriet Eaton's life and to several of the Mainers mentioned in the biographical dictionary. Elizabeth Leonard of Colby College and the late Marli Weiner of the University of Maine in Orono helped me make connections with Mainers who could be of service, and I thank them for their critical feedback. My thanks are due also to Judy Bielecki for sharing her knowledge of Isabella Fogg; to Brian McCarthy, a descendent of the Eatons' housekeeper in the 1850s; to Patricia Burdick, special collections librarian at Miller Library, Colby College, in Waterville; and to Michael C. Lord of the Androscoggin Historical Society in Auburn. The reference librarians at the Portland Public Library, especially those in the periodical and microforms room, made my hours of poring over old local newspapers far more congenial on surprisingly hot Portland summer afternoons.

Archivists and librarians outside of Maine were also quite helpful: Fran Blouin, Karen Jania, and Shannon Wait at the Bentley Historical Library of the Michigan Historical Collections in Ann Arbor; Richard C. Malley and Cynthia Harbeson of the Connecticut Historical Society in Hartford; Thomas Wilsted and Laura Katz Smith of the Thomas J. Dodd Research Center at the University of Connecticut in Storrs for their help with the Eaton letters housed there; Cynthia Harris of the Jersey City Public Library in New Jersey; Suzanne Hahn, director of reference at the Indiana Historical Society in Indianapolis; Edward L. DeSanctis of the Oneida County History Society in Utica, New York; John J. Devine, Jr., of the reference department at the Boston Public Library; Conrad E. Wright and Peter Drummey, archivists at the Massachusetts Historical Society in Boston; Paul Carnahan, librarian at the Vermont State Library in Montpelier; Rebecca Federman of the New York Public Library; the archivists at the New-York Historical Society in Manhattan; Zachary W. Elder of the Duke University libraries in Durham, North Carolina; Kathy Shoemaker of the Woodruff Library, Emory University special collections in Atlanta; and Greg Cohen, a 2007 graduate in history at Emory and a young man I have known since he was *in utero*, for his assistance with the C. B. Thurston papers. I also wish to thank the reference librarians at the Martin Luther King, Jr., Memorial Library in Washington, D.C.; Mike Klein, senior reference librarian, and Rodney Katz of the humanities and social sciences division at the Library of Congress, Washington, D.C.; Stephen Greenberg of the history of medicine division at the National Library of Medicine, National Institutes of Health, in Bethesda, Maryland; and Deborah Van Broekhoven of the American Baptist Historical Society in Atlanta. John Brinsfield of the U.S. Army Chaplain Corps in Fort Jackson, South Carolina, and Benedict Maryniak of Buffalo, New York, helped me with biographical information about the chaplains Harriet Eaton encountered. Ben, in particular, deserves thanks for his timely aid.

I had the pleasure of completing the last portion of the labors associated with Eaton's diary while I was on sabbatical at the University of Sydney in 2007. My greatest debt is to History Department member Dr. Frances M. Clarke for her extraordinary generosity on many fronts and for the sheer originality of her ideas about social constructions of suffering during the American Civil War. In Frances, I found a friend, colleague, and hiking partner with whom I look forward to collaborating on many projects in the future. For intellectual inspiration, I thank Frances' colleagues Robert Aldridge, Penny Russell, Judith Keene, Alison Bashford, Nick Eckstein, Clare Corbould, Kirsten McKenzie, Julia Horne, Stephen Robertson, and Iain McCalman; and Susan Thomas and Penny Gay in the Sydney University Deparment of English—all of whom made me feel at home at the other end of the world. Angela Woollacott, director of Women's Studies at Maquarie University in western Sydney, a scholar whose work I have admired for many years, and Tom Buchanan of the History Department at the University of Adelaide both provided academic venues for me to present ideas connected with this project, and for these opportunities I am grateful. Sydney University staff members Carolyne Carter, Elia Mamprin, Joanne Harris, Nikki Whipps, and Mervyn Ui smoothed my transition to a new university and library system with informative good cheer.

I am blessed with generous colleagues and students at Indiana University-Purdue University-Indianapolis without whose help in all manner of areas from technology to bibliography and back again this book would have been the poorer. Nancy Eckerman of the Lilly Medical Library of Indiana University spent days helping me identify the three-score surgeons with whom Harriet Eaton interacted during her months in Virginia. Sharon Fish, Tina Baich, and Becky Mock of IUPUI's interlibrary loan staff made it possible for me to find the many nineteenth-century books about Maine that the Hoosier State lacks. Reference librarians Karen Janke, Kristi Palmer, Jaena Hollingsworth, Jim Baldwin, and Delores Hoyt helped me with a bevy of questions as I prepared annotations. I hardly know how to thank Diana Dial Reynolds for her help with census data. Diana provided research assistance out of all proportion to the time she had available with nary a complaint. Thanks to the incomparable Bridget Brown for indexing services.

Joy Kramer, Mike Scott, Bill Stuckey, Wayne Husted, and Michael Maitzen, Indiana University School of Liberal Arts technologists, eased my way in the brave new world of computing and digital reproduction. A bushel of thanks to English Department secretaries Pat King and Wanda Colwell for administrative assistance with this project, as well as Sharon Peterman, Rick Hanson, Merle Illg, Gen Shaker, Edith Millikan, Becky Renollet, and Annette Hill in the Dean's office of the School of Liberal Arts for helping with fellowship money so that I could travel twice to the Maine Historical Society and state archives. Associate Dean for Research David Ford and Dean Robert White of Liberal Arts encouraged and supported my travel, even as I struggled in 2004 and 2005 with breast cancer. Medical Humanities Program colleagues William Schneider, Emily Beckman, Judi Izuka-Campbell, Fran Brahmi, and Dr. Margaret Gaffney were also generous with their time.

Several friends offered hospitality and several others, their professional expertise. My friend of thirty-five years, Dr. Robert H. Kieft, former head of the Haverford College libraries and now at Occidental College, put me in touch with archivists who could answer my esoteric questions and provided me many a web address when I was on the sleuthing trail. Sarah Stanbury of the English Department at Holy Cross College in Worcester, Massachusetts, answered questions about Boston-area geography. I had the good fortune to find Erik Jorgensen, Director of the Maine Humanities Council, who, along with his wife Tamara Risser and son Will provided me a guest room in their sprawling Portland home for two "down East" weeks free of charge. Lisa MacFarlane of the University of New Hampshire also provided hospitality. How glad I am to have been acquainted with Kitty Hauser and Peter Wilson of Sydney, Australia, for a room with a view.

After the initial publication of this volume, Nicholas P. Picerno of Bridgewater, Virginia, contacted me with further information about several Maine regiments and material about Frank Eaton's life. I am indebted to Chief Picerno for his generosity in sharing his archive, especially the photograph of Frank.

The greatest debt scholars incur is to those who read and critique the manuscript. Thanks to the three anonymous readers engaged by Oxford University Press, and to Frances Clarke, Lyn Sudlow, Amanda Porterfield, and Phil Goff. Nancy Toff, Sonia Tycko, Leora Bersohn, Jaimee Biggins, and Michael Philoantonie at Oxford University Press were models of diligence and good humor as we journeyed from manuscript to book. If I have been foolish enough not to implement their suggestions, I will undoubtedly regret it later. My sister-in-law Chyai Mulberg helped me with countless details from her home base in Fairfield, Connecticut. She, my parents, Bobbye and Bud Schultz, and my friends Shawn Kimmel, Kathleen Junk, and Gina Laite are good as gold and unconditionally contribute peace and richness to my life and work. Thank you all.

Introduction

Harriet Eaton of Portland, Maine, was thirty-eight when her husband Jeremiah, a Baptist minister, died in 1856 of a respiratory illness resembling tuberculosis. Left to raise their three children (aged thirteen, seven, and one), Eaton managed to support the family for nearly six years with help from friends and fellow congregants of Portland's Free Street Baptist Church (FSBC). In October 1862, when Maine had already sent twenty-one regiments of soldiers to war and while the disastrous human losses at Antietam three weeks earlier were still freshly felt, the Free Street Church organized the Maine Camp Hospital Association (MCHA) to provide relief services to Mainers in the field. Harriet Eaton and Isabella Fogg, a thirty-nine-year-old working-class widow from Calais, Maine, were the first women dispatched by the MCHA to go to those soldiers.[1] Eaton closed up her home, left one of her daughters with friends in nearby Gorham, and sent her other daughter to school near Boston. Her eldest child, nineteen-year-old Frank, had recently volunteered with a Maine regiment; Eaton undertook her service in the hope that she might occasionally catch a glimpse of him. She reasoned that if she cared for other women's sons, perhaps her own would meet with better care.[2]

Women all over New England responded quickly and in large numbers when news reached them that sick and wounded men were perishing for want of aid in tent and field hospitals far from home. In the political landscape of the Union, every soldier was a son of the nation, and those laid low by wounds or disease deserved a full battery of domestic comforts. The women who ultimately performed relief labors in Union military camps participated in the largest mobilization of wartime benevolence up to that point in the history of the United States. They brought their homely talents to the war front by cooking, carrying, and cleaning; in effect they domesticated medical work.

Like scores of other educated nineteenth-century women, Harriet Eaton charted her wartime life in a diary, assessing the significance of the national events around her even as they were unfolding. As one of more than twenty-one thousand northern women who performed domestic and administrative tasks in military hospitals throughout the war, Eaton was motivated by a sense of religious obligation and a political mandate that freed her from typical constraints on middle-aged, middle-class widows to lead retiring and unobtrusive lives of usefulness. Women like Eaton were "summoned to war, charged to patriotism," encouraged to move beyond the script of republican motherhood into a more direct relation with civic agency, resulting from a patriotic groundswell of support that placed men's and women's duty to the nation before their domestic obligations. Whereas women's public visibility had excited comment and even criticism in the first decades of the nineteenth century, it was now central to the project of waging a civil war.[3]

This was not a sudden shift, but a gradual one in which the domestic realm of women's influence expanded to accommodate the more public channels of their war service. Though this visibility gave northern women identity as a national body, it was local groups that provided the foundation for women's war work. Even as the United States Sanitary Commission (USSC) was building a national reputation by taking charge of local aid societies, war goods were still prepared in homes and churches by women with a stake in their local communities. And despite the USSC's growing power and influence, hundreds of women like Eaton sought relief positions through churches and unaffiliated state agencies, having little to do with the federal network of benevolence.[4]

Beyond her wish to be near a son at war, Harriet Eaton's reasons for volunteering to care for soldiers from her state are complex and not plainly expressed. Not only was she witness to the growth of women's patriotic action on behalf of Union soldiers, she was also a deeply religious wife and mother who had endured personal loss and believed that easing the suffering of Maine troops would heighten and consecrate her devotion to God. Eaton had spent more than fifteen years in a prominent congregational position when the war began—three of those nursing her ailing husband—and was therefore well situated to become the FSBC's chief deputy in the cause of soldiers' aid. Eaton's religious convictions, best understood against the backdrop of unprecedented growth in the New England Baptist Church twenty years before the war, impelled her to serve God through tending those who had willingly resigned their domestic comforts and familial base.[5] As a Baptist, Eaton was conversant with a theology that represented the war as both a penalty for the "corruptions of mammon" and a test of faith that could galvanize and redeem the fractured nation's millennial destiny. Personal sacrifice in the form of war service thus provided individuals like Eaton the opportunity to become better Christians.[6]

The abolition of slavery also figured into Eaton's decision to volunteer. In an era when northern politicians and lawyers could not discover how to bring an end to human bondage, citizens looked to the clergy for guidance.[7] Under Jeremiah Eaton's leadership in the 1840s and in concert with many other New England congregations, the Free Street Church had taken a firm stand against slavery, consistent with the denominational schisms that had created the northern and southern branches of the church in the same decade.[8] Eaton thus viewed her service as a kind of mission whereby she might, in addition to nursing soldiers, extend charity to slaves, who by 1862 sought safe harbor by the thousands in Union military camps.[9] However, once white New Englanders were forced into close quarters with runaway slaves, or "contrabands" as they were called before Emancipation, their idealized view of racial equality began to unravel.[10] If Eaton was more liberal than other white women in her willingness to work with African Americans, her diary entries surely confirm that people of color were at best cultural novelties and at worst, nuisances. Though initially fascinated with black religious services in the camps of the Army of the Potomac, she came to avoid these meetings, which she associated with the quaint and primitive.

Eaton's work, and that of others who provided wartime relief, constitutes a transitional period in the history of American nursing. Before the war, "nurse" was an unstable term, referring to a broad range of domestic activities. Women with husbands and children would have spent substantial time nursing their intimates, and many would have witnessed death—though not on the unprecedented scale of the war years.[11] As a result of the war, antebellum perceptions of nursing as exclusively domestic work began to change. Before 1870, those who had been connected with the wartime bureaucratization of care discussed how professional nurse training might benefit medicine. By 1873, they sought to open the first U.S. schools of nursing in Massachusetts, New York, and Connecticut based on a model already pioneered by Britain's Florence Nightingale in the wake of the Crimean War.[12] American educators hoped to gain scientific credibility for nursing as a profession connected to, but distinct from, medicine. This mandate was pivotal in moving nursing from its domestic status as Everywoman's vocation to a scientific course of study that produced female professionals.

Eaton's diary provides an open window into the early (dis)organization of Union medical and relief systems. It was not uncommon in the first two years of the war for churches to send volunteers to minister to soldiers in camp and field hospitals. The MCHA, formed by parishioners at the FSBC in the autumn of 1862, deputized Eaton and Isabella Fogg to be its representatives in Virginia. By 1863, Maine legislators had established a centralized relief organization, which became a clearinghouse and command post for all of the local aid groups in the state. Thus, even as the MCHA perfected its supply procedures, it was subject to the authority of the Maine State [Relief] Agency (MSRA), which meant that Eaton's reports from military camps went first to MSRA chief executive John H. Hathaway and afterward to MCHA workers in Portland.

This model of grass-roots organization reflects what happened at the national level as well. A federal relief bureaucracy emerged only after local groups had begun to supply men in the ranks. In May 1861, after scores of women had answered ads in their local papers calling for nursing volunteers, Acting Surgeon General R. C. Wood appointed asylum reformer Dorothea Dix to handle the appointment of Union nurses. Dix worked steadily to appoint women she deemed respectable and sober, but it soon became clear that vetting a nursing staff one individual at a time was impractical. In June, a group of well-to-do New Yorkers formed the USSC to centralize the distribution of supplies and to appoint its own stable of workers. Although the USSC wished to coordinate the efforts of small-fry aid groups, its leaders came to discover that many groups—like the MCHA and the MSRA, which had already sent workers into the field—had little interest in being managed by a larger body. Though many local and state groups did cooperate with the USSC, others did not. Because the MCHA remained independent of federal benevolent groups, Eaton was not compelled to pass muster with Superintendent of Army Nurses Dix or with the legion of USSC gatekeepers when she first went to Virginia in 1862. By 1864, however, when Eaton worked at City Point, military administrators held a tighter rein over the haphazard nature of voluntarism in an attempt to regulate the entry and exit of relief personnel.

Military camps and hospitals were thronged with civilians from all walks of life, which created frustration and discipline problems for military leaders attempting to wage war, even when the presence of those civilians was not disruptive. With multiple bodies at the local, state, and federal levels formally and informally authorizing relief personnel, not to mention individuals who volunteered independently, benevolent work was chaotic in the war's early years. Although citizens and government collaborated to provide more efficient relief efforts by mid-war, the sheer scale of a war fought in several theaters made centralization impossible. Into this hive of civilians, who sometimes worked at cross purposes, came Maine's Harriet Eaton.

EATON'S DIARY IN CONTEXT

Eaton's diary is a rarity in the constellation of Civil War nursing accounts. Though thousands of women active in the service wrote letters, fewer than sixty wrote full-length narratives of their medical relief work.[13] Of these, only five, including Eaton's, are unreconstructed diaries. The memoirs and reminiscences that constitute the balance of this canon were still being published in the first half of the twentieth century, and more recently as new sources have been uncovered.[14] Kate Cumming, the Scottish-born spinster daughter of a merchant living in Mobile, Alabama, was the only nurse to publish her own diary, and she did so in 1866 without much return on her investment. The diaries of Ada Bacot, Esther Hill Hawks, and Hannah Ropes were published in a fourteen-year span late in the twentieth century, indicating new scholarly interest in women's wartime medical roles.[15] These editions have brought to light the diverse circumstances of women who volunteered to do relief work. All of the diarists—Bacot, a widowed slaveholder from Darlington County, South Carolina; Hawks, a physician from New Hampshire who practiced among African American soldiers and Sea Island residents in 1863; and Ropes, a Massachusetts reformer and women's rights activist who had homesteaded in "Bleeding Kansas" in the 1850s—wished to relieve suffering, but each enunciated unique motivations, given her age, region, racial identity, marital status, and religious beliefs. Like Bacot's, Hawks's, and Ropes's diaries, Eaton's remained unpublished for more than a century after the war. In private hands until 1942, when Eaton's daughter Hatty Belle died, the diary landed in a Hartford bookshop and then in the Southern Historical Collection at the University of North Carolina, where scholars were slow to recognize its unusual eyewitness perspective on the web of Civil War medical relief services.

In this small field of diaries, Eaton's is distinctive for two reasons: First, it chronicles the challenges of roving regimental nursing in the field. "Roving" nursing differed from the experience of those stationed at one location in that traveling with and provisioning troops presented a variety of practical challenges. All field workers found transience wearing, but most were able to set up shop in a single place for days or months at a time in contrast to rovers like Eaton, who early in the war seldom knew two nights at the same location. When field hospitals moved to new locations, shadowing the movements of armies, nurses like Kate Cumming would pack up and move to a new semi-permanent location. Eaton's diary entries of 1862 and 1863 illuminate a different protocol: Instead of moving en masse to new, centralized installations where soldiers would come to the hospital, Eaton and her coworkers traveled from regiment to regiment, rendering mobile care and assistance to soldiers and surgeons, even as those regiments were on the move. Even though the second division hospital in Falmouth, which Eaton calls the "quarters," gave her a home base during the winter of 1862–63, she also traveled daily to two or three regiments, logging scores of miles every week. Eaton was responsible for men in more than ten Maine regiments and thus performed more administrative labor than women who went to war with specific regiments. Whether a rover, like Eaton, or the wife of a soldier attached to a specific regiment, such women were certainly the Civil War's original field nurses.[16] The far more common relief idiom was that of the urban general hospital worker, who neither lived the dislocations of war that field nurses did, nor were exposed to soldiers freshly removed from the field or too critically ill to be moved.

Second, Eaton's diary is noteworthy for its account of the work of state-sponsored relief agents who chose to remain aloof from the structures of federal benevolence, and in so doing exposed the political tensions implicit in the delivery of wartime relief services. Postwar narratives lionized the achievements of the two Union benevolent giants—the Sanitary and Christian commissions—because their authors frequently played a part in those organizations.[17] Eaton's critique of the USSC in particular shows a New Englander's mistrust of large, centralized bureaucracy, despite the success of that bureaucracy to convince most citizens of the Union that it had the best interests of their sons and husbands in mind. Mainers had a reputation for skepticism among USSC administrators. Abby May, secretary of the women's auxiliary of the New England Soldiers' Relief Association—one of the groups that worked in tandem with the USSC—attempted to convince Mainers that the USSC would responsibly distribute their contributions, but to no avail. Mainers wanted to collect and distribute on their own terms.[18] Although the federal commissions credited themselves exclusively for their wartime largesse, diarists like Eaton revealed that there was little agreement about who should be in charge of or take credit for soldiers' relief.

The five extant nurses' diaries share structural and thematic similarities, but the diarists' social positions and their political sensibilities make for striking differences. Only one, Kate Cumming's *A Journal of Hospital Life* (1866), was published during the author's lifetime, and it is also the most extensive account of relief work, covering a nearly continuous service of three years, from the April 1862 battle of Shiloh to her return home in late May 1865. As a single woman in her late thirties, Cumming brought out her diary in 1866 as a money-making venture to forestall scarcity and nearly went broke (and hungry) trying to find readers. Though she testifies that the account "is given without alteration," it is clear, since she anticipated an audience and discusses her preparation of the diary in postwar letters, that she edited the manuscript.[19] Her organization of the diary into chapters corresponding with sites in Surgeon Samuel Stout's "flying hospital" system is certainly one intervention, and the long narrative describing her return to Mobile in 1865 is another.[20]

Cumming's political candor and fierce Confederate loyalty are emblematic of the localism and exceptionalism that permeate her diary. Partisan passion is everywhere evident, from her criticism of Abraham Lincoln ("How long will the people of the North submit to this Moloch[?]") to her denunciations of Yankeedom ("Can such a people expect to prosper?").[21] Although antebellum pundits described elite white Southerners as placid and accommodating, especially where their men were concerned, Cumming's diary provides a signal defense of women's right to nurse and to confront surgical tyranny in Confederate hospitals—positions that align her more closely with northern reformers like Hannah Ropes and Esther Hill Hawks than her countrywoman Ada Bacot. All of the diarists, and Cumming is no exception, demonstrate their religious fervor through common rhetorical structures and frequent references to churchgoing. Despite their political differences over slavery, Protestant Americans in both sections of the country believed that they were fighting a holy war and that God would redeem the victor.[22] Like Eaton, Cumming notes which of her patients died as Christians and regularly quotes scripture, but she differs from Eaton in her insistence on divine retribution for the invading North. To Eaton's mind, the atrocities of war placed judgment at the doorstep of her own people.

The evangelical mood that swept the United States during the Second Great Awakening and was still much in evidence during the 1860s also punctuates the diary of Ada Bacot, who referred to herself as a "Soldier of Christ."[23] As with Eaton, widowhood was a spur to Bacot's service, and like Eaton and Cumming, Bacot sought the opportunity to nurse through church associations—in her case, the Episcopal Church of South Carolina. Just twenty-eight when the war began, Bacot had lost her young family in a five-year period during the 1850s: her husband in a brawl with their overseer and two toddlers to disease. Believing that she could find the personal satisfaction and redemption that had eluded her in domestic life, she traveled to the Monticello Hospital in Charlottesville, Virginia, to nurse men from the Palmetto State. Despite the difficulty of obtaining money for the trip and disapproving family acquaintances who feared the impropriety of her plan, Bacot began her service late in 1861 and kept a periodic account of her hospital life for slightly more than a year. Because the Confederate medical department never instituted a national aid auxiliary like the USSC or the Christian Commission, southern states remained powerful actors in the delivery of relief services. In the absence of a Confederate umbrella relief agency, Bacot's service, and that of most southern workers, confirmed the autonomy of individual states to establish their own procedures.

Turbulent social relations are the hallmark of Bacot's diary: She pores over the daily travails of the medical staff at the Charlottesville hospitals, all of whom were quartered in the same residence. She develops a close friendship with an attractive, married doctor whom she nurses when he contracts erysipelas (a streptococcal inflammation), and she takes a perverse delight in recording the less-than-ladylike behavior of a coworker to whom she feels morally and socially superior ("I never saw any one who could pervert things as [Esse] does. It is distressing to think we should have had such a person among us all this time, one whom we have shown so much kindness"). Though Bacot was thrilled to perform relief work, her responsibilities—cooking meals and attending to laundry—diminished her direct contact with soldiers in contrast to other female relief workers on site.[24] Still, Bacot's diary is significant because it illuminates the lives of Confederate medical staff from the perspective of a planter whose dedication to her state ultimately trumped her aversion to slaves and people of lesser social status. As it did for many Civil War nurses, Bacot's service offered a welcome reprieve from family cares, and despite inevitable sorrow and inconvenience, she thrived in Charlottesville, bursting bonds that had confined her to a narrower sphere back home.

Esther Hill Hawks is the only diarist who had a husband during her term of service.[25] Hawks was working as a schoolteacher in Manchester, New Hampshire, when she married John Milton Hawks in 1854. Also a teacher, Milton sought a medical degree in the 1840s and graduated from Cincinnati's Eclectic Medical College in 1847, though he did not open a practice until 1852. Esther's own training as a physician began unofficially when she discovered Milton's medical textbooks. By 1855, she had enrolled in the New England Female Medical College in Boston, where the celebrated German-American physician Marie Zakrzewska became her mentor.[26] Although Milton was an advocate of woman suffrage as early as 1848, he was less enthusiastic about Esther's growing medical acumen, observing in 1864, "I wish Ette had never seen a medical book, or heard a lecture. It is not a businessman-like worker that a husband needs—It is a loving woman...."[27]

In spite of his jealousy, Esther was able to practice medicine during the war, thanks to Milton's military connections. In April 1862, after Union forces had invaded the Sea Islands, he was appointed to oversee the health care of blacks on the Edisto Island plantations, and by July, General Rufus Saxton had appointed him surgeon at a military hospital in Beaufort that served African American soldiers. When Esther joined him in October, it was after an unsuccessful attempt to pass muster with nursing superintendent Dix, who thought the twenty-six-year-old too frail and inexperienced. Sent initially to the Sea Islands as a teacher by the National Freedman's Relief Association, Esther cared for Milton's African American patients in his absence. Even though medical administrators would have paled at the unseemly prospect of a woman physician treating soldiers—and a white woman, at that—Hawks practiced with impunity because the patients were people of color who were of little concern to overtaxed medical administrators. "I performed the duties of hospital and Regimental Surg.," she wrote, "doing the work so well that the neglect to supply...regular officers was not discovered at Hd. Qrtrs. I suppose I could not have done this if my brother had not been hospital steward—or if the patients had been white men...."[28] Hawks was well aware that those who professed abolition often treated real African Americans with contempt. Though diary entries are periodic and not daily,[29] readers gain insight into the lives of black soldiers from the perspective of a northeastern white woman. Hawks's diary thus distinguishes itself not only because she is the only woman physician to have written one, but because the diary chronicles an interracial medical practice.

Like Hawks and Eaton, Hannah Chandler Ropes was an abolitionist, but one for whom the war was not the defining event in a life filled with reform activism. Ropes was born in 1809 to a large and prominent family in New Gloucester, Maine, not far from Portland, and by 1836, two years after her marriage to school administrator William Henry Ropes of Bangor, they moved to Bedford, Massachusetts, where Hannah's abolitionist sentiments simmered as she raised a family. In the late 1840s, William Ropes abandoned the family and moved to Florida, leaving Hannah to fend for her two children.[30] Increasingly involved in free soil debates over slavery, Ropes joined her son Edward in the frontier outpost of Lawrence, Kansas, in 1855 and toughed it out for six months before returning to Massachusetts, weary of the violent clashes between pro- and antislavery agitators. She published an account of this episode in 1856 and followed this with a novel, *Cranston House* (1859), which fictionalized the Kansas events and centered on a male hero patterned after her son. At age fifty, Ropes had been head of a household for nearly fifteen years, had published two books, and had traveled fifteen hundred miles across the continent to work for political change. She was an independent and worldly wise woman when she sought a nursing position in Washington in 1862.

Though Ropes served at Georgetown's ill-equipped Union Hotel Hospital for just six months before she succumbed to typhoid—the same affliction contracted by coworker Louisa May Alcott and that made Ropes the only one of the diarists to die in the service[31]—she lost no time in ameliorating conditions there. When her complaints to Surgeon General William Hammond about the graft and lechery of the chief surgeon and hospital steward fell on deaf ears, she took her case directly to Secretary of War Edwin Stanton with little concern for the political fallout that might result from sidestepping a male superior. Stanton, who was no friend of Hammond's, sided with Ropes, arresting the offending officers and subjecting Union Hotel to a medical inspection that resulted in improvements in patient care.[32] As Ropes fought this battle, she displayed an uncanny sense of her impending death, noting in late October that after fifty years of living, "the time left to anyone after that is very short at best." In her last diary entry, on December 27, 1862, she even refers to herself in the third person.[33] Literally sick to death of the continuing conflict with the surgical staff, Ropes could be stopped only by a pathogen. An early feminist, Ropes is the only diarist who was willing to confront surgical authority head on. While Eaton and the other diarists recorded their tiffs with surgeons and their dissatisfaction with a depersonalized medical bureaucracy, Ropes took action, revealing an astute insight into the politics of gender relations in the military fraternity.

All five diaries help us draw a fuller picture of the challenges implicit in medical relief work as women experienced it, each offering social, political, and religious observations that reveal the tensions implicit in the medical war—a scientific and cultural battleground in its own right. Seeking to repair bonds of family and community, women put patients at the center of their accounts, whereas surgeons were more often clinical in their observations. The eyewitness immediacy of nursing diaries has thus emphasized the soldier's experience of illness, a perspective that, by decentering medical authority, has made the patient's voice more audible. In this sense, Eaton's diary takes us places that have often been beyond reach: into ambulance wagons rolling over rugged terrain and into hospital tents, where the sounds and smells of suffering still have the power to bring tears to the eyes. In contrast to other relief workers who logged four years in camps and hospitals—Eaton's length of service appears modest.[34] But a daily account of just eleven months allowed Eaton to get at the heart of relief work. Women more ensconced in national hospital administration had little time to chronicle the day, but Eaton's distance from federal bureaucracy afforded her more time to write on a daily basis.[35] Only on rare occasions was she too taxed to write, some days jotting down minimal notes before she was overcome with fatigue.[36] Still, she sought the continuity of a daily regimen of writing to bring coherence to her desultory and unpredictable field work.

EATON'S FAMILY

Born Harriet Hope Agnes Bacon in Newton, Massachusetts, in 1818, Eaton was the last of the fifteen children of Josiah Bacon of Boston. Eaton's mother, Agnes Ramsay Hope of Edinburgh, Scotland, was herself a widow when she married Josiah

Bacon in 1803. Agnes was forty-nine years old when Harriet was born; Eaton's father Josiah was fifty-eight. Of Agnes Hope Bacon's eleven children, seven died before the age of two, leaving Harriet with two older brothers and a sister who survived into childhood.[37] Harriet also remained close to two of her four half brothers, born between 1783 and 1790. Both of Harriet's parents died in Newton, her father in 1831 and her eighty-six-year-old mother in 1854.

Details about Eaton's childhood are sketchy. She received a common school education during a period when girls' training was beginning to move beyond instruction in manners and the domestic arts, but before the standardization of a classical curriculum for both sexes.[38] In June 1840, Harriet married Jeremiah Sewall Eaton of Waere, New Hampshire, whom she met while he attended the Newton Theological Institution, a Baptist seminary founded in 1825 in her hometown.[39] Sewall, as Harriet called him, had graduated from Union College in Schenectady, New York, in 1835, and from Newton in 1839. In January 1839, he wrote from the seminary, expressing his wish to see her as often as possible, and he teased her about holding him captive: "Oh! Hatty," as he called her, "How can you be so cruel to exert such a tyranny over an innocent, unoffending creature like me? Does not your conscience trouble you sometimes? What matter it though you say 'I am no tyrant.' Does this weaken the bonds of oppression? By no means. If I am a slave, it does alter my condition, though my oppression says she is very kind to me & has my good in view."[40] Sewall easily adopted figures of speech relating to slavery to represent his plight as a suitor. In September, after he had graduated and was awaiting ordination in Hartford, Sewall was still pleading his case, now by long distance:

> I perceive that in my haste to close [my letter to you] this afternoon, I neglected to acknowledge the receipt of your very kind & excellent letter. I received it this morning. It was worth—why, it was beyond price. I feel much obliged to you for expressing your mind so fiercely on one point. I must confess that my feelings have been severely tried several times, on account of the apparent indifference you have manifested on the subject of our future union. I appreciate your motives. Still I think you are unnecessarily cautious & this may suggest an important principle of action on other subjects. In endeavoring to avoid the faults of others we should guard against an opposite extreme.

As the prospective wife of a minister, Eaton's emotional caution and circumspection befitted her situation, but Sewall desired a more ardent sign and lamented their separation, as Harriet took a September trip to Sandwich on Cape Cod, which was more than sixty miles from Newton. "It is only three weeks this morning since I saw you," he observed, "& yet I cannot remember any time when six weeks have appeared to me so long in retrospection."[41] Sewall's "enslavement" would endure nine months more, until he and Hatty married on June 3, 1840.

In the same month that he poured out his heart to Harriet and about six weeks before his ordination in November 1839, Sewall attended the trial of African captives who had commandeered the slave ship known as the *Amistad* before a U.S. Circuit Court in Hartford. The previous July, two Spanish businessmen with interests in the Cuban sugar trade had set sail from Havana to Puerto Príncipe (three hundred miles to the east) with a cargo of fifty-three adults who had been kidnapped from their west-African homes, brought to the New World early in 1839, and sold in Havana's slave market—despite the Cuban government's 1820 edict outlawing the importation of slaves.[42] After three days at sea, a Sierra Leonean named Cinqué, who himself had been transported to the Caribbean by Portuguese slave traders, led an uprising during which the captives killed the *Amistad*'s captain and ordered the Spaniards to sail the ship back to Africa. Two meandering months later, a time during which the Spaniards surreptitiously steered the vessel northward instead of eastward, a U.S. revenue cutter intercepted the ship near Long Island, New York, and towed it to New London, Connecticut. While U.S. judges decided who had jurisdiction in the affair, the Africans were imprisoned and tried in Hartford, where Sewall witnessed their trial. Ultimately, the Supreme Court decided in 1841—with American pro- and antislavery proponents at each other's throats—that imprisoning people who had never been legally enslaved could not be justified, and it granted the Africans' request to return to Sierra Leone in 1842. Sewall's proximity to these proceedings stirred righteous indignation, which he brought to his pulpit in Hartford.

The Eatons spent the first four years of their marriage in Hartford, where Sewall served the First Baptist Church. Harriet would return to this congregation thirty years later to continue doing mission work. Their son Frank was born in 1842, and two years later Sewall was hired by Portland's Free Street Baptist Church. In 1848, their daughter Agnes was born and in 1855, a third child, Harriet or "Hatty Belle," named for her mother. Sewall was a handsome, earnest man with luminous eyes; the only extant image of Harriet Eaton was one made by the First Baptist Church of Hartford sometime around 1880 when she was more than sixty. This photo shows her to be a small, pleasant-faced, dark-haired woman with an air of steely determination.[43] By the 1850s, when Sewall was only in his forties, respiratory ailments began to limit his activities, and he was obliged to resign his pulpit in 1854. In late 1853, the Eatons took a five-month trip to the South in the hope that a warmer climate would alleviate Sewall's symptoms, but he died in September 1856, at age forty-five. One of his parishioners remembered him as "a man of gracious and winning spirit," and added that "his wife was like unto him."[44] The death of Harriet's beloved mother in 1854 and her husband two years later were heavy blows that caused her to seek increasing consolation in her spiritual life.

Before Sewall's death, the household included a servant, Hannorah Cronin McCarthy, a fifty-three-year-old widowed Irish immigrant who had escaped the potato famine of the 1840s.[45] After Sewall's death, the Eatons lived without a servant and moved down the street to what was likely a smaller house on Spring Street. There is scarcely a trace of the Eatons' life between 1856 and 1862, though it appears that in exchange for some sort of legacy paid by the church at the time of Sewall's

The Free Street Baptist Church as it would have looked in the Civil War period. Today the building is used as the children's museum of Portland. MAINE HISTORICAL SOCIETY, PORTLAND

death, they were able to make ends meet. Eaton surely felt a moral obligation to the Free Street Church to relieve the wants of soldiers when it decided in 1862 to send representatives to the field with sanitary aid. During Eaton's absences at the front in 1862 and 1863, she left elder daughter Agnes at school in Massachusetts under the care of a brother's family and the younger Hatty Belle with Mary Webster Whittier in nearby Gorham, Maine—a friend whose military-aged sons, Ned and George, Eaton would see regularly during visits to the 5th Maine Battery. During the 1864 tour, Ruth Mayhew, one of Maine's vast army of female relief workers,[46] was the girls' guardian in Portland, where she had been teaching school since the 1850s. When Eaton came home for Christmas in 1864, the widowed Mayhew took her place at City Point and remained there for the last year of the war. In 1864, George Bosworth, who had succeeded Sewall Eaton in the pulpit and was on the board of the Portland Soldiers' Association, helped organize the Portland Soldiers' Home, located at 14 Spring Street, adjacent to the Eatons' residence. It is likely that Eaton worked in the home after her second battlefront tour ended in December 1864, since she was by this time a seasoned nurse and administrator. In May 1865, Eaton once again returned to the front, this time for two months to Alexandria, where she brought supplies and tended to those too ill to travel home to Maine. If she kept a journal of this last tour, it did not survive.[47] Eaton was also on hand after the war to nurse those injured in the great Portland fire of July 4, 1866.

Some time after 1868, Eaton moved to Tioga County, New York, to open a hardware store. Though no surviving documents illuminate her motives, it is likely that she took this action to be near a soldier whom she had met and had intense feelings for at City Point in 1864. By 1872, she had moved back to Hartford, where on behalf of the First Baptist Church, the place she had been a congregant early in her married life, Eaton became something of a lay minister. Moving among Hartford's poor, she visited the indisposed and dispensed physical and spiritual assistance. Resembling a Victorian embodiment of Hawthorne's Hester Prynne, Eaton avoided categorization as needy only because she aided those with even less than she had.

In 1877, a clergyman who had observed Eaton's war work and was aware of her mission work in Hartford told Clara Barton in the customary hyperbolic language that Eaton was "one of the sweetest and most saintly souls of all those who went to the front."[48] Happy to supply domestic comfort, but not always easy about her role as confidante, Eaton noted in 1879 that "while many seek advice from me with reference to cases of a personal and strictly private character, I often feel my own incompetency to counsel and in such cases can only carry them to my Heavenly Father to be directed from above."[49] That Eaton would have used a word like "incompetency" to refer to herself is puzzling: Might she have been alluding to the Tioga County episode as unfitting her to provide counsel to those seeking spiritual clarification? Or was it her characteristic modesty asserting itself, the default to deity in matters where Eaton wished not to meddle? Might the mission work itself have constituted penance for sins not divulged? Our current portrait of Eaton yields few answers, but her desire "to bring souls to Christ, to spend and be spent in such service" indicates that, as in former days, she was intent on using her energies to help others and thus reach a purer state of Christian identification.

Though she lived out her life with her daughters, Eaton never reunited with her son. Frank Eaton married a South Carolinian after the war and worked as a U.S. commissioner during Reconstruction. Frank lived with his wife Annie and their three daughters in Columbia and Philadelphia until his death from tuberculosis in 1886—less than two years after his mother's. Agnes and Hatty Belle, neither of whom ever married, joined their mother in Hartford apparently after her departure from the New York hardware store. Agnes's secretarial job and Hatty's income as a music teacher kept the household afloat, since Eaton earned no salary for her charity work.

After her death in 1884, she was brought back to Maine for burial beside Sewall in Portland's Evergreen Cemetery. A close friend eulogized her as "remarkably endowed with gifts and graces," a self-denying wife, mother, daughter, sister, and "good Samaritan," an "ideal of a woman, so pretty, graceful, gentle, dignified, industrious, spiritually minded, ready, not only with the needle and scissors,... but in the prayer and conference meeting—so filled with the spirit of God."[50] No New England woman remembered with similar adjectives at her death could have desired to depart from the path of rectitude that would have earned her such encomiums. Still, Eaton's postwar connection with Tioga County, New York, suggests an alternative reading:

that in an attempt to seek spiritual fulfillment, she might have swerved off the conventional path for a time.

A NEW ENGLAND WIDOW GOES TO WAR

Harriet Eaton's diary of hospital work offers a candid look at the physical and spiritual care of sick and wounded soldiers during three years of the American Civil War. As a civilian eyewitness engaged by a church-sponsored organization, Eaton served many masters. As a field nurse in Virginia, she negotiated the treacherous terrain between civil and military authority, all the while dedicating herself to the sort of mission work that was common among American Baptists of the era. As one of thousands of women who volunteered domestic services to soldiers in the field, Eaton traveled nearly six hundred miles from home by steamer and train to the military encampments of the Army of the Potomac in and around Washington. During her first tour of duty, she traveled a territory of approximately eighty miles from what is now Harpers Ferry, West Virginia, to Fredericksburg, with stops in Frederick, Maryland, and Falmouth, Virginia; the second tour would take her as far south as Hampton Roads, to the peninsula created by the James and York rivers and the immense Union hospital post at City Point, Virginia.

In her mid-forties at the time of her service, Eaton was a mature adult and an experienced household nurse, but nothing prepared her for the misery she encountered among Maine troops exposed to the elements in the Virginia countryside in the first two years of the war. Not only was the Army Medical Department ill prepared for the onslaught of wounded bodies, but poor sanitation, inadequate food, and a dearth of domestic comforts provided ideal conditions for camp illnesses like measles and smallpox to thrive.[51] Hundreds of soldiers from Maine and elsewhere died before they had ever shouldered a musket. The work of caring for sick soldiers demanded physical strength, but it also took emotional fortitude. Early on, Eaton noted the "hardening process" she was undergoing and regretted how quickly men passed away who, for more timely intervention, might have survived. Initially, she lacked confidence concerning the grim task before her, but in time developed a sturdy demeanor that enabled her to work among the dying with enough equanimity to retain sympathy for her charges while being useful to them—labors that put her in close quarters with civilian coworkers and scores of surgeons and officers. Strangers thrown together under medical exigency became intimate associates, and the forced intimacy bred tensions that could not always be resolved. Many surgeons won Eaton's admiration for their skill in seeing to soldiers' welfare, but others neglected their men and resented the public scrutiny that civilian relief workers represented. All hospital workers, Eaton included, had to learn the wisdom of both flexibility and obedience to military law if they themselves wished to survive in camp. Knowing when to remain silent and when to protest was vitally important where lives were at stake. Though publicly modest and self-effacing, Eaton came to understand the politics of the military-medical arena and in time became a more assertive and resourceful field nurse.

The religious climate of wartime New England was such that northern Baptists like Eaton felt obligated to alleviate the suffering of others in any way they could. Eaton's own religious devotion was, of course, one small piece of a larger fabric of Christian nationalism that emerged as a militant call to benevolent action during the Civil War.[52] Though soldiers away from home were susceptible to the secular temptations of camp life and many found themselves straying from the institutionalized religion of their local communities, the civilian population and the wartime press invested heavily in the metaphor of a warrior North taking up the call to arms to punish a morally deficient South.[53] This scimitar of self-righteousness, audible in Julia Ward Howe's 1862 anthem, "The Battle Hymn of the Republic," indicates the extent to which a formerly docile evangelism had been repackaged as Christian militancy; the nationalistic mandate of patriotism aligning itself with the Protestant imperative to do good. Patriotism was sacralized during the war and began to function like a denominational religion in its own right. Instead of viewing suffering as a conduit to Christian insight, citizens began to refashion suffering as the foundation of a moral (and patriotic) cause.[54] Together, a war-infused patriotism and Christian service produced a heady brew: one where national redemption was possible only through the sternest tests of character, which in turn were physically manifest in the battlefront death toll. In peacetime, religious leaders exhorted their flocks to walk away from provocation. In wartime—and in this, a civil war—Christian duty required a more activist response. Theologians were the first to turn the other cheek when met with the possibility of a gospel of peace. They supported the war and found religious justification in its conduct.[55]

Eaton's religious devotion penetrated to every level of her hospital work, from her decision to leave her home and children for months at a time to her tireless efforts to convert the soldiers in her care. Just as her obligation to do "the Lord's work" transcended her maternal and domestic responsibilities, she never lost sight of the religious objectives she brought with her, like so many pots and pans, to military camps. Eaton lamented the incursions of military time upon spiritual time, when fighting and marching disrupted scheduled camp meetings, but the periodic loss of this routine made her value it all the more. She regularly sought out chaplains in the hope of discovering how she might help mentor men poised for conversion, and she believed, like other churchwomen, that her presence at the front radiated a moral power that could turn men away from the vices and temptations that surrounded them. Indeed such women valued their role as moral arbiters, even clung to it as a kind of righteous shelter from the travails of military camps. Eaton was no different in this regard, hoping to set an example of Christian justice among her peers. However, this idealized depiction of women laboring in a righteous cause fails to acknowledge the precarious reality of flesh-and-blood nurses, who had to tamp down their desire for religious self-expression with the need for self-control.

Regardless of the difficult and unsavory work of caring for broken bodies, Eaton believed that her months of labor would not be in vain if her aid resulted in the spiritual saving of even one soldier. Although postwar nursing accounts trumpeted the success of numerous conversions—deathbed and otherwise—Eaton's experience suggests that they did not occur with frequency.[56] It might even be said that the soldier who became the object of Eaton's devotional energies in 1864, Maine infantryman Nathaniel P. Jaques, succeeded as much in converting her to his way of thinking as she did in converting him to hers.

Eaton's wartime nursing put her in the middle of a populous contraband community. Despite the Free Street Church's support of abolition, Eaton had had little to do with African Americans until she traveled to Virginia. She mentions interactions with several people of color: those who told stories of loss and prophecy to passersby; cooks, laundresses, and camp servants; and magnetic clergymen, especially in 1864 in the multiracial setting of City Point. Her curiosity about African American religious practices prompted her to listen to black preachers, but she sometimes came away from these outings peeved by what she perceived to be their lack of decorum. Though well aware of the plight of slaves and fugitives, Eaton, like many who supported abolition, was not convinced that people of color could ever achieve social or educational parity with whites—a racist perspective that was commonplace even among liberal thinkers in Eaton's time.

Because the Civil War antedated the professionalization of nursing, Eaton came to her work equipped with domestic knowledge but with little in the way of medical training outside of what she might have obtained from domestic observation—a fact that pertained as well to many state-appointed surgeons. In the pre-professional era, nurses were maids of all work whose duties extended beyond physical care of the body into the realm of the spiritual. Though today's nurses continue to perform custodial labors, their medical and scientific responsibilities have supplanted the collection and distribution of supplies that were integral to the Civil War nurse's daily routine. As a provisioner supplying food, medicine, and clothing, Eaton served as a conduit between the home front of Portland and the Maine regiments of the Army of the Potomac, communicating the needs of the latter to the households of the former. Her correspondence is full of lists recording the goods sent from towns all over Maine and of requests for supplies, like pillows, of which soldiers were especially fond. Occasionally she learned that her letters about Maine troops made it into local newspapers, bringing to her unwanted celebrity. Although Eaton was usually circumspect in her letter-writing, she sometimes complained about people and protocol—complaints that she feared were not consistent with her Baptist beliefs. Unhappy that the state relief agency had offered her letters to the papers without seeking her permission, Eaton endured the publicity by reasoning that her personal mortification paled in comparison to the good that might come of public appeals to alleviate war front suffering.

With obligations to her children, to individual soldiers, to military-medical personnel, to state relief managers, and to God, Eaton used her daily journal as far more than a supply register and medical chronicle. It offered her a safety valve for the political, religious, and emotional balancing act she performed during her months of military service. Though embarked on a labor that fused patriotic and religious motives, Eaton was no saint. Her humanity is most visible when she was agitated about conditions that were often, but not always, beyond her control. In particular, Eaton's relationship with coworker Isabella Fogg, whose rough manners and mysterious Canadian origins offended her, brings to light the personal conflict that was inevitable, even between those with the same munificent objectives. Indeed, Eaton's and Fogg's workplace encounters show how the gendered prescriptions of self-sacrifice and piety were strained—and even toppled—by wartime medical relief work.

PORTLAND AND MAINE IN THE CIVIL WAR ERA

Portland was an up-and-coming community, hopeful of challenging Boston or Hartford as a center of culture and commerce, when the Eatons moved there in the 1840s. Its position on Casco Bay, where the arrangement of islands provided a natural barrier, made it attractive to both commercial and military interests. In 1849, the last slave ship to enter an American port sailed out of Portland—a maritime harbinger of civil discord surrounding the growing abolition movement. Portland also produced a series of literary luminaries in the nineteenth century: poet William Wadsworth Longfellow; Sara Payson Willis Parton, a.k.a. Fanny Fern, the first successful American woman journalist, whose folksy critique of women's social and legal subordination gave her the star power of a modern celebrity; and African American literary pioneer, journalist, and magazine editor Pauline Hopkins. During three days in November 1850, Portland abolitionist Daniel Oliver had played host to runaway slaves William and Ellen Craft as they fled, disguised as an incapacitated white gentleman and his loyal slave, from Macon, Georgia, to the northern states, and thence to Canada and England.[57] Though it is unlikely that the Eatons knew about the Crafts' brief stay, their experience in Hartford with the *Amistad* captives had made them conscious about the plight of fugitives, and they brought abolitionist sentiments with them when they moved to Portland in 1844.

Throughout the 1860s, Portland was a destination for theologians, dignitaries, and artists and an important stop on the antislavery lecture circuit. In October 1860, the Prince of Wales made a brief appearance in Portland on the Victoria Docks, which quickly descended to comedy when a local maiden launched a bouquet that knocked off his hat.[58] A month before the firing on Fort Sumter, tragedian and future Lincoln assassin John Wilkes Booth performed Shakespearean soliloquies in a Portland theater. On Independence Day that year, Reverend William T. Dwight addressed Portlanders in their new city hall, urging them to eschew Protestant factionalism and embrace the cause of union—a sure sign that political loyalty carried the Lord's blessing. Two days before Christmas in 1862, political sensation Anna

Elizabeth Dickinson lectured Portlanders at City Hall on "The Lessons of the War," concluding that the demise of slavery was imminent and urging men to enlist to finish the job.[59]

On January 14, 1864, a packed house of Portlanders heard abolitionist Wendell Phillips criticize President Lincoln's leniency with slaveholders. The enthusiastic crowd sang Julia Ward Howe's "Battle Hymn of the Republic" and other patriotic songs; Phillips donated the proceeds to the Sanitary Commission. In what became a momentous year for Portland, the Union, and Harriet Eaton, Portlanders heard Frederick Douglass speak in April 1864. The *Portland Daily Press* recounted that Douglass addressed a packed house at City Hall on the subject of "The Races" and labeled the ex-slave and publisher of the abolitionist organ *The North Star* "a logician, an orator, and a man of research."[60] In October of that year—not two weeks after Eaton departed for her second tour of duty—William Lloyd Garrison spoke at Mechanics Hall, "skinn[ing] the copperheads alive" for their opposition to the war and confirming Portland as a place inhospitable to proslavery leanings.[61] Political events of this magnitude gave Portland citizens the promise of a more urbane destiny. Strangely, the much-touted defensibility of the port was breached in June 1863 when a group of Confederate mariners disguised as fishermen made off with the *Caleb Cushing*, a Union revenue cutter. When a group of alert citizens gave chase, the Rebels abandoned ship, but not before setting it ablaze. Though Portland's security was never again threatened, a spate of similar incidents occurred along the Maine seacoast in 1864, convincing Union officials to protect all major ports on the eastern seaboard.[62]

When Abraham Lincoln called for seventy-five thousand troops in April 1861, 4 percent of all the available men in Maine enlisted in less than two weeks. From her upstairs window, Longfellow's sister Anne Pierce observed crowds of people who filled Congress Street day and night. By the end of the month, five hundred soldiers were marching and drilling adjacent to the city center, and local women had produced sixteen hundred flannel shirts, eight hundred towels, ditto pocket handkerchiefs, ditto neckties, and bandages for these future heroes to carry with them into Dixie.[63] Because Portland was the state's point of embarkation for soldiers traveling to Virginia, citizens were accustomed to seeing Maine's recruits in high spirits. Though some regiments were mustered in Portland, others had been encamped for weeks in Augusta, the state capital, complaining of boredom and illness; the prospect of forward movement and an enthusiastic sendoff delighted them. Portlanders were known statewide for their laconic and retiring manners, but they met the departing troops with elegant provisions and emotive displays. In July, when the first regiments were leaving the state, hundreds gathered to see them off. By September, broadsides could be found around town advertising for "Riflemen" to try out for a company of sharpshooters—perhaps to repair the reputation of the recently disbanded 1st Maine Infantry. As was common practice early in the war, this regiment assembled for only ninety days, whereupon its Portland boys, who had seen no action, returned home sheepishly to local reporters' mock-epic accounts of their less-than-heroic exploits.[64] Civic enthusiasm persisted into the second year of the war. Twenty-two-year-old private John West Haley of Saco observed on August 18, 1862, as the 17th Maine prepared to head south, that "the ladies of Portland made us a dinner of pies, cakes, cold meats and other luxuries not mentioned in commissary supplies," undoubtedly some of the last substantial fare they would sample.[65]

Like people all over Maine, Portlanders read their newspapers—eleven in all—with great attention, combing the columns for news of their kinfolk at the front, especially after battles. The *Portland Daily Press* and the *Daily Transcript* regularly published lists of local men confined to Washington hospitals and accounts of relief efforts on behalf of regiments in the field. Citizens were advised how to direct letters to their loved ones and where to send donations of prepared food, clothing, medical supplies, and money. By mid-war, field relief agents were assuring the mothers of Maine that the grateful thanks of soldiers desperate for the issue of their larders would repay them a thousandfold, could they but see the joy their donations occasioned. In Portland, agents described the precision of the supply chain and publicized the sacrifice made by Harriet Eaton and Isabella Fogg, who ministered to troops in the harshest of conditions and "received no compensation for their services from any source." Irene Bosworth, wife of Eaton's husband's successor and secretary-treasurer of the Free Street Church's aid society, praised the duos' reports as "prompt, frequent, minute, and thrillingly interesting," emphasizing the extent to which eyewitness accounts from Virginia outposts became fodder for public consumption.[66] Portlanders remained upbeat, at least in the press, well into 1864, when Eaton, Bath's Sarah Sampson, and later Ruth Mayhew staffed a state supply tent at City Point. So sterling was the reputation of Maine's relief workers at the Point that soldiers brought in from the Petersburg trenches claimed to be from Maine (even if they were not), the high-quality care and liberal dispersion of quilts simply too good to pass up. One postwar commentator recalled the soldiers' wartime refrain: "Next time I enlist, it will be in a Maine regiment."[67]

The positive spin that pundits assigned in retrospect to the war's relief efforts looked less sanguine in 1862 and 1863, when the state had not yet standardized its collection and distribution procedures. Abba Goddard, an outspoken citizen and self-appointed hospital visitor, regaled Portland's newspaper readers with accounts of need and abuse in the hope of urging them to action on behalf of their defenders. Before Maine's Amy Morris Bradley took charge of the convalescent camp on the outskirts of Washington in 1863, Goddard wailed, "It is impossible to give you an idea of its utter unfitness for animals—much more for poor suffering humanity." It was popularly dubbed "Camp Misery," and Goddard heard soldiers refer to it as "Camp Convulsion," lamenting its disorder and the neglect of the Surgeon General's Office in contrast to more comfortable city hospitals like Armory Square. Goddard also deployed her correspondence to invoke patriotic pride in the sons of Maine: In a letter dated January 15, 1863 from Fairfax, Virginia, where she was in camp with the

10th Maine, Goddard reported that she had chanced to see the encampment of the 25th Maine the day before. This was in fact Frank Eaton's regiment, and Goddard waxed poetic about company A, to which he belonged:

> A fine manly set of fellows they are. I was proud of them.... Young [Lieutenant Charles B.] Hall looks every inch the soldier, as do the entire company. The Portland boys are fine specimens of young Americans.... Their encampment is a model. One can easily trace the line of Maine troops, or select their quarters, out of an entire army corps. Our sturdy backwoodsmen know how to hew wood and pile it, and their quarters show their handcraft.... I wish some of our Portland Ladies' Committee could be here to-night, to hear what our men say when a woman from home enters camp.[68]

Though used to being the object of male attention, Portland's spinsters and matrons were now consumers of the masculine military ideal. The heroic imagery embodied in such descriptions provided powerful leverage among potential producers of relief supplies.

Happy to read about exemplary men off fighting, Maine's citizens were also treated to less savory narratives of life at the front by soldiers themselves. Charley Oleson, a boyhood friend of Frank Eaton's and a steward at Eckington Hospital in Washington, spent listless hours composing gossipy letters to his friend Charlie Thurston about Portlanders in the service. One about Fred Bosworth, son of FSBC pastor George and his wife Irene, suggested a less than heroic bearing:

> You remark in your last about Fred Bosworth's enquiry in regard to whiskey—for one of his character he seems to be quite anxious in regard to that compound—I must in relation to this tell you a story: F. H. E. [meaning Frank H. Eaton] told me the other day, Fred you know used to loaf around Steph Knights in Union St. and so a short time since he wrote Knights a letter in which among other things he expressed a wish for some of his beer, stating that whiskey was getting played out and they had nothing to amuse themselves with but the little nigger wenches. Mr. B (Fred's father) heard of the note & went to Mr. K and requested to see it and for a short time it created quite a stir. Mrs. Eaton is still out here among the hospitals.[69]

Since Frank was the son of the *third* pastor of the FSBC, it stands to reason that the son of the fourth pastor might have provided him an apt target for ribbing. Although we cannot know how authentic this report of Fred Bosworth's drinking and womanizing was, the alleged lapses in his conduct—hardly anomalous given the restlessness of soldiers without a mission—would have been seen as serious infractions back home; indeed his family would have suffered from this chink in his honor.[70]

Morale among working-class soldiers from Portland began to suffer by the middle of the war. Altogether, more than half of the men in Maine regiments were laborers and mechanics. When a conscription act was implemented in 1863, those wishing to avoid service could do so for $300—the price of a substitute. Rank-and-file Mainers resented this practice because it obviously favored wealthier citizens, and they expressed their frustration in public demonstrations and personal letters.[71] Moreover, skilled craftsmen could make far more doing carpentry than soldiering, and thus found little incentive to reenlist once their terms of service had expired. So concerned were Portland's civic leaders that draft riots would erupt, like those that had brought New York City to its knees in July 1863, that they authorized the state militia to keep the peace.[72] It is probably no coincidence that trade unions formed in Portland during this period also—the typographers and coopers in 1863 and the carpenters, railroad engineers, machinists, painters, blacksmiths, and longshoremen in 1864—given public sentiment that leaned toward protecting industrial workers returning from the service.[73]

Like other Americans in the northern states, Portlanders were jubilant when Robert E. Lee handed over his sword to Ulysses S. Grant at Appomattox Court House on April 12, 1865, without any idea of the momentous assassination that would occur two days later. Ellen Usher Bacon, the sister of another of Maine's prominent nurses, Rebecca Usher, wrote about the end of the war as it was felt in Portland:

> What a world of events have been crowded into one week! I heard the first scream at midnight—looked at my watch, just 12. The watchmen whistled all round; the bells commenced ringing; pistols [going] off—sky rockets went up—I thought of Lee the first scream, told Dr. B[acon] it was not a fire, could not move him, talked of a riot and hearing the fire-arms rapidly firing he got up and went out. In two minutes came back with the news. In a short time the whole city was illuminated, the streets were rapidly filling with people. We shut up the house and went out.... Went around the corner to hear Governor Washburn. The people would not hear speeches but they could cheer for Grant—for Lincoln—for the Flag—for the Union—for everything that was good and patriotic.[74]

The carnival atmosphere on this night in 1865, complete with its celebratory if ironic fusillade, suggests the extent to which war-weary Portlanders embraced this news. In June, as troops began to march back through town for mustering out, they were met with the ringing of bells and the firing of cannon. Even as local boys still filled Virginia hospitals, Portland feted returning veterans. John West Haley, en route with the recently mustered out 17th Maine, noted that "an immense crowd assembled to greet us and they pressed us so hard that we had some difficulty even getting off the train."[75]

Portland's monument to the soldiers and sailors of the Civil War, dedicated in May 1889, still stands today in the open-air plaza at the commercial heart of the old city. A representational limestone image of soldiers at arms surrounding a grand personification of "Our Lady of Victories," it is typical of monuments erected in the 1870s and 1880s in its depiction of manhood and military valor.[76] Dedicated "To [Portland's] sons, who died for the Union, 1861–1865," the monument explains that of the four thousand soldiers who called Portland home, almost 10 percent perished from wounds or illness. "Honor and grateful remembrance to the dead," the stone letters proclaim. Just under these words is another phrase—one seldom chiseled on wartime statuary, but calculated to remind spectators that sacrifice was not the sole province of the dead—"Equal honor to those who, daring to die, survived." Whether or not city fathers meant to include this caveat in recognition of those who served Maine in noncombatant capacities is unclear. But historians and archivists have stood ready to show how the organization of state relief efforts may have earned for Portland's wartime citizens, in addition to her veterans, a portion of that honor.[77]

EATON'S NURSING SERVICE

Harriet Eaton served in the field with Maine regiments for seven months, from October 1862 to May 1863, when illness forced her to return home.[78] She served at the City Point hospitals from October 1864 through the end of the year, and she concluded her service with a trip to Alexandria in May and June 1865, where she helped nurse soldiers released from Confederate prison camps—in all, more than twelve months in the field. Eaton's diary and letters bespeak the experience of an able relief worker, but she was loath to call herself a nurse. This reluctance was tempered by the broad cultural transition in nursing underway during the war. Lacking any formal instruction in nursing, unlike a group of New Yorkers trained by physician Elizabeth Blackwell in 1861 and authorized by the Women's Central Relief Association (WCRA), Eaton shrank from the title.[79] Her belief that the state context of her work disqualified her from the esteemed title contributed to her hesitation. Because she was not employed by Superintendent Dix or a national relief organization, Eaton perceived her role in relief work to be ancillary. "I was a sort of nondescript," she wrote after meeting with an officious surgeon at City Point, "neither one thing nor the other.—I did not belong to Miss Dix, though Miss Dix sent me, I belonged to a Maine Agency but had no pass from Surgeon General Barnes."[80] As the USSC disseminated news about soldiers languishing for want of comforts, which only its national efforts could assuage, state relief initiatives, in the Union at least, appeared inconsequential.[81] As a clergyman's widow who abjured the limelight, Eaton minimized her actions. Even though she occasionally communicated with Dix and nurses whom she perceived as nationally prominent, even though she regularly saw President Lincoln and General Grant, and was more than an acquaintance of Maine's warrior hero, Joshua Lawrence Chamberlain, she wished to remain in the shadows. This may have been in part the result of introversion, but Eaton's marginal position also allowed her to be a critic, and to criticize with impunity— something she could not have done had she been employed by Dix or the USSC. Her snipes at USSC workers Helen Gilson and Frank Fay suggest that from her distance and perspective, she *could* be a critic—just enough out of the mainstream to avoid consequences.[82] Female relief workers with more bureaucratic responsibility, like Iowa's Annie Turner Wittenmyer, who developed the system of special diet kitchens, were obliged to internalize military prescriptions and regulations, however tempted they might have been to challenge medical wisdom.[83] Without the gravitas of federal authority demanding her obedience, Eaton could remain aloof. She was free to express dissatisfaction up to a point, but was careful not to judge others too quickly.

Even though she initially declined to call herself a nurse, Eaton nevertheless performed as a veteran nurse by the winter of 1863. She had been with the Maine troops for long enough to become sarcastic, like the rank and file, about political decisions that affected the command of the Army of the Potomac. Uncharacteristic cynicism, verging occasionally on a repudiation of the war, marked her association with the military. In early 1863, as the army congregated in winter quarters near Falmouth, Virginia, and "Fighting Joe" Hooker prepared to outflank Lee entrenched at Fredericksburg on the other side of the Rappahannock, Eaton began to refer to army headquarters and the 2nd corps division hospital as "home." On a brief visit to Frank in Washington in February, she even noted being "homesick to get back to my work."[84] After the nomadic existence she had led in the field, she now conceived of home as a place where armies located their command and where the illusion of permanence allowed Eaton and those around her to replicate a military version of domesticity.

Only once during the war did Eaton publicly refer to herself as an "Army nurse," even though the work in which she engaged scarcely differed from that of women more at ease with the title. It might be argued that Eaton had a greater claim, since she spent seven months in the field with makeshift regimental hospitals, in contrast to many who knew only urban general hospitals with regular accommodations. Conditions in the field in the first two years of the war required more flexibility and ingenuity than in general hospitals; troops were constantly on the move, making the delivery of goods a hit or miss proposition. Eaton often noted how difficult it was to locate transient regiments in the field and how exhausting was the work of cleaning and feeding men who had received little aid or attention for weeks at a time.[85]

When Eaton headed north a week after the battle of Chancellorsville, she was so ill and overwrought from lack of sleep that she had to stop in Washington for several days before resuming the 540-mile journey back to Portland ("I am in a burning fever, am I going to be seized with pneumonia? Pain in my side severe"). Having been turned away from the residence where Maine nurse Sarah Sampson boarded, a stunned Eaton reported fainting before she made it to a downtown hotel.[86] Before pressing on to Portland, Eaton was desperate to find out whether Frank had survived the battle, and with the help of state agent Charles Hayes, she planned to go to Chantilly, where the 25th Maine reportedly was encamped ("I know I am too sick to take care of myself," she wrote[87]). On the morning of May 12, she took district horse cars to the Potomac River, crossed to Alexandria, walked in heat to the rail superintendent's office; thence to the Provost Marshal's Office to secure a pass. Disgusted that she had to wait hours for the next transport without any courtesy from the administrator ("faint as I was he would not offer me a seat in the Office"), Eaton had had enough. As she boarded a train to travel west to Chantilly, guards attempted to search a suitcase in which she had stowed a brandy flask, and she spoke out: "Telling them I was an 'army nurse,' I warned them against meddling with any part of my 'side arms'."[88] Using language reminiscent of Alcott's Nurse Periwinkle in *Hospital Sketches* and unwilling to brook intervention, Eaton invoked both the tone and metaphor of the warrior; sick and used up, she hoped that identifying herself as a nurse would earn her free transportation to Frank who, as it turned out, had not been in the battle.

By 1866 Eaton was backpedaling. Approached by New-York Historical Society founder and editor Frank Moore to contribute a sketch of her labors for his commemorative volume about women's wartime benevolence, she replied that "the work in which we were engaged differed materially from that of a <u>nurse</u> in the Army." Characteristically understating her contribution, despite the hard service she had seen, Eaton directed Moore's attention to former colleagues in the Maine Camp Hospital Association "to prepare something for the book."[89] It is not clear what Eaton had in mind when she suggested that her relief work "differed materially" from army nurses' work. She was inclined to take offense at the brash conduct of women at City Point and therefore might have attached to the term something improper from which she wished to distance herself. It is important to recognize, however, that Eaton did the work of a nurse—washing and feeding patients, delivering medicine and supplies, doing laundry, maintaining bedding, and attending to the social and religious needs of those laid low by protracted convalescence or impending death.[90] Writing to patients' families, praying with the dying, and even making arrangements for the transportation of soldiers' bodies were also integral to her work.

LIFE IN THE FIELD

Eaton interacted with soldiers from most of the Maine regiments connected with the Army of the Potomac, including the 2nd, 3rd, 4th, 5th, 6th, 10th, 11th, 16th, 17th, 19th, 20th, 25th, 29th, 31st, and 32nd infantries; the 1st Maine Cavalry, the 1st Maine Heavy Artillery, and the 2nd, 5th, and 7th batteries of the 1st Battalion of Maine Light Artillery. Eaton was especially attached to the men of the 17th, many of whom were from Portland, and the 20th Maine, the regiment that catapulted Bowdoin College rhetoric professor Joshua Lawrence Chamberlain to a generalship and postwar political fame.[91] These two units, along with the 16th and the 19th, were workhorses that saw much action and sustained numerous casualties; less than three weeks after it was mustered in, the 20th was shouldering muskets at Antietam. Both it and the 17th were engaged at Fredericksburg, Chancellorsville, Gettysburg, the Wilderness, Spotsylvania, Totopotomoy, Cold Harbor, and operations connected with the siege of Petersburg. The 17th lost 199 men on the second day of Gettysburg alone, more than one-fifth of its total roster; throughout the war it lost 370 men to wounds and disease; the 20th, similarly, lost 376—mortality rates of approximately 40 percent.[92]

Eaton vastly preferred her first tour of duty in northern Virginia to her second, more sedentary, service at City Point.[93] Though travel and accommodations were primitive for Eaton in the field (she noted enthusiastically in her second month of service, "Slept on a bed last night!"[94]), she prized the opportunity to work one on one with Maine soldiers and surgeons, providing them with food and clothing, assuaging their anxiety in illness, and even occasionally having a "Portland chit chat."[95] While the work taxed Eaton's patience and endurance because of the difficulty of procuring supplies and then locating the far-flung regiments for which the supplies were destined, it was also more gratifying. The need for her services was clear cut; the mode of her communication with superiors quite direct. On the way to Washington three weeks after the battle of Antietam, she and Isabella Fogg, with whom she had traveled from Portland, encountered scores of soldiers left behind in huts and private homes as the Army of the Potomac retreated south from Sharpsburg—soldiers not caught in the wide net that the USSC had professed to cast. Here was a job for states: In Augusta, Governor Israel Washburn decreed that the sons of Maine should not have to suffer and die for lack of food and comforts during the second winter of the war.[96] If federal benevolence was not reaching Mainers, then state-sponsored benevolence would. George Knox, chaplain of the 10th Maine, put it diplomatically:

> The Sanitary Commission is doing a great and benevolent work; and yet there are hundreds of our suffering soldiers whom Hospital employees and agents of the Sanitary Commission cannot be expected to reach, or immediately minister to. There are many sick and wounded in temporary Hospitals, and in the track of a moving army, by the wayside, and in half-ruined buildings, who too often are dependent on the stinted charity of a people disheartened and desolated by actual war. These poor sufferers sometimes actually lie for successive days without medical aid, or any proper nursing.[97]

When Eaton traveled the field dispensing to Maine regiments under the aegis of the Maine Camp Hospital Association, she did so as an autonomous actor. She, Isabella Fogg, and Charles C. Hayes, the state-appointed relief agent responsible for overseeing package distribution from the capital to men in the field, took stock of what was needed and communicated with relief agents at home in Portland (George Davis, Harriet Fox, and Lewis Smith).[98] The Portland agents in turn helped coordinate the delivery of goods to Maine soldiers via the Maine State [Relief] Agency, located at 273 F Street in Washington and headed by Colonel John W. Hathaway—just down the street from USSC headquarters at #244. The links between Portland and other towns in the Pine Tree State were aided by newspapers like the *Portland Daily Press* and the *Eastern Argus*, which throughout the summer, fall, and winter of 1862–63 asked homemakers to prepare supplies and send them to Portland, whence they could be shipped to Washington.[99]

The system of supply and distribution presented a unique set of problems, in part because male relief agents initially resisted the idea that women could be partners. When the MCHA sent Eaton and Fogg to Washington in October 1862, they arrived without any assurance from the state of Maine that they would be able to serve its troops. Both Charles Hayes and John Hathaway took a dim view of women traversing the wilderness and subjecting themselves to the daily rigors of survival. A quartermaster attempted to scare them off by telling Eaton that the Rebels might take them prisoner during their regimental perambulations. Two weeks after the women's arrival in Virginia, the men, witnessing their firm intention to stay, began to relent, but only after the women determined to demonstrate how essential their services were by refusing to hand over their report on the status of regiments in the field. "Poor fellow," wrote Eaton about Colonel Hathaway, "it's a hard case, for he is only convinced [that we can stay] because he is obliged to be, but no matter, we do as we please, our expenses all paid."[100] Even at the outset, Eaton had already absorbed a useful political lesson about moving forward by disregarding naysayers. Despite the men's disapproval, she saw that they did not, in fact, have the authority to send her home. Since she and Fogg were already at work and not dependent on the state for their expenses, Colonel Hathaway would have been at pains to make them reverse course.[101]

By the time of Eaton's second tour of duty at City Point, female relief workers were everywhere in evidence. When she returned to the Army of the Potomac in 1864, after an interval of seventeen months at home, however, the system of provisioning state regiments had been superseded by a more rigid federal framework that left virtually no man behind, uncared for, in a hut. The Union ambulance corps was now experienced in removing soldiers from battlefields before they perished; and the Surgeon General's Office, with the help of USSC leaders, had designed evacuation procedures to dispatch wounded soldiers via hospital transports almost immediately to general hospitals in Washington, Baltimore, and Philadelphia without their having to lie unattended for days in the field.[102] Conditions for the soldier who fell in battle were far better in 1864 than in 1862, and improvements in sanitary procedures lessened mortality when men fell ill. Such advances made Eaton feel extraneous, however. She noted on October 28, 1864, "I am more than ever dissatisfied with this way of working, I reach the suffering and destitute so indirectly." Her feeling was similar to that of Clara Barton, who, after providing aid to soldiers during the battles of Antietam and Fredericksburg, landed in the Sea Islands in 1863 without a clearly defined mission.[103] Eaton's sense of not being needed was perhaps ironic in light of another Maine nurse's testimony that, even as late as February 1865, soldiers brought into the Point from the field "had not even a tent to cover them" and "almost perished with cold."[104] Yet in what was perceived as a more orderly process of relieving soldiers' needs, women like Eaton lost some of the independence they had enjoyed earlier, when the medical "buck" had to stop with them.

City Point offered a more bureaucratic and institutionalized setting for medical and relief personnel previously stationed in the field. Located at the end of a rail line from Petersburg, Virginia, twenty miles to the southwest, on what one nurse called "a barren, almost treeless country of untilled land," it featured a supply depot for unloading ships, officers' headquarters, and hospitals for the cavalry and the 2nd, 3rd, 5th, and 9th corps of the Army of the Potomac. The built environment consisted of more than a thousand tents and ninety log cabins located on "immaculate" lanes of compacted soil, which turned to mush when it rained.[105] City Point's position at the confluence of the James and Appomattox rivers meant that supplies easily reached the ten thousand men who could be hospitalized there and, more importantly, that wounded men could be transported back up the Chesapeake Bay into the Potomac River for Washington, where more than twenty-five thousand hospital beds awaited.[106] City Point was just that—a relief city in which were concentrated hundreds of the eastern theater's medical and relief personnel during the summer of 1864 through the spring of 1865, when the most ferocious fighting of the war was under way: surgeons, orderlies, laundresses, cooks, quartermasters, sutlers, chaplains, nurses, people employed by the Sanitary and Christian commissions to distribute supplies, state relief agents, and contraband women and men eking out a modest existence. In such an environment, competition between workers was fierce and jealousy common.[107]

Compared to the transience of regimental hospitals in the field that Eaton encountered in 1862 and 1863, medical arrangements at City Point were more compact and closely supervised. While this configuration was a blessing in the sense that men wounded near Petersburg during the Weldon Railroad operations in June 1864 or the mine assault in July could be triaged and sent to a general hospital within a day or two, it was also a curse for those who desired greater autonomy in their relief labors. For a person like Harriet Eaton, used to catering directly to the men from her state and immediately able to see the results of her aid, the regrouping of men by army corps was a disadvantage. For obvious reasons, Eaton had an affinity for men in Maine regiments; the City Point hospital barracks were arranged such that Mainers were dispersed throughout numerous buildings, and Eaton was obliged to care for men from New Hampshire, New York, New Jersey, Pennsylvania, Massachusetts, and Vermont, as well as any Westerners who might have been transferred to the eastern theater.

In addition to the dispersion of her state's troops, Eaton chafed at the close quarters of City Point, which pitted state agents against the national commissions, and (to Eaton's mind) bona fide, veteran nurses against those without such pretensions. Eaton referred often to the officious conduct and parsimony of sanitary commissioners responsible for doling out supplies to imploring state agents; one prominent sanitarian noted that even among those within the organization, there was disagreement about whether relief workers ought to be able to draw food from commission supplies. Nurses without rations obeyed the letter of USSC regulations and went hungry, while well-fed tattlers promised to report them if any comestibles meant for soldiers went missing.

There is evidence that by late 1864, supplies were plentiful enough to lessen the stranglehold, but Eaton still chafed at discord in October: "Mr. Shaw formerly of Portland connected with the [Sanitary] Commission called here and I gave him my opinion on the importance of the Agencies working in harmony, as I have not felt since I came here, that there was that reciprocity of feeling that should exist."[108] Anxious to address the tension and more willing by 1864 to assert her views, Eaton sought out a potential ally with whom to register her displeasure. Despite her wish for greater harmony, the squabbling aid groups were unable to resolve their differences.

STAFF RELATIONS AT CITY POINT

If institutional configurations at City Point strained working relations, so did the experience of veteran nurses and surgeons working in a fishbowl. As long as relief workers were out in the field, their encounters with others were infrequent. But locating the eastern theater's hospital center at City Point compressed these usually distant workers into a relatively small area where egos could not always be suppressed and tempers were likely to flare. Eaton's complaints about the "beau-seeking, lady-hunting" climate of City Point are unremitting. Simply trying to stay out of the fray sapped her energies, as it also did for New York nurse Sarah Palmer, who confessed that she was "tired of noise; tired of the tongues which talk, talk, talk at the supper-table... tired of trying to be happy; and tired of everything." Palmer also observed that married soldiers at City Point sought liaisons with single nurses who knew nothing of their marital status.[109] After serving two or three years in field hospitals, women like Eaton had in effect been banished to City Point, which bore little resemblance to the field hospitals of yore. When a soldier was wounded at Petersburg, the staffs of surgeons John H. Brinton, stationed near the besieging forces, or Edward B. Dalton, head of medical services at City Point, saw him first, and when he was stable enough to be moved, ambulances would pack him off in a train for the two-hour journey to City Point. When the Army Medical Department had been less well organized, and before Jonathan Letterman and Charles Tripler had perfected the evacuation of wounded men by ambulance and train, finding those men in the field had been the centerpiece of Eaton's labors. Once the new system of evacuation had been tested and improved, women's triage skills were not often utilized.[110]

As late as the autumn of 1864, despite the now-public visibility of thousands of relief workers, Eaton was still encountering time-consuming road-blocks on her way to City Point. Even before her return to the army, such difficulties were already apparent. In late June, Frederick Burmeister, chief surgeon of the 2nd corps hospital at City Point, wrote to the Surgeon General's Office, requesting six additional female nurses. One week later, Surgeon Dalton replied in no uncertain terms that "there are already as many female nurses here as can work with advantage. An increase in the number would be detrimental to the service. In this opinion I have the full concurrence of every Surgeon in charge of [a] corps hospital."[111] Unaware of this correspondence, Eaton left Portland on October 12 and met rail delays in New York and Philadelphia. She arrived in Washington on the 15th, only to learn that coworker Charles Hayes had not obtained a pass for her travel to City Point. Charles Crane, acting as adjutant to Surgeon General Joseph Barnes, had made it policy that no civilians could travel to the Point without the express consent of Surgeon Dalton. "Well," wrote Eaton on the 17th, after her friend Charles Gilmore had put her up for two days, "we will see what we will see. I will, <u>in person, apply to every source</u> and be <u>refused</u> before I will give up going tomorrow."[112] Undeterred, Eaton prepared herself to do administrative battle.

The next day, she descended into a bureaucratic quagmire that would have thwarted a less determined individual. She took the horsecars from the Gilmore residence to the Maine agency on F Street, went in the company of a state agent to the War Department, and met with Major Louis Pelouze in the Adjutant General's Office, who passed her to Adjutant Crane. In addition to the earlier admonition, Crane insisted that Superintendent of Army Nurses Dorothea Dix would need to authorize any nurse's pass to City Point. Since Dix's exclusive authority to appoint nurses had been circumvented the previous October by General Order 351, which made it possible for any U.S. surgeon to appoint the nurses he needed, Crane's proclamation was dubious at best.[113] Before noon, Eaton sought Dix's whereabouts and was assured by Crane's staff that Dix could be found at St. Elizabeth's Insane Asylum Hospital far beyond the bounds of the city to the southeast, overlooking the Potomac and Anacostia rivers. Eaton boarded the horsecars for the Navy Yard—the end of the line; then played a game of chicken with three omnibus drivers in an attempt to learn which vehicle would depart first. After a three-mile journey, she arrived at St. Elizabeth's only to learn that "Miss Dix never stopped there" and was probably at home. Not willing to risk another futile ride on the omnibus, Eaton "footed it in haste" back to the Navy Yard, then took the horsecars to Dix's residence at 430 Fifteenth Street, a couple of blocks from the Gilmores', where she had begun the day's odyssey. In her first of only two meetings with the legendary reformer during the war, Eaton found Dix at home and procured her pass, certain that her middle-aged looks and demeanor favored her in the interview.[114] Before eleven that night, she had arrived by transport ship at City Point.

The protracted nature of what should have been a straightforward procedure, because Eaton had in her possession documentation proving her right to be there, indicates that army brass, with help from the USSC,[115] had erected informal barriers to keep even veteran workers like Eaton away from the action—unless, of course, they persisted. Officers wished to limit entry because City Point had become a magnet for meddling civilians. Without a pass from Dix, Eaton might have appeared to be a thrill-seeker. Gatekeepers could deny anyone access to the hospitals at City Point on any ground, and they could entertain themselves at the expense of earnest women. Despite Dix's diminished power and the contempt in which Dix was held by the Surgeon General's staff, Eaton was required to seek her permission. Since Eaton had entered field work through local and state organizations and not through Dix's national superintendence, she and Dix were not acquainted. But undeterred by what she understood as a new layer of red tape, Eaton persisted and obtained the authorization. The depth of Eaton's savvy and indeed her success were measured in the words, "Hav'nt I accomplished it?"[116] If Eaton had been tempted to acquiesce to authority figures at the commencement of the war, she had learned in time, like many veterans, how to ignore the officious and gain her objective.

Surgical authority presented a litmus test for nurses, who sometimes found that medical regulations were at odds with patient care. As New York nurse Georgeanna Woolsey put it, the Army Medical Department, "while not intentionally hard-hearted, would rather prefer to see a man die in the regular way, than to give him a chance of being saved irregularly."[117] Experienced field nurses like Eaton were cognizant of the delicate balance on which their relations with surgeons rested; they developed a precise sense of how to follow rules without surrendering patients' well-being or their own integrity. In other words, they became diplomats. Eaton's interactions with surgeons were cordial but variable. Inevitably, she liked some better than others. Surgical neglect frustrated her, and though she instinctively kept her own counsel, on some occasions she spoke out. When surgeons refused to discharge men whom they believed would recover and the same men died in field hospitals instead of at home, Eaton's ire was visceral. Working closely with the ill and wounded, she believed that she understood better than a skeptical surgeon which men could no longer be of use to the army and ought to be released to die at home.

Eaton was critical of the surgeon of the 20th Maine, Nahum Monroe, and would eventually take sides against him when the 20th's assistant surgeon, Nahum [sic] Hersom, of whom she was especially fond, found Monroe derelict in his medical duty. In March 1863, when Monroe refused to release a chronically ill soldier whom he believed was suffering only from "nostalgia," Eaton swung into action.[118] "I could not have believed Dr. Munroe [sic] would be so ugly or could be so ignorant," she wrote, after another 2nd corps surgeon had judged "Young Spaulding" a fit case for discharge and Dr. John Moore, a medical director in the Army of the Potomac, had rescinded Monroe's declaration—two actions that, in addition to sparking Eaton's courage, shed light on the professional one-upmanship of such negotiations.[119] Determined that Spaulding's sister should not be disappointed after she had traveled to Virginia from Kennebec County, Maine, to carry her brother back home, Eaton confronted Monroe four days after his pronouncement. She contested his written statements about Spaulding, "pick[ing] them all to pieces," and then begged him to stop procrastinating and release sufferers before they died.[120] Eaton recognized that she was risking her reputation for steadiness by speaking so plainly, but she succeeded in getting Spaulding discharged.

While Eaton reserved her most candid censure of the surgeons for the pages of her diary, the soldiers of the 17th Maine were more public in their criticism, questioning the courage of surgeons who shied away from the front lines. After the battle of Chancellorsville, Charles Mattocks, a lieutenant in the 17th, observed, "The wounded have in many cases been sadly neglected…from the cowardice of Surgeons. This doctrine of Surgeons remaining in the rear so far out of danger while poor fellows are suffering for immediate aid is about exploded in the minds of those who have seen the thing in the front." Mattocks went on to sing the praises of the young Annie Etheridge, a second Florence Nightingale in his opinion because he had seen her dress wounds under fire, "where few Surgeons dared show themselves."[121] Another disgruntled soldier from the 17th complained that surgeons were "whittler[s] of human flesh and sawers of bones, [who were] often moved more by their individual likes and dislikes than any medical knowledge. Some surgeons are no more fit for their position than a cow is for teaching the languages."[122]

It is no wonder that soldiers in the 17th grumbled, given the turmoil and instability of the regiment's medical operations. The middle-aged surgeon Henry Wiggin lasted only five months before he contracted malaria and was forced to resign, and the men were outraged when their assistant surgeon, William Wescott of Standish, Maine, was passed over in favor of an outsider with fancy medical degrees. That outsider was none other than Eaton's friend Nahum Hersom, a Bowdoin- and University of Pennsylvania-educated physician. Hersom entered the service in the summer of 1862 and fumed as he witnessed Surgeon Monroe's disregard for sanitary procedures in the 20th Maine. By December 1862—less than four months after the 20th had been mustered in—10 percent of the regiment had contracted smallpox; the highly contagious disease had decimated the regiment of unvaccinated men whom Monroe had not quarantined until nearly a hundred had contracted it.[123] At this troubling juncture, Hersom was promoted, ahead of Wescott, to surgeon of the 17th. Though Eaton was happy for Hersom's good fortune, the rank and file were not. They protested Hersom's appointment because their will had been ignored, and they continued to protest even after Wescott was dismissed for incompetence. Throughout the rest of his service, Hersom found himself in the unenviable position of having to win the loyalty and respect of men who associated his presence with the ouster of a favored comrade *and* of having to second guess his former superior, Monroe, whose men seemed unusually susceptible to disease.

If some surgeons were stubborn or inept, others were simply reckless. No sooner had she arrived for her first tour than Eaton heard of a surgical mishap in which an overdosed soldier died. An overzealous surgeon at Fairfax Seminary Hospital in Alexandria, attempting to punish a patient for raiding a liquor cabinet, stilled him with barbiturates instead.[124] Fifty-eight-year-old Isaac Wixom, a physician from rural Michigan, pursued Eaton for five months during her first tour, even as he was being court-martialed for misuse of "medicinal" supplies. Good-humored about

Wixom's strange manners (she was giving him no encouragement), Eaton found his scientific practices just as unusual. After their first meeting, he gave her the recipe for "Wixom's dose": "For a severe case of congestive fever, 40 grams calomel, 20 gr. quinine, 15 ipecac, 10 opium, 3 capsicum and 1 oz. [spirits] turpentine. Rub the body with 1 pint spts. turpentine, then roll the person in sheet wrung out in hot water and put them in bed where perhaps they may lie twelve hours, then work it off with a slight portion of phys[ic]. I told him that was kill or cure, he said certainly it would be kill if that did not help." Despite her mistrust of Wixom's medical knowledge and romantic intentions, Eaton was incensed when she learned of his court-martial, suspecting that he had fallen afoul of political ill will.[125] Put off by his idiosyncrasies but flattered by his attentions, Eaton had come to depend on the social outlet that Wixom and other surgeons and officers of her acquaintance provided—even if she also wished for more solitude at times.

In the aftermath of battles, medical relationships were pulled taut. Asleep at 4:00 a.m. in a field hospital during the spring 1863 battle of Chancellorsville, Eaton found herself in the midst of an artillery barrage that spared her and the surgeons but killed several patients. The next night, unable to traverse swollen streams whose bridges had been carried away in the heavy rain, she searched for a place to rest her head:

> Drenched to my skin, I rode up to a house, found it crammed full of wounded soldiers who were there on the same errand as ourselves. There was not even standing room, but the doctor managed to find me a corner long enough to lie down in an old attic full of old rubbish & wounded soldiers. There, as he gave me a dry blanket I rolled myself up in a corner, after one o'clock and lay in the dark, with our poor boys, not one of whose faces I had ever seen till morning.[126]

When Eaton called on Dr. William Hezless to attend a soldier whose arm had been amputated at the shoulder, the Pennsylvania surgeon disarranged the ligatures and the man bled to death. Apparently uneasy that Eaton had witnessed this slip of hand, Hezless, who would be court-martialed for drunkenness nine months later, told the shell-shocked Eaton that he hoped she would be killed before next they met. When she asked the surgeon why he would say such a thing, he replied, "why, I know you will go straight to heaven"—the taunt calculated to mock Eaton's piety.[127] That soldiers and surgeons should have been cynical about religious devotion amid the carnage of war is not surprising, but Hezless's thinly veiled insult suggests that some surgeons never adjusted to women's presence and continued to butt heads with them throughout the war.

RACIAL PRINCIPLE AND PRACTICE

The racial climate in the Army of the Potomac and particularly at City Point presented social challenges for blacks and whites alike. For African Americans seeking shelter with Union troops, City Point offered numerous opportunities for manual labor, but little in the way of social advancement. White relief workers like Eaton made a convenience of former slaves, exploiting their willingness to do char work and cooking when it might spare the nurses the trouble.[128] Assuming that ex-slaves were anxious to leave the South, some New Englanders even spoke of carrying home the newly emancipated and making servants of them.[129] If Eaton periodically felt bested by sparring surgeons, her interactions with Rachel, a contraband worker assisting Maine relief agents at City Point, gave her the opportunity to turn the tables. Rachel was already working at City Point when Eaton arrived in October 1864. Believing her to be more of an encumbrance than an asset, Eaton presumed the superior attitude of many elite white Northerners to black Southerners. When a white civilian came to the Maine agency tent looking for her wounded son, Eaton directed this lady to sleep in Rachel's bed and for Rachel to sleep on the floor; the presence of a white stranger trumping that of a black familiar. Unhappy with Rachel's "keeping tent," Eaton complained of her slovenly habits—unwashed tablecloths and bedding—and fretted about her inability to control her: "Scolding her has no effect."[130] It is probable that Rachel read Eaton's commands not as exigencies but as wishes that she might fulfill or not, depending upon her inclination. Punitive language would have had little impact on a person formerly in bondage. What Eaton interpreted as indolence was more likely willful disregard; it was of little matter to Rachel whether Eaton's fire was stoked or not, and her enigmatic presence—a commonplace identity for African Americans in positions of prescribed inferiority[131]—prompted Eaton's suspicion that Rachel was stealing supplies meant for sick soldiers. Before a month had passed, she inveighed, "I am sick of having Rachel about and the sooner she goes the better."[132] With no other reference to Rachel in the diary, it looks as if Eaton got her wish.

Eaton's interactions with Rachel must be understood in the larger context of race relations in Maine during the Civil War period. Though histories published after Emancipation celebrated the abolitionist spirit of Mainers, there was statewide controversy over slavery on the eve of and during the Civil War.[133] A mob fearing industrial competition from black workers broke into the print shop of a Bangor paper, the *Democrat*, and smashed its press when it editorialized in favor of resistance to war in 1861. Portland papers were similarly skeptical about sundering the Union over the cause of abolition.[134] Frank Eaton's acquaintance and Portland private, Charley Oleson, called local abolitionists "white livered" when he perceived their reluctance to enlist; Oleson also denounced the government's call for black troops in 1863: "They are enlisting 'Patriotic Colored Citizens' at a great rate[,] are they not. Government I see is going to raise 50,000 negro troops and officer them with whites. Willn't [*sic*] that be grand," he wrote cynically.[135] Surgeon Benjamin Buxton of the 5th Maine observed in 1863 that white soldiers fearfully anticipated a black invasion: "The Emancipation Proclamation is not generally well received in the Army. The officers say that the President had much better have declared that the war should end with the present year, but to us it looks ridiculous to declare negro freedom in a territory where we can hardly get a foothold for a white man."[136] Limitations on the racial tolerance of educated Mainers were much in evidence in the mid-nineteenth century, and soldiers proved no exception.

Eaton had written of her own limited interactions with African Americans long before she encountered the contraband Rachel at City Point. Portland's population in 1860 was 4 percent black, and that percentage would continue to decline into the twentieth century.[137] While Eaton would have observed African American dock workers in Portland, her war service brought her into more direct contact with a wider range of people of color, and with southern blacks in particular. Such individuals are reckoned as faceless and nameless throughout much of Eaton's account. As she traveled the countryside in the vicinity of Frederick in the autumn of 1862, Eaton met with "old Dinah's" who offered her refreshments and with "ivory Joe" who helped her carry a Christmas feast to the ailing men of the 20th. When African Americans are named, such as Lucy, to whom Eaton hands down an old dress, they are not distinguished by surname.[138] Boarding for a short time at the Richard Randall home near Falmouth, Virginia ("real secesh"), Eaton met Charlotte, a servant whose dialect she attempted to transcribe: "her children, grand children and great grand children, all but dis ere man had been sold from her right on the block by the door and 'pears like her heart would break when her last grandarter was sold three year ago."[139]

Moved by this display and the profession of faith that kept slaves like Charlotte going, Eaton was more adventurous during her second tour, attending services at the colored hospital at City Point soon after her arrival. She found the preacher "eloquent" and his sermon about denominational conflict perceptive, but expressed discomfort among "the colored bredren"; with its "strange mixture of black and white," it was "a queer place to be in." Later, Eaton found their meetings "noisy" and their singing "peculiar."[140] Though several of the white surgeons whom she befriended were attached to the 10th U.S. Colored Infantry, she declined invitations to see that regiment on parade and to dine with the officers.[141] Like other white Americans, Eaton kept her distance from blacks, representing them variously in the diary with pity, anxiety, scorn, or dismissal.

ISABELLA FOGG AND A PARTNERSHIP GONE WRONG

At the center of Harriet Eaton's relationships sat her coworker Isabella Fogg. Although the postwar reminiscences of former nurses praise female solidarity, Eaton's diary, with its greater immediacy, challenges that view.[142] Eaton's relationship with Fogg—cordial but sometimes strained to the breaking point—illustrates the rigors of field nursing, suggesting that the model of cooperation, so often celebrated in published nursing narratives of the Civil War, sustained its own wounds.[143] Eaton's diary reveals friction borne of the social competition in which these two women unwillingly found

Isabella Morrison Fogg, a widow from Calais, Maine, was Eaton's coworker during her initial tour of duty with the Army of the Potomac's second division in 1862–63. Eaton found Fogg indecorous and impulsive, and over time their working relations cooled considerably. MAINE STATE ARCHIVES, AUGUSTA

An agent for the state soldier's relief association, Charles C. Hayes was often at Eaton's side as she rambled through the Virginia countryside in search of Maine's infantrymen. Hayes sensed the tension between Eaton and Isabella Fogg. MAINE STATE ARCHIVES, AUGUSTA

themselves. Fogg's lack of formal education, her Canadian and Irish antecedents, her labor as a "tailoress," and her working-class assertiveness ruffled Eaton's genteel and retiring manners.[144] "An unwitting participant in the anti-Irish sentiment of the day," Eaton felt threatened by Fogg's can-do attitude and the boundless physical energy Fogg applied to her relief work, even to the point of making herself ill. Eaton's inclination to remain on the margins of regimental and hospital life did not endear her to Fogg.

With significant knowledge about New England's three urban jewels—Boston, Hartford, and Portland—Eaton was no small-town girl. Negotiating these cities made her at once more worldly but also more cautious. For her own part, Fogg resented Eaton's attitude of noblesse oblige and did not let it pass unremarked, scolding Eaton in the second month of their acquaintance for "[feeling] so far above Calais because [she] came from Portland" and "was not willing that [Fogg] should come near [her] that came from P[ortland]."[145] Add to this the circumstances of being thrown into physical proximity with a relative stranger and having to cope with deprivations (no place to sleep, infrequent shelter, exposure to the elements, inadequate food), and it is easy to see how even the best of friendships would have faltered. Widespread illness among Maine regiments during the fall and winter of 1862–63 and hundreds of Maine casualties from the battles of Antietam, Fredericksburg, and Chancellorsville left little hope, in the case of Eaton and Fogg, for a good outcome.

That both women had teenaged sons among the Maine troops provided, at least initially, a bond between them. A desire to be near her only child, the eighteen-year-old Hugh, a private in company D of the 6th Maine Infantry, impelled Fogg's work in the camps and hospitals, and so it was with Eaton, whose son Frank had enlisted in company A of the 25th Maine in September 1862 along with a group of his Portland friends.[146] When Eaton left for Virginia, ten days before Frank's regiment left Portland for Washington, she lived in hope of seeing him. Though the 25th was assigned to the defenses of Washington in 1862 and Frank was stationed near Long Bridge, the mile-long timber structure spanning the Potomac from southwest Washington to Alexandria, Eaton would see her son only twice during her service. These rare sightings and Frank's rejection of religion suggest that he may have been less devoted to his mother than she to him.[147]

Isabella Fogg would see Hugh more often because of his illnesses. He contracted both malaria and syphilis in the service and was so seriously wounded at the battle of Cedar Creek in October 1864 that his left leg had to be amputated two inches above the knee.[148] By the autumn of 1864, Isabella was working for the Christian Commission, having been dismissed by the MCHA. She journeyed from New England to Baltimore, where Hugh was recovering from surgery, and stayed at his bedside for more than two months. Fogg herself would be confined to a hospital bed in Cincinnati for two years beginning in January 1865, when she fell through a hatchway and sustained a back injury aboard the transport vessel *Jacob Strader* as it floated up the Ohio River.

From the first of their acquaintance, Eaton decried Fogg's questionable self-control and lack of caution. Fogg herself chafed at Eaton's arrogant self-satisfaction, her circumscribed sphere of action, and her formal etiquette. As early as the third week of their service together, Eaton was vexed by Fogg's inability to "cast her burden on the Lord" when a search for Hugh, who had been reported sick, ended fruitlessly. Bickering was evident by the second month, with Fogg telling Eaton that "she supposed I felt that she was <u>my</u> cross."[149] Throughout the diary, Eaton berated her coworker's domestic ineptitude: she charged Fogg and her contacts with failure to pack boxes properly and resented having to clean up their condiment jars, which had "gone to smash." By the end of 1862, Eaton's patience was wearing thin: On the eve of the battle of Fredericksburg, Fogg borrowed Eaton's boots, ostensibly to locate an ambulance to convey them into the field for the day's work, but instead of returning to their tent, Fogg went on to Aquia Creek for supplies, preventing the unshod Eaton from visiting the regiments for several days. When Fogg finally returned, harsh words were exchanged, though Eaton does not relate them, choosing instead to record Fogg's rejection of a proffered cup of tea and concluding, "I had much rather go to a Regt. by myself and act for myself" than in company with Mrs. Fogg.[150] Even Charles Hayes, who worked with them in the field, was aware of the feud. He wrote to John Hathaway of the MSRA, "I find that Mrs. Fogg works away from Mrs. Eaton much better than with her and for the future I shall endeavor to have their labors divided so that they can work in two different regiments."[151]

They were still at odds a month later when Eaton, homesick, blue, and cold since it was January, kept her seat in the ladies' ambulance while Mrs. Fogg conducted business with General Sumner at 2nd division headquarters. Such a gesture suggests that Eaton neither wished to be seen with Fogg nor to present an allied front in their relief labors—a physically telling symbol of their growing rift. Alluding to her internal struggle to coexist more peacefully with Fogg, Eaton redoubled her efforts to remember her mission of Christian succor: "The caring for our suffering soldiers I came here for and I love the work, but there are things I little dreamed of."[152]

Eaton had an opportunity to reconcile with Fogg in the fifth month of her service, when they joined forces to protest the conduct of Alden Litchfield, the "wicked, profane, cruel, and unprincipled" quartermaster of the 20th Maine, who bragged to peers about "hustling" the recently expired into the ground and charging to their corpses new clothing requisitions that landed on the backs of his cronies.[153] Eaton and Fogg collaborated on a letter, written in Eaton's hand but signed only with Fogg's name, in February 1863. Eaton's decision not to sign the letter—though she was most likely its author and not merely a scribe—signaled yet another layer of enmity between the two. Not wanting to be seen as a troublemaker, Eaton characteristically strove for invisibility; Isabella Fogg's willingness to own the critique of the quartermaster's graft and other plain criticism she leveled at officers and coworkers is likely to have been what led to her ouster from the MCHA in November 1863.[154] Eaton, always aloof and more politic, fared far better in public evaluations, exhibiting a style of conduct that military men and their elite supporters in Maine found more suitable. The ladies' petition appears to have been unsuccessful, since Litchfield was

Known familiarly as "Sewall" to his wife Harriet, Reverend Jeremiah Sewall Eaton brought his young family to Portland in 1844 when he was named pastor of the Free Street Baptist Church. Forced to resign because of illness in 1854, he died of what appears to be tuberculosis in 1856. MAINE HISTORICAL SOCIETY, PORTLAND

not mustered out until June 1865. Working in tandem apparently did not improve their mutual regard.

As they pleaded their case against Quartermaster Litchfield to military officials in late February 1863, Fogg fell seriously ill, probably with typhoid. By March 4, Fogg was unwilling to remain in bed and insisted that she ride with Eaton to the regiments in the field. From March 9 to 11, in bone-chilling weather, Fogg made a trip to and from Washington for new supplies, unwilling to stop when she saw so much work to be done; by the next day the exposure had completely incapacitated her. Though she asked for Dr. Hezless to attend her, rejecting the consultation of Dr. Wixom, she refused to endure the blistering process Hezless recommended.[155] She agreed to let Dr. Hersom cup her—a process by which blisters were raised through the vacuum created when heated glass cups were applied to the skin—but declined his mustard poultice. Assigned to nurse Fogg, Eaton was beside herself, wondering how to appease the capricious patient: "What shall I do?" she wrote. "The Lord direct me. Dr. W[ixom] says I must not leave her two or three days, while she says, if I do'nt go to visit the Regt. she will start for Washington tomorrow. Here lays the powder, she will not take it, and there is the mustard draft [*sic*], she will not have it on."[156] According to Eaton's testimony, Fogg kept four surgeons running, refusing to rest and thus delaying her recovery. Eaton's resentment was palpable, her tone shrill, when Fogg went on the offensive against Eaton's military friends: "Mrs. Fogg had Dr. Moore to call on her to night and he told her, she <u>must</u> have fresh air, and not gobble down medicine but take good, wholesome food. The Major [Charles Gilmore] was here, but what an effect it had, he was not attentive enough, said Portland people were '<u>human beings</u>' in answer to her remark that all they cared for her was that she might be out of the way. I am not easily frightened at <u>hysteria</u>."[157] In a state of mental and physical debility, Fogg lashed out again and again, souring alliances upon which she had depended while Eaton took the high road.

A report from Charles S. Wainwright, colonel of the 1st New York Light Artillery, accused Fogg of giving preferential treatment to soldiers of the 5th Battery, the only Maine regiment present in the Union Army's 1st corps, as it encamped near Middleburg, Virginia, at the end of August. "Our doctors curse the old woman up and down as a meddling pest," he complained, "doing ten times the harm she does good. Her bringing [Lieutenant William F.] Twitchell over here at last excited the General's ire, so that yesterday he ordered her out of the corps.… The sanitaries no doubt do some good…but when…their agents go still farther than this and attempt to run against regulations, they become a nuisance not to be borne."[158] Clearly, Eaton was not the only person who found Fogg's initiatives presumptuous and inappropriate. The November meeting of the MCHA in Portland resolved that "in consequence of reports prejudicial to the character and usefulness of Mrs. Fogg, as a nurse now under the patronage of this association, having been received, it was voted that the President with Mrs. Fernald and [Ellen Usher] Bacon, be a committee to inform Mrs. Fogg that the Association deem it for their interest and the good of the cause, to dissolve their connection with her."[159] Though Eaton never admitted any role in Fogg's dismissal, she certainly believed that she had sufficient cause to see Fogg undone.

This chilly détente marked the end of Eaton's and Fogg's partnership. Only two other times does Eaton mention Fogg in the diary: first, in October 1864 at City Point, when the returning Eaton discovered that Fogg, who had been working for the Christian Commission since her ouster from the MCHA, had become an object of derision among Portland veterans in the 5th Maine Battery—the same unit to which it was alleged she had given preferential treatment ("Poor Mrs. F has to take it from all of them"); and second, on her way back home in December, when she learned about Hugh Fogg's amputation and wished that she "had letter paper with me this morning," presumably to write a note of condolence.[160] Eaton's reaction to this news, best described as fleeting regret, provides one small shaft of light in an otherwise dark room.

Now that Isabella Fogg was out of the way, Eaton might feel a glimmer of remorse for what was surely her part in Fogg's undoing. Eaton's feeling of pity, earnest though it might have been, provides further insight into this psychodrama: If Eaton sensed that she had engaged in a witch hunt, there was no better way to be chastened, and thus reinstate herself in her good opinion, than by performing an entirely private penance. Though this parting of ways strongly suggests that Isabella Fogg may have been more sinned against than sinning—after all, she was hardier and more hardworking than Eaton and did not fold up her tent and go home when self-proclaimed social superiors rejected her—Eaton was not about to capitulate to this view. But the nuances and insinuations are all in Eaton's firsthand account, not erased or expunged as they might have been had Eaton sought to publish her diary after the war. From the soldiers' reckoning, women like Eaton and Fogg had been "ministering angels." Eaton's rendering of the anatomy of the relationship reveals mutual fault, intractability, and prejudice—qualities as distant from harmony and perfection as postwar hagiography was from lived wartime experience. Indeed, these proceedings revealed the Janus face of the "lady with the lamp." Whereas postwar accounts dubbed the nurse as a paragon of self-sacrifice, obedience, and delicacy—a "woman of valor" whose moral compass guided her in dealing with soldiers and surgeons[161]—the struggle played out in Eaton's diary reveals just how hard it was to live up to the ideal.

THE SPIRITUAL QUOTIENT

Chastening was habitual with Eaton and served as a constant reminder of submission to a higher power. The diary is punctuated with declarations of such submission, demonstrating Eaton's wish to model Christian deportment for those she met in Virginia. Within five days of her arrival there in 1862—on a Sunday after services—Eaton was lamenting time spent in "careless conversation.... Oh! let me remember what I am here for," she scolded.[162] Repeatedly expressing regret that the Union Army ignored the Sabbath by commencing military movements on Sundays, Eaton initially felt guilty for not reserving the day for the Lord.[163] In time, however, she became inured to the practice, rationalizing her work with soldiers, Sunday or any day, as a quintessential and temporal expression of Christian charity. Dying men particularly drew her interest. The first deathbed she attended on her twelfth day of service contained a delirious officer from the 19th Maine, whom she "tried to point...to Jesus but to earthly appearances such attempts were vain."[164] Though perhaps more of a consolation to Eaton than to some of the men she tended, helping soldiers die lent welcome structure to the chaos governing relief work in the field.[165]

Helping to save the soldier's soul was no less important than saving his body, and true patriotism required Christian workers to attend to both as a moral imperative.[166]

In fact, few relief workers would have seen the redemption of the soul as distinct from the healing of the body. It was a privilege to attend the passing of a soul into eternity and a great consternation to witness a death devoid of spiritual peace. Even worse was not to witness a death at all; families bereft of sons and fathers without the evidence of the body were tortured at the prospect of a soul having departed without its customary human emissary.[167] Eaton and others like her did their best to ensure that no soldier would face eternity unprepared. If they sensed that death was nigh, they ascertained a soldier's religious convictions. If they found the sufferer spiritually wanting, they exerted themselves urgently in his behalf lest he die without the grace that Protestant watchers believed was integral to a good death.[168]

Anxious to see evidence of soldiers' desire for conversion, Eaton began her service confident that she would bring men to God. By late 1862, the Army of the Potomac was awash in revivalism. Even though men in the ranks continued to drink, swear, whore, and gamble, attendance at camp meetings soared, suggesting that churchgoing provided weekly redemption for those who did not finally intend to renounce their vices.[169] Several Maine regiments constructed chapels, including one well known to Eaton, the 16th, which featured a canvas roof and pulpit as well as evergreen boughs and scriptural excerpts adorning the walls.[170] In accord with the northern Baptist revivalists' position opposing the consumption of alcohol and the use of profanity, Eaton was hopeful early on that she could serve the greater good by bringing lost lambs back into the fold, but instead she found resistance.

On a snowy night in November 1862, Chaplain George Knox of the 10th Maine lamented that conversion opportunities were scarce, and Eaton concluded philosophically that "this [was] not a war under God's direction." Two days later, she renewed her efforts by distributing tracts, but soon discovered that the men used them to light their pipes.[171] Gratified in February 1863, when Chaplain John Adams of the 5th announced that three Mainers had recently undergone conversion and several more "gave evidence of seriousness," Eaton waxed beatifically, "Oh how precious to feel that the spirit of the Lord has not ceased to strive in this scene of corruption and moral death."[172] Eaton pressed on, though not without doubts that such transformations might be short-lived. As General Hooker amassed a force of more than 110,000 men around Fredericksburg in April 1863, movements that would culminate at Chancellorsville in May, Eaton worried about her son Frank, whom she believed would be ordered to join the troops gathering for battle.[173] Anticipating the worst, Eaton framed the religious conundrum over which she was struggling: "Oh why this dreadful war! [Frank] bears no malice to his Southern brother, can he deliberately take his life? I cannot bear the thought. Can a Christian nation conscientiously kill each other? Will our Maker approve?...Why is this, let me ask, why?"[174] While contemporary theologians went on record proclaiming the divine sanction of their Christian militancy, Eaton's private musings illuminate the contradiction that many devout Christians must have observed. How, she wondered, could the demands of war ever transcend the dictates of the Ten Commandments?

Unable to resolve these questions, Eaton continued to dedicate herself to the Lord's work and remained hopeful that she might convert soldiers during her second tour of duty. The more complex social fabric of City Point—its population density in contrast to the diffusion of regiments earlier in the war—made for a greater concentration of men, many of whom, as convalescents or administrators, had time on their hands. In the fourth year of the war, the novelty and alacrity that guided officers and their men in 1861 and 1862 had morphed into lassitude and boredom. Though it would be reasonable to assume that the horrible cases of illness Eaton witnessed in the fall of 1862 would have created religious fervor conducive to conversions, the fact remains that she made more missionary progress later in the war, when relief systems had been more successfully centralized, and with men who were not desperately ill. In late November, just five weeks before Eaton returned to Portland, she met the convalescing Nathaniel P. Jaques, a grey-eyed, dark-haired, five-foot-nine-inch private in the 19th Maine Infantry from Bowdoin. Jaques had been in the ranks through Fredericksburg, Chancellorsville, Gettysburg (where the regiment had been instrumental in repelling Pickett's Charge), the Wilderness, Spotsylvania, Cold Harbor, and now Petersburg; Eaton saw in him a soul ripe for awakening and, in his moment of spiritual vulnerability, a surrogate son.

In what can best be described as a series of ecstatic encounters, Eaton pursued the twenty-seven-year-old with a fervor that threatened to outstrip its religious sanction. After first meeting him in the Maine agency tent on November 19, she felt an immediate connection, hoping that Jaques would not "resist the evident strivings of the Spirit."[175] Eaton wrote him a letter because she was "burdened in spirit for him," and on November 21 was already referring to Jaques as "my dear J," with nomenclature that would become even more intimate two weeks later, in the abbreviated form of his first name, "N." Though such intimate forms of address were not unusual in nineteenth-century correspondence among familiars, the speed with which Eaton's solicitude accelerated is surprising, when we consider that she had met Jaques a mere two days earlier.

Within a week of forming the acquaintance, Eaton had made Jaques the focus of her chronicle, confiding that "his frankness interests me most deeply," praying that he might renounce strong drink, and declaring that her hand "trembled" as she wrote to him. Two days later, Eaton again chose the word "deep" to characterize their bond, a word that she seldom used up to this point in the diary: they had "a deeply solemn conversation" which prompted her to consider "how deep an experience I am permitted to have in his case."[176] On December 3, just two weeks to the day of their introduction, Eaton was enthralled that Jaques professed his willingness to be baptized, but worried that her emotional investment in him might compromise her strivings on behalf of her own son. "It seems as if my soul must burst this clayey tenement and soar away," she wrote jubilantly. "My dear J has found Jesus. Last night my agony was so great, that I rose to pray for him.... He went to meeting and on his return, with tears rolling down his cheeks, he told me of his happiness.... Now the thought comes, 'have I received him instead of my dear F[rank]?'" The next day, Eaton attended Baptist services twice, taking pleasure in the conversion of three soldiers who "were buried in the likeness of their Lord beneath the wave" and in hearing Jaques's public declaration of faith. Anxious to regain self-possession lest she wallow in the pride of having instigated Jaques's conversion, Eaton characteristically chastened herself: "Oh! that I may be kept humble."[177]

During her remaining days at City Point, the level of her intimacy with Jaques increased. They regularly enjoyed "sweet converse of heavenly things" and Jaques attempted to forestall his return to the Petersburg trenches by asking Eaton to intercede on his behalf with hospital staff. By the second week of December, he became Eaton's de facto assistant and spent entire days in her company in addition to several nights. Eaton now noted that she loved him "as an own son" and believed that he had stopped drinking as a gesture of his regard for her: "Oh, how can I realize the happiness I am permitted to enjoy. I am surprised at the similarity of our views and at his own maturity of thought on these subjects. He has decided to give up a bad habit, partly because the habit is bad, and partly to please me."[178] Inevitably, Jaques was called back to the front, and Eaton felt "robbed" of their last night together when two other visitors intruded on them. By December 14 Jaques was gone, but Eaton's ardor had not cooled. She arranged with Joseph Spaulding, colonel of the 19th, to send mittens to the men ("Dear N must have a pair") and reprised her correspondence with Jaques. "Have written to my dear boy," she noted on December 17, again invoking the language of familial relation. The next day, she mentioned twice having written to Jaques; whether she had actually written him two letters or was simply so forlorn at his departure that she mentioned the letter-writing twice is not clear. The following day she prepared a package of "goodies" that the steward of the 19th conveyed to Jaques and noted on December 21 that she had "just written to both of my dear sons." En route back to Washington, Eaton was thrilled to receive a letter from Jaques and hoped that by the time she reached Portland, another of his missives would be waiting for her.

Eaton's intense relationship with Nathaniel Jaques was the spiritual highlight of her "season with the army."[179] Though she was eighteen years his senior and referred to him as a son, it is apparent that Eaton felt more than maternally about Jaques. The religious rapture she described consequent to their numerous meetings and evident in their growing physical intimacy emotionally reimbursed Eaton for the things she had given up to go to war. Dedicated to an evangelism that northern Baptists understood to be synonymous with their profession of faith, the act of saving a soul for Jesus Christ paid personal dividends over which even the most pious had to be vigilant. We do not know whether Eaton and Jaques ever experienced a sexual liaison; if they consummated their relationship, it is unlikely that they did so during their shared sojourn at City Point. However, the language of adoration was evident in Eaton's private record, spilling beyond its religious context into a more personal realm. In effect, for Eaton, the gift of spiritual awakening was tantamount to the most deeply fulfilling of human experiences, which by no means excluded the sexual. It was clearly powerful enough to last beyond the war and to give Eaton another chance for personal happiness.

The U.S. census of 1870 indicates that Eaton and Jaques were living in a boardinghouse with four other adults in Tioga County, New York, between Elmira and Binghamton, more than five hundred miles from Portland. Eaton was the proprietor of a hardware store there and Jaques was the store's clerk. At this time Eaton's twenty-two- and fifteen-year-old daughters were living with family friends Samuel and Elizabeth Whitney in Windsor, Vermont, away from their mother. A month before the Tioga County census appeared, Jaques was also listed in the Newton, Massachusetts, census—in Eaton's hometown—where he was selling stoves and furnaces. The thirty-three-year-old Jaques had been living in a Newton boardinghouse at least since 1868; the 1860 Newton census indicated that he had a wife, Charlotte, and a nine-month-old son, Claude.

Having never mentioned this young family to Eaton, we might suppose that they had perished before the war began. But a later document trail suggests otherwise: In 1881 Jaques filed a veteran's pension application from Nevada; he was living in Reno when the 1890 census was taken. By 1910, at age seventy-two, he was a resident of the Malibu, California, Soldiers' Home, one of many such facilities for single or widowed veterans who desired the camaraderie and needed public assistance.[180] The 1910 census also lists him as a member of his son Claude's and daughter-in-law's Los Angeles household, which suggests that he had both government and family support in his later years. We do not know whether Jaques's wife Charlotte was still alive and who was caring for his son when he and Eaton shared an address in upstate New York. All that remains to link Jaques with Eaton in the postwar years is the provocative census of 1870, from which it might be inferred that something more than friendship existed between them.

These facts are extraordinary. The profound spiritual connection that Eaton had forged with Jaques in 1864 over the prospect of his baptism did not end when he was mustered out of the service in 1865. How had Jaques come to move to Eaton's hometown? Had Eaton tried to connect him with members of her family who might help him get a start in business? If Jaques was a husband and father, what was he doing living at a second address—indeed the same address as Eaton—in a community hundreds of miles away from his young family? What was the origin of his and Eaton's commercial alliance, and was it fueled by some romantic understanding? What exactly was the nature of their relationship? Had Eaton's ecstatic language about her meetings with Jaques at City Point led to a secretive cohabitation? Since Jaques was listed in the 1870 censes for both Tioga County and Newton, one wonders whether he moved regularly between these locations or if the Newton address was a cover offered by a wife who wished to maintain respectability in what must have been, at the very least, an awkward position. While it may well be that the relationship between Eaton and Jaques was entirely innocent—after all, she had characterized him as a second son at City Point—we also know that Eaton left her daughters with friends in Vermont and that she would never again return to Portland. At a time when idle gossip or merely the *appearance* of a loss of virtue could tarnish a woman's reputation, even if she were a fifty-two-year-old widow, it is reasonable to conjecture that Eaton might have moved to Hartford to escape notice after the connection with Jaques had run its course. There is no hard evidence that Eaton and Jaques were lovers, but their (d)alliance was certainly unconventional. The true nature of the friendship, while offering us a glimpse into the well of religious ecstasy, remains just beyond our reach.

Just before her departure from City Point in December 1864, Eaton recorded regret at having to leave "this birth place of souls." As a Baptist and an evangelical, Eaton strove to point men toward God and hoped that she might be used as an instrument of their conversion and redemption. Her concern for soldiers who teetered on the brink of eternity unwittingly and unsaved had been keen; the figure of birth amounting to an antidote for the cosmic reckoning that stole away the unwary too soon. Eaton's "birth place of souls" inserted hope into a mass spectacle of death but also referenced her nursing experience. Her own soul has been birthed in the crucible of war. Leaving a former life behind, she explored a region of the United States that she had seen only cursorily years before, she had attempted to forestall the toll of human misery with physical and spiritual aid, and she had witnessed the mystery of self-regeneration as she grew to love her work and formed attachments that a society at peace could not have tolerated. Eaton made the last entry in her diary on Christmas eve 1864; she arrived back in Portland that evening to spend the holidays with her daughters. Son Frank was still a soldier, his whereabouts unknown. But by 1868, he was a married resident of Columbia, South Carolina.[181] When he died at age forty-three in 1886, two years after his mother and a year before his sister Agnes, he left a widow and three young children—an uncanny reprise of his mother's fate.

The voice of Harriet Eaton, by turns incisive, discerning, plaintive, and tender, reminds us what it was to be a civilian with family ties during the Civil War. Though the conflict tested Eaton's religious mettle, it made her a more thoughtful and grateful Christian. Not inclined to challenge the civil, religious, and medical authority that sponsored her work, Eaton nonetheless found ways to assert her will as a field nurse. Like other female relief workers, she invented a flexible diplomacy that gave her room to make improvements in soldier care while she followed military rules. Neither a paragon nor a pariah, she found fortitude where she least expected to and could not jettison her prejudices as much as she might have wished to. Eaton was, above all, human in her strivings and failures, in her conscientious application of religious principles, and in her desire to do the best she could under less than ideal circumstances. The extent to which the contested ground of medical care is visible in Eaton's diary urges us to move beyond the two-dimensional perspective that has for too long characterized our understanding of civilians' role in wartime benevolence.

Though the content and meaning may sometimes be obscure, we can reassemble enough of the story, as if by time travel, to enter a past that eludes us, even as it continues to evolve.

NOTES ON THE TEXT

Harriet Eaton's "journals," as she called them, have belonged to the Southern Historical Collection at the University of North Carolina (UNC) since 1942, when UNC's Wilson Library purchased the diary from a Hartford bookshop. That was the same year that Eaton's youngest child, Hatty Belle, who had kept the diary, died. Having outlived her sister Agnes and brother Frank by fifty-five years, Hatty Belle was the lone guardian of Harriet Eaton's legacy. Given the paucity of extant Civil War nursing diaries, it is fortunate that UNC acquired the journals and that I found them in 1991 while I researched *Women at the Front: Hospital Workers in Civil War America* (2004). Long before I had completed work on that book, I determined that the diary should someday be published because of its candor and its behind-the-scenes look at the tensions that animated state relief work in the shadow of federal benevolence.

Harriet Eaton's journals consist of five worn tan leather volumes, four by six inches in size, with ruled gray pages. Eaton's cursive penmanship was admirably legible, despite its small size—the equivalent of today's twelve-point type. Eaton used pencil in the first volume; in later volumes she wrote in black ink, now faded in places and water-stained. Volume 1, not included in this edition, contains Eaton's diary of the sea voyage that she and husband Sewall took to Florida and Alabama during the winter of 1853–54 to alleviate his respiratory distress. Their journey began on December 5, 1853 in the Portland harbor on a ship bound for Mobile, Alabama—coincidentally the home of Kate Cumming. Though Cumming and Eaton probably never met in Mobile, Eaton mentions meeting Mrs. Williamson and her daughter Margaret on March 18, 1854. Eight years later, Margaret Williamson would accompany Kate Cumming to Okolona and Corinth, Mississippi, where they would begin their hospital work with the Confederate Army of Tennessee.[182] During an arduous journey from Portland to the South, which took four weeks because the winds were not favorable, the Eatons stopped in Washington, Savannah, Gainesville, the Bahamas, and several of the Florida Keys before they reached the port of Mobile on January 3, 1854.

As they crossed and recrossed Dixie, the Eatons spent some weeks in Gainesville, where Sewall gave sermons and Harriet observed at first hand the lives of slaves and their white owners. On March 4, 1854, she noted derisively, "The happiness of many planters seems to consist in making cotton to buy negroes and buying negroes to make cotton. The state of public morals is frightful." Her many interactions with slaves convinced her that the peculiar institution degraded southern manners and kept the entire region in educational and cultural stultification. Scornful of slaves who had no notion of their age or even of numbers, Eaton would carry both indignation and frustration with her when she traveled to Virginia in 1862, remarking at the masks of indifference worn by the bondspeople she worked with in military camps.

On April 26, the Eatons left Gainesville and began an overland journey home, which included a stop in Atlanta, "a city, so they say." Almost prescient, Eaton reconsidered: "Well I suppose it is destined to be a city of some importance as being a great gathering place for rail roads."[183] As they worked their way up the Atlantic seaboard, the Eatons met with other church friends spending the winter in southerly latitudes—an indication that nineteenth-century New England had its share of snow birds. A highlight of the journey home was a stop in Mount Vernon, where Eaton was thrilled to see the last resting place of George Washington and where she bristled at countrymen who failed to regard the place with appropriate reverence.[184] After recording stops in Washington, Baltimore, Philadelphia, New York, and Hartford, the first volume of Eaton's diary ends abruptly, in mid-sentence, on May 27, 1854. The last page of the volume features a list of expenditures for goods that Eaton purchased and another list with names of women and dollar amounts, perhaps for the Eatons' board or laundry. Extant accounts from the 1850s show Sewall to have been a careful accountant of his young family's purchases; Harriet would be no less careful in her cataloguing of supplies in reports to the Maine Camp Hospital Association eight years later.[185]

Volumes 2 and 3 record Eaton's first tour of duty in the Army of the Potomac, beginning on October 6, 1862 with her trip to Washington, and ending on May 12, 1863, as she fumbled her way home in illness, six weeks before the battle of Gettysburg. Volume 3 has lost its covers and has significant water stains, rendering many of its pages difficult to read. It begins with Eaton's entry for December 20, 1862, in the frozen drizzle following the battle of Fredericksburg, and ends with the Maine wounded from the battle of Chancellorsville struggling to survive. Exhausted from more than seven uninterrupted months of hard field service and overwrought until she gained the intelligence that Frank had survived the battle, Eaton left Virginia barely able to sit up.

Volume 4, which picks up seventeen months later, in 1864, covers Eaton's second tour in the Army of the Potomac's immense hospital installation at City Point, Virginia, from October through December, as the siege of Petersburg interminably reached its sixth month. Little did Eaton know when, homeward bound, she and Sewall passed through Petersburg and Fredericksburg in May 1854 that she would return to repair the broken bodies of soldiers in both places a decade later. On the first page of Volume 4 she wrote, "Journal of a second tour to the Army now lying before Petersburg and Richmond." Bound in blue-gray cardboard, the inside of the front and back covers features notes concerning patients Eaton cared for from all over the Union states—a change from her earlier tour as nurse for Maine troops alone. This informal list includes the name of Nathaniel Jaques—the soldier from Maine whom Eaton believed she had been called to save. Although Mainers were dispersed among soldiers from other states at City Point, Eaton never lost track of boys from home. Indeed Jaques would figure prominently in Eaton's postwar years.

we are told. we must leave the ground, a general order has been given. Mrs. T. was determined to cross the river, although Col. Chamberlain wrote a note discouraging it. She left us and took an ambulance while we started for the Smith house. I had no sooner arrived there, than I received a note that a hundred men, were then on the way who needed a dinner. Mrs. Husband had come and was dressing wounds. Mrs. McKay soon made her appearance from across the river, ie. I procured a detail of men and cooked them broth over a camp fire We fed the men, but as there was another train coming Mrs. Fogg determined to remain and get a supper for them, while I went on with the team.— Soon after we started a tremendous thunder and hail storm commenced the ambulance leaked like a sieve and notwithstanding I had two quilts I was drenched to my skin. I met the 6th Maine and Capt's Furlong and Busford assured me of Hugh's safety. He was with the Colonel.

<u>Wednesday, May 6th</u> Well, last night I had an adventure. The streams were so swollen that the bridges were carried away and after being

An excerpt from Eaton's diary. SOUTHERN HISTORICAL COLLECTION, UNIVERSITY OF NORTH CAROLINA-CHAPEL HILL

mixed up with supply, ammunition and ambulance trains in all sorts of ways, we were at last left alone, lost our way, learned that the bridge near Stoneman's Switch was carried away, so there was no help for it, and drenched to my skin, I rode up to a house, found it crammed full of wounded soldiers who were there on the same errand as ourselves. There was not even standing room, but the doctor managed to find me a corner long enough to lie down, in an old attic, full of old rubbish & wounded soldiers. There, as he gave me a dry blanket I rolled myself up in a corner, after one o'clock, and lay, in the dark, with our poor boys, not one of whose faces I had ever seen, till morning. At five I rose, and impressed men to go into the old cook house and build me a big fire, bring camp kettles and fill them with water, and there I made a good, warm breakfast for 150 men, and they assured me they had enough. — I gave four shirts to shivering literally naked men, and slippers to others. As soon as possible I left and reached home about ten o'clock. Mrs. Fogg and Mrs. Husband came in, in about an hour and a half. We were all sleepy and we laid down and were sound asleep when who should march in without knocking but Dr. Harley, and woke us up ex-

Eaton was also an inveterate letter-writer, corresponding with friends and family as well as with local Portland and state relief agents about her work with soldiers. Her letters to MCHA officials were occasionally reprinted by the *Portland Daily Press* and the *Portland Transcript*—a subject that caused the modest Eaton consternation. When officers teased her about her journalistic celebrity back home, Eaton was distressed beyond measure. Still, she found time to write to friends—many of whom were involved in the supply train from Portland to Washington—and to relatives. Eaton's letters to her daughter and namesake, Hatty Belle, archived in the Josephine Dolan collection at the University of Connecticut, are particularly poignant, revealing Eaton's regret at having to leave her youngest in the care of others. The letters, which are cross-referenced in the diary, are reprinted in Appendix I.

Most of Eaton's orthographic peculiarities have been maintained. She consistently put the apostrophe in contractions before instead of after the *n*, as in "ca'nt" and "do'nt," and put a space between "Mc" and the rest of a surname, as in "Mc Intyre." She spelled names as she heard them—not always accurately, as in the case of Dr. "Bermister" for Burmeister and "Fobes" for Forbes. Though Eaton hailed from the Boston area, Mainers in her midst would have elided the *r* in Forbes to make it sound like <Fawbs> and thus to make its correct spelling uncertain. When citing large numbers, Eaton inserted commas to the right of the hundreds instead of the thousands column. Despite these anomalies, Eaton was a good accountant and an able speller with a good ear. She frequently used abbreviations—for company, regiment, hospital, Maine, and for officers' ranks, among other things. Eaton also used shorthand for her familiars by referring to them with the first letter of the surname, as in "Mrs. F" for coworker Isabella Fogg, and "Mr. H" for Maine state relief agent Charles Hayes. Eaton's underlining has been maintained; though she occasionally underlined for emphasis, her most frequent use of underlining flags the letters she wrote—a quick way for her to peruse the diary text for an update on her correspondence.

Minor corrections and insertions in the text have been made when, for example, a letter or word was inadvertently left out, or to correct a name or reference when it is certain that Eaton meant something else. Serial commas have been inserted in diary entries. In the matter of misspelled place names, Eaton's initial spelling is indicated in brackets, as in "[Frederic]" for Frederick, Maryland. Subsequent uses have been corrected and are signaled by enclosing the corrections within brackets or by using "[*sic*]" when Eaton's original spelling is retained. Quotation marks have been added to indicate her attempts to represent the dialect of contraband slaves at City Point in 1864.

The diary is followed by an extensive biographical dictionary of most of the five hundred people to whom Eaton refers in these pages. Each entry in this alphabetical roster includes not only the service record of soldiers and the wartime activities of civilians, but also information about an individual's prewar and postwar lives. Individual entries for which I have not been able with certainty to ascertain birth and/or death dates do not include this information. For people with identical surnames, given names are included in brackets for clarification; similarly, most surnames that Eaton indicated with only a

Eaton's son Frank enlisted in the 25th Maine Infantry in September 1862, less than a month before she left Portland for her first tour of duty in Virginia. Frank complained of chronic respiratory distress throughout his three years of service with the Army of the Potomac. He married a Southerner in 1866 and became the father of three daughters. At the age of forty-two, in 1886, Frank died of tuberculosis, the same disease that killed his father. COURTESY OF NICHOLAS P. PICERNO

single letter are spelled out to avoid ambiguity. Generals whose military achievements Eaton mentions are not identified unless she saw that officer in person. In individual entries, the age given is that of the soldier when he first joined a regiment. The town from which a soldier joined a regiment is not necessarily his birthplace. Unless otherwise mentioned, all regimental numbers refer to the infantry. Cavalry, battalion, and artillery regiments are explicitly designated to distinguish them from the infantry. People mentioned in the diary whom I have not been able to identify positively are not included in the biographical dictionary. In most cases I have not been able to identify the civilians who accommodated Eaton along the way, so they are not included.

The Diary

These two women, ready to board an ambulance from a canal boat on Antietam Creek, are likely to be Harriet Eaton (left) and Isabella Fogg (right) in 1862. Relief workers in the vicinity of the Army of the Potomac sought access to such conveyances as they moved among regiments in the field. COURTESY OF U.S. ARMY MILITARY HISTORY INSTITUTE, CARLISLE BARRACKS, PA.

Journal Book

HARRIET H. A. EATON

PORTLAND, MAINE

1862: OCTOBER 6 TO DECEMBER 31

WASHINGTON, OCT. 6TH 1862

Monday morn.—Bade farewell to my precious boy, and took the cars, in company with Mrs. I[sabella] Fogg, for Washington. Found pleasant companionship in the cars, but on arriving in Boston found Norwich road obstructed by transportation of Regiment. Took Stoughton route but on our arrival at Boat found that also obstructed in same way.—While seated in the Ladies Saloon discovered my shawl had been forgotten, and alone, at 1/2 past 12 at night, rushed on shore and through the cars, in the darkness, to hunt up what I had so carelessly left.—Of course it had been appropriated, and in the mean time the Regiment were passing on board the Boat, & to the tune of "Glory, Hallelujah" I made again for the Boat on the double quick all surrounded by bayonets.—Found Mr. Drake searching for us with the welcome news that by taking the Ferry we might take the shore route and not lose our connection in the morning.—After crossing the river, quite a little incident took place in the shape of some enraged drunken soldiers, one of whom, a man of Herculean frame, fixed his bayonet and commenced flourishing it round in altogether too close proximity for pleasure. I was calm, thought I must not be afraid of soldiers at the outset.

TUESDAY MORNING OCT. 7TH 1862

Took breakfast at the Astor House at the polite invitation of Mr. Coffin alias "Carlton" of the Journal.—Told him I was glad to make his acquaintance, from impression received that "we learn the truth when Carlton speaks." Mr. Drake <u>very</u> attentive and kind, never left us till we were safe on board Phil. cars. From Jersey City we had one delay or change excepting crossing the city of "brotherly love" in horse cars till we arrived at Washington.—On the way, talked with many officers who all approved our mission. Dust between Baltimore and Washington almost suffocating.—Camps, squads of soldiers, and guards meet the eye at every turn. How quiet and unconcerned are the people of Portland, so far removed from these scenes.—Reached Washington about seven [in the] evening and took lodgings at Mrs. Williams, corner of 4 1/2 and C St. Expense of trip from B[altimore] to W[ashington] $12.25, hack hire 84 cts.—

WEDNESDAY OCT. 8TH 1862

Heat intense, sacks out of the question, borrowed shawl. Mrs. Williams called on Mrs. Mc Intyre. Then went to the Post Office to find the rooms of Mass[achusetts] Asso[ciation]—Agent informed us that their goods were transported by Express to W[ashington] and from thence free of charge to Frederic[k] or Harpers Ferry, also that an ambulance was detailed for their service by government, free. Went to the Patent Office, visited the Rooms of the Michigan Asso[ciation] through the politeness of Judge Edwards, their Pres.[1] They keep constantly employed five ladies visiting Michigan soldiers in Hospitals, besides all the gentlemen. These ladies have a room where they can cook for the sick men and daily carry to them their supplies. One of them expressed great satisfaction that Maine boys would at last be looked after, and gave us the name of one in Douglas Hospital.[2] From this went to Armory Hospital, perhaps the best in the city, every thing in fine order, talked with many Maine soldiers, found the nurses warm hearted and kind.[3] Mrs. D[rake?] was to leave for P[ortland] that day, had manifested discontent all the time, evidently not inspired by patriotism and not followed by many blessings from those who witnessed to her expressions of feeling.—Left card for Dr. [W. C.] Robinson who was also to leave for home to day.—In this Hospital each ward has a separate building, and each bed a musquito [*sic*] netting over it, every thing sweet and clean. Every day they have a printed Hospital bill of fare from which to choose their meals.—Hence proceeded to Douglas Hospital, a fine brick block in the yard of which roses and other plants were blooming brightly and at the side of it a large number of Hospital tents.—Here we found the young man referred to by the Michigan lady, whose leg had been amputated. His emotion was too great for utterance that some one from Maine had come to see him, and it was not diminished when I gave him one of

---

[1] HE mistakes the name of Judge James M. Edmunds.

[2] Douglas Hospital was at the corner of I Street and New Jersey Avenue; Surgeon Peter Pineo presiding.

[3] Armory Square Hospital was located on 7th Street; Surgeon D. W. Bliss presiding. Among the women who nursed there was Amanda Akin Stearns, whose memoir, *The Lady Nurse of Ward E* (1909), details the hospital environment.

bro[ther] Greenough's pears.—Saw eight or nine men from Maine in this Hospital, among them one from Cape Elisabeth and Dr. Carey's son of Gorham. They seem to feel great horror of entering [the] Convalescent Hospital.[4] Men look very comfortable here. Saw a beautiful <u>drawing</u> made by a New York man who was asleep. The Maine sick men are nearly all of them very young.—Returning home found Dr. Robinson had called in our absence. In afternoon Edward W[hittier] came, and we had a delightful chat, promised to send an ambulance next day to take us out to his camp.—In evening had interesting conversation with a boarder, Mr. Smith, refugee from Va. near Culpepper [*sic*], formerly from Maine.—His domain has been run over by three armies. Wife and family still remain.—Federals, perfect vandals in their destruction of his property. Been for months a prisoner in Richmond as a spy but released for want of evidence. Gen. [Oliver Otis] Howard did not prevent devastation, also [General John] Pope, General [Robert E.] Lee <u>obliged</u> respect for his property, though he made his house his Headquarters.—Mr. S[mith] does not believe a spool of cotton could be bought in the vicinity for 50 cts. Pd. $3.50 for coarsest kind of leather shoes (made by negroes) for his little girl eight years old.—

[See *Appendix letter 1. HE to Agnes Eaton, October 8, 1862*.]

THURSDAY MORNING OCT. 9TH 1862

Lieut. [Edward] Whittier came with ambulance, took us first to Arlington Hospital, then to their camp.—Hospital, confiscated residence of a secesh,[5] delightfully situated on an eminence in a grove, and taken care of by sisters of charity as in Douglas Hospital. Took poor Charley Oleson completely by surprise, he was <u>so glad</u> to see me, is better, they tell me, though he is sadly emaciated and looks <u>very</u> weak, no appetite. How I wish I had a mint of money—I should like to tempt the appetite of these poor fellows. Nurse a fine young man, says their food is good though but little variety, scarcely any fruit. George W[hittier] now took us to his

---

[4] Established after 2nd Bull Run in August 1862 to contain the overflow of casualties, the convalescent hospital near Alexandria, Virginia, was dubbed "Camp Misery" by the rank and file. Under the purview of officers in the Army of the Potomac who had more important business to conduct, it was a filthy and ill-equipped way station for men en route back to their regiments from field and general hospitals—not unlike the stockade that was built to imprison Union soldiers at Andersonville, Georgia. By the end of 1862, public indignation about the camp led to plans to relocate it on higher ground and to build barracks and outbuildings. The camp showed signs of domestic improvement as soon as Amy Morris Bradley, a nurse with the 3rd Maine Infantry, was reassigned there to bring order out of chaos. It ultimately had barracks for five thousand men, houses for officers, a library, a kitchen, and a twelve-hundred-seat church. Bradley was the impetus behind a camp newspaper and other activities that helped men pass the time. Under pressure from the Medical Department, the convalescent facility was suspended in February 1864 and the institution became known as the "Rendezvous of Distribution."

[5] Slang term for "secessionists."

tent, under the noble trees, showed us his bed not long enough for him to stretch in, short though he is, but he seems happy.—Looked over his traps that he brought from home and into the whites of the eyes of his piece of "animated ebony."[6]—In officer's tent sat on a trunk and mailed a <u>letter to Mrs. Bosworth</u> from Gales Oaks, Leppein Battery, enclosing one for <u>Mrs. Whittier</u> and <u>dear Frank</u> [Eaton]. I <u>hear</u> to day that the 25th Regiment is to go to Baltimore.—Returning from this beautiful spot, not having time to visit Finlay's Hospital,[7] we rode through clouds of dust and trains of army wagons to No. 17. Here I remained to meet one Agent while Mrs. Fogg went in search of Mr. Fobes [sic], a Maine man connected with some of the Bureaus.—At three o' clock Mr. [John H.] H[athaway] made his appearance. He was still very decided on the impractibility [sic] of our plan, said he had made it the subject of thought and inquiry and as a result could not cooperate. Mrs. F came in, showing no intention of giving up. He asked me if I had selected a Hospital, I said <u>no</u>, my earnest desire was to labor for <u>Maine</u> Soldiers if possible.—He said if we would give up the service for Regiments, he thought my wishes on this subject might be carried out for those in Hospitals. We do not yet see our way clear. Mr. H will call again at 1/2 past 3 tomorrow.—In evening Mr. and Mrs. Mc Intyre called, seemed interested in our plan and offered any aid in their power to bestow. He will see Mr. Hathaway tomorrow, also inquire rent of a room. Had another pleasant chat with Mr. S[mith], more and more interested in the trials he is passing through.—

FRIDAY OCT. 10TH 1862

Have been to the Depot to get our trunks, and with those under our control do not feel so utterly destitute of conveniences. Mrs. Fogg has gone to see the surgeon general to know if an ambulance can be detailed.[8] It is after twelve o' clock and I fear we cannot visit a Hospital to day. My mind is much on my dear soldier boy. The Father of fatherless, guide and protect him.—Had the pleasure of hearing yesterday through the Whittiers that darling Hatty Belle was feeling happy and contented on Monday. <u>Wrote to Agnes</u> yesterday morning. Evening Mr. Hathaway appeared in great haste, wishing us to visit the Hospitals at Georgetown, particularly the Seminary Hospital for officers. Found there a <u>very</u> sick man, Capt. Rand of Waterford Me. belonging to 16th Maine Company D. Do'nt believe he is having suitable medical treatment, sat by him about two hours. Found about eight of our Maine

---

[6] HE means an African American servant. This kind of racialized language is typical of elite whites, who would have seen themselves as socially superior not only to former slaves, but to any person of African descent.

[7] Finley [sic] Hospital was located on New York Avenue near what at the time was Gales' Farm; Surgeon J. Moses presiding.

[8] Fogg's request was not the sort of thing a surgeon general would have deigned to handle.

men there. Thence went to [Columbian] College Hospital[9] and there found about seven men from Maine, some of them very sick, but very glad to see us. One of the 7th eating his supper of tea, bread, and preserves & in a great hurry to rejoin his Regt. who were on their way home. Mr. Mc Intyre called, bringing a welcome <u>letter from Agnes</u>, also one from Dr. Fitch. Mr. M has been inquiring for a room for us.

SATURDAY MORNING OCT. 11TH 1862

Started out to find "lodgings," came near getting in the wrong place, had a nice call on an old lady, who sent us to Dr. Smith Presbyterian minister whose lady was very affable. Called on Miss Dix, not at home at first, chatted with Miss Metford till she came, the latter quite severe on "Gilson and Fay." Most happily disappointed in Miss Dix, found her remarkably affable and genial, she expressed quite a desire to keep us, tried to help us in the matter of "rooms," said she was going to make arrangements for reaching the Regts. and ended by saying "let me see you again ladies."[10] She wore a broach and chain, dressed simply in black with lace inside kerchief.—Saw Mr. Hathaway, reported with reference to the Hospitals in Georgetown, he requesting me to go again in afternoon to see Capt. Rand. Found the Capt. more comfortable and better taken care of. Surgeon said he might have a peach.—But this matter of rooms is a hard business, do'nt know what we shall do.

SABBATH OCT. 12TH 1862

Attended church in the morning at Mr. Sunderland's Presbyterian. Pleasant church but smooth dull preacher, text "They have no danger therefore they fear not God."—Afternoon, visited Trinity Church Hospital,[11] found nine Maine men, the day cold and they not provided, part of them, with suitable clothing.—Saw Miss Sarah Prentice of Paris Me. who is Matron of Hospital.[12]—One of the sick boys told me he was glad to see <u>Maine acting</u>, if it was only for the name of the thing, for while ladies from other states had been visiting the Hospitals he had been <u>ashamed</u> to say that no one looked after him.—Heard preaching from their chaplain Rev. Mr. Raymond of New York State, who entered the service as a private, and an address from Rev. Mr. Gregory from same state, who left his church as Capt. of a company, both Baptist ministers. Their

---

[9] Columbian was on 14th Street; Surgeon T. A. Crosh presiding.

[10] Thomas Brown notes that Dix attempted, before her powers of appointment were effectively stripped in October 1863, to be a maternal figure for nurses, making her home a retreat for them and buying them small gifts. See Brown, *Dorothea Dix, New England Reformer*, chapter 13.

[11] Trinity Church Hospital was located on C Street at the corner of 3rd; Surgeon A. J. Baxter presiding.

[12] That is, Trinity Church Hospital.

text, "I do remember my faults this day." Plain earnest preaching, attentive, thoughtful listeners. Building well ventilated but I am afraid the poor fellows do'nt have much to tempt the appetite. Evening remained at home, and I fear spent my time <u>very unprofitably</u>, in careless conversation, must guard against it and remember it is "the little foxes that spoil the vines."—Oh! let me remember what I am here for.—

MONDAY OCT. 13TH 1862

Went out house hunting in company with Mr. and Mrs. Mc Intyre, quite early in the morning. We walked and we walked but found ourselves of little account, nobody wanted "ladies." After searching some two or three hours to little purpose, parted from Mr. & Mrs. M and went in search of Dr. Perry and lady.—Here we found sympathy in our proposed plan of operations and a decided approval. Thence to Judiciary Square Hospital[13] to see the Maine men, one poor fellow who had been wounded in the head, felt pretty hard towards his own state but very glad to see us. After dinner went back to "Judiciary" to see the doctor to inquire what stimulants might be afforded him, could'nt find the doctor, but through a Mass. lady did find a poor, sick dying man who had had his leg amputated, was suffering from a relapse, and would not probably live through the night, relapse caused by hearing of the death of a twin brother, killed in battle. He was from Cherryfield Me. Evening Mr. Hathaway called, we are to receive our sentence tomorrow.—Calling at Mr. Mc Intyre's he again went out with us and we succeeded in finding a room for $10.00 at the home of an old gentleman named Piggert, family consisting of himself and two daughters.

TUESDAY OCT. 14TH 1862

Have moved to our Rooms, C St. 399.—Have also seen Mr. Hathaway who very quietly told us that nothing had been done at that meeting and they had adjourned to Wednesday. I informed him we should immediately write to Maine and report the existing state of things, also requested stimulants for a young man from Maine in whose behalf we had called three times to find the doctor. Mr. H[athaway] was for sending us back again for a written order, but we declined and the wine was forthcoming. Had some pretty plain talk with Mr. H which resulted in his writing for us, a certificate of good character, &c. Called at Mrs. Williams' & Mr. Mc Intyre's in evening.

[*See Appendix letter 2. HE to Mrs. Bosworth, October 14, 1862.*]

WEDNESDAY OCT. 15TH 1862

Commenced letter for Mrs. Bosworth in morning and started for Frederick and Harpers Ferry at 11. Nothing special till we reached the "Relay House" where we

---

[13] Judiciary Square Hospital was located on E Street between 4th and 5th; Surgeon A. J. Marsh presiding.

were detained till five o' clock and I filled up the time by finishing <u>my letters to Mrs. Bosworth</u> and <u>writing for Mrs. Fogg to Mr. [Jedediah] Jewett</u>.[14] At the Relay House were finally invited to partake of the dinner by a sutler who was interested in our mission. Proceeded to Frederick, mid a perfect rush of people, rather discouraged as to finding a place to put our head for the night but again providence provided, my attention being directed to a Maine lady who was seeking for her husband, a gentleman sitting near her kindly offered to find lodgings for us which he did, though falling into the hands of the "Philistines" we had to pay 50 cts. for each meal and the same for a bed.[15]

THURSDAY OCT. 16TH 1862

Capt. Snow of Maine 19th of Rockland, quite sick where we lodged, ulcerated throat and fever. Called on Col. [Samuel] Allen of 1st Maine Cavalry, saw Capt. [Zemro A.] Smith and Lieut. [Greenlief T.] Stevens. Col. Allen went with us in ambulance to visit his Regt. Made gruel for the sick in Hospital, and found some very sick there though comfortably provided for, also found several sick in their tents and made gruel for them also.—Col. Allen wished us to visit sick in Hospital at Comp[any] A. Detailed Lieut. [William P.] Coleman of Lincolnville Me. to go with us. Found some parts of Hospital in very bad condition, filthy, betraying but little attention to the sick, and some of the men from Saco & Biddeford represented themselves as almost starving, having five loaves given out for seventeen men. Found one poor fellow without any shirt, only thin linen coat. Had with us supplies for his wants, I am thankful to say.— Poor fellow from Michigan, covered with flies, in a sad condition without any care. Stopped over night at farm house on the bank of a little stream where was boarding a Capt. Cowdin from Biddeford of Cavalry and Quartermaster. They entered earnestly into our plans, but Quartermaster thought we should find it too arduous and if we did not look out would be taken prisoner on Virginia side. <u>Unlike</u> the night before, the woman here asked but 50 cts. for what we had paid $1.50 for the day before.

FRIDAY OCT. 17TH 1862

Rode into Frederick, only in time to save ourselves and take the cars which we found left at nine. Frederick seems a very pretty thriving place except for the war. But all the Hotels but one, all the school houses and all the churches but one, are taken for Hospitals.—Cars crowded as on to Harpers Ferry is the word. Yesterday we heard the distant booming of cannon at intervals all day, and hear there was a skirmish

---

[14] It was common for HE to write letters at Mrs. Fogg's behest; whether because Fogg was a poor writer or too fatigued to write is unclear.

[15] Profiteering on the part of people with lodgings in the vicinity of military camps was common.

about eight miles distant.[16] At the farm house at Fred[erick] they told us when the Confederates were there, the secesh farmers hid every thing because they would not have "secesh" money, but when the union men came they had enough and sold at the rate of four cts. an egg. The ride along the Monocacy and by Ellicott's Mills was beautiful in the extreme, then came "Point of Rocks," rightly named indeed.[17] But we came through Sandy Hook to Harpers Ferry, made by our Creator so lovely by nature, oh how awful are the devastating effects of war as here exhibited! Bridges destroyed, and houses with the bare walls standing meet you at every turn. All in confusion worse [sic] confounded. As we alighted from the cars, there stood Lieut. Coleman, who informed us he had received a telegraph the night before that his brother was very sick here.—He procured a carry all and took us to Bolivar to see his brother, and I immediately decided to remain with him and do what I could, while Mrs. Fogg went to Sharpsburg to see the Regts. and find her son.

SATURDAY OCT. 18TH 1862

Poor Lindley M. Coleman Capt. of Comp. B is no more. Another noble young man has been sacrificed for his country. Delirious with fever, neither any effort of mine, or earnest pleading and groaning from his brother could draw naught from him, but ravings like these "march on my men, march on" and the like. Glad am I that by my presence I could impart comfort to his brother and absent friends, I tried to point him to Jesus but to earthly appearances such attempts were vain. I was permitted to close the dying eyes, and attend to the last kind offices and there we must leave him.—Went with the ambulance with his remains to the Ferry, where as the Lieutenant bade me farewell, he seemed almost broken hearted.—Did not find Mrs. F at the "Ferry," could not stop over night in such a fighting, brawling, hole, so I walked up to the hill to see what might befall me. Oh, how impregnable and commanding are those Maryland Heights where Miles ordered the white flag of surrender to be raised, and then fell by some <u>well</u> aimed shot, a <u>traitor to his country</u>.[18] No one who views the region can doubt his ability in that commanding position, to have held Loudon and Bolivar Heights, and with those all the country around.—And, here let

---

[16] On October 16, McClellan ordered a reconnaissance that began at Harpers Ferry and ended at Charles Town, with intermittent skirmishing.

[17] Point of Rocks, Maryland, was located on the Potomac River; the Baltimore and Ohio Railroad ran through it. The Monocacy River is a tributary of the Potomac, running north to south through the state of Maryland and to the east of Frederick.

[18] Dixon S. Miles is remembered infamously as the commander who surrendered Union defenses—twelve thousand strong—at Harpers Ferry to Stonewall Jackson on September 15, 1862, the day after the battle of South Mountain and two days before the battle of Antietam began. Understood as a strategic linchpin, the loss of the Union position at Harpers Ferry served an invitation to Lee to reestablish a presence on nearby Antietam Creek. Dixon was mortally wounded during the skirmish.

me say, that viewing the shallow waters of the Potomac as they appear now, we need not be surprised that Stuart's Cavalry raid could have been effected.[19]

SUNDAY OCT. 19TH 1862

Saturday's journal left me walking towards Bolivar Heights. I had thought best to return to the house where I had taken my meals and accept this invitation to tarry all night.—But such a night!!! The night before, I had slept but little on a soldier's cot, with valise for a pillow, so being weary I thought to retire early. Mrs. Tacy volunteered to light me to bed, so on reaching the stair head I found myself in a small unfinished attic, and was coolly informed, she supposed I would not mind sleeping in same room with herself and husband. I found I was in for that and more too. With the man and his wife, lay their youngest child and to my horror, when they were about to retire, there came also their dirty, grown up daughters, and camped down on the floor, just at my back.—I do'nt know how many live inhabitants they brought with them, but one thing is certain, sleep departed from my eyes and rest from my body. As they thought I slept, their conversation was any thing but gratifying. One thing, I will say their cooking was quite respectable.—Oh! How I longed for morning and then what an hour I spent, with the old man alone, who seemed to sleep while I dare not move as I waited for him to go down stairs.—After breakfast, be sure I took up my line of march, making for the Regt. of the 19th Maine, Col. Sewall of Balt[imore] commanding, Rev. Mr. [Edwin B.] Palmer, chaplain, and Dr. A. J. Billings of Freedom, surgeon. I visited Col. [Sewall's] tent then accompanied by chaplain, walked to the parade ground where on a camp stool detailed from Col.'s tent, I was seated within the hollow square formed by the Regt. and listened to a very good discourse from the words, "watch and be sober."—After service visited the Hospital found it very neat, but too much crowded, men all suffering for want of flannel shirts, surgeon seemed deeply interested in our work.—Chaplain kindly procured a lodging place for me with Mrs. Potts where were boarding a Capt. Plympton of 19th Mass. Regt. with his wife and child.—Mrs. Fogg returned this afternoon, feeling much distressed at learning that her son had been left sick at Seminary Hospital, Alexandria.

MONDAY OCT. 20TH 1862

Morning visited the Regt., also went in ambulance to Sandy Hook for medical supplies, and returning were forced back by guard, because we were in a light ambulance and had no pass, would not even let us walk over pontoon bridge without a gentleman with us. Ordered us to cross at "Ford's of the Potomac."[20]—Close under

---

[19] On October 10, 1862, with Union wounds still smarting from Antietam, J. E. B. Stuart, cavalry commander of the Army of Northern Virginia, crossed the Potomac River from Virginia into what is now West Virginia, with eighteen thousand troops, on his way to wreak residential havoc on the small town of Chambersburg, Pennsylvania.

[20] Also known as United States Ford.

Maryland Heights, and along the banks of the Canal over a horrid road we made our way, only to find the path blocked up and obliged to return. Here Mrs. Fogg called to her assistance the officer of the guard and with a wave of the hand we were soon on the bridge. Went to the "Ferry" to get our pass (for Washington in the afternoon) of the provost marshal. Then back to Bolivar, and after dinner for which with three other meals Mrs. Potts asked twenty-five cents each and a levy for our bed.—The ride home was delightful, camp grounds all lighted up looked pretty in the distance. Reached our room about 1/2 past eight.

TUESDAY OCT. 21ST 1862

Have spent a strange sad, day. Took Omnibus about eight in morning for Alexandria, then Ferry (they say it is about eight miles across), then Omnibus again to Seminary Hospital.[21]—Here, Mrs. Fogg found her son had never been there, and after such a long search, to be wholly disappointed seemed for a time, more than nature could endure.—All were very kind, the head doctor took me over the Hospitals and through the cook room, was much pleased with the cleanliness of the wards and their fine ventilation. Dined with the doctors, they have over a hundred employees, dinner roast chicken and ducks, sweet and white potatoes, peas, tomatoes, and apple pie. Providence kindly ordered that an ambulance should be there for a Mrs. Harris of Mass. Association whose acquaintance I was happy to make, and who gladly gave us a seat to the Ferry as I do not know how I could have got Mrs. Fogg home. Oh, that Mrs. F might be enabled to "cast her burden on the Lord."—Just as I reached the Alexandria side this morning, heard a voice, "How do you do Mrs. Eaton," and to my great pleasure took Willy Manning by the hand, he had just obtained a furlough of thirty days and was bound home. Called on Mrs. Mc Intyre, she tells me Frank's Regt. are camped on Capitol Hill, arrived last Sunday but Frank and John Emery were still detailed for duty at Camp Lincoln. No letters for me, it is now 1/2 past ten, Mrs. Fogg has been asleep hours and I have such a sore throat and pressure on the lungs that I ought to have been abed long ago. Bought some milk, biscuit, and cheese for supper to night, but have no fire to my sorrow. Why ca'nt somebody write me a letter from home when I am so anxious to hear?

WEDNESDAY OCT. 22ND 1862

Have received three letters, a nice long one from Mrs. Whittier of six pages that did my heart good, a letter and note from my precious boy, who is still in camp, I wish he had the long letter now that I have just mailed to him. I have also written to Mrs. Whittier and Hatty. Frank also enclosed to me a letter from Augusta and an

---

[21] Fairfax Seminary Hospital near Alexandria, not to be confused with Seminary Hospital in the Georgetown district of Washington.

introductory note to Mrs. [Rebecca] Pomroy.[22] I am rejoiced to say that Mrs. Fogg has found her son safe and sound. He is in one of the Hospitals in Washington, Mount Pleasant,[23] and has been to see her. Now, I trust we shall be all right again with God's blessing and what do we without it?

THURSDAY OCT. 23RD 1862

<u>Spent last evening in writing to Mrs. Bosworth</u> till eleven o' clock, oh I have so many letters to write. Went to see Mr. Hathaway this morning, Miss Fobes[24] present which I think rather perplexed him, our documents from officers seemed rather startling, he proposed to keep them but we had no idea of giving them up, so he took copy. Bill of fare for dinner to day, as our stomachs crave a sumptuous repast. Pig souse[25], bread, cheese, and crackers, newspapers for a plate, one mug for our drinking comfort and Mrs. F's inevitable jack knife to cut our repast. The souse was our extra delicacy and we laughed over it and enjoyed it, verily one can use themselves to almost any thing.[26] <u>Mailed Mrs. Bosworth's letter</u>. Introduced ourselves to Mrs. Bigelow by inquiring the location of some of the Hospitals and she kindly invited us to go with her to them in her ambulance, accordingly this afternoon I went to Columbian Hos., Mrs. Fogg to Mount Pleasant Hos., and Mrs. Bigelow to Carver Hos.[27] Had a most delightful call on sweet Mrs. Pomroy, found her every thing she had been described, returning met the Pres. with his body guard, going out to Soldier's House, his summer residence.— Mrs. Bigelow in the warmth of [her] heart invited us to dinner and we remained nothing loath, for meat is a scarce article with us now. This evening I have written to <u>Sarah [Caduc] in London</u> which I shall forward with one for Perkins & Anna. It is ten o' clock so good night to my journal. Mrs. Pomroy says she has had over thirty Maine men and they were the most temperate she ever had under her care.

[*See Appendix letter 3. HE to "Mrs. Bosworth," October 23, 1862.*]

FRIDAY OCT. 24TH 1862

While Mrs. Fogg went with one of the ladies from Mrs. Bigelow's to visit her son in Mount Pleasant Hospital, I called at Mrs. Mc Intyre's. Returning we decided to

---

[22] The War Department required prospective nurses to present letters of reference from two surgeons and two clergymen. See Brown, *Dorothea Dix*, 290; and Schultz, *Women at the Front*, 60–61.

[23] Mount Pleasant Hospital was located on 4th Street near Boundary Street; Surgeon C. A. McCall presiding.

[24] Ellen Sarah Forbes Tolman.

[25] Usually pigs' feet or ears, pickled in spiced wine or vinegar.

[26] HE uses the word "use" in its more archaic form—to mean "accustom."

[27] Carver Hospital was located on 14th Street, near Columbian College Hospital; Surgeon O. A. Judson presiding.

visit the 25th Maine, just as we were starting on invitation of Miss Sharpless, we first accompanied her to Eckington Hos.[28] I saw Charley Oleson again, only wished I had had something for him, he speaks highly of the "sister" who has looked out for their ward, wants her photograph. Found several Maine men, one too sick to converse and two more who will not live long. One had formerly attended Free St. Church, name Stubbs, the one who was dying's name was Quint, the former expressed his trust in God, and said that was his only comfort, but he was too feeble to make himself understood but little. A young fellow of the 6th Maine who was detailed as nurse mentioned this fact. He had recently come from Fairfax Seminary Hos. Alex[andria]. While there one of the soldiers in Hos. managed to get some liquor and became somewhat noisy, the doctor in attendance said, I'll soon still him, at the same time administering some medicine, and sure enough he was still in twenty minutes, he was dead. So much for the poor soldiers.—Returning we rode over to Capitol Hill, Camp Casey, there we found the 25th, 23rd, and 27th Maine Regts. The 25th was on dress parade, so we only saw the surgeon Carr of Lewiston. He has seen service, was gentlemanly, and interested in our plan. Dreads the acclimating process very much for his men. Oh! my poor Frank! I must trust.—Went to the Hos. of 23rd but found it empty, as they are making preparations to move, though they have between twenty and thirty sick men whom they are leaving in Hos. and private houses. Surgeon Lovett Brownfield says he will not leave Washington till he has Hos. supplies if he has to put every man of the Regt. on the sick list. Returning home at six, found Mr. Hathaway's card, requesting our attendance at his room at seven o'clock. Arriving there, he said, well ladies, Mr. [Leonard W.] Watson will leave for Frederick tomorrow, and the evidence you brought with you on your return is of such a character that I do not feel at liberty to resist your claim any longer. Of course we laughed at him a little about being brought over. Mr. Watson came in, and said, are these ladies to go with me? "Well," said Mr. H[athaway], "they will go with you as far as Frederick and then take their own course poking round among the Regiments." He says when you write to Maine tell the people that I think as you do now. Poor fellow, it's a hard case, for he is only convinced because he is obliged to be, but no matter, we do as we please, our expenses all paid. While I write this, let me ever remember that my duty is to labor and toil for the poor soldiers, let me hourly seek grace and hold my Father's hand. I need patience, especially.—Called at Mrs. Mc I[ntyre's]. Wrote two letters to Frank one to P[ortland] and one to camp. Ate our supper and dinner too of sausages, biscuit, cake, cheese, and preserves. A sumptuous repast. Had knives and forks too!! Had a call about eleven from Mrs. Elliot, sister of Mrs. Robinson of Mass. Asso. who sat till 1/4 past twelve midnight. I entertained her sitting on the floor myself. Oh 'tis hard, 'tis hard to leave W[ashington] without seeing my more than ever precious boy, but duty calls, I must not refuse.

[28] Eckington Hospital was located in Gales' House, a hotel on New York Avenue; Surgeon S. A. Storrow presiding.

SATURDAY OCT. 25TH 1862

Stopping at Mrs. Yonson's again, it seems so much like home.—Nothing special on the road, fare from W[ashington] to F[rederick] $3.25, distance from W[ashington] to Relay House 24 miles, from thence to Fred. 46, thence to Harpers Ferry 30. Arriving at F[rederick] we called on Capt. Snow of the 19th Maine, Rockland, who is recovering, and who very politely took a carriage and carried us to our lodgings in company with Capt. [James W.] Hathaway of [the] 19th who is about resigning on account of his health.

SUNDAY OCT. 26TH 1862

A decidedly rainy day. Lieut. Col. Doughty[29] boarding here, also Lieut. [Black Hawk] Putnam, with the Quartermaster and Capt. who were here before. But one opinion is expressed with reference to the Regimental Hospital here, viz,[30] an improper man for surgeon,[31] and nurses who are cross and even profane to the poor sick men.— Mrs. Fogg secured some apples which we had baked by Mrs. Yonson and then we carried them to the Hospital. They have 32 men sick in Hos., two have died since we were there before, the men seemed very happy to see me, and to the outside view presented a very comfortable appearance. They have no chaplain and have not had any for a long time. They nearly all have nothing but cotton shirts, one poor fellow is just getting over the measles, with only a cotton shirt, when he has been accustomed to wear woolen, must attend to his case.—Hospital steward said they had a Hos. fund of $51.00 that they had gathered at some time previous, but Capt. Cowdin[32] tells us, "_it is good but it ca'nt be got_," so of what use is it? Capt. C and Quartermaster Griffin very much dissatisfied at the thought of doing nothing and going into winter quarters. Was amused _last night_ at a conversation about the _bounds of the Regt._ and the manner in which these officers come within the regulations. "_Of course we do._" No Sabbath here except as we may always keep it in our own heart in communion with our ever present Father. Oh! how I wished I had religious reading with me this morning. Wrote a long letter to Samuel & Elisabeth [Whitney], also one to Mr. & Mrs. [Jedediah] Jewett for Mrs. Fogg. At table to day Col. Doughty told of a young surgeon who said to him rubbing his hands, "we performed a splendid operation to day, splendid operation, took off a man's arm at the shoulder blade," "ah, how does the man do," said the Col. "Oh, of course the man's dead" was the composed reply.— Mrs. Yonson says a man came here the other day for a poultice (from Comp[any] A) for his hand and on her insisting on putting it on for him, she was shocked to find three of his fingers were off and nothing but a little plaster stuck on the stumps,

---

[29] Calvin S. Douty.
[30] An abbreviation for "videlicet," meaning namely, or to wit.
[31] The surgeon of the 1st Maine Cavalry was George W. Colby.
[32] Louis O. Cowan.

while the palm of his hand was all maturated and yet not a particle of attention was being paid to it.—³³

MONDAY OCT. 27TH 1862

Wrote to Mrs. Hart this morning as it was raining very hard and we could not go out. After dinner, carried some broth from Mrs. Yonson to the Hos. and fed the men. They seemed very glad to see us, and enjoyed their dinner, they had also some toast and butter, this latter a great rarity. Made a request that the men should put on flannel shirts, those on the floor must be attended to and cots got for them. Walked in to Frederick, found the box standing in the entry of the house, (the box that ought to be sent to the Maine 19th) but it is not packed at all, if this is the way they do things at the Sanitary Commission and the way Mr. W[atson] attends to it, I think the less we have to do with the whole concern the better.—Then we went to see about the requisition for ourselves, the man said it was cancelled and Mrs. F felt any thing but—about it. We tried twice to find Dr. Steiner but he was not in, and I was determined that poor boy who had had the measles should not be without a woolen shirt to night and I purchased one and gave $1.25 for it, and returning left it at the Hospital. Saw a Maine man of the 10th Regt. named Burch of Saco.³⁴ He had just received a letter from his wife and a box with the children's daguerreotypes, his little boy about two years old taken with his mouth wide open was very funny. Poor fellow, he had enlisted but two months and was shot in the hip, he feared he should never have the use of his leg again.

TUESDAY OCT. 28TH 1862

Mrs. F went to town about the boxes while I remained at home to receive Mr. [Leonard W.] Watson and make out our bills.—When Mr. W came, I talked pretty plain. After dinner visited Comp[any] A. We carried some milk, tomatoes, and sour kraut [sic] which we soon disposed of. Oh these poor men, they have to dress their own wounds, wash themselves if they are washed at all, and eat _____.³⁵ I wish I could attach one of their rations to this book, that it might be seen at home. The poor fellow, Edward B. Warren of Standish Me. to whom I gave the shirt when we were here before, heard my voice and called to me. It is discouraging to go into this Hos. for the poor men are most starved I have not a doubt of it. Coming home we saw a poor old German woman, Vickley she called herself, carrying her basket

---

³³ The hand wound was suppurating, or discharging pus. In the era before infection was understood to cause harm to human tissue, many physicians believed that pus augured healing. But in this case, HE lamented that the soldier had not received prompt medical attention.

³⁴ Of the 567 Union soldiers from Saco, none was named Burch. Nor did any man in the 10th have that surname.

³⁵ In leaving the space blank, HE most likely had an expletive in mind.

loaded with crackers, cheese, &c. for the "boys," she scorned the thought of <u>selling</u> to them. Next we saw a poor fellow who had lost his right arm, trying to knock an apple from the tree with his left and Mrs. F tried to help him but in the attempt sprained her foot badly, I am afraid she will have a sorry time of it. We also visited Regimental Hos., saw surgeon Colby, and were glad to find those bedsteads have at last arrived, and a new Hos. tent is also being pitched. One poor fellow who has had typhoid fever took cold in the storm of Sunday, pneumonia set in, and he will not probably live but a day or two.

WEDNESDAY OCT. 29TH 1862

Mrs. F will have to keep still to day, if not longer. I went into town this morning, first however going to Hos. with a pillow for the sick one, but poor fellow he had passed away at five o' clock this morning, his name was Carter. His body is to be embalmed at the expense of his company and sent home. Lieut. [William P.] Coleman got his furlough to day to go home with the body of his brother. Called on Col. Sewall of the 19th Me. this morning, his wife has come, an agreeable lady, think the Col. will be obliged to resign either his post or his life. As for that box for the 19th, if the San. Com. or Mr. W[atson] or Capt. Snow or Col. Sewall cannot get it to the men who are suffering and dying for want of the things, I shall almost wish I was a man. I bought some crackers in town, came home, and after dinner made some cracker toast for supper for Cav[alry] Hos. and carried it to them, they seemed to relish it much. Six new ones have been put in the new tent. One of them when he saw me said it seemed like a streak of day light to see a lady's face. I found in Hos. to day Charles Hamilton, widow Hamilton's son of Portland. He was <u>right glad</u> to see me, said he was acquainted with my dear Frank.

THURSDAY OCT. 30TH 1862

<u>Wrote to Mrs. Mc Intyre</u> this morning and gave it to Mr. [Leonard W.] Watson to take into the city, also sent our bills against the State to Mr. Hathaway by Mr. W. Wrote also a <u>letter to Agnes</u>.—After dinner took a large pail full of soup to Hos., enough for all the boys, went in and talked with them all, and tried to cheer them up. Find hardly any of them have pocket handkerchiefs. Promised one or two of them lemons. Rode into the city in Cavalry ambulance and visited the Barracks Hospital.[36] Found one young man Charles Dunlap of 5th Maine from Brunswick very low, he has been shot through the lungs, can only whisper, seems very peaceful in his mind but thinks it would be too much for him to see his friends. By his side lays a young man wounded in six places, when I asked him where he was from

[36] HE means Frederick, Maryland. Most of the hospitals HE was visiting were regimental ones in the surrounding countryside.

he said, "Louisiana, and if I had been on the right side I should not have been wounded so badly." There are plenty of rebels in this Hos. Saw two of the Maine Cav. Comp[any] F. Capt. Boothby, one Tewksbury from Portland, the other [Charles] Walker of Yarmouth. They both gave me their names in testimony against Surgeon Colby, bearing witness to his profanity. Saw one of the most painful sights I ever witnessed, a lady from New York who had just arrived to visit her husband & found he had died the night before, and she must go alone to the dead house to look at his cold remains. It was dreadful to hear her shrieks of agony.—Our ambulance having left us, we were obliged to procure another, as Mrs. Fogg could not walk home. Called at Adams Express only to be disappointed, as that box has not come yet. Bought six lemons for 25 cts., put Agnes' letter in the office and came home.

FRIDAY OCT. 31ST 1862

Wrote a letter to Mrs. Lancey in the morning. Proposed to Mrs. F to carry handkerchiefs and lemons, &c. to Hos., dividing them and each taking to separate tents.—Quartermaster [Griffin] gave me a paper with the name of his son, sick in Smoketown Hos. Sharpsburg,[37] afternoon visited Hos., found the men could not have lemonade because they were out of sugar, made a little stir, nurse promised to get it.—Flooring the Hos. to day.—Nurse wished me to tell one young man he must eat nothing but flour porridge, in tent they told me they had brought him nothing but Indian meal to eat. I do believe it has done them some good to have us here. Started for the city and met our Maine Committee, Mr. W[atson] & Mr. H[athaway] returned to the house, talked till almost dark with Mr. Hayes, decided to go on to Sharpsburg tomorrow, found it necessary to walk into town to see Col. Allen, a splendid moonlight evening, warm like summer.—From Mr. Hayes' account Miss Fobes deems our plan quite chimerical, one comfort, we are not to be controlled by Washingtonians. Several boxes on the way, Mr. H[ayes] saw one advertised as having started for us from Free St.

SATURDAY NOV. 1ST 1862

Started about 1/4 to ten o'clock for Sharpsburg. Arriving in Frederick found our box of supplies had arrived, with them on board and Mr. Hayes on the bag of oats. Took our departure for the pike, day summer like, scenery beautiful indeed, autumn tinted foliage covered the mountain tops while villages nestled in the valleys. Stopped

---

[37] Smoketown was a tented field hospital established after the battle of Antietam. Bernard Vanderkieft was surgeon in charge. Female staff included Maria M. C. Hall, Mary Morris Husband, and Ellen Orbison Harris. Wrote Isabella Fogg of the place, "The effluvia arising from the condition of these grounds is intolerable, quite enough to make a man in perfect health sick, and how men can recover in such a place is a mystery to me." See Isabella Fogg to John Hathaway, November 10, 1862, MSA.

at Middletown and took our lunch, biscuit, butter milk, and apples, provided by Mrs. Yonson (we paid her $3.50 for our week's board). From Middletown, Pleasant Valley where we visited a Hospital and found the men enjoying good dinners provided by the kind ladies of roast chicken, broth, &c. One man Jones who had lost a right arm wishing he had another that he might keep on fighting, from thence we continued our way over the mountain through Crampton Pass, the scene of one of the battles.[38] Here were the marks of bullets and shells, 24 graves with head boards where our men fell and a trench where lay 15 rebels. One little house where lived an old man who had three union flags shot down on that day and three rebels killed in his little door yard, while his house remained wholly unharmed. Magnificent view as we crossed over the mountain into the valley, thence through Boonesboro a pretty little village, from whence the sick had all been removed a day or two, we went on to Kedarsville,[39] here we visited four Hos[pitals], found a good many Maine men, all the poor fellows had been brought here within a few days and were in a state of great destitution, the poor fellows lay on a little straw without pillows, much as they did on Bolivar Heights. But we could not stop, it was near night and we missed our way in trying to find Smoketown Hospital.—We arrived just at dark, smoke had indeed settled down, it was almost suffocating.—Mrs. F and driver amused me with a discussion about the horses being watered, over a horrible rocky descent she thought it safer to walk. Arriving at Hospital, and driving to Headquarters we were directed to a farm house, so over stumps through holes without roads we drove to find our lodging at Mr. Slowman's. The house was full, we slept on floor in the sitting room or rather lay there, had no sheets. A wounded southwestern Virginia rebel boarding there, why can he be provided with private quarters, when our own men are not allowed to leave Hos.? All the day before we had met straggling soldiers and government wagons, camps were all broken up and Regiments moving on. Firing heard through the day.

SUNDAY MORNING NOV. 2ND 1862

Started early to visit Smoketown Hos., was quite disgusted with the place. Stench and filth dreadful. One ward, having bad head ache, I could not enter. Men have not enough to eat. Dirty rags and other filth meet you at every turn. Men well enough to be up laying in bed for want of clothes. Saw the renowned Mrs. [Ellen] Harris, and went into her tent, she was very polite to me, had a large tent with hospital stores and a very large cook stove. Miss [Maria M. C.] Hall was with her. Saw also a Mrs. [Mary Morris] Husband who seemed very active in the fever wards. The young man Roscoe Griffin, Quartermaster's son, is doing well.

[38] Also known as Crampton's Gap, it was one of the sites of the battle of Antietam, which had taken place a month and a half earlier.

[39] Keedysville, Maryland.

When Harriet Eaton met nurse Maria Hall of Washington, D.C. (center, in apron), at the field hospital called Smoketown two months after the battle of Antietam, she complained, "Stench and filth dreadful." Situated in a grove of oak and walnut trees, Smoketown held more than five hundred patients by October 1862. Eaton could not imagine why, in light of ample food and nursing care, men were confined to bed for lack of clothing. COURTESY OF EDWARD G. MINER LIBRARY, UNIVERSITY OF ROCHESTER SCHOOL OF MEDICINE

By the time she was twenty-five, Maria M. C. Hall was already a seasoned battlefield nurse.
COURTESY OF U.S. ARMY HISTORY INSTITUTE, CARLISLE BARRACKS, PA.

Smoketown is just the place for malarious diseases to prosper. Do not feel satisfied with traveling on the Sabbath but I believe we must go on. Hence to Bakersville to a school house where we found 23 men of the Maine 5th who had been left by some mistake without any supplies. Promised to see that they had Sanitary supplies from Sharpsburg.—Reached Sharpsburg in time for dinner and partook of it at a private house, called on Capt. Hill who is slowly recovering from the measles.[40] Decided, as the Hospitals here had been emptied, to proceed to Harpers Ferry, was deeply

---

[40] Measles were common among men from rural areas who had not been exposed to the disease as children. In 76,318 cases of measles among Union troops, there were 5,177 deaths overall—approximately 7 percent—with a higher rate of mortality for black soldiers (11 percent) than for white (6 percent).

affected to find myself riding over the battle field of Antietam. There were the graves, the trenches, scattered all over the field, friends still seeking the graves of dear ones. There was the famous cornfield where the battle was so fierce, the orchard where our Maine 10th tried to fight under cover of the trees, the hay stacks, the riddled school house, the trees with the branches broken in all directions, and the field far across still covered all around with dead horses making the air in some cases offensive in the extreme. Oh! I tried to realize the scene of that awful day but how little could I do it. Mr. Hayes pointed out to me Col. _____['s] grey horse as he lay on the field.[41]—Hence we rode onward through the most beautiful and romantic scenery I had almost ever seen, on the sides of mountains where the road was built under the precipices that overlooked the Canal and the Potomac. The forests are magnificently tinged with their autumn hue, this was very striking on the mountain where McLellan [sic] stood to view the battle of Antietam.—Then came the moonlight scenery, and do'nt let us forget the awful road so full of holes and pitches, that threw me, as I sat on my box of supplies, in all directions.—I thanked the driver, for going so grandly over the very top of the stumps and stones.—Finally, we reached Sandy Hook, then came the tug of war, in the shape of a place to sleep for the night.—Up a long flight of steps we wound our way, the woman refused but the man lying in bed proposed to go up stairs, give up their own room to their boarders, and let us sleep on the floor in the parlor. Mr. Hayes and driver slept in the ambulance.

MONDAY NOV. 3RD 1862

Crossed over in two sutlers' teams, over the pontoon bridge, left our valises in the Sanitary Rooms, and went on to Bolivar Heights. Called on Dr. [Edwin B.] Palmer, then visited Hos. of the Maine 19th. They have left 51 there, but Dr. Hawes seems very attentive. Told him there was probably a box of supplies for them that we had been working hard enough to get to them, so they immediately sent down to the Express, and that box has at last arrived at its place of destination, in the time when it was sadly needed. Thence we went and partook of a dinner at 50 cts. each, and then called on Gen. Jackson, a queer old codger, saw also Lieut. Stratton of Portland, and had quite a chat of home, he is now acting adjutant for the General's staff. Came down from the Heights to seek for an ambulance from Dr. McNulty but did not succeed in getting one for to night. There has been cannonading for three days and we were quite amused to day to hear the sutlers making arrangements to skedaddle (as the rebels are to be seen in large numbers from the Heights and the inhabitants really fear an invasion) for the sake of securing government stores of which they are sadly in need. One man said he had no doubt they would be here in 24 hours. If I should be taken prisoner it is more that I bargained for, but I do'nt believe there is any danger. We have the promise of a bed on the floor in the dining

---

[41] HE left an underlined blank space. Oliver Wendell Holmes makes a reference to the "colonel's gray horse" in a July 1863 article in *Atlantic Monthly*, but does not identify the officer.

room of a house over the rooms of the provost guard. The woman says they are refugees from Virginia to save her son and husband from being forced into service.

TUESDAY NOV. 4TH 1862

In the morning went first to Dr. McNulty to beg for our ambulance, was not successful, thence proceeded up, up, up to Gen. Slocum's Headquarters, oh what a <u>splendid</u> view! Gen. Slocum could not provide transportation except to Berlin but advised a visit to new <u>convalescent</u> camp in Loudon Valley, we accepted invitation, took in a <u>large</u> load of Hos. stores, crossed the Shenandoah on pontoon and pursued our winding way under rocky crags, over precipices, still onward, missing our way but at last arriving at camp, found many poor men but none from Maine, without any doctors on the ground, had fires made, washed their faces, made corn starch gruel, and coffee, supplied the present necessities of some 50 men, returned over the Shenandoah passing by hundreds, I do'nt know but thousands, of men from convalescent camp [in] Washington bound for their Regts. Then over the Potomac through Sandy Hook, over a fine farming ground, we reached Berlin and our Maine 10th just about sunset. While looking for the convalescent camp this morning which we had passed by mistake, were stopped by our pickets who told us we were quite far enough as the rebels were within a quarter of a mile.—Stopped for the night, with Mrs. Jordan, who amused us much at being so much shocked to find there were two of us instead of one, took tea there, find the sutlers in great trouble as they hear the rebels are in Hagerstown on the road to Boonesboro and will probably take Frederick with its government stores. Do'nt believe it! Mrs. Jordan looking after the bread plate as hungry men kept coming in, exclaimed that that must have been eaten too. Expect tomorrow to find the way our suffering men are treated by our government, I mean our <u>sick</u> men. Why ca'nt they be discharged?[42]

WEDNESDAY NOV. 5TH 1862

Slept on a bed last night! Visited the Maine 10th, saw Dr. [Horatio] Howard, went with him to Regt. Hos. in the negro church, find the men there very comfortable. They have a good nurse, but he has the duties of Hos. steward, nurse, and every thing to attend to. Found a grandson of old Mrs. Brackett's there, but not very sick. One poor man from Norway[43] will stand it but a few days without he receives constant attention. Went to the old school house on the hill, found one old man there of the Maine 12th who has been knocked about from pillar to post till he hardly knows where he belongs, only that he belongs to the govt. and ca'nt go home without his discharge

---

[42] HE expresses here and elsewhere frustration about the protracted nature of processing paperwork for disabled soldiers, who would have been better off dying at their homes. Overtaxed surgeons were often an obstacle to the timely departure of disabled men.

[43] Norway, Maine.

papers.⁴⁴ Mr. Hayes will try and get them for him. Visited four other miserable holes called Hospitals, mostly filled with Penn. men. In one old hut without doors or windows we found seven men, one of them from the eruption on his face I immediately suspected of having small pox. We went down to the main street and after a long search found a surgeon who went with us, examined the case, pronounced our surmises correct, and ordered the men all up into the loft by themselves. We then reported the case to Col. Fillebrown who sent with us the officer of the day, Capt. Jordan, and he took the case in charge.⁴⁵ While Mrs. F made some gruel for the 10th Hos., I went over to the Regt. to see Joseph Down[e]s. One of the men showed me his tent, he was not there, so I made a call on <u>Mr. Knox</u>. He went out and found Charles Tibbets and Lieut. [John M.] Gould, and they with the Advocate⁴⁶ made quite a Portland chit chat. Returned to Hos. with Mrs. F and dispensed the gruel to the sick. Returned to Mrs. J[ordan]'s and tried to write a <u>letter to Mrs. Bosworth</u>, amid the constant clamor of an army of sutlers that we thought it very desirable should be sent to the front. One man, who we thought was a sutler but who pretends to be a captain of one of our Regiments in N[orth] Carolina, in my opinion ought to be in Fort Lafayette.⁴⁷ Capt. Sargent gave him some pretty heavy doses, I do believe he became a little frightened.

[*See Appendix letter 4. HE to "Mrs. Bosworth," November 5, 1862.*]

THURSDAY NOV. 6TH 1862

<u>Very sick all day</u>, a violent attack of cholera morbus.⁴⁸ We have taken a little room in a log hut consisting of two rooms, and are comfortably provided for.

---

⁴⁴ Though this soldier's name remains a mystery, HE and Fogg reported that he was fifty-seven years old, had been injured in the spine (probably in Mississippi where the 12th was stationed), brought back to Fortress Monroe, and left with a New York regiment that had abandoned him. It was not uncommon for men to falsify their ages in order to collect bounty money, but injury, illness, or exposure soon brought them low. The National Archives (Record Group 53) indicates that four men in their fifties belonging to the 17th Maine were dishonorably discharged in December 1862 and forced to forfeit their pay and bounty for having claimed that they were only forty-five. One of these, Benjamin Morrill, who was fifty-six, had fought in the Seven Days battles and lost a son there. Morrill blamed recruiting officers, who knew full well that the men were older than forty-five, but felt compelled to meet their enlistment quotas. See Isabella Fogg and HE to John W. Hathaway, November 10, 1862, MSA; and Lowry, "An Epidemic of Geezers."

⁴⁵ Capt. William P. Jordan of Portland.

⁴⁶ *Zion's Advocate* was a weekly religious newspaper published in Portland from 1828 to 1920.

⁴⁷ Located in New York Harbor adjacent to Brooklyn, Fort Lafayette, built during the war of 1812 and named for Revolutionary War hero the Marquis de Lafayette, housed Confederate prisoners of war and northern citizens who publicly expressed southern sympathies (also known as Copperheads).

⁴⁸ Cholera morbus was characterized by vomiting and diarrhea; it might have been the cause of food poisoning. Diarrhea and dysentery were soldiers' most common ailments, resulting in nearly forty-five thousand deaths among Union soldiers alone.

FRIDAY NOV. 7TH 1862

Better this morning. Thanks to my kind Father who knows the discipline I need, and truly I am in a peculiar manner, which it is not best to write about, being subjected to severe discipline. O for patience to bear and forbear while I labor for the soldier's good. Mr. Knox was in last evening, also Mr. Hayes and Capt. Sargent. Mrs. F has gone in company with Mr. Hayes to Kedarsville, Smoketown, and Hagerstown. I do'nt know when they will come back, perhaps not for a day or two,[49] but I do know one thing, it is a <u>luxury</u> to be alone.—A sick soldier has just been in for me to make him some gruel, and he ate it as if he enjoyed it. His name is Wright of Lewiston, had a sister, Miss Wright, who taught school in P[ortland] with the Misses Cumpston.—The sick soldier in the other room wanted me to write for him to his sister Mrs. Shepherd of Laconic, N. H. His name is Fullerton. I think him very sick with diphtheria. The soldier for whom I made the gruel says he has never drunk liquor, except one 1/2 pint of gin which he put in some bitters his mother sent him, since he enlisted and he has borne the marches, as well if not better than most of the men. <u>Quite a snow storm</u>. I think the snow is nearly an inch deep on the ground.—Made farina gruel for the man who is so sick in Hospital, also for the sick one in the other room.[50] While sitting in the dark in the evening, enjoying the luxury of quiet, Mr. Knox called and stopped till nine. He was very cold so I built a rousing fire. He says he does not know why it is, but his faith does not extend as far as <u>conversions</u> in his Regt. I am afraid this is not a war under God's direction, only in so far as he <u>permits</u> evil.

SATURDAY NOV. 8TH 1862

Felt tried [sic] with myself last evening for not having done more for the poor sick boy in the next room. Thought of my own dear boy. This morning I went in and carried him gruel, heated bricks for him and was just going to wash him, but the woman with whom he boards did it. Made gruel for Charles Matthews of Norway[51] who is sick in Hos., then went down into the village after going to the Hos. to see the men, carrying them some herring, and rubbing the poor sick one, then went to the old cabin. There lay a poor fellow very sick with pneumonia on the floor with his feet to the fire, in another corner sat a poor woman, mourning as if her heart would break for the death of her only child, and in the next room lay the little innocent who had not seen two years of this world's troubles, with arms folded on its breast, its freed spirit having fled the clayey tenement. And such is life, the woman talks very well, like a Christian. Her husband is a soldier. I inquired if they knew any thing of his

---

[49] In fact, Fogg and Hayes returned on November 10, after a three-day absence during which they visited Maine soldiers in Hagerstown, Bakersville, and Burketsville, Maryland, and at Russell Springs and Smoketown Hospitals. Many were suffering from exposure with only muslin shirts to keep them warm, and a number had already contracted diphtheria.

[50] Farina was a hot cereal resembling cream of wheat.

[51] Norway, Maine.

relatives, but they said his mind wandered so that they could get nothing from him. First I roused him, asked him where he lived, he said "no where," asked him where his wife lived, replied "where I left her," then inquired where he left her, reply "on the line," but I finally succeeded in rousing him sufficiently to get the direction, his name Archibald Reath, his wife's Phebe Ann Reath, Mechanics Grove, between Coleraine and Drumore Penn. He wished me to write to her and I have done so, poor woman this is the last she will probably ever hear from her husband. Surgeon has promised me he shall be removed to Hos. Returned home and made gruel for a man who came to the house and the sick man here. Hos. nurse came for some for Matthews, afterwards went into Mrs. Jordan's and ate a miserable cold dinner, returned, made beef tea for "James." Heard a noise in his room, went in and found two rough looking Irish soldiers with the door thrown wide open, and a stretcher in the room, telling him to get up, and go to the cars with them to go to Harpers Ferry and from there he should go home. He told them he could not move, after expostulating with them I went to the house for the woman who boards him, who told them if they attempted to take him away he would be a dead man before they landed him at any Hospital. Hearing this they desisted. Oh! can this be the way our sons are to be treated when through weariness and sickness they fall by the road side! What will become of officers who become so careless of the lives of their men? Went to the Hos. again to carry stimulating gruel for Matthews and prepared some beef tea also for them. Returning, Mrs. Ridenburg brought me in a pan of biscuit. Have had the misfortune to break my watch spring, so sorry for I shall have to wait till I go to Washington to have it fixed! Capt. Sargent has been in and spent part of the evening. I am told that Brig. Gen. Jackson is a hard drinker and very profane and I should think it from his appearance. Saw Gen. Ricketts the other day at Col. Fillebrown's tent. Do'nt believe Mrs. F will be home to night, well I'm quite content. I should be happy to spend the Sabbath alone. The snow that fell yesterday has not all melted yet.

SUNDAY NOV. 9TH 1862

Went early in the morning to the Hospital, carried gruel, had a little talk with the men on the Sabbath and left them some tracts. Was woke the first thing in the morning by young man in next room, went in as soon as possible, and found him in a pitiable condition. Indeed, I could not help him alone and called to the soldier boarding at the next door to assist me, this he refused, saying he knew nothing about the man or what was the matter with him, Mrs. Ridenburg then came to my assistance, but who cares for the poor soldier? Made milk punch and gruel for men in Hospital, went over to camp to get a doctor for James.—In the afternoon attended a short service at Hos., then went after the surgeon of the district for a watcher of the night, did not succeed, went for Dr. [Horatio] Howard, who not very willingly said he would try to send somebody, but poor James died about eleven o' clock. I had talked a little with him during the day, but I do not think he knew he was going to die. Mrs. Fogg came home, all wearied out. <u>Wrote a letter to bro. Greenough to day</u>. Mrs. Fogg brought me six letters from home, wish she had had one or two, she would have felt better.

MONDAY NOV. 10TH 1862

Have written <u>copied</u> letters all day till I am completely worn out. In the evening they sent for me to the Hos. to make them some gruel for Matthews. They have sent away all the sick from the general Hospital.

[*See Appendix letter 5. Isabella Fogg (HE) to John H. Hathaway, November 10, 1862.*]

TUESDAY NOV. 11TH 1862

I am but just able to enjoy my letters from home, I have had so much to do. James was buried this morning in a soldier grave. I have been <u>writing a letter to his mother</u>, to send with the little things that were in his pocket. This afternoon we shall go to Frederick to look after our boxes.

WEDNESDAY NOV. 12TH 1862

Arrived in Fred[erick] just at night. All seemed delighted to see us at our "home." Found the Quartermaster [Griffin] there, ready to leave in the morning. He was feeling very anxious about his son.—This morning went over to see the men in Regt. Hos. and glad were they, there has been one death and many removed to Frederick. I did not carry that <u>porridge</u>. Went over to Comp[anies] A and B, distributed one pr. drawers, seven pr. socks, and some eight or ten handkerchiefs, also crackers. Dr. Mc Gregor was very attentive, condition of things much improved, though there is still a want, Comp[any] B is in better order.—One man, I do'nt know how many more, has <u>bought</u> all his poultices this long time because he could not get them without. Tents are all floored and warmed now.—At Comp[any] B went to office to get the names of Maine men, and unexpectedly met Dr. Turnbull's son of H.[52] Knew him from his resemblance to his mother, and sent a little note to Annie Howard by him. Went into Frederick, but found it too late to visit Hospitals.

THURSDAY NOV. 13TH 1862

Ambulance took us in town at 1/2 past eight, was much vexed on going to our boxes to find that through a blunder in the manner of sending our boxes and through the spite of the Sanitary Com. we had to pay for freight $2.35. Visited Hos. during the forenoon, nothing special, men seem well cared for except in the German

---

[52] HE's reference to "H" is cryptic, since the hometown of the Turnbulls' son Franklin was Frankfort.

Reformed[53] where Bond is, there they complain sadly of starvation. Sent out two bottles of shrub[54] to Pav[ilion] Hos. Strange when there was such a "great work" to do there that that is the last I hear of it. Afternoon, again visited Hos., attended to other business, called on Misses Weisson, took tea there and returned to Berlin, vexed that our boxes did not come on with us in the night train.

FRIDAY NOV. 14TH 1862

Shall not go to Washington to day. Hear sad news. Three of the men of the 10th have died since we left, two were very sick when we left, but the other was very sudden. In Frederick saw a Georgia man laying [sic] on his bed outside the barracks, enjoying the air and two ladies ministering to him. I have never seen that done for our own men. Hear that our 20th Regt. at Baltimore who were sent there sick are dying very fast. I have no confidence left in anything, none in the movement of our army, none in our government, but this only increases the suffering of our poor men. Made wreaths for the coffins of Corporal Irish and Gurney,[55] also cut off a lock of their hair and prepared it to be sent home in their letters.—Attended the funeral, they were buried in one grave, had singing for a part of the service. Gurney had two <u>brothers</u> in this Regt. who remained in camp, not caring to attend the funeral! Does war make us worse than the heathen?—Capt. Sargent asked if they would not like his ring to send home, but they declined, saying "it was of no account".—The canal boat has gone and we are still here, as we wished to see there a little righted in the new Hospital.—Mrs. F after telling me to night that I felt so far above Calais because I came from Portland, that I was not willing that she should come near me that came from P[ortland], and some other similar remarks, seeing that I <u>would not</u> be drawn into a controversy with her, remarked that she supposed that I felt that she was <u>my</u> cross. Oh! how many a true word is spoken in jest.—I would gladly write to Agnes to night but I shall not be able to with this candle.

SATURDAY NOV. 15TH 1862

The men have all been removed to new Hos.—On going there this morning found the Hos. steward examining one of our boxes which had been opened partially, reckon he was somewhat ashamed.—Made soup and farina for the men, they have their new cook to day. Gave the doctor eight quilts together with shirts, towels, stockings, drawers, &c.—Mrs. F went in company with Mr. Knox on horseback to

---

[53] The German (later Evangelical) Reformed Church of Frederick was established in the colonial period and was used as a hospital during the war.

[54] A cordial made of fruit juice, vinegar, sugar, and either brandy or rum.

[55] Michael Gurney died on November 12 and Nathan F. Irish, on November 13, 1862.

see two sick men, I declined being one of the party. Wrote a letter to Mrs. Whittier and Hatty Belle.

[*See Appendix letter 6. HE to Hatty Belle Eaton, November 15, 1862.*]

SUNDAY NOV. 16TH 1862

I hope while I live never to spend another day like this. Read in my Bible this morning, "Let this mind be in you who was also in Christ Jesus." "Do all things without murmurings and disputings."—A poor soldier belonging to the Battery was buried to day, having been stabbed by another the night before, while under the influence of liquor.—There are one or two men in the Hos. that I think are sinking.—Gave Mr. Knox a few things for his comfort.—

MONDAY NOV. 17TH 1862

I am satisfied our work is done here and I want to leave as soon as possible. Hope to get our boxes all fixed and ready for the first canal boat.

TUESDAY NOV. 18TH 1862

Nothing of importance. Made about five quarts of gruel and carried it to the quarters for the sick men there. Mrs. Fogg went off on horseback to see two sick men. In the evening, old Mrs. Singafuse sent in word that she thought 50 cts. a day would be about right for her room. We were thunderstruck. I have about 25 cts. a day for my whole house, and here we have been living in this old hut, deprived of every comfort in this wonderful Berlin![56]

WEDNESDAY NOV. 19TH 1862

Boxes all packed and ready for a start. Good riddance to Ridenburg and Singafuse. We watch for a boat. Paid the old woman $2.00 for her room.

THURSDAY NOV. 20TH 1862

Here we are in the Chesapeake and Ohio Canal. A coal boat, the Dutch Hen, Capt. Mc Mullen, every thing about it ugly and dirty. This is romantic, what a cabin and what a state room!! Capt. and I take the bed turn about, or rather the shelf, there is no bed. It rains in torrents, and drip, drip it goes in all directions over head, Mrs. F sits with a handkerchief folded on the top of her head to catch

---

[56] Berlin, a small town near Falmouth and Fredericksburg, was in Stafford County, Virginia, in the northeastern part of the state.

the drops and I have an apron folded in my lap to catch them. They seemed to feel very bad at the Hospital to have us leave them.—We passed two forts, one in Seneca, and also Dam No. 2. We are very much disappointed that we have got to tie up to night, do'nt know when we shall get in to Georgetown. <u>Have written to Mother Shaw to day</u>.

FRIDAY NOV. 21ST 1862

Such a night! Horrors! "John" turned in till 1/2 past one, then after washing the dishes and the <u>dish cloths</u> (Charles [Hayes] having found some soap in an old blouse by the road side) he made breakfast and turned in again till six o' clock. Then came the tug of war, Mrs. Fogg had as much as she could attend to, to rouse up all hands, keep the fire agoing, the hatch ways & windows open and shut to keep from roasting & then freezing, the pumps agoing to keep the old hulk from sinking, while I sat up all night on one of the benches, my head on my goose rolled up for a pillow.—Now we have stopped for those old pontoon bridges again at the 7 locks, the 6 locks was a wild place. Hurrah for boating on the Canal. We are out of provender too. Mrs. Fogg went ashore at one of the locks yesterday and found some <u>ham</u>, round cakes, and cheese, we soon made way with that and now we must go hungry till we get to Georgetown. <u>Have written a long letter to Sarah Caduc to day</u>.

SATURDAY NOV. 22ND 1862

We arrived at Georgetown just at sunset, and with our noble captain went on shore to find a place to store our boxes. He, as I expected, had his bottle filled the first thing. They, no doubt, had a high time on board that night. Found our home, called at Mr. Mc Intyre's, received two letters from Gorham, my dear little Hatty does not forget mother. Hear that a check has been sent from P[ortland] for me. Mr. Hathaway had six letters waiting for me, a feast indeed, if I could be permitted to enjoy it in peace. Letters from Frank, Agnes, Sarah Caduc, Maria, Samuel and Elisabeth [Whitney], Mrs. Hart, Mr. Greenough, Elizabeth Whiting, and Mrs. Lancey besides Hatty Belle's, Hatty Whittier's, and Mrs. Whittier's last evening. Thirteen letters waiting for me, I ought not to complain, but an important one is missing, also the Free St. box.—Visited the Casparis Hospital[57] this afternoon, saw four of the Maine 18th, one of them will die and he is delirious and can understand nothing. Poor boy!

---

[57] Casparis Hospital was located on A Street, southeast of the Capitol building; Surgeon W. E. Waters presiding.

SUNDAY NOV. 23RD 1862

Yesterday I supposed all day that this was Saturday and when Mr. Hathaway made his engagement to meet us at eleven o' clock in the morning, I did not realize that it would interfere with the Sabbath service. Truly I am in a trying place and I need <u>special grace</u>. My trials are great, I little understood where my greatest trials were to be. But oh I want to bear for the sake of the poor soldier. <u>Have written to Mrs. White and Mr. Bosworth to day.</u>—

MONDAY NOV. 24TH 1862

This morning went first to Mr. H[athaway]'s office, saw there one of the men whom we had seen on Saturday and had to send the sad word to the other two that the brother of our Joshua Mitchell of Jay and the cousin of the other were among those who had fallen victim to the awful mismanagement of Smoketown Hospital.—From the office, I took 7th St. cars for Maine Cavalry. Had a pleasant walk to camp, found the men ready for a start. Quartermaster Griffin could hardly speak for deep emotion, in view of what we had tried to do for his son. Lieut. Coleman also seemed most happy to see me but was deeply affected as he talked of his mother. I love the Maine men. Took 7th St. cars and went to 4 1/2 St. calling on Mrs. Williams. A pleasant call, her son very sick.—Mrs. F has had her son with her making her a call. Made a few purchases such as stationery and a map of Virginia, some gloves for a levy [*sic*] a pair,[58] and postage stamps, then went over to office and selected our supplies to take to Annapolis in the morning. Mrs. Bigelow & Miss Sharpless sent in a large basket of supplies to take with us in our new trunk.—Did not retire till twelve.

TUESDAY NOV. 25TH 1862

Was up before five to be ready for a start, but the man failed to come for our baggage, went over at eleven but found we could not make the connection and remained till three. Called on a Mrs. Stewart with Mrs. Fogg, her daughter walked with us to the public gardens.—<u>Wrote a letter to Sarah Caduc</u>, and mailed it at Annapolis Junction where I am now writing this.—Chat in the cars with Rev. Mr. Henries, a Maine man, chaplain at Annapolis, an excellent man, did'nt he ask me some pretty close questions! He understands well how <u>some</u> matters stand.

WEDNESDAY NOV. 26TH 1862

Arrived in evening, all safe, went with Mrs. Fogg to a Mrs. King's where we passed the night, sleeping on the floor, in the same room with herself and infant a week old, also

---

[58] HE emphasizes the expense of the gloves.

her sister and another child. Verily I am going through a hardening process, and I trust also an unexpected purifying process. Was told yesterday by chaplain that he never had the first particle of sympathy with some workers who if they could not lead would do nothing. Have to day visited College Hos.,[59] seen six Maine men, one Russell of Portland but all, I am happy to say, comfortable. Thence to Navy Yard Hospital, a beautiful place indeed. Found here a warm hearted company of nurses consisting of "Mother Grey" (Lydia B. Grey) of Boston, Mrs. Boutelle, an accomplished teacher of Albany New York, Mrs. Sayres (New Jersey I think), Miss E. Thompson, Ellington Ct., Miss Quinby, Biddeford, and Miss Pearson and [Adeline] Walker, Portland. Have taken the names of our Maine men in Hospitals here, numbering about 50. In morning visited part of them, afternoon, through the politeness of Quartermaster, had an ambulance detailed for visiting camp of paroled prisoners, it was very cold, snowed some, but no matter. Reaching camp, called first on Lieut. L. E. Estes who has our Maine men in charge. There are but four in Hos. and only one very sick, will try to get him into Hos. in town. Our Maine men about 140 in number are all in one section of the camp and this enabled us to give every one a short call. Saw Frank Tibbets, he looks finely as do all of them, we were proud of our men, they have the credit of being the best behaved set of men in camp, an example to the others. We were happily disappointed in their condition, but they have been paid off and have supplied themselves with little comforts, some two bbls.[60] of apples in their tent, and several kegs of cider. They have fires, &c. One Irishman (the only drinking man among them as Lieut. informs us) when we were leaving, came out to the road, with several others and in the exuberance of his joy exclaimed, "Bully for the State of Maine, she'll take care of her men." We left at disposal of surgeons about 1/2 bush[el] apples, two gallons cranberries, a lot of stockings, &c., and distributed handkerchiefs among the prisoners.

THURSDAY NOV. 27TH 1862

Thanksgiving day. And oh how much I have to be thankful for, a year of mercies! A year too in which I think I have been led more into the <u>depths</u> of Christian experience than any hitherto. Thus far the Lord hath led me, I <u>desire</u> to trust <u>all</u> to the control of a kind Father, <u>my own</u> will swallowed up, and I purified, this poor sinful body made a meet temple for the Master's use.—Made it our home with the ladies of Hos. and to day I have made it my business to call on <u>every</u> Maine man, about fifty in number, all were glad to see me, they are comfortable so far as warm rooms, &c. are concerned, but there is a great deficiency in variety as well as quantity of

---

[59] Annapolis was home to St. John's College, used during the Civil War as a Union medical installation. Twenty miles from the Capitol and renamed College Green Hospital, it held convalescing soldiers from 1862 through the end of the war. After significant renovations, the college reopened as St. John's in 1866.

[60] Abbreviation for "barrels."

food, how men are going to get strong on sour bread, weak coffee and tea, a little beef once a day, rice and sauce, I know not. Poor fellows, it was any thing but Thanksgiving day to them.—I have not had a great deal of time to think of my precious family. I trust them, I know they think of mother and home.

FRIDAY NOV. 28TH 1862

Have finished up our business in Annapolis, had a visit pleasant indeed with the ladies, dined on a Boston Thanksgiving dinner, by invitation, with Mrs. Gibbs and Stone and another lady of the College [Green] Hospital, and left in haste at 1/2 past two for the cars for Washington. I am very weary, almost sick, would be quite so at home, must soak my feet in mustard water to night, and hope to be well again tomorrow. It is no little [*sic*].

SATURDAY NOV. 29TH 1862

Went to the "Rooms"[61] immediately after breakfast and found that our box that had been among the missing had arrived, also that our large box had been opened by Mr. Hathaway and various articles abstracted [*sic*] therefrom. Our packages were scattered hither and thither, but Mr. H seeing my indignation soon gave directions for them to be returned to their rightful place. We have worked all day, with the assistance of Mr. [Leonard W.] Watson, have packed two barrels and two boxes, with what we already have on hand, we shall be ready to start on Tuesday. Miss Morrill made quite a stir this afternoon by appropriating two pair of private socks to her own use after being informed to that effect. I shall not let this matter rest, those socks must be given up.

SUNDAY NOV. 30TH 1862

Have attended church to day and heard Dr. Robinson of Harrisburg preach a most admirable sermon from the fifty-first Psalm, the sermon and reading of 1 Peter 1st chap. did me a great deal of good. Called on Mr. Mc Intyre and procured my watch, received letters from Mrs. Rea, Mrs. Barbour, Mrs. Greenough, Mrs. Griswold, &c. Wrote a long letter to Mrs. Griswold.

MONDAY DEC. 1ST 1862

Wrote to Mr. Bosworth and also to Frank Henry by to day's mail.[62] Received letter from both of them this morning and feel very anxious that Frank should be doing

---

[61] The "rooms" of the Maine State Relief Agency, located at 273 F Street.
[62] HE means her son.

something.—Mr. H[athaway] still thinks we had better leave tomorrow and in that case we shall have enough to do to be ready, no time for journalizing. The stockings have been returned. Lucky for those ladies! Called on Mrs. [Sarah] Hathaway in the evening.

TUESDAY DEC. 2ND 1862

After a tremendous hurry, going out early and purchasing two dozen [cans] condensed milk, 1/2 dozen canned chicken, alcohol, and candles to the amount of $13.80 cts., then, purchasing an army knife for self, went back to room to work, finished up by reaching the wharf <u>in season</u> for the *Wilson Small* to start, or rather, long before it was time for her to start.[63]—Have seen Mayor Fay and Miss Gilson, I forbear comment, also Mrs. Barton with her supplies.[64] We had quite a time to get ourselves on board the boat, they doubt the surgeon general's pass. However, we were at length passed, stores and all, <u>free transportation</u>. But lo and behold, when we got to Aquia Creek, it was a Creek sure enough, no houses there, not one to lay our heads in, but the floor of the *Wilson Small* answered every purpose.

WEDNESDAY DEC. 3RD 1862

This morning Capt. went on shore with us and introduced us to Quartermaster [Theron E.] Hall whom we found very polite, he as well as Dr. Letterman advise us to store our supplies here and for this purpose he has assigned part of his own barge to our use, we have lost one of our boxes. We were surprised by meeting poor sick Capt. Cowan, who having received his discharge is on his way home. How glad we were to be able to make him a good cup of tea & some biscuit and butter, he was so overcome he cried like a child. Mrs. Fogg went to San. Com. to get some milk and they offered her enough for <u>one cup</u>! <u>She thanked and left them, getting the milk somewhere else</u>. <u>Wrote to Mr. Hathaway</u>. We left for Falmouth at noon in baggage car and at Falmouth, what was our surprise to find ourselves landed in a camp, no houses there. A col. of a Maryland Regt. kindly took our trunk in charge, no thanks to the Mayor or the lady,[65] he also sent the officer of the day with us to Gen. Sumner's Headquarters, from which place we were sent [in] ambulance to "Burnside's" Headquarters, thence through Dr. Letterman, Medical Director of the Army, to Hooker's Headquarters, where

---

[63] A hospital transport operated by the Sanitary Commission.
[64] HE sees the forty-one-year-old Clara Barton, who never married.
[65] HE means Frank Fay and Helen Gilson, who were working for the Sanitary Commission at this time.

after a good jouncing we arrived in evening. An orderly was immediately sent to procure us lodgings, and we have them indeed, down stairs are laid out the remains of a hog, and up stairs, through the chinks the stars peep through, and that is the only means of lighting our sleeping apartment. The family consisting of a man and his wife and two children seem very civil. I have left my valise at Aquia Creek.

THURSDAY DEC. 4TH 1862

Called this morning on "fighting Joe [Hooker]." Were received very politely, he complained of newspapers and their false statements, but very politely ordered an ambulance for our use while we should be visiting his division, so we availed ourselves of it and started for our Maine 20th. Here we have spent a most delightful day. We first called on surgeon, find they have 65 men undergoing treatment. The officers made a reconnaissance to find lodgings for us and at length made a demand on a family by the name of Boller for a room. Col. Ames and Lieut. Col. Chamberlain very gentlemanly and with Adjutant [John Marshall] Brown full of fun over their table, &c.

FRIDAY DEC. 5TH 1862

The family where we stop have three sons and son-in-law in the rebel army. They say they have nothing for us to eat. Have been to Aquia Creek to day in a tremendous storm of rain and snow, making an attempt to get a box and barrel from the cars, sent a letter to Mrs. Whittier by Mr. Pendleton of Gorham.—Lost sight of the box and barrel and fear it is lost.

SATURDAY DEC. 6TH 1862

Have suffered much to day in going to Falmouth Station about the missing box, and to my great disappointment have not found it, they say a car broke down on the road. Find that Col. [John] Hathaway is in the neighborhood. Mr. Hayes called this evening and says they need us at the 17th Maine.

SUNDAY DEC. 7TH 1862

Have spent the day (after making gruel in the morning for the 20th) with the 17th. Officers seemed pleased to see me. Col. [Thomas A.] Roberts and his son the Adjut[ant Charles W. Roberts] with Lieut. Col. [Charles B.] Merrill, Surgeon Wiggin, &c. They have 16 sick in tent, over a hundred under treatment, have been very busy to day putting up a new Hos. tent. Buried one man to day. Sick men in a more comfortable condition than the 20th. Left with them six papers of corn starch.

Saw Fred Bosworth, he is very well and is quartermaster's clerk. Saw John White, he looks sick, very much fallen away. Their chaplain seems to have absconded, they have written him unless he returns and does his duty he had better retire.[66] Mrs. Fogg and Mr. Hayes have gone to Aquia Creek to day.

MONDAY DEC. 8TH 1862

Opened stores brought up last night, find apples in a horrible condition but they are glad of them any way. Surgeons Munroe and Hersom <u>kind men</u>. Went in afternoon to Potomac Station to look up a house, but did not succeed, though Brigade Quartermaster Howland advises us to live tent fashion, he thinks the first gun will be fired tomorrow, every thing looks like a movement speedily. I dread it yet desire it. One of the sick men of the 20th died last night, buried to day. Made gruel for the sick men to night, also made gruel and cracker toast for them this morning. The 20th have gone on picket for 48 hours except the sick and those with bad shoes who have been excused by surgeon and Col. [Ames].—Men are suffering sadly for vegetables. Commissaries have just received a few potatoes and desiccated vegetables.

TUESDAY DEC. 9TH 1862

Have opened the Gorham box this morning and find it in good condition except the two bottles of tomato ketchup, which had both gone to smash. Are now waiting impatiently for ambulance to take us to the 17th. Mrs. Fogg proposing to go to the 5th but I am afraid it will be too late to accomplish any thing. Dined with Col. [Thomas A.] Roberts, Dr. Wescott, and Col.'s son [Charles W. Roberts], the Adjutant.—Mrs. Fogg and Mr. Hayes went to visit the 5th while I have remained to attend to the wants of the 17th. One of Capt. [George W.] Martin's comp[any], named [Joseph] Drew of Fryburg has died this afternoon. I have made about two gallons of corn starch gruel and a large quantity of buttered milk toast, no conveniences but an out doors fire. Have seen Stillman Robert's son[67] and Mr. Yeaton [*sic*] to day.

---

[66] Harvey Hersey of Portland was the Universalist chaplain of the 17th Maine. Private John W. Haley (1840–1921) of company I wrote that "he no sooner arrived in camp than he joined himself unto 'the sons of Belial' and could soon guzzle more whiskey than the fattest of them. As he couldn't get enough to drink in legitimate ways, he resorted to illegitimate ones, even to stealing. He also stole a horse when we marched through Maryland in the fall of 1862. On the whole he acted so much like Satan that his career with us soon ended" (See Haley, *The Rebel Yell*, 250).

[67] Stillman Roberts of Portland had two sons of military age: Charles H., born in 1835 and Edward A., born in 1838. HE must mean Edward, who was a private in company B of the 17th.

WEDNESDAY DEC. 10TH 1862

Mrs. Fogg did not return last evening and I had the honor of sleeping in the Col.'s tent, most kindly vacated for my use. A nice bed was made for me, the floor had been newly carpeted with cedar, but I was dreadfully cold, did not sleep at all. The poor men coughed all night in all directions, and there was a constant tramp of troops and army wagons. On going to the Hos. this morning every head was raised with exclamations of pleasure, one said "there comes our angel," others said they would soon get well if I would only stay. This morning I baked apples for them all in the Col.'s tent on some flat rails before the coals, and oh how glad they were to get them, even with a little ashes. Yesterday I gave all of them some of "grandfather's" peppermints, and they about cried because it brought home so near. One of them said the nearest like civilization of any thing he had seen in this country, except my face. I took a long walk to find the 5th Battery but they had moved. I however went to [the] 1st Mass. and saw Willy Manning. This afternoon, left immediately after dinner as they have marching orders at sundown and seeing the ambulance was still missing, I had a frightfully muddy walk before me. Mrs. Fogg arrived just at night, having seen the Maine 16th on the road and the 5th Battery. She brought me a letter from Hatty Belle to George Whittier. On her arrival we went over to Gen. Hooker's Headquarters, for advice as to our location in case of battle and he thinks we had better remain where we are. He is exceedingly polite, a Maine gentleman was with him. Returning Lieut. Col. Chamberlain called, feeling a longing for a little preserved ginger. He seemed very thoughtful in view of what might be on the morrow, but still showed us how to toast hard bread. The Col. did not get any peppermints from me.

THURSDAY DEC. 11TH 1862

At dawn that awful cannonading commenced, how could I bear it! We rose early & went to camp of the 20th but they had left, except the sick and <u>quartermaster, who took the apple to day.</u>—Returned to the house and prepared our things for a sudden move, then Mrs. Fogg took cars to learn the condition of things with reference to wounded while I went to camp and gave each man a little marmalade to put on his hard bread. The men, poor fellows, were exceedingly busy, <u>examining</u> the condition of their flannels. Apropos of this, I have this moment stopped writing to make a reconnaissance over my own person, and it has not been an unsuccessful one. So much by way of episode. Sitting on an old bread box before Lieut. [Augustus H.] Strickland's camp fire I <u>wrote a letter to Mr. Hathaway</u> to day, and this afternoon after <u>writing to Miss Lucy E. Barbour</u> of Gorham, I made gruel and prepared crackers and marmalade for Steward Pendleton who had returned from his Regt. and is going to Hos. at Washington. We are told to night that Fredericksburg is burning and our army has crossed the river, if so we shall probably leave tomorrow. <u>Wrote a letter</u> this evening for Amanda Boller to her soldier boy <u>Samuel Williams of Co. H</u>

Eaton enjoyed the company of Bowdoin rhetoric professor Joshua Lawrence Chamberlain and his wife Fannie, when the 20th Maine was in winter quarters during 1862–63. Eaton knew him as a jokester, but his military valor led him to postwar political prominence. MAINE STATE ARCHIVES, AUGUSTA

56th Regt. Penn. Vols. Now I must try and write to Mrs. Bosworth. Well it is written and it is striking small hours.

[*See Appendix letter 7. HE to Mrs. B[osworth], December 11, 1862.*]

FRIDAY DEC. 12TH 1862

Have written to Margaret O'Brian [*sic*], and a long letter to my precious Agnes,—I am vexed with Mrs. Fogg, she started out for an ambulance and the next thing I knew she

The 2nd Maine Infantry, on parade at Hall's Hill, Virginia, during the winter of 1861–62. Led by George Varney and full of men from the Penobscot Valley, Eaton regularly attended the sick of the 2nd, as many as thirty at a time. NATIONAL ARCHIVES AND RECORDS ADMINISTRATION

had gone to the Creek for supplies and worn my rubbers thus preventing my going out all day. To be sure I can write letters but that is not very pleasant when there is so much else to be done, I have made gruel for a good many here at the house.

SATURDAY DEC. 13TH 1862

<u>An awful day</u>. The battle began early in the morning, and has continued all day.[68] While Mrs. F went to see about an ambulance I went over to the Division Hos. and there I found the sick men of the 2nd Maine about 30 of them. I staid there during the afternoon, made whiskey punch and provided crackers, butter, and marmalade for all the Maine men.—Returned to camp of the 20th intending to work for them but found Mrs. F with an ambulance ready to go forward. Accordingly we drove over to the Lacey [*sic*] House,[69] about 1/2 a mile from the battle field, where they were bringing the dying and where lay the dead. It was my first experience and an awful one it was, but I find my nerves strong to endure where I can be of service. One poor fellow who had had both legs shattered called me to him and said "do let me see

---

[68] Battle of Fredericksburg.

[69] The Chatham plantation, purchased by planter James Horace Lacy in 1857 for his wife and five children, was known as Lacy House and used as a Union headquarters and field hospital in conjunction with the battle of Fredericksburg in December 1862. The 1771 house, which had nine rooms and a two-story veranda, had been the home of planters for three generations and served as the venue for Burnside's battle strategy meeting on the evening of December 10. Just outside the city, its porticos featured a view of the Rappahannock River. Significant vandalism made the house uninhabitable after the war.

your face tomorrow, I am growing childish" and he burst into tears. Another from Worcester Mass. wanted me to write home a letter to his mother with my pencils, so that she might hear from him as soon as possible, as only his left arm was shattered and he was not killed. Two shells struck the house while we were in it and the noise of the musketry and cannon's roar and flash was perfectly terrific. Mrs. Barton there with four ambulances and seven men.[70]

SUNDAY DEC. 14TH 1862

Another sad day. Not a day of rest for me, though I am thankful to say there has been no fighting or very little. We have however been to one of the tent Hospitals all day. (Saw there Miss Gilson and Mr. Fay, and I must say they were exceedingly uncivil. They were manifestly unwilling that my trunk should remain under the protection of their tent.) I spent the day in washing wounds, oh! how many frightful scenes I have been witness to. The sight of the dead becomes a familiar one. Col. Varney of the 2nd Maine with his Adjt. and one of his captains among the wounded. Mrs. F has gone to Washington to get more supplies. How I wish I could hear from our Maine Regts.

MONDAY DEC. 15TH 1862

Went out early in the morning to camp of the 20th with my basket of supplies, also to Division Hos. where I found the 2nd Maine glad enough to see me. One poor fellow very sick. While at the camp of 20th an old gentleman came to me who said his name was Blanchard from the town of Cumberland, he was looking after his sick son in Hos. of the Maine 17th. I went with him to three Division Hos. without success, then walked over to Quartermaster Morse who sent him in [an] ambulance to another. Poor man I very much fear his son is dead. Oh! I am so tired, I wonder how many messes of gruel and punch I have made to day. Hear nothing from the army that seems favorable. One poor fellow of the 2nd came straggling into camp with his face badly bruised by a shell.

TUESDAY DEC. 16TH 1862

Poor Mr. Blanchard returned last night and so I had company to tea and to breakfast this morning. For breakfast I exchanged with Mrs. Boller hard bread for a flour cake. We had a terrific blow last night and a very hard shower. Just after breakfast, who

[70] Throughout most of the battle of Fredericksburg, Clara Barton assisted in caring for wounded soldiers at Lacy House. Before the battle began, she resided there as a guest of 9th Corps commander, General Samuel Sturgis. She had managed also to slip into Fredericksburg under Confederate fire during the battle to help at various dressing stations, according to Stephen Oates. By December 13, she described Lacy House as bestrewn with wounded men, leaving hardly a place to walk. See Oates, *A Woman of Valor*, 116.

should make me a call but Adjt. [John Marshall] Brown. The Regt. are all returning, have evacuated Fredericksburg, a perfect failure after such a terrible loss of life. It really seems good to see them back, I told Lt. Col. Chamberlain my presentiments about him and he said I must be his good angel. They have lost but four, seven missing, and about 30 wounded but not severely. Mr. Blanchard has returned this evening and my fears are confirmed, his son is dead, he will remain here again to night. The 17th have lost but two and a few wounded. Mrs. Fogg has not yet returned. Men in Hos. are in a suffering condition. They must have better care. I must write a letter for one of them in the morning.

WEDNESDAY DEC. 17TH 1862

Procured an ambulance from Lieut. Ayres of the Ambulance Corps and went this morning to the Division Hospital in Berry's division at the Thrashley House[71] and found there about 300 men mostly wounded. Col. Carver of the 4th Me. in charge. Of his Regt. of 223 but about 111 remain. The sick and wounded of the 17th and 3rd are also here. Made about four quarts of gruel, four gallons of chicken broth, and as much hot broma[72] with crackers spread with marmalade for the sick. I had a regular siege preparing it with the wind and snow blowing all ways burning my dress in five places with the flying cinders. Went among the sick and gave our men some peppermints and a few apples. One poor fellow shot through the lungs begged for another apple tomorrow. Mrs. Fogg returned in evening. Mr. Blanchard here again. This last army movement I have no patience to write about it, as Gen. Hooker told Mr. Blanchard, "it is all of a piece with the whole war, a succession of blunders from beginning to end." Have written to Frank this evening, I had letters from Frank, G[eorge] R. Davis, Colchester, Brookline, and London by Mrs. Fogg.

THURSDAY DEC. 18TH 1862

Again went to Thrashley House Hos., saw Col. [Thomas A.] Roberts there, had a call also from Col. Hathaway who said as he saw me stirring about 16 gallons of chicken broth, contained in the camp kettles and a huge cook pot that if I was only ugly enough I should answer for Scott's Meg Merrilies.[73] It has been one

---

[71] A private home and tent hospital in Stafford County, Virginia, seized after the battle of Fredericksburg, serving approximately four hundred soldiers. HE noted that "amputations were constantly going on, and deaths occurring" as she cooked for and fed the hordes. See HE to Mrs. Bosworth, December 22, 1862, MCHA, Collection S-61, MHS.

[72] Broma was a light cocoa made from the powder that remained when cocoa butter was separated (known as the broma process).

[73] Archetypal gypsy character associated with life in the wilderness in one of Walter Scott's Waverly novels, *Guy Mannering* (1815).

of my most satisfactory days, for by hurrying I succeeded in providing dinner for those poor wounded men before the ambulances carried them to the boat for W[ashington]. Mrs. Fogg returned from Aquia Creek with all our supplies between ten & eleven o' clock. I offered to get a cup of tea for her which was declined, and therefore I spent the time in <u>writing to Mrs. Whittier, Hatty Belle, and Mrs. Greenough</u>. I am anxious that the children should hear from me before Christmas, my darling children, how I long to see them. Mr. Blanchard here again to night.

FRIDAY DEC. 19TH 1862

Went over to camp of the 2nd early this morning to make a call on Mr. Hathaway and carry my letter, this was cause for offence in one quarter. Then returned and after breakfast, received our large boxes of supplies. Mr. Boller's family in great trouble lest the house should break down, and I had to manage in all sorts of ways to stow them away. Found Mrs. Fogg's box from Calais in sad condition, pickles all gone to smash. In the afternoon went over to the camp of the 20th and made whiskey punch, while Mrs. Fogg prepared oysters for them. I had much rather go to a Regt. by myself and act for myself. <u>Writing to Mrs. Rea</u> last evening.

SATURDAY DEC. 20TH 1862

According to <u>Mr. Hathaway's request</u> we started to day in ambulance accompanied by Mr. Hayes, I for the 19th and Mrs. Fogg for the 16th. The roads were perfectly awful, but we had a first rate dinner and <u>I</u> did not fear to ride. The road led over Falmouth Heights and past the ugly batteries, very silent now, Fredericksburg lay as quiet in the valley below as if it had not been the scene of such awful bloodshed. Dr. Hersom, now a paroled prisoner, says the fury of the inhabitants knew no bounds when they returned to F[redericksburg] and found their houses ransacked. They have 24 men in Hospital of the 19th. I have been able to supply all that had pressing need with drawers, stockings and shirts, giving away 12 shirts, 12 pr. drawers, and 15 pr. socks. Prepared tea with milk in it for them, and as they had just got soft bread I toasted it and spread it with butter and marmalade.—I also carried a basket of apples among them, and of one thing I am certain, I had the blessing of many. Their Hos. is in the best condition of any I have seen of the Regt. Hos. and they have been there but three days. In the evening I walked over to the house of a family by the name of Carter. They were from New York, a fine family, consisting of an old lady and her daughter Sarah. There are also two brothers here name of Morrison who have been imprisoned in Richmond for Union sentiments, have lost every thing, their families have returned to Delaware. Here at last I have found <u>real, thorough going</u> Union people, notwithstanding the abuse they have received from [the] Union army.

SUNDAY DEC. 21ST 1862

I am out of patience waiting for the men to come for me to go over to the Regt. The family here have gone to visit their daughter Mrs. Primer while I seem to be left to keep house. I am afraid my poor men will not get their chicken broth for dinner to day. It is the Sabbath, still I wished to minister to the sick. Well, I am here in Dr. Billing's tent before a good fire, waiting for my water to boil and the men shall have a good dinner if I can make it. One man sitting by me now says he has three brothers at home and he would rather bear that some one had shot them down with a rifle at home than to hear that they had enlisted in the army and sickened and died. One good requisition of the surgeon I wish to notice, he will not prescribe for any man in the morning who comes for medicine till his face and hands have been washed and his hair combed. A grand idea, the very act makes them feel more like men. The doctor says their chaplain [Edwin B. Palmer] is a valuable man and rendered most efficient aid on the battle field. Now for the dinner.

They seemed to enjoy it thoroughly, also the handkerchiefs and the peppermints. I have enjoyed myself very much in working for this Hos. and I believe I have done the men some good.

MONDAY DEC. 22ND 1862

Returned last evening and soon received a call from Col. Chamberlain, who wished me to call on Col. Ames who was threatened with fever. Though exceedingly weary I walked over and found him quite comfortably laid down before the fire in his table [sic], turned wrong side up.—On talking about going to the Creek in course for Washington, Mrs. F proposed to accompany him to take care of him. Mr. Hayes is very sick and stopped here last night. I have finished Mrs. Rea's letter and written a long one to Mr. Bosworth. Went to the Maine 2nd with supplies and found them breaking camp. Their surgeon Dr. Morrison, very polite and desirous that we should visit their Regiment as soon as they were regulated.—Have been having Mr. Hayes soak his feet and put mustard on his chest, he has not sat up any all day. Mrs. F has had quite a time with the surgeon's department of the 20th, one of their men died to day.

[See Appendix letter 8. HE to Mrs. Bosworth, December 22, 1862.]

TUESDAY DEC. 23RD 1862

This morning carried hot tea and crackers to the men in quarters, for which they seemed very thankful, some of them are very sick. It is with great satisfaction that we see a Hos. tent going up to day and a stove on the ground. This afternoon we have been trying to find [the] Hos. of the 5th Army Corps without success, so we went to the one belonging to the 3rd Army Corps. As soon as Lieut. Shields saw me, he exclaimed have you brought my apples? to which I was most happy to reply in the affirmative and gave him <u>two</u>! Took a cup of tea in the cook room of two Aunt Dinah's, attended a soldier's funeral, where we met the chaplain and assistant surgeon of the 19th.[74] Then went over to [a] little negro cabin where we were told the men of the 17th were sick. How glad they were to see us, but to my sorrow I found John White there, it made me very sad to see how sick he looked. Oh! how his poor mother would feel if she should know he was there.—Found Mr. Hayes sitting up before a <u>hot</u> fire when we came home. Mrs. F returned from [the] 20th with a <u>big</u> kettle in which she prepared some apple sauce. Have <u>written to Mr. Hathaway</u> this evening, all have gone to bed and to sleep too, I believe. What a luxury to feel <u>alone</u> once in a while.

WEDNESDAY DEC. 24TH 1862

This morning Mr. Hayes and myself took an ambulance, Mrs. F not feeling well enough to ride, and visited the 2nd, 3rd, & 4th Regiments. A gentleman, Rev. Mr. Fowler of North Yarmouth called on us, he having come out in behalf of a Mrs. [Emaline] Herrick whose son [Henry P.] belonging to the 16th had been killed at Fredericksburg. Found the 2nd Maine all confusion, just settling their camp. Hospital tent put up but very damp, I am afraid poor Hodgkins whom I have been so long nursing in the Div. Hos. will die from this exposure. Dr. Morrison very kind and attentive. In the 4th Maine, I met with Dr. [George W. [*sic*]] Martin, a fine young man, and the only surgeon they have. He tells me they have in Hos. no very sick men, as soon as we arrived he said, "have you been to dinner?" and we were soon seated at a table where there was corn bread, <u>very</u> nice hot biscuit of wheat meal, which he had winnowed and bolted under his own hand, beef steak, beans, and tea. I have not had such a dinner since I have been in the army and besides that, we were invited to a Christmas dinner with them tomorrow, but declined. Left with them some stockings, brandy, condensed milk, &c. Then rode to the 3rd and called on Dr. Hildreth who gave the same report of the health of his Regt. The Col. made some stricture on the internal appearance of the doctor's tent while a "detail" were in attendance outside, getting ready for Christmas. Left there some corn starch, after calling on the Colonel.[75] At the little log cabin without windows called again on the sick of the 17th. Found them rejoiced to see me, stopped and made them some gruel, but was very sorry I had no jellies to leave them. Left them a can of chicken and a few

---

[74] In 1862, the assistant surgeon of the 19th Maine was Henry C. Levensaler [see listing in biographical dictionary] and the chaplain, Eliphalet Whittlesey (b. 1821) of Brunswick, a graduate of Yale College, and a professor of rhetoric and oratory at Bowdoin College.

[75] Moses B. Lakeman was in command of the 3rd by this date, Oliver O. Howard having been promoted to major general.

tamarinds.⁷⁶ Two of the men very sick indeed. Walker must die. Perry I think a kind nurse. Poor John White, he must learn to deny himself or he will die. Mr. Fowler joined us again.

THURSDAY DEC. 25TH CHRISTMAS DAY 1862

Weather so warm as to be almost summer like. Busy at work to day assisting in Sanitary movements for the removal of the sick men of the 20th into their new Hospital. We are supplying them with new shirts, drawers, and stockings. I made chicken broth for their dinner, then returned home and made five pillows, filling them with <u>leaves</u> for want of <u>any</u> thing else, and took "ivory Joe" over to camp with me in the evening to distribute them. Such a time as we do have! Carlton inquires "who bosses the job?" Dr. Munroe has gone for Sanitary supplies. Another man died this morning, and one last Monday. I closed his eyes, bound up his face, cut off a lock of his hair, and wondered at my indifference as I passed back and forth by his body all day. Saw a man buried from the Division Hos. on Monday without a coffin.

FRIDAY DEC. 26TH 1862

Still occupied for the 20th. This morning carried hot tea and crackers spread with butter to the sick men in quarters. Returned home for some condensed milk and nutmeg for Hos. use. Made three more pillows and filled them with leaves and carried them over for the men. Several more of the men will die. One of them will not live through the night I think. Went to the Commissary Department to Capt. [Charles] Walker and purchased supplies at government prices, such as hard bread 20 lbs. for a dollar, &c. As soon as they spied me coming to the Hos., they asked if I would let them have some stimulant, so I had to go home for brandy. The <u>Sanitary Commission</u> gave them almost nothing. Col. Chamberlain called my attention to a piece in the "Press" about our work at which I was very much annoyed. This publicity of my name is really <u>too bad</u>.⁷⁷ My darling, darling children, how I wish I could see them to night. The Lord keep them, make them His, and make me more faithful, above all things, giving me patience for peculiar trials.—I loaned the Adjutant [John Marshall Brown] a <u>sheet for a table cloth</u> for Christmas!

---

⁷⁶ Processed from the pod of the tropical *Tamarindus indica*, tamarind is prepared by crushing the acidic but sweet pulp of the pod and was used medicinally in the nineteenth century.

⁷⁷ The *Portland Daily Press* carried a piece about the Maine Camp Hospital Association, on December 22, 1862 in which officers endorsed the work of Harriet Eaton and Isabella Fogg. On November 15, 1862, the *Press* had published a letter of Eaton's written from Berlin, Virginia, on November 5, without her permission.

SATURDAY DEC. 27TH 1862

All things seeming to work favorably, we took [an] ambulance, Mr. Truell driver, with a load of supplies, to visit the Maine 6th and the other Regts. in that vicinity. It was a long ride, some eight or ten miles. We first stopped at [the] 20th and took our basket of shirts and drawers, then on past Burnside's Headquarters and the <u>Post Office</u>, on, on, to "White Oak Church," an old dilapidated building much like a barn, but one of the guide posts for this part of the country, still on to the 6th Maine.[78] Dr. Holmes not well, saw the assistant surgeon, Dr. Blossom, went down to the Hospital where they have 15 sick, only two very sick, about 50 sick in quarters, gave a large apple to each one in Hos. Mrs. F made tapioca gruel for them, while I made tea and spread crackers with butter and jelly for men in quarters, & carried it round to every sick man's tent, also gave part of a green apple to every man sick in quarters. They are fixing up for winter, with hewn logs, plastered. Dined with Capt. Haycock on beef and hard bread, left with them dried apples, wine, brandy, corn starch, condensed milk, a can of chicken, one of oysters, and some jelly, also handkerchiefs, dressing gowns, four shirts, four pair of drawers, 1/2 dozen towels, and stockings. Lieut. Flint said he was certain if we did not give it to the men ourselves, they never could get it. Cooks seemed to understand their work, sick men were raised from the ground, had mattresses, and looked very comfortable. Lieut. Furlong escorted us to a lodging place for the night, we had quite a walk to get there & it was well it was the Lieut. who gave one of us such a tramp, at length we were ushered in to a Miss Catlett's, where was a maiden lady, tall and cross eyed, an old grandma, a secesh daughter with her children, and two <u>very smart</u> secesh ladies who seemed to be visiting there. We had bacon and eggs for supper with some <u>awful tea</u>, though I gave them some to make it with.

SUNDAY DEC. 28TH 1862

Slept on the floor in the garret last night, this morn Mrs. F met with a provoking accident by the door swinging back. Got some <u>cotton in the pod</u> there, from the negroes. Rode over to the 6th and thence proceeded to the 5th. It is the Holy Sabbath and yet I had forgotten it, early in the morning. As we rode up to the 5th, it was a pleasing sight to see them assembled and their chaplain Mr. [John R.] Adams preaching to them, a death had occurred that morning and Dr. Buxton their surgeon said it was the <u>first</u> that had taken place (under his immediate care) in the Regt. They still have Mr. [William S.] Noyes of Bakersville memory for their Hospital Steward, every

---

[78] After the battle of Fredericksburg, "The [Union] army went into camp on a line from Falmouth to Belle Plain: the 6th Corps occupying nearly the center of the line, at a place called White Oak Church, from a little whitewashed meeting house, without bell or steeple, in the midst of a clump of white oak trees" (See Stevens, *Three Years in the Sixth Corps*, 173).

thing about the Hospital and grounds was in fine "police order,"[79] kitchen utensils remarkably neat but Dr. Buxton so profane, even in our presence, that I deem him unfit for such a work. I do not believe such profanity excusable on any ground. We left with them a bottle of brandy, a can of milk, one of chicken, a paper of corn starch, some preserves, towels, handkerchiefs, stockings, shirts, drawers, tea, and handkerchiefs [sic]. Did not go through the quarters, left them also dried apples and a pail full of green apples. Saw Lieut. [Daniel C.] Clark.—Left with the chaplain a taste from Gorham, also butter and marmalade for Hos. Hence proceeded after taking dinner with Dr. Buxton, on soup and wheat bread, to the 5th Maine Battery, there I had made up my mind to go and there I went. The Whittiers delighted to see me. Capt. Leppein a very fine man, also Lieut. Twitchell. Took tea with them and luxuriated in hot biscuit, cold beef, sweet cakes, not forgetting that famous salt cellar and mustard pot with blue glass lining.—Gave them two shirts, two pr. drawers, two pr. stockings, one doz. pr. mittens, one paper corn starch, a few dried and green apples, jelly, preserves, condensed milk, handkerchiefs, towels, butter, &c. George [Whittier] will deal it out to the men. As it was bright moonlight, we remained awhile in the evening, then escorted by Lieut. Twitchell and Mr. Hayes, rode about a mile to Mr. Richard Randall, real <u>secesh</u> all but the old lady, she likes the old flag and the "green backs." "<u>Charlotte</u>" told me in the morning that her children, grand children, and great grand children, all but "dis ere man" had been sold from her right on the block by the door and ["']pears like her heart would break when her last grandarter was sold three year ago. She dreamed two year ago about wading to her knees in blood, the Spirit of the Lord told her two year ago and she told it to the church, Joseph was sold into Egypt, they meant it for evil but the Lord meant it for good and he became a king, and so it would be with them yet.["]

MONDAY DEC. 29TH 1862

Took breakfast with the 5th Battery this morning, first Mrs. F determined to sit in [the] ambulance, though Mr. Truell said he had his horses to feed, finally Capt. Leppein said he would bring the breakfast to her and she decided to come to the breakfast. George & Edward [Whittier] had a letter from their mother last night, so I suppose Hatty is well. Went to the 2nd Battery, Col. Rose[80] absent but Lieut. glad to see us, they have seven sick men, left with them two papers corn starch, some jelly, butter, dried and green apples, brandy, condensed milk, handkerchiefs, stockings, shirts, drawers, & mittens.—Did not cook any thing for them but at Mrs. Fogg's special request left for the 16th Maine, where we took dinner, with Lieut. Tilton[81] and Dr. Baxter. Saw young

---

[79] Archaic usage of "police" as adjective meaning highly scrutinized.

[80] It is likely that HE meant Colonel Adrian R. Root (1832–99) of the 94th New York, who was artillery commander at Antietam and under whose orders the 2nd Battery served.

[81] HE means Charles Tilden.

Cleaves of Bridgton. Dr. Alexander surgeon, they have a larger proportion sick than any other Regiment. Arrived home about dark, very weary, Mrs. Fogg quite sick but unwilling that I should do any thing for her. A report that the army will move.

TUESDAY DEC. 30TH 1862

Went over to camp this morning with a pail of hot cocoa for the boys and crackers, found them laying out two more who had died this morning, carried my supply as far as it held out and returned to make more, on going back with hot tea found the Regiment had struck their tents. They were going off in a hurry, they knew not where. Capt. [Joseph B.] Fitch asked if he might come to our room till the bustle was past, I could not refuse though I understood it very well. Received six letters by the hand of Lieut. Waite, <u>two from George R. Davis</u>, two <u>from Mrs. Whittier, and two from Mrs. Bosworth</u>. Am glad to know more boxes are on the way but am so anxious about my precious Agnes that I know not what to do, my last from her was received Nov. 22nd, more than a month since. Now I have a sick man at the house, and it is no fault of the Major and chaplain, that there are not <u>two</u> here. I call it a perfect imposition when they saw plainly how I was situated. Mrs. Whittier is so kind to write so often, and she makes me feel so easy about Hatty Belle. Mrs. Bosworth had just heard from Fred that he had seen me.

WEDNESDAY DEC. 31ST 1862

After getting breakfast for my sick man, I made a lunch for those in camp and attended the funeral of the two who died yesterday. They were buried in one grave, oh how sad was the scene with <u>all</u> the circumstances attending it. Came home and made chicken broth for the Capt. [Fitch], then prepared more tea and crackers for the men, and gave several of them a package of tea for which they seemed truly grateful.

1863: JANUARY 1 TO MAY 12

THURSDAY JAN. 1ST 1863

A delightful day for New Year. Have carried all the sick men in quarters hot cocoa and crackers or gruel, also the men in Hos. Capt. [Joseph B.] Fitch still here. Mrs. Fogg gone to Washington.

FRIDAY JAN. 2ND 1863

Went over to the 17th to day and carried with me a supply of shirts, drawers, stockings, &c., also a supply of condensed milk, pepper, ginger, preserves, farina, and passing through the quarters gave each man who was sick a paper of tea, a cracker, and some dried apples.—One poor fellow was brought in to Dr. Wiggin with his toe chopped off, it rolled from his stocking on to the floor, and I assisted in trying to quiet his nerves while it was being dressed. Poor fellow! He did not swear any while I was present. They have 14 men in Hospital, two or three of them very sick, of typhoid fever. As a whole I think the Regt. remarkably clean in the face.

SATURDAY JAN. 3RD 1863

Mrs. Fogg returned this evening. In the morning I made broma for the men in quarters, then walked over to the 2nd Maine in company with Mr. Hayes. We missed our way going and coming but the day was pleasant and even though we came out at Potomac Station, if I had not gone far over my shoes in yellow mud I should not have minded it.[1] Wrote letters to Mr. Bosworth, Mrs. Hart, and Mrs. White and received one from my darling Agnes, for whom I had been so anxious, the Lieut. [Waite] having carried it by mistake all through this reconnaissance. At the 2nd Maine, their camp has more appearance of comfort through the industry of the men in hewing logs, even making doors of them with latches, and one I saw with a stirrup for a knocker. I think Hodgkins will live after all his being banged about from one place to another in the height of his fever. Carried over tea and dried apples, also crackers, and distributed to the men in quarters. Dr. Morrison going round with me. Col. Varney has a palace of a tent, floored and a very nice fire place, most could do as well if they tried, only four men in Hospital.

SUNDAY JAN. 4TH 1863

This morning carried to the men in quarters hot tea, crackers, salt fish, and baked apple, Mrs. Fogg carrying it to the Hospital. Returned to the house about twelve, and sat down to read a little, but Mr. Hayes came over and told me there was to be [a] service at the camp and I gladly availed myself of the privilege. Adjutant [John Marshall Brown] politely provided me with a seat, the Col. [Ames] & Lieut. Col. [Chamberlain] standing on either side, sermon on the immortality of the soul. Went home and prepared hot tea, crackers, butter, and marmalade for men in Hospital. Skillings and Grinnell very sick. Mrs. F gone to Burnside's Headquarters to see about a flag of truce for the recovery of Capt. Hutchins' body.

MONDAY JAN. 5TH 1863

This morning Mrs. F wishing to go to the region of Belle Plains [sic] to see Col. Tilden of the 16th, we took an ambulance load for that Regiment and the Maine Cavalry, but having many stoppages did not reach the Cavalry till night, and was carried to Richard Randall's secesh ranch to stop, Mrs. F having returned home by the way of Burnside's Headquarters.—"Dick" wishes we were all at home, he looks but his wife says he is deranged.

TUESDAY JAN. 6TH 1863

Early in the morning Quartermaster Griffin sent his big team for me, driver was one we had visited at Trinity Church Hos. Dr. Colby had at first few wants but finally he was very glad of 1/2 dozen flannel shirts and drawers, as many pr. of socks, soft

---

[1] HE's comment about the mud foreshadowed what was to come in little more than two weeks, as Burnside, attempting to get to the other side of the Rappahannock after the disastrous loss at Fredericksburg, took the Army of the Potomac on the infamous "Mud March" of January 20 to 23, 1863. The inclement weather so demoralized the troops that Burnside was no longer considered an effective leader and soon relieved of command.

George Varney, a businessman from Bangor, was only twenty-eight when he was named colonel of the 2nd Maine. A veteran of thirteen battles, he was wounded in the head at Fredericksburg, but lived to become a politician and railroad tycoon. MAINE STATE ARCHIVES, AUGUSTA

crackers, apple jelly, two cans condensed milk, farina, peppers, and spices. I went all through the camp, giving tea, apples, and crackers. Capt. [Black Hawk] Putnam very attentive, he lost one of his men found dead in his tent Sunday, he was buried <u>without</u> coffin through surgeon's orders while Capt. was absent with his Regt. on picket. When he returned he made them take up the body, had a coffin for it and had him buried with religious services. All honor to Capt. Putnam whom we met at Mrs. Yonson's. Now came the opening of Mrs. B[osworth]'s can of chicken, it was so nice as when first prepared at home, and made a grand dinner for the 14 men in Hospital. The Regt. in a good state. Returned to the 16th. Found their chaplain Mr. Bullen had married one of Prof. Ripley's daughters. The 16th have 48 sick men in Hos. and 146 sick men in "quarters." Dr's Alexander and Hunter said they might have chicken broth for their supper and the camp kettles went on but the rain came down and I could not pay much attention to it. Dow, ward master, and [William] Eaton, Hosp. Steward, both sick. Dr. jokingly remarked they would probably remain sick while the jellies lasted.

WEDNESDAY JAN. 7TH 1863

Mrs. F did not return till near night, making it necessary for us to stop with "secesh Randall" again, when he saw me he said, "Now we shall have to have another quarrel this evening." On our way home the Cavalry charged on our poor ambulance, stopped at 17th and left canned chicken enough for a dinner for them. Two of their men buried to day and another very low. Called on our way at Gen. Sumner's. I do'nt like that man's face, though he was very polite. Saw Generals Franklin and [William F. "Baldy"] Smith on the road, also Gen. Birney with his horse gaily caparisoned, reviewing between 25[,000] & 30,000 men, but had not time to admire the pageant.
[See Appendix letter 9. HE to Mrs. Bosworth, January 8, 1863.]

THURSDAY JAN. 8TH 1863

To day as Mrs. Fogg must again go to Gen. Sumner's, I took with me supplies for the 4th Maine, saw there Dr. Whitington [Whittingham] medical inspector who asked our sympathy for the Regulars. Went to the quarters and carried the sick men an apple, tea, and crackers. They have but four men in Hos. Took dinner there and in company with their new doctor [Dr. George W. Martin] walked over to the 3rd carrying with me tea, soft crackers, and apples. Returned in time to <u>write a letter to Mrs. Bosworth</u>.

FRIDAY JAN. 9TH 1863

Have to day made chicken broth for all the sick men in Hos. of the 20th as well as many of those in quarters. Poor fellows, they thought it was a long time since they had seen my face. [Abel] Jackson (the old man) died this morning and Skillings will die before night.—It is really alarming to think of the frightful mortality in this Regiment.

SATURDAY JAN. 10TH 1863

Wrote last night to Mr. Bosworth about Miss Van Horne and Miss Pogen. Also wrote to Mrs. Whittier, Hatty Belle, and Frank. Skillings died last night as I expected. It is a rainy day, still we have managed, rigged out in our repellents to go and see the sick men, they inquire if we ought to be out in the rain but we tell them if they can assure us the men will not suffer we can remain quiet and not without. To night Mrs. F and myself have been looking for "army appendages"[2] and not without success. While at the quarters to day saw Capt. [Joseph B.] Fitch making a coffin for Skillings, he said he was making it from bread boxes out of which the poor fellow had eat [*sic*] his rations.[3]

SUNDAY JAN. 11TH 1863

Weather delightful after the rain. Another man died in the Hospital last night, I was talking with him yesterday about his cough as I handed him a cracker while he sat eating his dinner and although I did not expect him to recover, I little thought he was so soon to pass away. Carried apples to the men in quarters, then assembled with the men for service, but preaching was dispensed with, they had only singing and a prayer. Had a long call from Dr. Wixom of the 16th Michigan this morning, the way he puts medicine down a man's throat would frighten a Northerner. He gave us the recipe for "Wixom's dose." For a severe case of congestive fever, 40 grams calomel, 20 gr. quinine, 15 ipecac, 10 opium, 3 capsicum, and 1 oz. [spirits] turpentine. Rub the body with 1 pint spts. turpentine, then roll the person in sheet wrung out in hot water and put them in bed where perhaps they may lie 12 hours, then work it off with a slight portion of phys[ic]. I told him that was kill or cure, he said certainly it would be kill if that did not help. Pendleton has got back to the Hospital and Hersom is coming. Halleck having decided that his imprisonment by the rebels was illegal. After service carried tea and crackers to the Hos., also to Hos. of the 16th Michigan. They have managed since we have been here to get up a great talk about "stimulants" given to dying men, and for one I am glad to say my skirts are clear. Have written to Agnes, my precious Agnes to night, oh how I wish I could see the dear girl. Have heard through [Capt. Charles?] Walker to day that another of my letters has appeared in the "Portland Press," I ca'nt bear to think of being thus made public, every thing I write is done in the most hurried manner.[4]

---

[2] "Army appendages" was a military euphemism for forage, wagons, ambulances, and any other equipment used for the support of troops. See Townsend, "History of the Sixteenth Regiment, New Hampshire Volunteers," 137. HE meant food, clothing, and medical supplies.

[3] "Eat" is an obsolete past participle for "eaten," pronounced ĕt.

[4] Letters from HE appeared in the *Portland Daily Press* on December 30, 1862 (from December 11 and 16) and on December 31, 1862 (from December 22).

MONDAY JAN. 12TH 1863

A delightful day. With Mr. Truell and the ambulance well provisioned, we went to the 19th to day, carried dried apples, green apples, tea, canned chicken, currant and rhubarb wine, and apple jelly, also soft crackers. Visited the camp, finding far more sick men than the doctor named, perhaps because they like the tea. One old man from Fairfield said he was 68 years old and his name was [Samuel] Emery.[5] I like the Hos. attendants here, they understand their business and then they do it. Returned back by way of Falmouth, having "seceshdom" in full view, and passing the Lacy house were afresh reminded of that fearful battle.[6] First to the station and then to Sumner's Headquarters, where I sat in ambulance waiting for Mrs. Fogg to get through with her interview with the Gen. He came out with her and politely inquired why I had remained in the ambulance. Mr. Hayes returned from [Aquia] Creek this evening and brought with him a stack of letters for me. One to the firm from Mr. Jewett, also from Lewis Smith, Miss Harriet Fox, Mrs. Greenough, Frank, and Mrs. Whittier, enclosing one from my darling Hatty and her dear little picture. The sight of that little face completely overcame me, and what with Frank's letter, I could not help having a good crying spell. I think if I ever again get where people love me and are affectionate and kind once more, I shall know how to appreciate it. The caring for our suffering soldiers I came here for and I love the work, but there are things in connection with this mission I little dreamed of. Perhaps I was sent here to learn patience. That sweet picture, I kissed it again and again.

TUESDAY JAN. 13TH 1863

Have written to day to Mrs. Lancey, enclosing a line to Mr. Bosworth. To day we have been to the 2nd Maine, and I had a very pleasant time, though some things were annoying and mortifying in the extreme, it was after the pattern of the 5th Maine Battery['s] performance[7] and with not a shadow of reason for it that I could see. I do feel encouraged to hope that Hodgkins will get better, notwithstanding all the disadvantages. The nurse told me that the last strawberry I carried over was a "real God send to him" and it had lasted till yesterday. I was so glad I had some more of the same to day and some apple jelly. Just as I thought we were about to leave, Mrs. F stopped out of the ambulance to make a call on Col. Varney, so I went to his tent also. Wrote to Mr. Hathaway.

WEDNESDAY JAN. 14TH 1863

Mrs. F gone to Washington, have sent by her a letter to my dear Frank, also written one for Lieut. Enslend, for Amanda. Have had a violent head ache, unfit for doing much to day, still we went through the quarters with tea and crackers, and found a great many very

---

[5] Emery gave his age at enlistment as forty-four.

[6] Fredericksburg, December 13, 1862.

[7] It is likely that HE was referring to soldiers' use of profanity in her presence.

sick men. Young Cummings died this morning and his brother came here before Mrs. F was up to make some inquiries about sending the body home. Poor fellow, he feels sad indeed. Dr. Wixom called. For a wonder [*sic*] spent the evening downstairs talking with the Lieut. Mr. [Charles B.] Hall, a young Englishman and Mr. Christie, the guard. I was glad to forget the war for half an hour.

THURSDAY JAN. 15TH 1863

This morning carried Capt. Keen[e] his breakfast of tea, toast, apple jelly, and salt fish, then returned home, and prepared small papers of tea, these with crackers, salt fish, and apple sauce, I carried over to camp and to my surprise found the sick men had all been hurried off to take the cars, so I had to carry my supplies home again. The appearances of a move seem so distinct that I went to work packing our boxes to be in readiness. Wrote to Lewis Smith about Mr. Lombard of the 16th whom Mr. Hayes found was well, he also found the young man that Mrs. Greenough wrote about and gave him the apples. The weather is so warm that a fire is really disagreeable, but the wind shakes the old house almost to its foundation. On carrying the letter to the Office, was surprised to see many of the sick men back again, some were completely exhausted, so I ran home and made tea and toast for them. I am told that an individual whose name may be passed by in silence has talked of me in this Regiment[8] as being "the petted widow of a clergyman, who perhaps did well enough at home, but was unfit for the camp & yet was trying to get the reins in this business." Well I am willing to bide my time. Have had some little keepsakes made for A[gnes] & H[atty].

[*See Appendix letter 10. HE to Lewis Smith, January 15, 1863.*]

FRIDAY JAN. 16TH 1863

Well I am tired enough to night. This morning very early I went over to camp with my two large pails full of broma, my pockets full of crackers, but I had to leave two companies unprovided, so home again I went, made another pail full, and carried over a basket of tea and apple sauce. In one tent, one young man with wet eyes said he never should forget me, in another tent where three were lying sick, one resembling Frank, they asked my name, and then said, when I asked them to come and see me, "all Maine will know you, we read your letters in the papers." Poor boys! If I can do them good by the letters, let them go imperfect as they are, though it seems as if I could not endure the thought of having my name before the public. Heard the Regt. had orders to move and went over to the Col. [Ames]'s tent to inquire, Col. Chamberlain received me very heartily, remarking it was not often they were so highly honored as to have a

---

[8] The regiment to which HE refers is the 20th Maine, but the source of the gossip is unclear.

call from me. Find the brigade have marching orders, with 60 rounds of ammunition and three days rations. The sick have had no orders. This evening have carried gruel and crackers to the sickest of the men, Walker says it varies now from the old couplet, "angels' visits, <u>few and far between</u>," I come so often. I mailed a <u>letter to Samuel and Elisabeth [Whitney]</u>, and now I must write to London. Up to this date I find noted in my journal <u>62 letters</u> that I have already written since I came out.

SATURDAY JAN. 17TH 1863

The same story, orders to move tomorrow at one o' clock. Dr. Wixom made another long call this morning. After he left made chicken broth for the sick in quarters, while talking with the men in Hos. felt some one gently touch my shoulder, turned, and was met with the inquiry, "will you dine with me?" made in such a manner that I could not refuse. <u>That dinner</u>, I shall not soon forget it, oh! How my mind is relieved, 'tis well to try to do right & then <u>trust</u> for the rest.[9] Came home and made gruel for the sickest cases, sending it by Mr. Hayes. Mrs. Fogg has not returned, is she sick?

SUNDAY JAN. 18TH 1863

Have enjoyed great peace of mind to day, felt a nearness to my Heavenly Father, spent the morning in reading, then with crackers and papers went over to the Regt. for they have not left yet. I crept into one of the little tents and had a talk with two of my boys, oh I want to be more faithful, not letting opportunities slip.

MONDAY JAN. 19TH 1863

This morning very busy arranging our boxes & emptying a part of our barrels, preparatory to Mrs. F's return. At noon, after finishing a <u>letter to Sarah [Caduc] in London</u> I went to work preparing tea for the sick. While on my knees stirring in the milk, there came a little tap at the door, to which I said without rising, "come in," and who should stand before me but Dr. Wixom again. I was perplexed, for I did not want him to feel he must carry my pails, but I was relieved by a messenger coming after him. Soon as he had gone, I got ready for a start, when lo, who should I see coming toward me from the new Division Hos. but Dr. W, so in spite of me he carried my pails. Happy faces did it give to those poor men who got the tea, poor Bradford, Co. I, wants me to try and get his discharge through. Ingalls, Co. I, must have some dried apples. I do wish they would examine the tents and make the men fix themselves better. No move yet. Various camp rumors, not very favorable to Burnside, wonder if it is true that the other generals have refused to cooperate with him. Col. C[hamberlain] had a telegram from Mrs. F from the Creek, requesting him to send Mr. Hayes to the Station for her. He went, but she was not

---

[9] The gossiper mentioned on Jan. 15 apparently confessed and apologized.

in the three o'clock train. Somebody thought they had got into a "scrape." Saw two men of the 16th Mich. undergoing punishment, they were sitting on a horizontal pole raised about ten feet from the ground, with their feet tied. I asked Dr. W about it, and he said he had to tell the Col. (their punishment being to sit there six days, eight hours a day) the second evening, that he thought it would endanger their lives, and he was induced to alter it, to making them walk round a ring so many hours.[10]—Mr. Truell was here to day & asked about the side saddle. I have <u>written to Sarah Caduc</u>. Mr. Boller's folks have had their horse & cart stolen, two different nights lately, but the cart has been found at the 12th N. Y. Mrs. B has heard from part of her children, I am so glad and I must write again for her.

TUESDAY JAN. 20TH 1863

What shall I do? It seems as if I could endure it no longer. To stay in this room and look at those decrepid [sic] men as they come to this new Division Hos., so many of them must suffer on, growing more and more feeble, till they feel as one told me yesterday, "it is better to be laid away in a box and covered up." I expostulated with him, asked if he had a wife, "yes" said he "and three dear children." "And do you think she feels as you do?" He thought not, and I tried to encourage him in the dark hour. One poor young boy said he thought of his mother most of the time, only sometimes when he thought of me. Another in the same tent said he should call me "Aunt" and I willingly accepted the title. Mrs. F returned last evening, but she was quite in trouble as her boxes had gone to Falmouth in spite of her. She brought me letters from Mrs. White, Mrs. Wilson, with $23.00, Mrs. Caduc, Mrs. Mariner of Sebago, who has <u>four</u> boys [in] the army (God have mercy on her), and would be glad to come out here. Mrs. Fogg thinks there is to be a breaking up in the existing state of things in our Maine affairs and I don't feel like meddling with it, there are so many different opinions afloat. I had also a letter from Mrs. Sarah Shaw, saying that through the solicitation of Mother Shaw, they had forwarded a box mostly for my individual self.

WEDNESDAY JAN. 21ST 1863

Were all day trying to relieve the suffering of the men in Division Hospital and at the Camp. That Quartermaster Litchfield of Rockland is in my opinion a great rascal, a man void entirely of principle, he buried a man to day before the body was cold, detailed some poor sick men to dig the grave with thr[eat] of putting them in a similar hole and then boasted to Mr. Hayes that he hustled him into the ground ———

---

[10] The colonel of the 16th Michigan was Thomas B. W. Stockton of Flint, who had been taken prisoner in May 1862 and exchanged in August 1862, when he became a brigade commander. It is possible that Wixom referred to Lieutenant Colonel Norval E. Welch as colonel.

quick.[11] He asked Capt. S[12] the other day to draw a pair of pants for some one connected with him and charge it to one of the dead men. He orders the sick sergeants to do guard duty, threatening to tie them to a cart wheel. Are our sons to be under the tyranny of such an awful man? I wish I had power, I would quick send him to Thomaston.[13]—To the Div. Hos. I carried chicken broth and gruel. Major[14] is coming to our house tomorrow, it is pouring rain, Oh our poor soldiers!

THURSDAY JAN. 22ND 1863

The elements are against us, dreamed last night, and woke up with the words almost audible on my lips, "Headquarters are above." Major [Gilmore] very sick, he is Mrs. Fogg's patient and I can find abundance to do at the Hospital and in "quarters."

FRIDAY JAN. 23RD 1863

The army are coming back, the Batteries and Ambulance Corps have already returned to their old place.[15] Went to day to the Depot with Mr. Hayes intending to go to Hos. at Windmill Point.[16] After waiting at the Depot from 1/2 past nine till 1/2 past one, or rather standing in the car after being pulled in, I decided there would not be time to go and return that night so I gave it up. On coming home found Mrs. F had been making tapioca, chicken broth, and tea for the sick in quarters and had two or three of the sick men there at the house to carry it over. I went with them and dealt it out.

SATURDAY JAN. 24TH 1863

Have written letters to Mr. Jewett and Mrs. Wilson and sent them yesterday. To day I have been (in company with Mr. Hayes, by the first train to which I was hurried by Mrs. F without my breakfast) to the Windmill Point Hospital. First, we went to Aquia Creek, thence by "Fairy" [sic] to the landing, thence through 2,000 head of cattle to the Hos. Dr. Hunkins met us first and showed us attention, soon the steward of the 2nd Maine came to our assistance. He first took us to Hodgkins, but poor Grinnell died this morning and was already dead, yes, starved to death, nothing but

---

[11] HE leaves a dotted line, implying Litchfield's use of profanity.
[12] Probably Edward Snow of the 19th Maine, who was from Rockland, and who was a hospital resident during this time.
[13] Thomaston was the site of the Maine state penitentiary, built in 1824 and described by one witness as "a high wall enclosing several acres of ground."
[14] Major Charles D. Gilmore of the 20th Maine was a Portlander.
[15] This signaled the failure of Burnside's "Mud March."
[16] Windmill Point Hospital was located on Marlborough Point in Potomac Creek, on the state line between Virginia and Maryland.

hard tack and salt pork for 4,000 poor sick men! Just like all the army movements, No Kettles to cook with, not even wash basins for washing, nothing, nothing, nothing, but indifference. When a man is sick, no longer effective as a soldier, what does government care for him! I really believe Hodgkins will live through it all, how glad he was to see me, and how happy the men were to see my face again, they showed me (some of the 11th)[17] the handkerchiefs I gave them in their Regt. Hos. and all exclaimed at my following them up. I told them I was going after them, either to Richmond, the Gulf of Mexico, Washington, or home, some added, "Texas too." We found about 136 from Maine, saw them all, and left with them soft crackers, some farina, jellies, shrub, lemons, and a few oranges. It was time to return, taking our walk back by the beach, were deeply interested in the geological formation of the shore and the petrifactions. Very curious shells are imbedded in what has now become solid rock. After sitting with some officers on the end of the wharf for some time, waiting for the "Fairy," we decided discretion would teach us to wait no longer, and we started to walk to the Creek, three miles.—Some one at the Hos. however procured us a famous ride in a great uncovered army wagon, four horses. Some one asked our driver if he would be down again the next day. His reply, "no, it is Sunday and I keep Sunday." Another man rushed out and stopped him as we were starting, saying, "Do give us a lock of your hair then."—A pleasant unique ride brought us to Aquia Creek, where we had a trial of our patience as the cars backed and filled [sic] till eight o' clock. We had a seat on the outside of a freight car. My seat was about three inches square, between a Battery wheel and half a barrel of souse pigs' feet. Had very pleasant company, a gentleman connected with the balloon corps being on board. By way of [a] joke they frightened one old man, so that in view of combustible matter on board, and the bridge we were coming to, he left the cars before we started. We did not reach home till about 1/2 past nine.

SUNDAY JAN. 25TH 1863

The Major [Gilmore] quite sick, have been looking over the "tracts" received from London, and find a very interesting variety. Mrs. F wished me to assist in unpacking a box which invitation I respectfully declined, she remarking, she hoped I would never do any thing worse.—Dr. Wixom came, I made tea, and with Smith to carry the tea and I with crackers and tracts went to every tent. The men seemed pleased with the reading, especially the tract "that will do to light my pipe." Some of them were singing the hymns before I left. In the evening wrote to Mrs. Griswold, acknowledging the receipt of two boxes, also to Mrs. Sarah Bond of Haverhill, Mass. whose husband requested me to write to her from Windmill Point Hospital.

[17] This is HE's only mention of the 11th Maine in the entire diary. Its men had traveled to Washington in November 1861 and they were serving in the 2nd division of the 1st brigade of the Army of the Potomac at this time.

MONDAY JAN. 26TH 1863

Last night a box that Mrs. F brought from Washington for the 10th Maine was stolen from the door at this house.—I have to day been to the 17th and to the Division Hos. of the 3rd Army Corps. At the Regt. I left a paper of corn starch, one of farina, some dried apples, and soft crackers. Went to the Hos. where their sick men have been carried, where Mrs. Mc Kay and Miss Sharpless are at work. They seemed glad to see me, I dined with them and Dr. Morrison. After dinner left with them seven shirts, three pr. drawers, three Hos. caps, two papers farina, 1/2 bush[el] dried apples, a jar of raspberry preserves, one of shrub, a bottle of currant wine, four oranges, eleven pr. socks, one can chicken. Returned home in time to visit the 20th Maine after baking a little pie for Hodgkins and filling it with guava instead of apple. Carried the Hos. men some crackers, and put cologne on their handkerchiefs, those that had handkerchiefs. Promised the others some tomorrow.

TUESDAY JAN. 27TH 1863

To day have been to the 19th. An awful road, was pitched all over the ambulance and into the top of it where I struck my head, making quite a cut. At the 19th they have 14 sick in Hos. and one in steward's tent. Dr. Billings gone home on a furlough. Gave the men three shirts, two pr. drawers, three pr. stockings, and handkerchiefs with cologne, also soft crackers. Left with Hos. Steward six papers farina, &c., some nutmegs, apple jelly, currant shrub, and rhubarb wine, also nearly half a basket dried apples, six lemons, four oranges. The men were pleased at receiving each some cough candy or lozenges.—Arrived home safe and immediately, accompanied by Dr. Hersom, carried some barley broth which Mrs. F had made, also crackers to men in Hos. Mr. Hodgkins a little better, he remarked it always made him feel better to see me and he hoped I would come every day. Gave each of them a new fragrant handkerchief.—When I was returning, [Edward P.] Merrill came to me and said, "there were" (as one of the men told him) "but two pleasant things out here, one was to hear the crows in the morning, the other to see the Ladies of the Sanitary Commission round." Have <u>written to Miss Fox</u> this evening. The Major still very sick, but Mrs. F has the care of him. My back aches laying [*sic*] on the floor, I know that much. Last night we had quite a time about Mrs. F's being sick. Dr. Wixom, Col. Chamberlain, and Dr. Hersom were present. Afterwards the poor Major was thoroughly rubbed in cayenne and alcohol which nettled him not a little, though he declared it made him <u>smart</u>.—Major talks of a furlough and I think he had better have it. <u>Wrote a letter for Mrs. Boller</u> to her son in law George this evening. Oh! I do want some letters so much, I know there is a package waiting for me in Washington and I am almost homesick to hear from my precious children. How precious home will be when I get there once more if all our lives are spared. "They said" last night that Burnside had been removed and Hooker taken his place, to night they say that Maclellan [*sic*] is reinstated, I wonder where the truth lays [*sic*].

WEDNESDAY JAN. 28TH 1863

Major still sick, no improvement. Have been to the Hospital with hot tea and crackers, though it is a severe snow storm. The poor boys thought they should know it was a Maine woman who ventured out in such a storm, I had quite a talk with them about their families and a whole lot showed me the daguerreotypes of their wives and babies. Hodgkins made some of the blackberry cordial. He is uncle to Hodgkins of the 2nd Maine.

[*See Appendix letter 11. HE to Harriet Fox, January 28, 1863.*]

THURSDAY JAN. 29TH 1863

Wrote to my dear Frank to day. A deep snow. Have not been out of the house. We have an addition to our number this evening, a Mrs. White, another lady seeking the body of her son, who belonged to the 17th. She will stay here to night. How I wish people felt as I do about the remains of their friends.[18]

FRIDAY JAN. 30TH 1863

To day I wanted to go to the quarters but was prevented by the storm, have however been to the Hos. and carried the men chicken barley broth. As the cook saw me coming, he exclaimed with joy that there was something the men could eat. They absolutely had nothing but bean soup. I gave them their barley soup and hastened home to make gruel for the sickest of them, returned to Hos. and carried two shirts, two pair drawers and five pr. stockings, a few days before I had given handkerchiefs to all of them. Wrote to Mrs. Whittier and Hatty Belle, met Mr. Hayes who had with him a package of letters for me from Mrs. Whittier, Hatty Belle, Frank, Mrs. Bosworth, G. R. Davis, and Mr. Hathaway. Wrote to Mr. Hathaway to send by Mr. Hayes when he goes to W[ashington] in the morning. Mrs. White of Otisfield cannot have the body of her son, he having been dead nine weeks, his disease malignant typhoid fever. Had a talk with Dr. Munroe about food for the men, he acknowledges they have nothing, not even flour for gruel for the men. Colonels Ames & Chamberlain were here this evening prying into every thing that they had no right to, even under the table looking for preserved ginger. They have before the door of

---

[18] It is likely that HE believed that bodies were buried in hallowed ground and should not be disinterred for reburial elsewhere, especially given that so many died of disease.

the Hos. an extra coffin waiting for the next occupant. I am glad to see [Edward P.] Merrill doing so well.

[*See Appendix letters 12 and 13. HE to Hatty Belle Eaton and HE to John W. Hathaway, January 30, 1863.*]

SATURDAY JAN. 31ST 1863

This morning carried broma and tea to the men in camp. I think they seem better than usual. In the afternoon took tea and crackers to sick, also paper and envelopes with some lemons. True is very sick. Town told me he thought the soldiers would always remember me if they lived to get home.

SUNDAY FEB. 1ST 1863

A miserable sick head ache all day, good for nothing and a house full of company.

MONDAY FEB. 2ND 1863

Major [Gilmore] still very feeble. Mr. Hayes has come down, brought a letter from Mr. Loring inquiring about a young man named Bridge at Windmill Point Hospital, also letters from Mr. Davis, Mrs. Bosworth, Miss Fox, and a Mrs. Fabyan, also in one of the boxes a letter from Mrs. Griswold. Have been to the Hospital of the 20th. Tried to get to Windmill Point.

TUESDAY FEB. 3RD 1863

To day have again been to Windmill Point. Am distressed at the condition of things there. A portion of the men are suffering sadly from neglect. They are dying and who cares? The 16th and 19th especially are in a sad condition. In the boat saw a Mr. Prince of China Me. who was seeking his son of the 19th.[19] Arriving at the Hos., he found he had died the night before and he had only to take the cold remains home with him. He was a good old man and calmly attended to the sad duty, only saying he could bear it but it would kill his wife. Capt. [Willard] Lincoln of the 19th with him and seems an excellent man. Oh! why cannot these poor fellows have their discharge before they die? Found the young man I was seeking for in a pitiable crippled condition, but the surgeons inform me they must go back to their Regiments in order to get their discharge and I do'nt believe it. Was obliged to return by the six o'clock train and had a <u>romantic</u>? [*sic*] moonlight ride (the moon rising o'er the Potomac), while I sat on the top of an open freight car loaded with bags of grain. That Potomac bridge is anything but agreeable.—Capt. [Willard] Lincoln walked as far as the 20th with me, it being very dark, after nine at night.

[19] There was no soldier in the 19th Maine named Prince.

WEDNESDAY FEB. 4TH 1863

Could not sleep for thinking of that Hos. last night, a severe storm but I have managed to get to the quarters of the 20th and carry them some dried apples. It is so severely cold that Mrs. F has kept a fire all night for the Major and we have laid down on the other bed with our clothes on.

THURSDAY FEB. 5TH 1863

Several of our boys are about having their discharge, I am thankful to say.

FRIDAY FEB. 6TH 1863

There is a Rev. Mr. Marstins here who has come for his nephew [John A.] Bates of Comp[any] A. I had just gone to Bates' tent to see about his clothing, that he as well as the others might be protected on going to our Maine climate. Then I went to Brocklebank, [Richard P.] Powers & Bosworth, also Town, Hodgkins, and Knights in Hospital. They will all want something.

SATURDAY FEB. 7TH 1863

Mrs. Fogg has been away some this week to try to hasten the Major's furlough. Hodgkins has been over to the house and fitted himself to clothing from head to foot outside and in and oh, how pleased he was. Part of them start tomorrow. Col. Chamberlain has gone home on a furlough. Lieut. Bailey is quite sick, needs constant attention. Wrote a long letter to Mrs. Griswold this week in which I mean at least to give that rascal Quartermaster Litchfield his due. Fred Bosworth called last Wednesday. The roads are in such a dreadful state that we have not been able to go anywhere in [an] ambulance for more than a week.

SUNDAY FEB. 8TH 1863

Mr. Hathaway called last evening. Gen. Strickland has been here, gave us each four 25 cts. pieces for change. He was a fine old gentleman, also Col. [Gorham] Davis of Bangor called. Gave reading to quar[ters] & Hos.

MONDAY FEB. 9TH 1863

To day I took [an] ambulance and visited the 3rd & 4th Maine.—Dr. [George W.] Martin not at home but Hos. Steward very attentive. They have indeed a <u>model Hospital</u>. The best one I have yet seen in the field, raised cots, quilts, sheets, pillows with cases.—Seven men sick, gave them three pr. drawers, two shirts, nine pr. socks, one cap, handkerchiefs to each, saw 19 men in quarters. Left with them about one peck dried apples, two papers farina, one maizena,[20] black pepper, one paper broma, one can condensed milk, one of chicken, soft crackers, &c. At the 3rd, they have none sick in Hos. but I left with them five pr. socks, four shirts, three pr. drawers, handkerchiefs, one paper farina, one corn starch, one can milk, one can chicken, dried apples, & soft crackers. Returning home, Mrs. F was desiring we should start for Wash. in the morning as the Major's papers had come. I do'nt see how I can be ready and yet I must see my Frank.

TUESDAY FEB. 10TH 1863

We have made out to reach Washington and are stopping at the Washington Hotel. Corner of 3rd Street and the Avenue. Coming down in the cars Col. _____ of the 3rd met with quite an accident, having his shoulder dislocated by the concussion of the cars as they attached the engine at the station.[21] Dr. Munroe, being on board, took it in hand and after a long time had it in place again. I was thrown down myself by the concussion. Col. [Thomas A.] Roberts of the 17th came on, on a furlough. I had a long talk with him about the scantiness of our supplies and our efforts to deal just[ly] by all. Went to the Rooms but did not find any one there but Mr. Loring.

WEDNESDAY FEB. 11TH 1863

Have been trying to find my precious boy but have not yet succeeded. Called on Mr. Hathaway this morning and Mrs. F talked so long that by the time I reached the "Rooms" the ambulance had gone. Repacked several boxes when I was surprised by receiving a call from Mrs. Dyer of Portland, after chatting awhile she told me how to find dear Frank and I took first the 14th St. cars & then 7th for Maryland Avenue and Long Bridge. There I saw lots of the boys, Capt. [Frank L.] Jones, Bernard Hobbs, Abbot, [Charles O.] Cole, Wetmore, [Lewis G.] Robinson, [Charles R.] Shaw, Han[son] Hart, but no Frank. Waited till three o' clock, but he did not come and I returned with a sad heart to Hotel. Han. Hart walked with me to Willard's to see Mrs. Shurtleff, but they said she was not in.[22]—Went out again to do some shopping and called on Mrs. Mc Intyre at 460 D St. between 2nd & 3rd, but she too was not in. Mrs. Dyer spent the evening with us. Received letters from Agnes,

---

[20] Maizena was a brand name for corn flour used as a thickening agent. Like farina, it was used to make gruel for ill men on a low diet. The first noted usage of the word was in 1862, suggesting that "Maizena" was a new product when Maine relief agents used it in the field.

[21] Moses B. Lakeman was colonel of the 3rd Maine. HE left the space blank.

[22] Willard's Hotel was a landmark at 1401 Pennsylvania Avenue—a block from the White House—during the war. It had been a popular meeting place for politicians since the 1850s. Nathaniel Hawthorne once commented that Willard's "may be much more justly called the center of Washington and the Union than either the Capitol, the White House, or the State Department."

Mrs. Hart, Mrs. Lancey, Sarah Caduc and Margie together with two notifications from [George R.] Davis.—

THURSDAY FEB. 12TH 1863

What shall I do? Here I sit, it is nearly one o'clock. I cannot find my boy. I have been to his quarters and he has been to the Hotel, he has a "pass" for the day, so he must come soon. I have written to Mrs. Sarah Shaw and a short letter to Sarah Caduc. Evening. Well, I have had the joy of seeing my dear son once more. He looks well, he dined with me & then we went to the Post Office, did a little shopping and called on Mrs. Mc Intyre. Capt. Hill there. I do not like my son's captain any better than I expected to.[23] Have had a letter from Mrs. Whittier and Hatty Belle to day, she is getting to be a famous seamstress and she certainly improves in writing.

FRIDAY FEB. 13TH 1863

Find we cannot get transportation for our boxes tomorrow and must wait over another day, perhaps two or three. Feel very unwilling to do this, especially as I fear it will involve the Sabbath. Have been down to the Bridge to see Frank and the other boys and look a little at their food and sleeping accommodations. Dear Frank has one of his hoarse colds coming on, otherwise I have no fault to find except with the dissipated habits of his Captain. Have promised to meet Frank at the Institute tomorrow.[24] We have nine barrels and twelve boxes to take down with us.

SATURDAY FEB. 14TH 1863

On rising this morning I was so homesick to get back to my work that I took French leave of Washington, glad to part with all but my dear Frank, whom I have not seen to say good bye. I called yesterday on Mrs. Bigelow and Miss Piggert. Coming down in the boat to day I met five ladies, wives of persons connected with the army. Mrs. Gen. Wheaton, a real rebel belonging to the F. F. V.s.[25] Mrs. Dr. Smith whose husband is surgeon in Windmill Point Hospital a Vermont lady, Mrs. Norris, who is in great distress and I fear will not find her husband living, he is a captain in 1st Mass. Cavalry. A young woman seeking her husband in an Ohio Regiment and Mrs. Kearnan, wife of the Adjutant of the 26th Penn. We had a pleasant time on board but only arrived at [Aquia] Creek in season to take the three o' clock train. Arriving at Stoneman's Station, I telegraphed to Mrs. Fogg, then stopped at the Hos. and came home.

[23] The captain of company A in the 25th Maine was Frank L. Jones, who resigned his commission on March 7, 1863. HE is not referring to Capt. Lysander Hill who was in the 20th Maine.

[24] The Smithsonian, which was founded in 1846.

[25] Abbreviation for the artistocractic "First Families of Virginia."

SUNDAY FEB. 15TH 1863

I hoped for a quiet day, but had callers, made gruel for Major [Gilmore]'s man (Baker), then Dr. Wixom came and talked, said he had killed a man since we went away. Am rejoiced to hear that Windmill Point Hos. is being broken up. Went to the Hos. and carried apples, crackers, and herring, two very sick men in Hos. Lerman & Emory. Mrs. F has returned, also Mr. Hayes and Major G[ilmore]. It was just as I expected about the return on the Sabbath. One box of condensed milk and candles stolen at the Station.

MONDAY FEB. 16TH 1863

Getting our boxes in shape all day. Packing and repacking. Fred Bosworth came over for his box and we had quite a search to find it, and to find the articles in one barrel, opened nine barrels at each end, finding what was wanted on taking out the 18th head. Had a nice time examining the Portland things, tongues, cakes, pies, and preserves with all the names on them. Saw Mrs. Norris on the rail road and ran over to her, find her husband is still living and to her joy gave her lemons, apples, jelly, crackers, &c.

TUESDAY FEB. 17TH 1863

As I expected, a miserable sick head ache all day. We have a Hospital tent for our stores.

WEDNESDAY FEB. 18TH 1863

Half sick and so have employed myself writing to Mrs. Nellie Gustin, Windham Me., Mrs. H. W. Walker, Peru Me. (I don't know which is which of the towns they live in), Miss H. L. Fox Sec[retary] of C[amp] R[elief] Asso[ciation]. Agnes for their circle [sic].[26]—Mrs. Fogg has come from Hos., says Emory died yesterday and Lerman to day. I made a pail of gruel for Hos. and some for Bailey. I should not be surprised if that rascal Litchfield ran clear yet. Col. Ames places too much confidence in him.

THURSDAY FEB. 19TH 1863

Sent a little package to my dear Frank by Matthews, also wrote a letter to him. Have been to the Hos., gave oranges to the men. They are trying to fit up the new Hos. tent. Our "guard" has been detailed: Charles Mero of Waldoboro. Like his looks very

---

[26] HE's reference suggests that her daughter Agnes participated in the MCHA's manufacture of soldiers' clothing.

much. Have been finishing the making out of our bills to night. The last four months every thing inclusive amts. to $138.77 for both of us.[27]

FRIDAY FEB. 20TH 1863

This morning rode to the Regt. and found they were not making much haste about the Hos. Returned again and carried 14 quilts and 14 pillows.—In afternoon visited the 17th Maine and carried them six shirts, six pr. Drawers, one doz. stockings, two doz. handkerchiefs, one doz. oranges, three doz. lemons, apple jelly, currant jelly, three doz. apples, tea, soft crackers, farina, broma, chocolate, one bottle currant wine, one can chicken, one doz. combs, also apples [sic]. They have some very sick men. Three have died within a week. Regiment out on picket. Saw Fred Bos[worth], also Willy Manning who has his discharge and is on his way home.—We have our stove in the tent, no thanks to the Quartermaster. Saw at the 17th Fabyan Charles, whose mother wrote to me.[28] I must answer her letter. Our horses or one of them came near foundering in the deep, deep mud coming home. Lieut. Lewis came in (as he said) "for something to eat," gave him a little jar of jelly, some salt fish, an apple, lemon, and orange, also made gruel for Sergeant Overlock. I do'nt know what will become of the Maine 20th and their officers.

SATURDAY FEB. 21ST 1863

When our ambulance reported this morning, our driver said he must be back at four o' clock, so I went over to the Ambulance Corps and got another one that we could have till evening. We have been to the 5th Maine over such awful roads, we have to travel in perfect zig zag style, one moment lunging into a "run" almost to the floor of the ambulance when we got stuck and had to jump out, the next thing on to a stump and out again while our driver applies his shoulder to the wheel. But at last, about two o' clock we reach the Regt., find a most cheerful reception from Col. [Clark] Edwards, Chaplain [John R.] Adams, and Dr's [Francis] Warren & [William S.] Noyes, the latter recently promoted. An invitation for dinner was immediately extended, but we thought best to go first to the Hos. They have 19 men sick, not very sick. We gave them apples, a piece of orange, candies, handkerchiefs with cologne on them, and left with the Hos. six shirts & drawers, 12 stockings, six towels, 24 handkerchiefs, salt fish, herrings, tea, broma, chocolate, nutmeg, pepper, six mittens, farina, corn starch, six combs, marmalade, currant jelly, elderberry wine, soft crackers, lemons, can chicken, & can mutton. Chaplain quite affected about his daughter. They honored us with a dress parade, the men appeared well, spoke with Capt. [Albertin P.] Harris.—Lieut. [Daniel C.] Clark home on a furlough. Sent

[27] HE means the expenses that she and Mrs. Fogg incurred on behalf of soldiers' relief.
[28] HE inverts the soldier's name.

some apples, oranges, and lemons to the 7th Maine. Arrived home safe and gave our new driver Beals credit for going round the stumps. Met Mr. Hayes on his way to the 5th and aided him through Gen. Patrick about the transportation of his boxes.

SUNDAY FEB. 22ND 1863

A tremendous snow storm. Have <u>written to Mrs. Fabyan and Mrs. Bosworth</u> to day. Read more than usual to day, also went into the tent and called on Charlie [Mero] and had a little talk with him about his soul's interest. When at the 5th yesterday Mr. [John R.] Adams gave me the cheering intelligence that there had been three recent cases of conversion and several more who gave evidence of seriousness, their prayer meetings were well attended.[29] Oh how precious to feel that the spirit of the Lord has not ceased to strive in this scene of corruption and moral death.—Went out to the tent to get some more quilts for the Hos. of the 19th and gave them four quilts and ten caps. In going to the tent I went over the top of my rubber boots in the snow.

MONDAY FEB. 23RD 1863

Rode in ambulance to the 20th and carried a pail of crackers and marmalade, and found Jennison and Parker hoping to go to Wash[ington]. Went home to get a vest for Jennison and a towel for another. The Hospital wonderfully improved by getting the men into separate bunks. <u>Wrote a letter to Mrs. Bosworth to day</u>.

TUESDAY FEB. 24TH 1863

Prepared a load of things to carry to the 6th to day, our ambulance failing to come in season we sent for another, the other failed us as Lieut. Ayres thought, and wisely too, that the roads were not in a fit state for horses to travel. Mrs. F went off on horseback and I took Tomlin with me and walked down to Potomac Station, carrying with me some niceties for Mr. Norris (Sergeant Parker's wife is with him). Found her at Mrs. Alexander's and had a pleasant call. That bridge has but a single plank part of the way, but I am not at all afraid. Returning found Dr. Wixom here, he is becoming an abolitionist, he says. Mrs. Norris was so thankful for these little attentions to her husband, says she shall write to me when she gets home. Was stopped by guard for a pass on my way home, but I laughed at him and passed on.

---

[29] The 5th Maine developed a reputation as a pious regiment; it held weekly religious services in a chapel tent. According to Bell I. Wiley, "A 'strong revival' was said to have occurred in the Fifth Maine Regiment during its encampment in Virginia in the second winter of the war" (see Wiley, *Life of Billy Yank*, 274).

WEDNESDAY FEB. 25TH 1863

Was surprised by a call from the Major [Gilmore] this morning, also Col. Chamberlain. Made an attempt to find the Maine 6th with a large load of supplies, but after wandering about in the mud first to Gen. Sickles' Headquarters, then to Gen. Carr's, we could not succeed in finding them. We broke our ambulance, took refuge in an army team driven by five negroes who were going for wood, they putting a pail down bottom up in the mud for us to step on it. It was a famous ride, but we could not find the Regiment and were obliged to come home. Mrs. Fogg quite sick. Returning, Dr. Wixom said as he received an orange for a sick man xxxxxxxx.[30] Major and Mr. Hayes staid here all night. Did expect Mrs. Chamberlain & Mrs. Harris. Major says I directed Frank's box and letter to the 20th Maine and he recognized my handwriting in both cases and altered them.[31]

THURSDAY FEB. 26TH 1863

Have been very busy this rainy day in assorting our boxes, taking a sort of account of stock. I have tied up the handkerchiefs in bundles of one and two dozen each, also the towels. Now I know what we have.[32] They seem to be in a hurry to get rid of the "green backs" to day, since this little skirmish at Hartwood Church.[33] Gave Lucy an old dress. Mrs. Fogg very sick to day, she has not set up [*sic*] scarcely any all day, I have written a letter for her to Hon. George W. Dyer about the Quartermaster.[34] The snow will soon go off with this rain. We like Charlie [Mero] very much. Dr. Wixom here again to day, but he will not prescribe for Mrs. Fogg. Our ladies have not come yet. Col. Chamberlain has spent the whole evening with us, he really looks sick, we have given him two quilts and a pillow for his bed.

[*See Appendix letter 14. Isabella Fogg (HE) to George W. Dyer, February 26, 1863.*]

FRIDAY FEB. 27TH 1863

This morning Mr. [Alvah J.] Bates, Chaplain of the 2nd Maine called inquiring if it would be a Sanitary measure to give his wife lodging here to night. We could not refuse, though as a Sanitary measure, I do'nt think it will pay to get us up in the morning to get breakfast for her. Baker, the Major [Gilmore]'s man, was here this morning and when talking about the deception of that rascal of a Quartermaster

---

[30] Wixom's words have been scratched out.

[31] Frank was in the 25th Maine, serving at Long Bridge as part of the defenses of Washington at this time.

[32] Line scratched out following this sentence.

[33] John Haley of the 17th Maine described Hartwood Church, near Falmouth, as "a small brick structure" that had been desecrated by Union cavalrymen.

[34] The letter, dated February 26, 1863, is written in HE's hand and signed "Isabella Fogg."

[Litchfield], said [that] to hear him talk to your face seemed like sliding down hill on a silk handkerchief, but behind your back [he] was going up hill on a harrow. This afternoon went over to the "quarters" and carried apples, lemons, crackers, gruel, and oranges to the men. Saw some who are really <u>very</u> sick, two or three burst out crying when I spoke to them, one in Comp[any] I, I must see again. Three of them were reading in their Testaments. Stopped at the Hospital and gave to the men their apples, lemons, and cologne with a few handkerchiefs. I believe the men do enjoy having me come in to see them, and the attendants too are all glad to see me. Osgood Hodgman is my boy.

SATURDAY FEB. 28TH 1863

Mr. Loring has been here this afternoon and brought me three notifications from G. R. Davis, two letters from Miss Fox, one of which speaks of a dress for me from Mrs. Wingate, how singular that she should be thus interested for me! Also letters from Mr. & Mrs. Bosworth, Sarah [Caduc] in London with the photographs of Perkins and Anna, Perkins is first rate but I never should know Anna's. I have been over to the 2nd Maine to day and carried them drawers, socks, mittens, and Hosp. supplies. Visited the sick in quarters in company with Mrs. Bates, the Chaplain's wife. She is from Lincoln. She is here to night and going to spend the Sabbath. A very pleasant lady, I have given up my bed to her. Went over to the 2nd first to see about some apples—four barrels that I do'nt believe belong to us, though matches to Mrs. Fogg's name, then I went over with some gruel to a sick man and some oranges, lemons, and cake to the sick. Mr. and Mrs. [Alvah J.] Bates were shocked to see so large a Hospital.

SUNDAY MARCH 1ST 1863

To day I have carried gruel, crackers, lemons, and cake to the Hospital and then I went to the quarters to have a talk with some of the sick men. Called on Mr. Sylvester Murdoch of Comp[any] C of Buckfield. Find him a most lovely Christian full of faith, although he feels sadly tried at present as his own health has failed and his wife is lying very low with consumption, with the care of three little children. He told me of some striking answers to prayer he had had in former years, once when their last morsel of food had been eaten and they knew not where to look for more. This evening we have as well as Mrs. Bates, Mrs. Chamberlain and Mrs. Harris. The latter a gay, lively Washingtonian.

MONDAY MARCH 2ND 1863

A dreadful sick head ache to day, have hardly felt able to rise from my bed. This evening I am much better, shall be able to do something tomorrow.

TUESDAY MARCH 3RD 1863

Mrs. Bates still here. Mrs. H[arris] and Mrs. C[hamberlain] stopped at the Regt. last night, and to day after I had carried hot tea and tapioca to the sick in "quarters," I called on the ladies at Col. [Ames's] and Lt. Col. [Chamberlain]'s tents. Mrs. H thinks the Quartermaster a fine fellow and that she shall never pity these officers any more, they are so much better off than she expected. Mrs. C on the contrary seems to think it a dreadful place. There is a Mr. Turner here who has been getting the discharge of his son, he is from Durham,[35] and leaves tomorrow with his son for home. We have supplied him with two shirts, one pr. drawers, one pr. socks, one pr. mittens, one handkerchief, some wine, crackers, and jelly for his son. Chaplain [John R.] Adams called yesterday and I gave him some "tracts" for his men. Also two doctors from the 6th Maine called and we sent dried apples, green apples, lemons, and oranges to their sick.—I feel sad for Sergeant [Charles A.] Clark (who was so abused by the Quartermaster), he has never been able to do "duty" to any extent, since the battle of Fredericksburg. He thanked me earnestly for calling and talking to him. I must remember to go and see him again, but what I want more than any thing else now, is to get to the more distant Regiments. The mud is drying up finally. Mr. Turner said to day to the Chaplain, "you have good help here from these ladies," and the Chaplain had to say "yes." We shall lose our nice guard Charlie [Mero] as they want him for a fifer for the Regiment.

WEDNESDAY MARCH 4TH 1863

This morning Mrs. Fogg procured orders for an ambulance, that we might visit the distant Regts. We started with a large load for the 16th and the two Batteries [2nd and 5th]. First, to the 16th in their Hos., they have 25 sick and 18 in the Division Hos. close by. To those in the old church we gave such things as they wanted, but when we went to the Division Hos. there came near being a row between Mrs. Fogg and Dr. Coventry about giving supplies ourselves instead of through the matron, Mrs. Latham, and while they disputed, I gave the figs. Dr. Alexander seems about discouraged [sic], while Dr. Eaton bears his new honors very well. We stop at the Colonel's tent to night and it is too bad, for by so doing we oblige Colonel Tilden, Lt. Col. _____,[36] and Major Leavitt to vacate their quarters. Slept very comfortably on the nicest bed I have seen in the army. Every thing in their tent is in pimlico order.[37]

---

[35] Durham, New Hampshire.

[36] HE leaves the space blank, but the lieutenant colonel at this time was Augustus B. Farnham of Bangor, who had been promoted from Major on February 5 when Tilden assumed the colonelcy.

[37] Pimlico, known for its tidy houses and postage-stamp gardens, was a middle-class London suburb bordering on the more exclusive neighborhood of Belgravia and contained within the city of Westminster. Londoners aspiring to a more elite social status moved in droves to Pimlico in the 1830s; the expression "in pimlico order" suggests social status, cleanliness, and orderliness.

THURSDAY MARCH 5TH 1863

At surgeon's call this morning we went to the Guard tent where Dr. Baxter presided and we acted as [his] assistant. A Mr. Fiske of Boston was present. While the Dr. prescribed pills and powders, we prescribed dried apples and salt fish, much to the gratification of the men. From here we went to the 2nd Battery, Capt. [James A.] Hall & Lieut. Paine. They have no Hospital, but the sick men came up and we gave them dried apples, salt fish, lemons, oranges, and candy, leaving the rest of the supplies in charge of a Lieut. From this we went to the 5th Battery, and I had the pleasure of seeing the Whittiers,[38] Charles Hunt, Lieuts. [Greenlief T.] Stevens and Twitchell. Gave the stores in charge to George [Whittier] and he seemed deeply interested in the sick.—His own private matters were discussed by us. He seems to take his trials bravely. Ned [Whittier] intends to take a furlough for home next week. Going home Mrs. F was anxious to find her way home by the 6th, so we got lost and wandered about in a valley where we took four roads and found them all to be wood roads, so Truell was finally obliged to make a new path through the woods and we came out "all right" by White Oak Church, though we had to ride as much as seven miles after sundown, but Providence protected us and we arrived safely. Chaplain [John R.] Adams was with the 5th Battery. Arriving home I found a letter from Augusta awaiting me.

FRIDAY MARCH 6TH 1863

I had a tremendous job packing up to day, for I have all that to do, and we were ready for a start for the 6th at one o' clock. We passed the 2nd and called a moment on Mrs. Bates, then came the roads, <u>such roads</u> whereof I never saw any thing like them, we walked about half of the way, the ambulance had to be lifted out by a detachment of 3rd Maine men, and though it was about three and a half miles we did not arrive till five o' clock. We find 12 men in the Hos., the tent is finely warmed by a flue that passes the whole length of the floor. To night we have given the men handkerchiefs and reading matter.

SATURDAY MARCH 7TH 1863

Last night we slept in Dr. Holmes' tent, he being absent on a furlough. We each had a stretcher for our bed, and our stove was made of two old camp kettles. The quilts and pillows brought for their Hos. [were] very convenient for our use. In the night the rain poured and I thought of the road home. This morning we prepared buttered toast, poached eggs, and salt fish for breakfast for the Hospital, then at the Dispensary tent under the care of Dr. Buck we prescribed as at the 16th to between 40 and 50. Dr. Blossom is the assistant surgeon. We breakfasted with Capt Bas[s]ford, Capt.

---

[38] Brothers Edward, also known as "Ned," and George were Portland friends.

Haycock also present. They have a little boy named Jerry who joined the Regiment when they came out at Worcester Mass.—Leaving the 6th we visited (after a funny roundabout ride) the Maine Cavalry, they have 18 in Hospital. Dr. Colby very polite, he seemed much gratified with our visit and our supplies. As there was every appearance of a dark night we hurried home, met Lieut. [Edward] Whittier, talked a few moments with old Richard Randall, stopped at White Oak Church, took a piece of it, while Mrs. F cleaned her boots before going to Headquarters. When we reached home Saturday night we were well used up, and glad to think Sabbath was coming.

SUNDAY MARCH 8TH 1863

Dr. Hersom has resigned, they have had another row with the Quartermaster [Litchfield], he complained of Baker[39] and had him punished by making him walk his beat and carry a log of wood. There are two very sick men in Hospital, I have made them gruel and also cranberry jelly and carried some to [Albert] Roberts and Murdoch in the quarters. Sabbath day we always have callers, Dr. Wixom for instance, he came to vaccinate the family. I wish they would keep away. Poor Allen will die and I am afraid Morrill too. Wrote to Frank.
[See Appendix letter 15. HE to John W. Hathaway, March 8, 1863.]

MONDAY MARCH 9TH 1863

Mrs. Fogg has gone to W[ashington]. Mrs. Bates called to bid us good bye. Dr. Wixom yesterday said he vaccinated Joe, solely on my account and we had a great laugh at him. He made rather a peculiar remark as he went out. Charlie [Mero] has been removed to day and a Mr. Foster occupies his place. I have completely examined the tent to day and put every thing to rights, also opened the Brookline boxes and barrel. On coming to the house received a request from Dr. Bennet for tapioca gruel and milk punch. Made enough gruel for all the sick, and carried them, also currant jelly, 20 pr. Hos. slippers, three caps, candy, cake, and crackers. Was intending to call on Mrs. Munroe but heard she had gone to ride. Dr. Hersom is all right again, but an apology has been tendered him by the Colonel.

TUESDAY MARCH 10TH 1863

To day I have been writing letters all day. Have written two sheets to Mrs. Bosworth, one to Mrs. Lancey, one or two sheets to Sarah Caduc, and one to Augusta.—I also wrote one to Mr. Hathaway Sabbath evening and sent by Mrs. F.—My arm is numb to day and part of the time I cannot feel my pen at all. This evening I have called on Mrs. Munroe, a real good lady.—Major [Gilmore] has returned and I called on

[39] Major Gilmore's "man" servant and presumably an African American.

The boyish-looking Surgeon Nahum Hersom was a favorite of Eaton's during her first tour of duty. When Hersom, an outsider, was appointed surgeon of the 17th ahead of an insider, the rank and file protested. MAINE STATE ARCHIVES, AUGUSTA

him.—Dr. Wixom was here to day. He is a strange man. He had some <u>special business</u> with me to day and I think he will understand my answer to his inquiries.—Tomorrow I must be ready for more boxes and barrels.

WEDNESDAY MARCH 11TH 1863

Mrs. Fogg returned, but our boxes will not come till morning. To day I sent for the sick men that could walk to come over from the 20th, and I gave them dried apples, green apples, tea, salt fish, a few lemons, oranges, some stockings, handkerchiefs, &c. Had a talk with them all, and they seemed to go away cheered. Made a pail full of gruel and carried [it] over for their supper. I had letters from Mrs. Whittier and Hatty Belle, Frank, Mr. and Mrs. Bosworth, Miss Fox, Mr. Davis, &c.

THURSDAY MARCH 12TH 1863

Had a busy day unpacking our boxes and barrels, there were ten barrels and five boxes. Mrs. Fogg confined to her room all day. The articles were quite well packed, except one for Mrs. Fogg from Mrs. Flint. In that a bowl of jelly and jar of damson had made sad mischief.

FRIDAY MARCH 13TH 1863

To day I have visited the 19th Regt. Had a very pleasant interview with Dr. Hawes. Drs. Billings and Leavenseller [Levensaler] absent. Dr. Hawes told the men Thanksgiving day had come, and he permitted me to give each man in Hospital an orange, lemon, apple, fig and some candy, a handkerchief, and some cologne.—I had a new ambulance driver, and never came so near tipping over, but I am bound not to do that. When I arrived Dr. Hawes came out, rubbing his hands and saying, "just in time for dinner."—On arriving home, I went over to the 20th with some niceties for their supper.

SATURDAY MARCH 14TH 1863

When I went into the Hospital to day, one of the men exclaimed, "How do you do, Mother?" and they all chimed in. I reckon I shall feel pretty old with such boys as some of these for my sons.[40] Six more have got their discharges, among them Parker, Jennison, [Greenlief] Herrick, and Hingston. I have been looking after their clothing to day but they will not leave till Monday.—Had a long chat with Mrs. Munroe to day in their tent. She is a very pleasant lady, full of feeling and energy.

---

[40] HE was forty-four years old at the time, and some of her charges were in their thirties and forties.

SUNDAY MARCH 15TH 1863

Mrs. Fogg very sick, sent for Dr. Wixom, but he had been kicked by his horse, so instead I called on him, he does not know me yet. Mrs. F sent for Dr. Hezless, connected with the 3rd Penn. Cavalry and Medical Director of the Division, he is a very pleasant man, but he has ordered a blister and Mrs. F utterly refuses, I do not know what the result of it all will be.[41] As I was walking over to call on Dr. Wixom, I saw them approaching for the burial of Morrill who died of typhoid fever, Allen had been buried in the morning, so I went to the grave and there seeing a few comrades, wiped away the falling tear, and Dr. Munroe read the burial service. So another widowed mother left to mourn her son by this awful war. They sent over to day Mr. Hooper of the 2nd Maine for some crackers for Dr. Morrison, also Lieut. Benson called and took some things in his saddle bags for the 7th Maine. I have written to day to Mrs. Whittier, Hatty Belle, and my dear Frank, and I am very anxious about him and his cough. His company seem unfortunate about their officers. Gen. Hersey called with Major Gilmore.

[See Appendix letter 16. HE to Hatty Belle Eaton, March 15, 1863.]

MONDAY MARCH 16TH 1863

Mrs. Fogg still very sick, sent this evening for Dr. Hersom to "cup" her which he did, but I have no faith in it.[42] He thinks she needs a blister, I do'nt know where Dr. Hezless can be.

TUESDAY MARCH 17TH 1863

Have mailed a letter to Miss Fox to day in reply to hers of the 13th and 21st February. I have received one since from her that has not been answered. Mrs. F sent for Major Gilmore this morning to talk on matters of business, and when he returned to camp, Mrs. Chamberlain and Mrs. Munroe called, then Dr. Hersom, then Col. Ames & Col. Chamberlain and we had a room full. Before they went away, came a Mrs. Clark, whose husband is City Marshal in Portland and her son, and before we had time to

---

[41] "Blistering" was used for inflammatory diseases, where the release of fluid build-up from the blister was thought to relieve the symptoms of the disease. Sticking plaster made from soap and resin was applied on porous fabric to a coin-size section of skin until the skin was sufficiently irritated to raise a blister—a process that could take up to twelve hours. Then the blister was lanced to release the fluid and swabbed with an ointment made from spermaceti oil to aid healing.

[42] Cupping was a form of blood-letting. Fuel in a curette or small glass pipe was ignited and placed at the junction of the skin and the rim of a glass cup which had been placed open side down on the surface of the skin. Though the flame usually burned the patient's skin, it used up the oxygen within the cup and created a vacuum. When the skin beneath the glass turned dark red or blue, the vacuum was released long enough to lance the engorged protrusion and replace the cup to catch the blood specimen.

breathe, came a Miss Spaulding from Kennebec County looking for her brother's discharge. Mrs. Clark and son have gone to the 17th, Lt. Col. being her cousin.[43] I went to Dr. Munroe to procure an ambulance for them, though she thought she could walk any where. If she can walk as fast as she can talk, she will do well. Miss Spaulding, I sent to Mrs. Grigsby's but she is back again to night and they will accommodate her here.

WEDNESDAY MARCH 18TH 1863

Dr. Wixom came over to day and he tells Mrs. F that her disease is not dangerous, that it is bilious pneumonia, or congestion of the liver with an irritated state of the lungs. Dr. Hersom also called, medicines have been left, and mustard ordered on the chest.[44] What shall I do? The Lord direct me. Dr. W says I must not leave her two or three days, while she says, if I do'nt go to visit the Regt. she will start for Washington tomorrow. Here lays the powder, she will not take it, and there is the mustard draft [sic], she will not have it on.—Dr. Wixom examined young Spaulding and pronounced him a subject for discharge.

THURSDAY MARCH 19TH 1863

To day has indeed been a trying one, as Mrs. F persisted in her previous determination till long after Dr. W came. He positively forbade her going and she is yet here. I try to do the best I can, and oh may I be directed and have patience. I have unpacked four boxes and two barrels to day and am very tired. Barrels were from the Camp Relief Association, one box from Westbrook, one from Steven's Plains, one for Mrs. Fogg from Mr. Whitman sent originally from [the] Soldier's Aid Society, Portland, and a fine large one from Free St. Church, which came nicely packed and contains among other things three nice kegs of pickles. It also contained a letter from Mrs. Griswold.

FRIDAY MARCH 20TH 1863

Mrs. Fogg very sick to day, Dr. W gave her a cathartic with which was a small portion of ipecac and this has made her very sick. To night he has obliged her to take medicine that she did not choose to have and a scene has been the consequence. Dr. Hersom has been appointed surgeon of the 17th. I do pity the poor 20th.

---

[43] The lieutenant colonel of the 17th Maine was Charles B. Merrill [see listing in biographical dictionary].

[44] A mustard poultice, plaster, or draft was used to ease the symptoms of respiratory illnesses. The poultice was made by mixing equal parts of dried mustard powder with linseed meal or oatmeal, then wetting the dry ingredients with boiling vinegar or water. After the boiling liquid had cooled sufficiently, it was applied to the chest over a piece of muslin so that it could be easily removed after thirty minutes. Applying directly to the skin created removal difficulties and caused the patient to "suffer a martyrdom."

SATURDAY MARCH 21ST 1863

A very unpleasant, stormy day, snowing and raining by spells. Dr. W has been here three times, Mrs. Fogg is very weak and feeble to day. I have been writing some to day for Mrs. Fogg. I watched last night with her, did not lay [sic] down at all, or let her sleep more than half an hour at a time.

SUNDAY MARCH 22ND 1863

Company all day. Dr. Wixom of course, and Dr. Hersom and Dr. Hezless, Mrs. Fogg wrote for Dr. Hezless.—Yesterday too Col. Ames called in answer to a request by note from Mrs. Fogg. Then came Col. Chamberlain and his wife, and so they keep a continual running while the Dr. says she must not talk.

MONDAY MARCH 23RD 1863

To day I have had one of our famous ambulance rides. I have been to the 7th and 5th. We were three hours getting to the 7th, that is Mr. Truell (our driver) and myself, but when once there found a hearty welcome. First saw their chaplain, Mr. Parinton, who was sick in Dr. Anderson's tent, then the Hos. Steward Mr. [Henry B.] Powers, (brother of one who had his discharge from the 20th with a lame hand) came and invited me to the Hos. They have a nice walled tent or rather two, with doors. There are 12 sick in Hos. After dispensing of my "goodies" to them, such as an apple, orange, lemon, some candy, a handkerchief, and cologne to each man, I went with Lieut. Benson to accompany me with a pillow case over his shoulder to the quarters and dispensed there. I called also on the Lieut. at his tent, he read me part of Miss Robinson of Portland's letter to him about the Levee[45] & showed me his Christmas presents. I like Dr. Anderson, he seemed so kind. After tea, I left for the 5th Maine, their Regt. out on picket, but Dr. [Francis] Warren urged me so hard that I stopped long enough to go into the Hospital and give each man a treat. Now, in full view of White Oak Church, we lost our way, although we were told by a man of whom we made inquiries that if we could find White Oak Church we could go any where from there, as if we were green. Mr. Hayes brought me a letter from Agnes, also one from Mrs. Downes with reference to a package that I have for her son. When I was going for the ambulance this morning I saw Adjutant [Charles W.] Roberts of the 17th and Lieut. Houghton. The latter saw Frank last week and said he was quite well again. Oh I want to be thankful for all God's goodness to me and mine.

[See *Appendix letter 17. Frank Eaton to HE, March 23, 1863*.]

TUESDAY MARCH 24TH 1863

A real rain storm. To day Mr. [Benjamin A.] Chase, chaplain of the 4th called here, he is now at the Division Hospital, also Mr. [Orson B.] Clark, chaplain of the 84th

---

[45] The Portland levee was a community social function to raise money for the troops.

Pennsylvania.—Dr. Wixom of course, <u>what a man</u>! and Dr. [John] Moore, Medical Director, also Mrs. Munroe, and in the morning Lieut. Lewis and wife. Dr. did not come,[46] consequently the "council" did not come off as expected. Mrs. Fogg is better I think, though still weak.

WEDNESDAY MARCH 25TH 1863

This morning went over to the Ambulance Corps, saw Lieut. _____ running off when he saw me coming,[47] Mr. Truell hardly thought it best for me to try the roads to the 3rd and 4th Maine to day, so I will wait till tomorrow.—Dr. Wixom called this morning by 1/2 past seven! What did he want to come here for so early, I should like to know. Dr. [John] Moore called again to day, also Dr. Hersom who is about being transferred to the 17th. Then came Mrs. Lieut. Lewis, also Dr. Wixom again and just as I was ready for Division Hos., Griffin's Division. After I went into the tent came Chaplain [Benjamin A.] Chase of the 4th, Mr. Alvord, and Mrs. Mc Kay.—I found the men in the Division Hos. very comfortable and very glad to see me, also men from the 2nd and some that saw me at Windmill Point. Poor Goodwin will die, and Jones and that pretty bugler ought to have their discharge papers.—Dr. Wixom in again this evening and Miss Spaulding has come in, after riding, with the promise that her brother's papers shall be in tomorrow.

THURSDAY MARCH 26TH 1863

Have been to day to the 3rd and 4th Maine. The Doctor was here this morning before seven, but I reckon I was ready for him, he said the <u>reason</u> of the early call was because he was to be out on Review. We traveling in the untrod path where Mr. Truell measured the distance between the stumps before taking the ambulance while I reached over the trunk, held the reins, and called out "whoa" to the horses as the Cavalry passed. In one place the <u>yellow</u> clay came near swamping the horse. At the 4th Dr. [George W.] Martin had gone home on a furlough, Dr. Cobb was absent on picket till just as we were leaving, then he very kindly cut across to the top of one of the hills to show us our way to the 4th. At the 4th they have seven sick in Hos., Mc Cobb [sic] acting Hos. Stew. and Clark; the old gentleman magnifying his office. There are none very sick, after delivering my stores and feeding the men with candy, I went in company with Mc Cobb and the ward tender with three pillow cases, one pillow case of dried apples, one of green apples, oranges, and lemons, and one with soft crackers, a box of butter, and my pockets with tea, handkerchiefs, cayenne, and candy to the "quarters." There were 20 sick there, I saw going Clifford who drove

---

[46] Probably a reference to Nahum Hersom, surgeon of the 17th Maine.

[47] HE leaves an underlined blank space, though it can be inferred that Lieutenant Ayres of the ambulance corps wished to avoid her.

me to and from the Hospital and gave me the <u>ring</u>, poor dear boy, he has been sick in Hos. at Washington. He belongs to Comp[any] A. From the 4th we went, after meeting the Regt. coming from review, up, up, up, then down, then up again, through stumps and mud to the 3rd. The doctors seemed very glad to see me, they have but four in Hos. with three doctors in attendance, Hildreth, [William] Jewett, and [James D.] Watson, I had a very pleasant chat with them in their tent, Major Lee coming in, having been wounded at Fredericksburg, he went home on a furlough and got married. I do'nt know when I have had such a jovial time.—Gov. Curtin and staff passed while I was there. Returning as we passed through the Cavalry, a fine brass band was discoursing rich music under the pines.—Had a letter from my dear Frank to night, I am worried about his cough, though he seems in pretty good spirits especially about the "wild turkey."—Dr. [John] Moore, Medical Director called and Dr. Wixom again. <u>Wrote to Mrs. Bosworth</u> this evening, in which I mentioned Mrs. Mc Kay and spoke of Mrs. Whitman.

FRIDAY MARCH 27TH 1863

To day Mrs. Fogg has had Dr. Hezless, Dr. Hersom, Dr. [John] Moore, and Dr. Wixom. Dr. Wixom was here bright and early, all in a heat and excitement about Miss Spaulding's brother's papers. I could not have believed Dr. Munroe would be so ugly or could be so ignorant. He has made out the papers, stating that "in his opinion the disease is 'nostalgia,' his pulse quickened by excitement of examination, some appearance that may lead to remote pulmonary disease."—This being the case, what has he blistered the young man for? Dr. Moore's eyes snapped when we told him about it and he has given orders that Dr. Munroe's certificate should be ignored utterly and new papers made out for signature.—Mr. Hayes came in this evening. I have been to the Hospital to see the boys and carried them oranges, lemons, apples, cake, crackers, fish, handkerchiefs, and cologne. My boy, Osgood Hodgman, suffers severely with his head, how I wish he had his discharge. They are all out of every thing in the shape of gruel again, and I have given them five lbs. potato starch for gruel, one paper corn starch, one can condensed milk, some indian meal, and one and a half dozen nutmegs.—Fred Bosworth was here to day for his "picallilly"[48] and made a long call. He is being promoted rapidly. I have had a short letter from my <u>precious boy</u> to night and find they were under marching orders several days ago, so I suppose he is now sleeping in a shelter tent, with that dreadful cough. O for patience to bear the existing state of things in the country.—Am surprised to learn of the death of Gen. Sumner, he seemed so full of vigor when last I saw him.—<u>The ladies</u> are all ordered off before Monday.[49]

[48] A relish of pickled vegetables.
[49] Likely a reference to soldiers' and surgeons' wives who were visiting in camp and were usually asked to return home before the start of spring campaigns. There were skirmishes all April leading up to the battle of Chancellorsville at the beginning of May.

SATURDAY MARCH 28TH 1863

A severe rain storm. Unable to accomplish much to day. Dr. [John] Moore here.

SUNDAY MARCH 29TH 1863

Oh how I wish I could attend some service to day. This afternoon Dr. Hersom was in and Mrs. F had a present from him of four buttons for sleeve buttons. I did not go to the Hospital to day for the wind blew almost a tempest.

MONDAY MARCH 30TH 1863

To day Mrs. Fogg has been very sick, I went to the Hos. to see about the men who have their discharge papers and provide clothing for them. Lieut. [Joseph W.] Lincoln is very sick, I fear will not live.

TUESDAY MARCH 31ST 1863

After the fine day yesterday we have had a snow and rain storm, but this afternoon I went to the 20th, called on Mrs. [Addison W.] Lewis and Lieut. [Joseph W.] Lincoln and then paid [Dr.] Munroe a visit. He read the papers he had prepared for Spaulding's discharge and I picked them all to pieces, I also begged him not to "watch" the men to see if they ought to be discharged till they died and then cited poor Allen's case. I never talked plainer to any one in my life, but I am afraid Capt. [Joseph B.] Fitch['s] description of him is true and he will receive my reprimand quietly and let it pass. The Regt. are in a bad enough condition as the vaccinated men are apparently breaking out with varioloid,[50] and they are trying to get a tent for them. Col. Chamberlain was in the doctors' tent. I robbed the Colonel's tent yesterday of the rocking chair belonging to Mrs. Boller, sending it to Lieut. [Joseph W.] Lincoln's tent.

WEDNESDAY APRIL 1ST 1863

The 17th have received my services to day.—They have 20 sick in Hospital and about the same number in quarters, but to day they were out on inspection and tomorrow they break camp and move to a new camping ground near the 3rd and 4th. Mr. [Albert] Roberts in Hos. was very glad to see me and I had a long, earnest talk with him on his soul's interest. I think he has met with a change. Col. [Thomas A.] Roberts, very kind but feeling quite unwell. Dr. Wescott seemed pleased to see me, said he felt

---

[50] A mild form of smallpox usually contracted after men were inoculated with smallpox vaccine.

Eaton confronted Nahum Monroe, surgeon of the ailing 20th Maine, when he refused to discharge a gravely ill soldier. "I could not have believed Dr. Munroe would be so ugly or could be so ignorant," she wrote. MAINE STATE ARCHIVES, AUGUSTA

as if we had brought them a large supply this time, he feels very bad about Dr. Hersom's being appointed over him, although he does not blame Dr. H for it and I think is disposed to treat him kindly. Mr. Hayes brought me letters to night, from Sarah Caduc, Mrs. Lancey, Miss Fox, two from George R. Davis, and one from my dear son, from the 20th. I am greatly relieved to feel that Frank is going [*sic*] so well in his new trial of army life. Oh how thankful I ought to be. Received a note from Dr. Hawes of the 19th to day, also one day before yesterday. Mrs. Fogg does not gain very fast.

THURSDAY APRIL 2ND 1863

Col. Ames was here this morning before we ate our breakfast, and such a time as there was about the buttons. Eva really <u>bought</u> them, she cut four from his new coat and promised to <u>pay on demand</u>, he offered to sell to me, but I am too old now to <u>buy buttons</u>, though a present would be quite acceptable.—Eva had better be careful or Dr. Hezless's prophecy may have more truth than poetry in it, before this is <u>settled</u>. I have <u>written to my precious boy</u>, Mrs. Fogg had Dr. [John] Moore to call on her to night and he told her, she <u>must</u> have fresh air, and not gobble down medicine but take good, wholesome food. The Major [Gilmore] was here, but what an effect it had, he was not attentive enough, said Portland people were "<u>human beings</u>" in answer to her remark that all they cared for her was that she might be out of the way. I am not easily frightened at <u>hysteria</u>.

FRIDAY APRIL 3RD 1863

To day I have spent with the 5th Maine. But first this morning, as there was a little "bossy" came to town yesterday, some of <u>this new milk</u> was wanted by somebody for their breakfast. Next we, that is, Miss S[paulding] and myself were ordered to eat it because it was unpleasant, even disgusting to us, or else somebody would not taste theirs, and so somebody went without till they came to their appetite.[51] The 5th Maine are in a very healthy condition, have but 12 in Hospital, and none in "quarters" really sick, only five report for medicine. Dr. Waterhouse of the 7th was there and dined with us, we had coffee, ham, potatoes, biscuit, doughnuts, and cheese. Chaplain [John R.] Adams seemed very happy to see me, showed me his family daguerreotypes. To night I have <u>written to Sarah Caduc</u>. Col. Ames called while I was away to day, and <u>took the interest on the debt which Eva has incurred</u>, charging three per cent. Would'nt I like to have been there to see!! But he was too cunning and looked out for that.

SUNDAY APRIL 5TH 1863

Yesterday morning at nine o' clock I started with Mr. Haskell our driver for the [2nd and 5th] Batteries and the 16th. He had never been farther than Gen. Hooker's, not

---

[51] The "somebody" in question was Isabella Fogg.

even to White Oak Church, so I had to be cicerone. All of a sudden, having changed my usual route a little, I found myself with the 2nd Battery. [Lieut.] Col. [James A.] Hall so earnestly urged my dining there that finding I should not be able to return that night, I accepted the invitation. About seven came up to the sick call to whom I distributed some comforts, leaving the rest with one of the Lieuts. About two o'clock after a pleasant visit I rode to the 5th Battery. Here, it does not take long to feel at home. Edward [Whittier] had just returned the night before from his furlough home, and I had pleasing accounts from Hatty Belle. Never was there a finer, more congenial company of officers than are to be found here. Capt. Leppein (who has been promoted to Lieut. Col. of Artillery), Lieut. [Greenlief T.] Stevens, Lieut. Twitchell, and Edward.—After a little chat, I decided to go immediately to the 16th and return by special invitation to the Battery to a six o'clock dinner. George [Whittier] rode over with me to the 16th. As usual they have plenty of sickness, 20 in Hospital and about 100 under medical treatment. The Hos. did not look very neat and the grounds around are in a sadly rough state. One man died of the small pox this morning at the "pest tent" put up specially for that purpose. How different from the 20th, really I do'nt know what will become of them. They have 100 cases of varioloid and small pox caused by inoculation[52] and the men are left, many of them, right in the tents with the other men. Left my supplies with the Hos. Steward, Mr. Dow, and there I had my first bouquet of spring presented to me by Mr. Dow, a bouquet of daffodils and jonquils. Men in Hos. as usual very glad to see me, though my stock of niceties was rather small.—Dinner at the Battery, stewed oysters, hot doughnuts, and biscuit with very pleasant conversation, but I was a little uneasy, the wind blew almost a tempest, they had to remove the ambulance to the valley and stake it up.—Spent the night at Richard Randall's, very pleasantly, I believe they really like to have me come.—Waking this morning when Richard came in to make the fire, he said the snow was to his knees and I began to think of getting home. Went down to breakfast, piggy being taken to have his first, after breakfast Edward [Whittier] escorted me to the 5th [Battery] to have breakfast there. Poor Capt. Lep[pein] did not make his appearance at the table and I had a nice chance to teaze [sic] him, he very politely <u>gave</u> me his photograph which I shall prize more than <u>buying buttons</u>. Our road home was a trackless waste nearly half way, but a kind Providence kept us from accident & we arrived safe about 1/2 past three. Found Mrs. Fogg about as when I left.

MONDAY APRIL 6TH 1863

Miss Spaulding was to have gone home, but she finally decided to stop and see the Cavalry Review to see the President and the mud. Honest old Abe was conspicuous

---

[52] Vaccine supply was often ineffective and resulted in the full-blown emergence of smallpox through exposure to another sufferer. The deep cut made with an unsterilized knife to deliver the vaccine sometimes resulted in blood poisoning or the transfer of some other blood-born disease to the patient.

with his stove funnel hat, Mrs. Lincoln was present in a carriage.⁵³ <u>Gen. Hooker</u> looked finely, also Mead and Stoneman. Letters from [George R.] Davis, Miss Fox, Mrs. Whittier and Hatty Belle, and Mrs. _____ of Yarmouth requesting an answer,⁵⁴ also one from Mrs. Lancey. Have <u>written to Agnes</u>, dear child. Small pox cases are more decided. Dr. [John] Moore quite indignant, he has been having a blow up with the Quartermaster about the tents. Col. Ames came after principal and interest for the buttons and received pay in full. Received by Remick $55.00 for <u>our</u> use, <u>wrote Mr. Bosworth</u>.

TUESDAY APRIL 7TH 1863

Miss Spaulding and brother started for home this morning. She was a real good girl and we shall miss her much. Col. Chamberlain called this evening. <u>Wrote to Mrs. W[hittier] and Hatty</u>.

WEDNESDAY APRIL 8TH 1863

Lieut. [Joseph W.] Lincoln died last night and I am informed his last words to Dr. Munroe were these, "I die a victim to your neglect." This afternoon I tried our new team, riding over to the Division Hos. Poor Jones, I am afraid the doctor has "<u>watched</u>" him till now that he has his discharge papers, he will never live to see his poor widowed mother. The boys were glad enough to see me, whether Maine boys or not. A Pennsylvanian showed me the photograph of his wife and little daughter. Mr. Ford got the dressing gown. They have no sugar at all to night and this shows lack of care for a Division Hospital. <u>Smith</u>, the nurse, it seems is the one who was kicked by the Colonel some time ago, he showed me his breast, which has had ever since that affair a large protuberance as large as an orange.

THURSDAY APRIL 9TH, NO, FRIDAY APRIL 10TH 1863

Mrs. Mc Kay called this morning and spent a pleasant half hour. Then I went to the 4th Maine, as Dr. [George W.] Martin had called the day previous and expressed a wish for some <u>sheets, &c</u>. The horses took me over that awful corduroy past Sickle's Headquarters, in a great hurry.⁵⁵ It did seem as if there would be nothing left of me. I found only seven sick in Hos. and <u>they</u> all getting better. Dr.'s had gone to follow the Resident as he had just passed.—In the afternoon I visited the Hospital of the 20th once more, then I called on Mrs. [Addison W.] Lewis and invited her to walk with me to the 32nd Mass. There I made inquiries about Lucius

---

⁵³ The review took place in the vicinity of Hooker's Headquarters.
⁵⁴ HE leaves an underlined blank space.
⁵⁵ The reference is to the bumpy surface of a corduroy or planked road.

Trowbridge [and] saw his captain, he said Lucius died very unexpectedly, was sick but nine days, did not know that he was dangerously ill. I am much pleased with the appearance of Dr. [Zabdiel B.] Adams, their surgeon, a Boston man, their Hos. a pattern of neatness and pictures all hanging round to make it cheerful. This morning the Major [Gilmore] sent over Baker with a note and a box of honey to Mrs. Fogg, but she seems "intensely disgusted" and wo'nt touch the honey. Mr. Hayes brought me letters to night from Sarah and Libbie, with photographs of brother Joshua [Bacon] and his wife,[56] a real nice photograph of dear brother, also letters from Mr. and Mrs. Bosworth, Mrs. Whiting, and George R. Davis. Mr. Hayes is very much vexed with the Maine Agency movement and [Leonard W.] Watson's having the superintendence.

SATURDAY APRIL 11TH 1863

I tried to get away to the Cavalry to day, but it was first one thing then another and finally I was obliged to give it up. Chaplain Knox and surgeon [Horatio N.] Howard called, then Dr. [John] Moore, and Mrs. Fogg asked for his photograph and said, "Mrs. E. would like one, <u>I know</u>," so I should. Chaplain [Alvah J.] Bates called also, and he told me that he attended Lucius [Trowbridge]'s funeral, and they had a solemn time. Staff officers all present. <u>Major Gilmore</u> and Col. Chamberlain here this evening.

SUNDAY APRIL 12TH 1863

Contrary to my usual custom I left home to day to visit a Regt. notwithstanding it was the Sabbath. I have been wanting to visit the 10th Maine at Stafford Court House for weeks and as Mr. Hayes wo'nt be here to day and knew the road I decided to go. We arrived about seven, a ride of some six or seven miles. The appearance of the country is better than that portion we have been over during the winter. There are some fences left around the farms. We also passed two camp burial grounds that were very neatly fenced in and very prettily ornamented. How glad I was to see such marks of thoughtfulness for those they were to leave behind in this vast burial spot: We passed "<u>Stafford Court House</u>" containing a Court House, Jail, <u>one</u> large dwelling house, and a few old buildings. The Regt. are on a hill with a Hospital away down in the valley in the most unhealthy place that could be found, it seemed to me. I did not like the appearance of the Hos. at all, as it respects neatness, one man had died the night before and his funeral was attended with the Sabbath services, the Regt. being in attendance. The officers seemed pleased to see me, I left such supplies as they needed, and started for home but met with quite an

---

[56] HE's half-brother, Joshua Butters Bacon (b. 1790), married Sarah Ann Perkins on May 4, 1817. Two of their five children were named Sarah and Elizabeth—nieces Sarah and Libbie to whom HE refers. Joshua would die in October 1863, less than six months later.

adventure. Going over a steep pitch down hill, a circular attachment to the pole near the axle broke all to splinters, we all sprang out, a kind Providence preserved us from injury, our horses proved gentle. Mr. Hayes started for the woods and procured a pole and a grape vine, and with this and straps and chains that Johnson had taken the precaution to take with him, our vehicle was mended, but it was growing dark and beginning to rain. Just then Mr. Alvord of the Christian Commission appeared coming over the hill, returning from attending a meeting at Major General [Oliver O.] Howard's camp. He kindly offered to take me with him, exchanging seats with a Mr. Bliss who waited for the ambulance in my stead. Mr. Alvord and I had a nice chat about Newton,[57] as he resides there somewhere near "Mount Parnassus." It grew so dark that part of the way, he had to lead the horse and feel for the stumps. When we reached the 20th I asked if he had not an evening meeting, so I, at my own request sent him to the meeting and took an orderly with me to accompany me home. Mrs. Fogg was much alarmed at our being so late. A letter from my precious son awaited my arrival, he is still <u>well</u>, thanks to my Heavenly Father. Oh! God, be thou his shield.

MONDAY APRIL 13TH 1863

To day I have had a wild goose chase for the Cavalry, when <u>we got to them, they were not there</u>, nothing but a deserted camp, two brick chimneys where the Hospital once stood, all gone, but two or three men guarding forage. One of them gave me a Testament brought from Fredericksburg. Finding my effort a failure, I rode over to the [2nd and 5th] Batteries, and as I told Capt. Leppein, came on purpose to make a call, which he said should be remembered somewhere else, than as my usual Hos. visit. Edward and George [Whittier] [are] well, I shall not probably see them again till after an onward movement. Humphrey has the small pox. The road is filled with Cavalry and pack mules, the Cavalry of the Army of the Potomac move to day, I suspect toward Culpeper.—One old, stubborn mule laid down under his burden of bread boxes and grain. George and Ned [Whittier] gave me a whole package of their mother's letters to read. Poor Major Gilmore, does'nt he have to take a blowing up![58]

TUESDAY APRIL 14TH 1863

Notwithstanding my two days of severe head ache and my long, long rides, I found this morning that Mrs. Fogg was feeling very anxious about Hugh [Fogg], and I decided to go over to the 6th lest they might move, and she not know whether he was here or not.—Lieut. Ayres refused an ambulance, but Dr. [John] Moore soon set him right.

---

[57] HE's hometown in Massachusetts, approximately twenty miles southwest of Boston.

[58] HE's reference is cryptic, though it is likely that she's alluding to squabbling among the officers of the 20th, including Dr. Monroe, whom HE believed was less than sympathetic to his patients, and Quartermaster Litchfield.

I had a rough Irish driver and a rough team, but I got along very well. Called on Dr. [George W.] Martin and found him right sick, hope he is not going to have the small pox. At the 6th saw Dr's. Holmes and Buck, inquired into their wants and left with them milk, nutmegs, jelly, shrub, herring, black pepper, oysters, &c. Called at Capt. Bassford's tent and saw himself, Capt. Furlong, Lieut. Waite, Sergeant Flint. They did not think much of being called the Light Brigade and carrying eight days rations and 50 rounds of ammunition to a man.[59] Saw also Major Haycock and visited the Hos., only ten sick.—Arrived home safe after meeting on the way three ambulance trains carrying away the sick. Major Gilmore came over, I suppose, to bid us good bye. There have been two deaths of small pox at the 20th. Now I believe I will go to my bed.

WEDNESDAY APRIL 15TH 1863

I have written a letter to my precious boy, enclosed six postage stamps. I felt very sad as I wrote, in view of the anticipated army movement, perhaps I may never see his noble form again. Oh why this dreadful war! He bears no malice to his Southern brother, can he deliberately take his life? I cannot bear the thought. Can a Christian nation conscientiously kill each other? Will our Maker approve? To day He has sent a tremendous rain storm which will derange present army movements. The streams will not be fordable. Why is this, let me ask, why?

THURSDAY APRIL 16TH 1863

Johnson received orders last night from Capt. Bliss to turn in our team this morning, and I have sent a note to Col. Myers Assistant Quartermaster General with reference to it. Major Gilmore called yesterday, and Mrs. F in her way told him we had nothing for supper, although she had just eaten two saucers of tapioca pudding and milk and a cracker. The poor man, to save us from starvation, went home and sent over a cake and apple pie. Dr. Munroe has been requested to resign, when he told Dr. [John] Moore such was his intention, the reply was, "I do'nt know that any body has any objections. I have not." What between Dr. Moore and the Quartermaster

---

[59] The soldiers were carrying munitions in expectation of the movement that would launch the Chancellorsville campaign and understood HE's joke as an ill omen regarding their fate. Immortalized in an 1854 poem of the same name by Alfred Lord Tennyson, the charge of the Light Brigade was an ill-advised British cavalry sortie at the battle of Balaklava in the Ukraine during the Crimean War (October 24, 1854). Of the approximately 670 Englishmen engaged, 118 were killed and 127 wounded in the assault. Though a 36 percent casualty rate is high, the number of men who perished, for example, on June 3, 1864 during the Army of the Potomac's assault on A.P. Hill and Robert E. Lee's forces at Cold Harbor, where more than eighty-five hundred men fell in less than ten minutes, or on June 18, 1864, when the 1st Maine Heavy Artillery lost 685 of it nine hundred men (to death and wounds) at Petersburg, seems tame. The 1st Maine "Heavy" had the dubious distinction of being the single unit that lost the greatest number of men on any one day of the war.

and Dr. Munroe, I think they have a lovely time of it at the 20th.—Major Gilmore has sent to his wife[60] to have two of his photographs forwarded to us, so I hope to get one and I <u>deserve it</u>, for I begged for it.

FRIDAY APRIL 17TH 1863

This morning Mrs. F announced her intention to go to the 6th to day, although she has not set up [*sic*] an hour at a time yet. The <u>reason</u>, Hugh returned to his Regt. and came over here to see her yesterday. She was distressed beyond measure to think he should have returned just at this time and she determined to get him out of it.[61] I offered to go in her stead, so John and I started on our break neck excursion that took us from the corduroy hill, with holes in it that threatened the horse's legs. Dined on baked beans with Capt. Furlong and Lieut. Waite, Capt. F[urlong] told me all about his marriage and the snow storms, took Hugh to Dr. Holmes who did not give much encouragement but after laying the matter before Colonels Burnham and [Benjamin] Harris and Major Haycock, they decided that they needed another man to take care of their horses and said that Hugh should have the place and I came back light hearted. Mr. Hayes came down this evening and brought me letters from Mr. Davis, Miss Fox, Mrs. Dyer, Miss Roberts, a Mrs. Jackson of Brunswick, Mrs. Whittier, and Hatty Belle. That letter from Brunswick deserves honorable mention, or rather the <u>officer</u> that went home and reported the wants so <u>few</u>, ought to be remembered by us with the kind of gratitude he deserves.[62]

SATURDAY APRIL 18TH 1863

The new cases of small pox in the [20th Maine] Regt. are rapidly showing themselves. I hear there are seven to day and one more has died, making three in all. I went to Division Hospital this morning to see about exchanging our guard, Mr. Poole seems so very feeble. Mr. Hayes brought five barrels and four boxes. This afternoon [I] took about a six mile ride after this fashion ⁀ to find the 17th in their new camp as I wanted to see [Albert] Roberts. He is improving. Dr. Hersom was right glad to see me and moreover I secured my <u>shoulder strap</u>. We had a long chat together about the 20th and matters and things in general. Mrs. Fogg rode out to day, for the first time in five weeks. <u>I have written to Mrs. Whittier, Hatty Belle</u>, and <u>Col. Hathaway</u>.

SUNDAY APRIL 19TH 1863

A most delightful day, warm as June. Mrs. F rode off this morning and never stopped till she reached Hooker's Headquarters, but alas for her the General had gone to

---

[60] Mary Jane Whitney.

[61] Fogg was attempting to thwart her son's participation in the Chancellorsville campaign on the pretext of his illness.

[62] That is, not much.

Aquia [Creek]. She saw Butterfield, <u>secured</u> the wagon, brought home a bouquet that had been sent by Mrs. Lincoln to Gen. Butterfield. The general gave it to her to give to the General Hospital of his old brigade.—The sick are being carried by all day to day in ambulance trains. Major Gilmore was here this evening with Capt. Spear, last evening with Capt. [Atherton] Clark, and the night before with Capt. _____.[63] He is making quite a business of it. Fred Bosworth spent nearly two hours with me to day. A young man came this afternoon who is clerk in the provost office to make inquiries about our Sanitary movements and said he wrote for a newspaper in Penn Yan[64] and wished to make statements. <u>Wrote to Mrs. Hart, Miss Roberts, and Mem Sahib.</u>[65]

MONDAY APRIL 20TH 1863

To day I have spent in the tent unpacking boxes and barrels. To day we have had four boxes and five barrels. The barrels from the Camp Relief Asso[ciation] and the boxes, one from Yarmouth, Turner, Monmouth, and Brunswick.—Most of the things came well, but the cider made a mess generally. I headed up a few of the barrels to be in readiness for a move. Mrs. F's head aches to day, wonder if she will take another ride like yesterday's.

TUESDAY APRIL 21ST 1863

Nothing would satisfy but going to the new General Hospital to day, now, what was the use? Every thing was in confusion, could not get the names, could not find the 5th Corps to leave that famous bouquet, saw Mrs. Mc Kay. Found the 2nd, 3rd, 6th Corps coming home, stopped at the 2nd Maine and left them some dried apples. I went to the 20th this morning and carried some apples and reading matter for the poor small pox men. Poor, dear Osgood Hodgman has got the small pox, all through carelessness, in letting those sick with it be carried into [the] Regimental Hospital. Found Dr. [John] Moore here on my return, soon Dr. Wixom came in, and afterwards the Major [Gilmore] & Capt. [Atherton] Clark, and in the evening the Colonels [Burnham and Benjamin Harris].

WEDNESDAY APRIL 22ND 1863

Our guard taken very sick and carried to Hos. We have our fears, though he says he has had varioloid.[66] The 20th had marching orders to day, so they have struck camp

---

[63] HE leaves an underlined blank space.

[64] A village in upstate New York, incorporated in 1833 and approximately sixty miles southeast of Rochester, in the Finger Lakes region. Its name was derived from the equal distribution of Pennsylvanians and Yankees in its population.

[65] The title "Mem Sahib" was reserved for European matrons in colonial India. HE may have meant Mr. Hathaway, who was her superior.

[66] Men who had had varioloid developed a natural immunity to smallpox.

and we saw them winding over the hill to their new camping ground. Mrs. [Addison W.] Lewis had their tent pulled down at short notice and was obliged to come here. Dr. Wixom has been dismissed from service and sentenced to lose his back pay and be fined besides, I am perfectly indignant.[67] Mr. Hayes came in and brought letters to me from Mr. Greenough with draft from Mr. [John B.] Foster in Waterville for $50.00 for the soldiers, also a letter from my darling boy. He is a really good boy to write me so often, but he need not be in such fear that I shall be harmed in battle. I am very anxious about his cough. He is off duty now on account of it. I do wonder who will take my place and live through what I live through. There is a report that Hooker has resigned because he could not be let alone. If that is true, I want to go straight home, indeed I want to go anyway.[68]

THURSDAY APRIL 23RD 1863

A powerful rain storm. Confined to the house all day but have spent the time in writing letters to Mrs. F. G. Putnam, wife of a Rev. in Yarmouth, Miss H. L. Fox, and Prof. J. B. Foster. I am homesick, I want to see my children, and I must get to them. I do not believe there will be an immediate army movement. Mrs. Capt. [Addison] Lewis of Boothbay and Waterville still here. Have been astounded to hear the sentence they have passed on poor Dr. Wixom. Dismissed from the service in disgrace, forfeit his back pay and fined $150.00 in all amounting to $1590.00. So much for spending about $3000.00 and raising three companies, besides statistics proving him to be one of the most official surgeons in the army. A fitting reward! Oh my country.

FRIDAY APRIL 24TH 1863

Another stormy day. Have written to Miss A. B. Jackson of Brunswick and my dear Frank.—Major [Gilmore] and Lt. Col. [Benjamin Harris] called this evening. Col. said he was waiting for Dr. [John] Moore as he would certainly call here before he went home. Whew! Was'nt he informed that the place to find Dr. Moore was his office![69] How pleasant it will be to be once more free from discordant sounds. Smith was here from the Division Hospital.

---

[67] On March 28, 1863, bad blood between Norval Welch, lieutenant colonel of the 16th Michigan, and Wixom led to a court-martial on the grounds that Wixom was less than fastidious in his management of regimental supplies. On this date, the court decided against Wixom, who was later dishonorably discharged from the service.

[68] Hooker had made enemies of Burnside and Meade after the battle of Fredericksburg, but he did not leave the Army of the Potomac until after the battle of Chancellorsville, still nine days in the future.

[69] HE is obviously sensitive about the implication of her fraternizing with John Moore, a married surgeon.

SATURDAY APRIL 25TH 1863

A terrible windy day. Mrs. [Addison] Lewis still here. Dr. [John] Moore called, advised Mrs. Fogg to ride a rail before trying a ride on horseback. Dr. Wixom called and bade us good bye, he was going to Washington to see what means of redress he could find.—[Albert] Roberts called to see about coming as "guard," straight out of the small pox Hos. He came, but was soon sent back. Dr. Eddy (their doctor) called, <u>came near</u> having a "spute" after he went away, oh these fusses, I must go home.

[See *Appendix letter 18. HE to Mrs. Bosworth, April 25, 1863*.]

SUNDAY APRIL 26TH 1863

Mrs. [Addison] Lewis still here. I have a dreadful cough, put on a mustard draft last night but I do'nt believe it has done me any good. Chaplain [Alvah J.] Bates called here yesterday, brought a letter directed <u>to Mrs. Eaton and Fogg</u>. Mrs. F told me this morning she had not read it yet. Dr. [Horatio N.] Howard sent over a note by Smith the nurse, directed to <u>me</u>, requesting quite a quantity of Hos. supplies for the 10th [Maine Battalion], they go home in about a week, except the three years men.—At the 2nd yesterday, two companies stacked their arms, because they were sure their time was out, and they were marched under guard to Gen. [James] Barnes, who gave them a talking [to] and there is no knowing what the result will be. Oh what a privilege it would be if I could go to church to day.

MONDAY APRIL 27TH 1863

Sudden marching orders for this (the 2nd Corps) this morning. They were all off between eleven and twelve except the 20th Maine and three Batteries. Mrs. F came in from Division Headquarters in a hurry and said we must pack up <u>immediately</u>. Last night I had a hard night with my cough and the disturbance it caused others. "Why! was you mad," said Mrs. [Addison] Lewis to Mrs. F this morning.—Capt. Lewis came over and told his wife she must leave in the first train. Mrs. Vicars [*sic*] was here trying to get lodging. Our new "guard," Albert Roberts, has come. All is commotion in the army and I was talking of going home tomorrow but now I must stop. The Governor [Abner Coburn] came down with his staff yesterday, was with the 20th Maine. Mrs. Fogg brought me from the Regiment three letters, one from Miss Fox, from Mr. Hathaway, and my darling Agnes, also two papers (perhaps from Miss Molly Crane). My dear Agnes does not think I shall be home for several weeks, oh my darling children, can I be absent from you much longer?

TUESDAY APRIL 28TH 1863

A foggy disagreeable day. I have the head ache. Mrs. F has had [Albert] Roberts up here packing bottles. She went over to the 20th yesterday and heard that the Gov. was coming here this afternoon, but he did not make his appearance. They say [Oliver O.] Howard is at the Front, Couch next, and then Meade, but Meade has the "right." No firing yet.[70]

WEDNESDAY APRIL 29TH 1863

To day we have packed one dozen quilts, one dozen large pillows, two dozen small pillows, two dozen shirts, two dozen drawers, two pillow cases of crackers and trunks, and baskets full of every thing. We are to be ready to start with the Ambulance Corps. Yesterday Mrs. Mc Kay called, how strangely she appeared, the doctors thought it would be "nice" for her to go to the Front, they (Miss Gilson and her) had by special effort on the part of the doctors, received permission to remain.

THURSDAY APRIL 30TH 1863

The Governor with Congressman Rice called on us this evening. Who would think he was a Governor? He seemed a little indignant that the "Dr." should have written him about our money when he had had no information of our movements. He, however, after receiving information partly through Mrs. Hathaway's letter to me, that we had really been under the employment of the State, gave us in part pay for our services $63.33 cts. and to pay $50.00 to me for what I had paid of my own money. Mrs. F has at last got her side saddle made. Major Gilmore had a good laugh over it, saying it looked like some horned evil thing that he should not like to mention.

FRIDAY MAY IST 1863

This morning when we found that the ambulance trains were about starting, we got ready for our May day ride, of about 14 miles to United States Ford, passing Hartwood Church, that famous place where the rebels rushed on last winter. On we came tremendously loaded, snap went a bolt, the Lieut. [Ayres] looked cross for we stopped the train, a new bolt was supplied, we passed the famous Eagle Gold mine,[71]

---

[70] At the battle of Chancellorsville, Gen. Howard was commander of the 11th corps, Gen. Darius N. Couch (1822–97) was commander of the 2nd corps, and Meade was commander of the 5th corps. After the battle, Meade was made commander of the Army of the Potomac, but rumors about his promotion were already afloat.

[71] Stafford County gold mine near Holly Corner, Virginia, where mining had begun in the early nineteenth century but was suspended during the Civil War.

looking ancient indeed, we ought to have a little of the dust to make us rich. At last the ambulance train "parked" and we turned up to Mrs. Graves' house.—Here we are, the poor woman's husband has been taken care of by Gen. Patrick.[72] The battle [Chancellorsville] has commenced, we hear the sound of war near at hand and do not know whether we are to cross the river or not.

SATURDAY MAY 2ND 1863

This morning we walked over to "Widow Burton's" as we heard there were wounded men there. They could walk and had left, then we went to the Smith house and I wrote a note informing Dr. [John] Moore where we were and asking his advice about crossing. Soon came a note stating that 50 wounded men would be sent there in ambulances and requesting a dinner for them. We went to work with a will and set all the rest to work, had the satisfaction of seeing Dr. Doolittle provide for them with a great deal of care. We had hot coffee, beef, chicken, and oyster soup.—We also gave them handkerchiefs. Fred B[osworth] was a nice assistant.—Our supplies being limited, we must return to have them replenished.

SUNDAY MAY 3RD 1863

The battle still rages, we barely hold our own, but at Fredericksburg Sedgwick has taken the heights. The 6th Maine has suffered severely, Major Haycock killed. We had a time of it last night. For about three miles the roads were in good condition and we passed a continual train of ambulances and army wagons, but at last we came to a stand point about nine o'clock, and from that time till broad day light we were obliged to sit in our wagon while the train passed. Arriving home, our horses and Johnson were both tired out, so we left them to return in the morning, and finding accommodations in an ambulance train going out, we took our supplies and started about two o'clock. It is a strange Sabbath. The battle has raged fiercely, as we rode up to our Hos. we saw on the field about 700 rebel grey backs who were prisoners. The lower part of the house was crowded with wounded. Capt. Goldman [Goldermann] and Lieut. [Edward] Moore are laying [sic] on stretchers. All round the house the ground is covered, and there is indeed work enough to be done. The poor fellows are so glad to see women here. Capt. [Atherton] Clark is here guarding telegraph.

MONDAY MAY 4TH 1863

Last night, I was cooking and feeding the hungry in the moonlight, till one o'clock, they are constantly coming in. This morning quite an event occurred, it was about

---

[72] Marsena R. Patrick was Union Provost Marshall General; the implication is that Mr. Graves had been imprisoned or worse.

four o' clock, I lay on the bare floor in the little attic with a quilt around me, when <u>bang whirrrrr</u> went the shells, a reb Battery had got the range of the Hos. in the night and commenced shelling us. I felt very calm, perhaps did not realize the extent of the danger. However, it seemed near enough to render it desirable to betake ourselves to a more remote place of shelter. The rebs gave one of their hideous yells, the wounded men, prisoners, ambulance drivers, horses, and mules made one rapid skedaddle. One young fellow came in hand, limping along, offered to take my valise, and begged us to feel that there was no danger, while we could see the shells as they screeched over our heads and burst around us. Two men were killed, several wounded. The firing soon ceased and we returned to the house and went to work preparing breakfast for the hungry. We hear the roar of cannon and musketry, but we are told that [a] Battery was taken. I walked over to the Hos. of the 12th Corps, they are greatly in need of help but I cannot go there, I saw the mangled remains of one of the poor fellows who was killed by the shell. I returned to the house and put up five papers of corn starch and farina, some crackers, a can of chicken, one of milk, and sent it over to the Hospital. Rev. Mr. [Royal C.] Spaulding's son of Houlton, full of mischief, has been very helpful. But oh! language cannot express my joy and gratitude to see Edward W[hittier] all safe and hear that George [Whittier] was safe also. But they have suffered severely, Capt. Leppein has lost a leg, Lieut. Twichell two fingers, and a severe contusion from a shell, and Lieut. [Greenlief] Stevens a severe contusion in the shoulder.—Oh! the awful scenes of suffering. Dr. Hezless called to day and while there I called him to look at a young man whose arm had been amputated at the shoulder, he tried to offer him a little assistance but the ligatures around the arteries became misplaced and he soon bled to death. Oh how sad I feel that I did not realize he was so near his end. Strange Dr. Hezless, he said in parting he hoped I should be killed before he saw me again, [I] exclaiming "how can you be so wicked doctor?" He replied, "why, I know you will go straight to heaven." Go on.—Dallas the ambulance "stretcher carrier" from Phil. is a fine little fellow full of mischief.—Glad enough was I to see Johnson and our team back this afternoon. We called at the Major [Gilmore]'s tent this evening and Col. Chamberlain came home with us.

TUESDAY MAY 5TH 1863

In the midst of our work we are told we must leave the ground, a general order has been given. Mrs. F was determined to cross the river, although Col. Chamberlain wrote a note discouraging it. She left us and took an ambulance while we started for the Smith house. I had no sooner arrived there, than I received a note that a hundred men were there on the way, who needed a dinner. Mrs. Husband had come and was dressing wounds. Mrs. Mc Kay soon made her appearance from across the river. We fed the men, i.e., I procured a detail of men and cooked them broth over a camp fire, but as there was another train coming, Mrs. Fogg determined to remain and get supper for them while I went on with the team.—Soon after we started, a tremendous thunder and hail storm commenced, the ambulance leaked like a sieve and notwithstanding I had two quilts, I was drenched to my skin. I met the 6th Maine and Capt's. Furlong and Bassford assured me of Hugh [Fogg]'s safety. He was with the Colonel [Burnham].

WEDNESDAY MAY 6_TH 1863

Well, last night I had an adventure. The streams were so swollen that the bridges were carried away and after being mixed up with supply, ammunition and ambulance trains in all sorts of ways, we were at last left alone, lost our way, learned that the bridge over Stoneman's Switch was carried away, so there was no help for it, and drenched to my skin, I rode up to a house, found it crammed full of wounded soldiers who were there on the same errand as ourselves. There was not even standing room, but the doctor managed to find me a corner long enough to lie down in an old attic full of old rubbish & wounded soldiers. There, as he gave me a dry blanket I rolled myself up in a corner after one o' clock and lay in the dark with our poor boys, not one of whose faces I had ever seen till morning. At five I rose and impressed men to go into the old cook house and build me a big fire, bring camp kettles, and fill them with water, and then I made a good, warm breakfast for 150 men, and they assured me they had enough.—I gave four shirts to shivering men, literally naked, and slippers to others. As soon as possible I left and reached home about ten o' clock. Mrs. Fogg and Mrs. Husband came in, in about an hour and a half. We were all sleepy and we laid [sic] down and were sound asleep when who should march in without knocking but Dr. Hezless, and woke us up exclaiming, "whipped again."—Oh! what can this mean? are we wholly defeated? I dare not think of it. The Regiments are all returning to their old camping ground and [Stonewall] Jackson has retaken the Heights at Fredericksburg.[73]

THURSDAY MAY 7TH 1863

Edward W[hittier] has been to see me to day, dear boy, how much I love him. Mrs. Husband left this noon. My cough is very severe and I have put on mustard, but I have persevered and written letters to Mrs. Bosworth, Mrs. Whittier, Hatty Belle, Frank, and Agnes.—Mrs. Fogg has been to see Dr. [John] Moore and to the 20th and has returned with the impression that there is to be an immediate movement of the army, so adieu to my brilliant hopes of getting home in a week or so. I trust I shall be directed aright. I hear that Colonel [Clark] Edwards of the 5th Maine was killed.—Oh horrid war.

---

[73] Though the Confederate general was credited with the victory at Chancellorsville, he had been wounded by his own troops on May 2 and would die on May 10.

FRIDAY MAY 8TH 1863

A damp, chilly day. Mrs. F is out riding but I do not envy her. My cold is bad. Hooper of the 2nd Maine was here yesterday and took 18 pr. of socks for their poor boys.—Their Brigade has marched out again, whether to go on picket or return to the picket I know not. Mrs. Husband says in their Div. Hos. of the 5th Corps they have prayer meetings, and the other night the head surgeon of that corps sent word to them to "stop their infernal noise."—

[*See Appendix letter 19. HE to Mrs. Greenough, May 8, 1863.*]

SATURDAY MAY 9TH 1863

To day I loaded the ambulance with as much as I could carry and went to the three divisions of the 5th Corps in Hos. and Brooks Station. They were glad indeed to receive my supplies, did not have much time to talk with the boys, except those belonging to the 20th who came out of their tents to see me, so many of them as were able.—Chaplain [Orson] Clark is indeed a good chaplain [even] if he is a Universalist and I am glad he has been detailed for service here.[74]—Mrs. Husband has left and gone to the 3rd Corps and they seem glad to be rid of her because she was determined to reign <u>King</u> or not reign at all.—I have to night received a package of letters and learn that my dear Frank has been dangerously ill in Hos. The first letter was written me by a friend of his, it was written nearly a fortnight ago, but he seems to be better now, as he has written a few lines himself, but I am <u>very</u> anxious and shall go to W[ashington] tomorrow, and thence to Chantilly. Oh how can I bear to think of his being so sick and I so near and yet ignorant of his illness!—If I find him better, I shall leave for home immediately, dear home! I am really almost sick.

SUNDAY MAY 10TH 1863

Sabbath day and a miserable sick, sick day it has been to me.—I parted with Mrs. F feeling a little bad to leave her alone, though I imagine she feels competent to take the whole charge and now she will have no check to her schemes.—Dr. Wixom went up on the boat, he was determined I should dine with him but I positively declined, partly because I did not wish to eat and partly because I was not willing he should pay for it.—I know I am in a burning fever, am I going to be seized with pneumonia? Pain in my side severe.—Mr. Hayes met us at the boat (I was glad), we went first to a private boarding house, where Mrs. Sampson boards (at her request), but they <u>would not take me in</u>, and fainting I at length reached the Metropolitan.[75]—Dr. Wixom

---

[74] Baptists and Universalists disagreed about salvation, the latter believing that all of humanity could be redeemed, the former, more in keeping with Calvinism, that only a select group would be saved.

[75] The Metropolitan Hotel in Washington, D.C., was located at the corner of 6th Street and Pennsylvania Avenue. In the tradition of luxury hotels built in the mid-nineteenth century, space was configured such that women traveling alone or with children inhabited separate parlors and dining rooms from men. See Brucken, "In the Public Eye," 211.

prepared medicine and brought it to me.—If I can stand up I shall go to Chantilly tomorrow.

MONDAY MAY 11TH 1863

Here I am still at the Metropolitan. I am unable to leave my bed, can only sit up a few minutes at a time. Dr. Wixom has been here three times to day. He feels my pulse, shakes his head and says, "Mrs. Eaton, you are not going to be sick." At the same time, I know he thinks I shall have a fever, but with God's help I shall start for Chantilly tomorrow, for my anxiety about Frank is so great that that alone will make me sick.—Mrs. Snow, the landlady is very kind, she has repeatedly sent a waiter with eatables, but I cannot eat anything. If I go tomorrow Mr. Hayes will accompany me for which I am very glad as I know I am too sick to take care of myself.

TUESDAY MAY 12TH 1863

How thankful I ought to be this night. I came home trembling, afraid even to inquire after my dear boy, lest bad news might be in store for me. But how mercifully have I been dealt with, on arriving at the camp the second person who came to the ambulance was my dear son, though it was so near night that I could only distinguish him by his voice.—I left W[ashington] early in the morning, taking the horse cars to the boat, then the boat to Alexandria. Then we had a long, long walk in the heat, from superintendent of the rail road to provost martial to get passes.—I had no certificates with me (like Mrs. F) and had to depend on Mr. Hayes for I was too sick to talk myself.[76]—We had to wait hours for the <u>cars</u> and the superintendent was anything but a gentleman, faint as I was he would not offer me a seat in the Office and I was obliged to take shelter in the nearest eating saloon I could find. The heat was dreadful, at last it was time to start. At the cars they overhauled my valise and there was my brandy flask. They took my valise from me and telling them I was an "army nurse," I warned them against meddling with any part of my "side arms." Arriving at Fairfax Station, we found ourselves again shelterless, besides I had been unfortunate enough to catch a spark in my eye. It was painful, but a surgeon connected with the Regiment who were doing guard duty at this place carefully removed the obstruction. The Colonel was absent, but the Lieut. in charge gave orders for an ambulance detail to carry us to the 25th Regiment near Chantilly, and after so many hindrances we were at last on the direct route.

[76] Isabella Fogg was careful to travel with endorsement letters from officers and surgeons. In the chaotic conditions of relief work, such testimonials often provided entrée to workers in the field. HE, who was critical of Fogg's assertiveness, chose not to ask any of the men with whom she worked to provide her with this safeguard.

1864: OCTOBER 12 TO DECEMBER 24

WEDNESDAY OCT. 12TH 1864

Left my dear home (which this morning seems dearer than ever), in the cars at quarter to nine for Boston. A pleasant day, nothing new on the route. Mr. Drake kindly offered every assistance in his power. Arrived in Boston 1/2 past two and immediately Mr. Hayes who met me at the Depot procured a carriage for the Old Colony Depot, where I remained without speaking except to procure a lunch of ham with a cup of tea till 1/2 past five, when our company, again assembling, we took the Fall River Road for New York.

THURSDAY OCT. 13TH 1864

It is a little singular that I start on my second trip to the Army just two years to a day from the first one.—Last night I had a first rate berth in the Ladies Saloon, wide enough for two, slept well but was sadly disappointed to learn that we should not connect with the Phil. train (too late), but must wait over.—Quite a company of us went to "Lovejoy's," our own party, with Dr. Hawes of the 19th, Lieut. [Charles B.] Hall of the 30th, &c., &c.[1] I have been out to Central Park to day, a place I have

---

[1] Lovejoy's Hotel, a New York City institution from the 1830s, was located on Park Row at the corner of Beekman Place. It was configured on the "European Plan," which meant that

long wished to see. It is beautiful indeed, not however much like an English Park, on some accounts more diversified, so many rocks, but the magnificent trees are wanting and the <u>deer</u> may not roam at will but are enclosed within a wire fence. The <u>swans</u>, however, and other water fowl have their freedom in their native element. It was about an hour's ride from Lovejoy's to the Park. Have formed a very pleasant acquaintance with a Mrs. Hyde and sister. Mr. H[yde] is <u>sutler</u> for the Campbell Hospital, Washington and they urgently requested me to call on them in W[ashington].—<u>Have written to Frank and the children</u> and this evening have had a very pleasant chat with an old gentleman who though a little "coppery" was very social and reasonable.[2] Sat till 1/2 past nine in the parlor and now find I have a very pleasant room. Hope to leave in the morning at seven.

FRIDAY OCT. 14TH 1864

Rose this morning before six and ordered breakfast, cup of tea, steak, potato, and French roll, for which I pay 40 cts. at this Hotel. We order what we please and pay accordingly. The air is very cold, <u>snow</u> was flying yesterday, and again I am disappointed. First, I learn that the cars do not leave till eight, and next that no "<u>military tickets</u>" are taken except in the <u>ten</u> [o' clock] train. Well, we shall get there by and by, only the most aggravating part is that I might have gone yesterday had <u>I</u> known of this train and I believe Mr. Hayes did know it. On arriving in Phil. about 1/2 past two and seating ourselves in the horse cars, the conductor announced that we were too late for the Washington train and must wait in Phil. till 1/2 past ten. What a commotion! Beside myself there were three ladies sitting beside me, Mrs. Camp and Miss Walker bound for Baltimore and Mrs. Franklin for W[ashington], who were without attendants and much perplexed. Soon the horse cars were off the track and as we rode about two squares corduroy style, it broke up all formality and we were quite acquainted. They all attached themselves to Mr. Hayes, who conducted us to the Continental.[3]—Thanks to Mr. Hayes, I was soon made very welcome in Mr. Spofford's family, one of the proprietors of the house, and Mr. and Mrs. Spofford,

---

guests could dine in or out as they wished. Horace Greeley ate there and claimed that it had good bread. A reference to the hotel in Horatio Alger's *Ragged Dick and Struggling Upward* (1868) confirms its reputation for good food and elite company. On November 26, 1864—not two months after HE dined there—secessionists set fire to the hotel twice during the morning. Foiled both times, they were apprehended and prosecuted. The building was not seriously damaged.

[2] HE's use of "coppery" is shorthand for Copperhead, the group of northern Democrats who opposed the war and counseled reconciliation with the Confederacy, even if it meant making slavery legal.

[3] Under construction from 1857 to 1860, the Continental Hotel was located at 824–838 Chestnut Street in Philadelphia.

with her sister, did all in their power to make me comfortable, assuring me that they were only too happy to do any thing for the soldier's friend. They have loaded us down with niceties for Gen. Connor. I have partaken of dinner and they would not let me leave without eating a hot oyster stew brought to their room.

SATURDAY OCT. 15TH 1864

Washington at last. A bright moonlight night with very pleasant company made the ride not unpleasant, although the wind blew round my head so, that I know I have taken cold. About 1/2 past six Mr. Hayes and myself took up our march for the Clarendon Hotel,[4] kept by Mr. Dodge of Maine who formerly kept the City Hotel, Portland. He professed an acquaintance with me through Frank, and I partook of breakfast free of expense.—Then I went to the [Maine State Relief] Agency and find we have lots of stores ready for the "Front." Mr. Hayes says he will not be able to leave till Tuesday. I have been to Douglas Hos. to call on Gen. Connor. Noble looking man, I was more indignant than ever at the work of rebel bullets.[5]—He seems very cheerful and hoping against hope, for they tell him it is very doubtful whether the bones will connect as they form. He showed me the pieces that had come out, some of which were the new formation. His leg is swung in a frame, which is a great relief to him. A Mrs. Clark gets him his breakfast and supper and he is well provided for. I wish the poor privates fared as well. Capt. [John R.] Myrick of the Cavalry is very sick at the Agency and ought to be in a Hos. but is on his way home on furlough and is unwilling to be removed. I have called at Col. Gilmore's this afternoon by his special request, but did not find any one at home but the daughter.[6] I have a nice room at the Clarendon with a sofa, rocking chair, two tables with all the rest of the necessary furniture. Musquitoes [sic] are very annoying but I have a canopied bed and can shut them out for the night.

SABBATH OCT. 16TH 1864

I am most happily provided for at Col. Gilmore's. How little I ever thought to reap the benefit of attentions paid him in the Army. Mrs. G[ilmore] is a lovely woman and he is as good as ever. This morning, just as I was locking my door to start for church, Col. G made his appearance and accompanied me there. Heard a young man preach named <u>Custis</u>, the name of the pastor is <u>Grey</u>. The text was on seeing, with

---

[4] The Clarendon was located at Pennsylvania Avenue at the corner of 6th Street. Both the Clarendon and Metropolitan were located in different quadrants of the same intersection.

[5] Connor had been wounded in the thigh at the Wilderness five months earlier.

[6] The "Major" had been promoted to lieutenant colonel of the 20th after the battle of Chancellorsville, when Joshua Lawrence Chamberlain became its colonel. Gilmore's wife and daughter had taken up residence with him in Washington after he began serving on court-martials.

the three men, as into the fiery furnace, the form of another like unto the son of God, walking with them.⁷ Subject, the prisoner of God with his people in their afflictions. A good, comforting discourse. After service Col. G would take no refusal for my going to his house. I have been this afternoon with the Col. and his daughter to Lincoln Hos., the largest in Washington, containing <u>2000</u> beds.⁸ They have a railway track with a car to furnish food for the sick with rapidity and every thing after the same style of complete order. Saw a number of the 20th Maine, one <u>very</u> low (young [Llewellyn] Cushman Comp[any] G). Wounded while lying down, ball entering the tip of the shoulder and crossing down through the lungs and body where it still remains. Poor fellow, he will not live many days, he wished me to see his brother Wales Cushman, same Comp[any] and Regt. Many of the men knew me and two or three were right glad to see me, shaking hands most heartily, particularly Meservy. Prescott I met at the Rooms, when he saw me he exclaimed, "oh! Mrs. Eaton, that mustard plaster you put on saved my life, I have the marks of it now," verily it must have been a strong one.

MONDAY OCT. 17TH 1864

Slept last night on the Col. [Gilmore]'s <u>camp bed</u> in the parlor. He wanted to sleep on it and let me occupy his, but that I would not consent to. It is a funny little affair that shuts up like a frame on which to reel silk. The prospect of getting to the "Front" looks a little dark.—Mr. Hayes has seen Dr. Crane, Adjt. to Surgeon General Barnes and he will not give the least encouragement, except an order comes direct from Surgeon Dalton, City Point, and this will delay me about a week. Well, we will see what we will see. I will, <u>in person, apply to every source</u> and be <u>refused</u> before I will give up going tomorrow.—I have been again to Douglas Hos. to day to see Gen. Connor and give him his pillow.—He is a little discouraged, says he has met with a great misfortune as Mrs. Clark cannot provide his meals any longer on account of her health. Called on Mrs. Morrill (Mrs. Mayhew's friend) by special request, she reminds me so much of Mrs. Shurtleff that it seems as if I must be talking to her.— Stopped and took dinner with them and finished another <u>letter for Agnes, Hatty, and Mrs. [Ellen Usher] Bacon.</u>

TUESDAY OCT. 18TH 1864

Hav'nt I accomplished it? There is something in a little determination or I should not be found this afternoon safely on board the *John Morgan* bound for <u>City Point</u>. I rose this morning with determination not to be foiled in the attempt if

---

⁷ Reference to the parable of Shadrack, Meshack, and Abednego in the Book of Daniel, chapter 3. Belief in God is tested when the three enter a fiery furnace and exit unscathed.

⁸ It actually had 2,575 beds.

perseverance would do it. Bade them good bye at Col. Gilmore's, receiving a most hearty invitation to make their house my home.—Took horse cars for Maine Agency, where I found Mr. Hinds just going to the War Department. Proposed to accompany him and was ushered into Major Pollouze's [Pelouze] presence, who in a very dignified manner declined any action and referred me to Adjt. Crane, Gen. Barnes being absent. Going to that Department I was informed, <u>no pass could be granted</u>, unless indeed Miss Dix might favor it. "Then I shall go," said I, "where can I find Miss Dix?" "She is at the St. Elisabeth Hos. Insane Asylum." So assuring Mr. Hinds I could find it, I took cars for Navy Yard which is quite out of the City. It was now near eleven. At the termination of horse rail road, I was told I must take omnibus three miles out of the city for Hos. After a smart quarrel with the driver as to which would go first, I took seat in one with my eyes on all three, and when I saw another starting I jumped out and in to that, while there took place a fight over my devoted head. However, I reached the Hos., marched up the walk, rung the bell, and on being referred to the surgeon was politely informed that Miss Dix never stopped there and her residence was 430 15th St., a few steps from the point I had left in the morning. I was so excited lest I should fail for want of time, that I waited for no omnibus but footed it in haste all the way back to the horse cars. By running a little I reached one that was just starting & back to the Treasury Buildings I went, thence to 430, where I found Miss Dix at home and very happy to meet me, said she "was only too happy to grant my request," fitted out an order expressly for me appended to a Fortress Monroe pass and sent me <u>free of expense</u> on my way rejoicing. At the Agency they were quite surprised at my success, but somehow I knew <u>she</u> would fancy my appearance, whether that is complimentary to me or not.—I hurried matters now and was ready for the boat and glad to feel perfectly independent of every one but Miss Dix in getting my pass.—The boat is a miserable affair.

WEDNESDAY OCT. 19TH 1864

A regular slow coach but we have fine weather and I hope to reach my destination sometime this evening. Ladies are scarce on this route but there is a Miss Willets from New York[9] on board, a volunteer nurse returning to Hos., and just as I was securing a corner in the dining room on a settee for my night's repose, she came offering a part of her stateroom. I had a miserable night with a terrible cold which I took going to W[ashington], but to day I am very much better, quite like myself. Have taken breakfast and dinner on board, neither of them good, paid 50 cts. for my breakfast and $1.00 for dinner, simply beef and vegetables, no pastry.—The weather is delightful but not so warm as I expected. Passed Point Lookout about 1/2 past

---

[9] HE met Georgiana Willets en route, who was from Jersey City, New Jersey. Willets had been serving at City Point in the second division hospitals since June 1864.

three this morning and reached Fortress Monroe at 1/2 past eleven, when the time for leaving that place for City Point is ten.[10]—But with no accidents surely I ought not to complain of the delay, but rather be thankful I am almost there. Saw Chesapeake Hos., but it is far from the landing and not at all accessible from the Boat, so I could only give Capt. Staniels my good wishes. My next, I hope, will be dated City Point.

THURSDAY OCT. 20TH 1864

About nine o' clock last evening found us at the Hos. I have on the Boat formed the acquaintance of Mrs. Dr. Bermister [Burmeister], he being surgeon in charge of the 2nd Corps. The ambulance came for her and took us all in. Arriving at the tent all was darkness, candle burned out.[11] Mrs. Mayhew, hearing an accident had happened to the boat, was out making a call and Rachel asleep, keeping tent.[12] All looks very strange, the tent is raised in a pretty spot on the banks of the Appomattox near its confluence with the James. In the foreground they are continually watering their horses and driving their army teams into the River, on the opposite bank of the cove are Gen. Grant's Headquarters, further in the distance is Bermuda Hundred,[13] while from Butler's Division comes the booming of the cannon. They have a "mess" consisting of Dr. O'Meagher, Div. Surg. of the 2nd Corps, and Dr. Terhune & this I do'nt fancy much, I had far rather live as I did before when with the Army. The fact is, I do'nt like the present work at all, we are not allowed to go to the Front, though there are continued calls. We have been into a few of the wards in this great village, but there seems to be but a few very sick ones here.—Mrs. Bermister called while we were out.

[10] Fortress Monroe was located on Chesapeake Bay at the mouth of the James River and at the tip of the peninsula where the peninsular campaign was fought in 1862. City Point was seventy miles upriver on the James from Fortress Monroe or approximately eighty miles south by rail from Fredericksburg and Chancellorsville, where HE had spent the latter part of her first tour of duty in 1862–63. The trip by water from Washington necessitated cruising southeast toward Chesapeake Bay on the Potomac River, past the mouths of the Rappahannock and York Rivers, and into the James at Hampton Roads.

[11] According to Rebecca Usher, who arrived at City Point in January 1865 just after HE departed, the MSRA presence there was "a stockaded tent with canvas roof & three rooms papered with newspaper. The first is the soldiers' reading room with an open fire, a table with newspapers & writing materials & long wooden benches—& three berths one above another—the second is our sleeping room parlor & store closet combined; & is heated by an airtight stove of unique pattern & the third is our kitchen & pantry" (Rebecca Usher Diary, January 19, 1865, Usher Family Papers, Collection 9, MHS).

[12] Rachel was an African American, most likely a contraband.

[13] The Bermuda Hundred was a line of Confederate earthworks in the vicinity of Petersburg, Virginia, that Gen. Benjamin Butler tried to assault without success from mid-May to mid-June 1864.

One of Maine's "vast army of women" relief workers, Ruth Swett Mayhew, pictured in a carte de visite from the war years, looked after Eaton's children in Portland in November 1864 while Eaton attended to soldiers at City Point. When Eaton returned home before Christmas, Mrs. Mayhew took her place with the Maine State Relief Agency. MAINE HISTORICAL SOCIETY, PORTLAND

FRIDAY OCT. 21ST 1864

Two calls this morning before we were through breakfast, for woolen clothing and canned milk, &c. for the Christian Commission. There were two or three calls yesterday from the same source. They say they have not a woolen shirt at the Point. Calls to day from the 20th and 19th at the Front. Chaplain [Samuel H.] Merrill stopped with us last night and breakfasted this morning. We had a very pleasant evening talking as if at home. He is on his way to Wash[ington] on business, and is strongly hoping that he may be able to perfect an exchange that will result in the release of his son. Mrs. Painter is a dear little woman with such winning ways that she gets all she asks for. She is building famous winter quarters.

SATURDAY OCT. 22ND 1864

We have Captain Twitchell dining with us to day.[14] He looks natural as life and brings up old scenes very vividly. Poor Mrs. F has to take it from all of them. Getchell, Hos. Steward of the Cavalry, was here and has taken quite a lot of things to them. Their term of service is about out, but they have been filled up by Barker's Cavalry.[15] More Christian Commission men here for clothing and canned milk. I have written [to] Mattie and Frank to day. Have had a call from Miss [Adelaide W.] Smith who was with Mrs. Mayhew and has been promoted to one of the kitchens. She is a bright sparkling lady full of wit and quick repartee. The Massachusetts agent has just been here and requested to find accommodations for a Mrs. Kipp who has come here to seek for the remains of her husband. Poor thing, I hardly think she will find him. We shall have to stow [sic] close here, she will have to take Rachel's bed while Rachel takes the floor. We have called on sweet Mrs. Bermister to day, a most lovely woman. Dr. Baxter and Dr. [Thomas C.] Barker returned the calls we made on them yesterday and begged so hard for album quilts that we finally gave them on condition that they made it up to us in blankets. Next came Dr. Lowenthall and he made an exchange after much pleading, sending us another quilt in its place which he had procured from the Sanitary.

SUNDAY OCT. 23RD 1864

Have written to Mrs. Bosworth to day. This morning I had fully intended to go to meeting at the Christian Commission tent, but could not leave at the hour, so was disappointed. Mr. Shaw formerly of Portland connected with the Commission called here and I gave him my opinion on the importance of the Agencies working in

---

[14] Adelbert Twitchell had been promoted from lieutenant of the 5th Battery to captain of the 7th Battery in the 1st Maine Light Artillery in 1864.

[15] Reference to Gen. Lafayette Curry Baker (1826–68) who led the 1st D.C. Cavalry on reconnaissance from the battle of Chancellorsville through 1864.

harmony, as I have not felt since I came here, that there was that reciprocity of feeling that should exist. Charlie Mero, our old tent guard has been to see me, and right glad he seemed to be too. Mrs. Kipp has been very fortunate in finding the remains of her husband in the Hos. yard; she is much relieved as she expected to have to go to the "Provost" to seek for it. Miss [Adelaide W.] Smith and Miss Blackmar have been here to day, also Mrs. Bermister and Uncle Richard.[16] Mrs. Bermister has begged another quilt.— I think I shall hear something further from the Christian Commission, for I talked pretty plain and one of their agents has been in again to say that they wished to see me. This evening we attended services at the Colored Hospital. The preacher was a sergeant in one of the colored regiments and an eloquent man he is too. He is proud of the army blue and the stripes too. The colored bredren [sic] and sisters were quite excited while he explained that there are <u>special seasons of salvation.</u>—It was a queer place to be in. Over head old bedding hung in festoons from the rafters, and the lanterns gave a dim light over the strange mixture of black and white. When he spoke of the breaking up of denominational differences, he showed a very clear insight into human nature. First the Baptist and Methodist, no longer disputing, next the Presbyterian, high over all, next the Episcopalian looking down with haughty frown, and lastly the Catholic crying out, "Avaunt, I will have none of ye."[17] Dr. Hammond, the surgeon in charge, seems much interested for the colored people.

MONDAY OCT. 24TH 1864

Mrs. Mayhew and Mr. Hayes have gone and left poor me all alone, but there is such continued work to be done that I shall not have much time to think, indeed it is almost impossible to get time to write one connected sentence. More things for the Commission, it is slippers now. Capt. Plummer of the 20th has been in to day from the Front, also Rev. Mr. Patten, chaplain of the 32nd. To the latter I have given a quilt, half a dozen towels, three shirts, and three pair of drawers for his Regiment. It is one continued call for crackers, fish, pickles, &c. besides the woolen goods. Mrs. Kipp will go home tomorrow, having had the body of her husband embalmed. I have <u>written to Agnes and Hatty Belle directing the letter to Hatty Belle</u>.
[See Appendix letter 21. HE to Hatty Belle Eaton, October 24, 1864.]

TUESDAY OCT. 25TH 1864

Mrs. Kipp has gone and Capt. Fogler of the 20th is here to dinner to day.—He was highly delighted to receive a quilt marked with his wife's name. A fine man, he is one

---

[16] Most likely an African American worker at City Point and a contraband.

[17] Although the preacher's words suggest that Catholics set themselves apart from other Christian denominations, mid-nineteenth-century anti-Catholic sentiment is a more likely interpretation. "Avaunt" is an interjection that means "Begone."

of those who I trust will come out <u>morally</u> unscathed by the temptations of the army. Gave him also some Bay Rum. Capt. Plummer was glad to take a can of peaches, a can of tomatoes, two pillows, and a quilt. This evening Miss [Adelaide W.] Smith, Miss Blackmar, Major [William] Baker, and Dr. Weevil [Wevill] called and I had a pleasant evening, and now I sit here alone questioning whether our supplies will be safe in the outer tent, really if the state of things was only known. I do'nt think there is honesty enough among our soldiers to save us from a guerilla raid. Here is our cellar, right out under the "fly" with no protection, and all our eggs and butter there. Miss Smith has been relieved by written order from her position in the cook house and Miss Hancock put in her place.[18] I have offered her the protection of our tent, for, poor thing, her purse with all her money and papers was stolen the other day.[19] She has been in again to tell me that Dr. O'Meagher had asked her to take a section and she had commenced her work. Dear little Mrs. Painter went out with Mrs. Vanderslice to day to seek for the body of the son of Mrs. V. While they were searching, with Dr. Burr the embalmer with them, a major rode up with a <u>very heavy</u> escort of Cavalry and inquired her business. She gave him the information when he informed her that she was three miles beyond our picket line and he would advise a rapid retreat. It did not take them long to meditate and effect a "skedaddle." Such a time as I have had supplying the wants of our Maine boys to day. Two or three of them have had a great time with their "comfort bags" and they all promise to write return letters.[20] Miss Smith, Miss Blackmar called. In the evening I went out to the cook tent and got John to come in and sit awhile with me, he seems so lonely, also Mr. Jones and Mr. Hall, nurse and ward master, came in.

WEDNESDAY OCT. 26TH 1864

All day the sick and wounded have been brought in from the Div. Hos. in the Front. The whole army seems to be in motion, some with five days rations and some with eight. I have <u>written to Samuel and Elisabeth</u> [Whitney] to day, also to <u>Sarah Caduc</u>.—For once we have sat down to our table with none but our "mess." They have been here from the 2nd Battery for supplies and I have given them crackers & pickles, corn starch, nutmegs, cider, tomatoes, blackberry cordial, towels & handkerchiefs, and Jamaica ginger. Miss Nye has also been in, she

---

[18] Hancock confirmed in a letter dated October 29, 1864 that she had "charge of the cookhouse," but in an earlier letter (October 17) complained that Dr. Burmeister had named Anna Morris Holstein to that post. She anticipated that this appointment would be short-lived because she had influential friends like Dr. O'Meagher. See Hancock, *South After Gettysburg*, 152–54.

[19] Curiously, Ada Smith reports in her 1911 memoir that someone attempted to steal her tentmate's (Frances M. Nye's) purse, not hers. See Smith, *Reminiscences of an Army Nurse*, 94–95.

[20] Women in aid societies in Portland and elsewhere supplied Maine's soldiers with early versions of the sleeping bag; grateful recipients could write a note of thanks to the seamstress, whose name was included with the bag.

came for gin and I gave her cologne and camphor. I have also given quantities of blackberry cordial, blackberry preserves, currant jelly, towels, comfort bags, apple sauce, crackers, pickles, &c. to the soldiers. Mrs. Price sent for crackers and I supplied her. Georgie Wheelock has been in and deposited $50.00 with me to be sent home. Uncle Richard made me a call. John is quite unwell to day. The stove smokes frightfully. Mr. Hall has come to sleep in and guard the front tent to night. This evening I thought surely some one was thieving in there and I rushed in, light in hand, when who should it be but Miss White Cat. Miss Hancock came rushing in this evening to see Dr. O'Meagher for information as to what she should do to feed the new men that had been brought in. They went to the Chris. Com. to get crackers but did not succeed, and he said she must make a cauldron of farina and mush for them. Two of the nurses have been ordered to report to the Provost Marshal, that they might leave tomorrow morning. The nurses seem to be full of jealousy lest one receive more honor than the other.

THURSDAY OCT. 27TH 1864

The continued war which makes the earth to tremble, announces that the battle has commenced.[21] God grant that it may be a decisive one for our beloved cause. I have been anxious for the movement to commence during the favorable weather, if we were ready for it and yet now I shrink. How quietly the doctors talked at the dinner table to day as to which wards should be reserved for the wounded as they were brought in, just as if they were arranging for an every day affair and it is right that it should be so. Miss [Adelaide W.] Smith came in this morning and <u>kept house</u> while I went to see Surgeon Dalton. He was not in and I reported myself to Dr. Collins, who seemed quite perplexed. I was a sort of nondescript, neither one thing nor the other.—I did not belong to Miss Dix, though Miss Dix sent me, I belonged to a Maine Agency but had no pass from Surgeon General Barnes. He turned my pass over and over, wrapped a paper round it to endorse it, then concluded not to do so, thought neither party had better be trammeled and so the conference ended and I bowed myself out. There comes a Christian Commission man, another flannel shirt wanted and half a dozen handkerchiefs. Oh! the roar, how many are passing into eternity! While I was out I called a moment on Miss Blackmar. I do'nt wonder they do'nt want their tent taken from them and all the pretty fixings removed. They have a carpet on their floor. Stopped a moment at Miss Hancock's department where she was ordering the alterations about her stoves.—From thence to make a call on Mrs. Bermister.—The Doctor [Burmeister] came in and sat a few moments but he was greatly disturbed at the loss of a plum pudding that "Aunt Betsy" had just been in consternation about, having found the ingredients sailing round loosely in the pot. Mrs. Bermister had <u>pinned</u> it into the towel and the doctor contended it should have

---

[21] Hatcher's Run, part of the Petersburg campaign.

been <u>tied</u> in. <u>I</u>, in this matter, agree with the latter. Returning I found Mrs. Dunbar here and three or four soldier boys. The Germans keep up a continual chatter in the next tent, they chatter me to sleep every night. Dr. Hawes called this morning, he has sent in his resignation which has not been accepted as yet, showed me a bullet that whistled past his ears the other evening as he sat in his bomb proof writing to his wife.— "Have you any tobacco?" "No, no tobacco." It rains quite fast, how pleasant it sounds as it pats on the tent, but it prevents the boys from coming to get their wants supplied. I have not had any thing like as quiet a day since I came out.—Mrs. M[ayhew] has gone off and carried the paper on which she drew her rations and which I was expecting to use.—The doctors try to make me feel easy about it, but I do'nt. Dr. Terhune says it's a pity if they ca'nt carry on this table, but I do'nt think so. It was so warm this morning when I went out to make my calls that I wore nothing but the large cape of my dress and my scarf.—Now the rain fairly <u>pours</u>, oh the poor boys! I am suspicious of that Rachel, she has got company in the front tent this afternoon and just now when she thought my back was turned, I saw her fussing with our boxes where she had no business to be.

FRIDAY OCT. 28TH 1864

I was indeed delighted yesterday afternoon to meet Dr. Hersom once more. He was on his way back to his Regt. Next came Chaplain [Samuel] Merrill from Washington and we spent a pleasant evening indeed, while the rain poured in torrents outside. The only trouble was a smoky stove, so as it was not cold, after shedding many tears over the disaster, we let the fire go out. About 1/2 past nine a most terrific cannonading commenced, the earth shook, and the heavens above and earth beneath were a scene of conflict.[22] Truly it was a war of the elements and I was glad I had company in the front tent. The large boxes filled with cans and bottles that are arranged for cupboards at the side of the tent seemed to waver as the bottles rattled together, I jumped up and partly dressed myself to be ready if the tent should go. This morning all is quiet and we are looking for the wounded to be brought in.—They are coming, but we cannot hear anything definite of the success of the movement. Dr. Hersom has gone to his Regt. He gave me his photograph before he left. I think him one of the best of surgeons. Lieut. [Hiram] Morse of the 20th has called and sat awhile.—Dr. O'Meagher brought two to dinner with him to day. Dr. Gladfelter [Glatfelter] has connected himself with our mess, but I am more than ever dissatisfied with this way of working, I reach the suffering and destitute <u>so indirectly</u>. I do'nt want to sit here and do the polite for a mess table, but would much prefer to live

---

[22] Seventeen thousand Union troops advanced toward Confederate lines at Burgess' Mill south of Petersburg on October 27, 1864 (Hatcher's Run). Union losses amounted to 166 men killed and 1,028 wounded. Confederate losses were not tabulated. Union troops were not successful in gaining ground.

on hard tack and a cup of tea and be untrammeled.—Dr. [William] Eaton, another of our <u>first rate</u> army surgeons, took dinner with us to day. He came down with an army train of wounded.—Miss [Adelaide W.] Smith was here a short time, she is still expecting her house to be pulled down over her head.

[*See Appendix letter 22. HE to Hatty Belle Eaton, October 28, 1864.*]

SATURDAY OCT. 29TH 1864

I do'nt know what I shall do with Rachel.—She has not a clean table cloth for tomorrow, and the bedding has been tucked away without being washed this week. Scolding her has no effect. Chaplain [Samuel Merrill] on his way from home to join his Regt. dined with me to day. Oh! dear what a discouraging repulse this last move has been to the army. I have written to <u>Frank</u>, <u>Agnes</u>, <u>Hatty</u>, and <u>Lizzie</u> to day, and received Agnes and Hatty's journals a day or two since.[23] Miss [Adelaide W.] Smith has come here to lodge as Miss Dix is on the place and she will have accommodations for her at their tent.

SABBATH OCT. 30TH 1864

Received a call this morning before breakfast from Miss Dix, she appeared at the rear of the tent just as we were about to sit at the table. We invited her to partake but she declined, evidently shocked to find herself in a doctor's mess. She made some remarks concerning our rustic table (a board on two barrels), then looking at my cupboards filled with bottles she remarked, "we seemed to have a restaurant." No Sabbath service for me to day. Chaplain Crawford of the 31st called yesterday and took some blackberry cordial to the Front with him. The boys all say he is every thing that is good. Lieut. [Hiram] Morse of the 20th and Dr's. [Thomas C.] Barker and Baxter called to day.—Hoped to have been able to have attended evening service but could not get away. Inspection day. Dr. Colic [Kollock] and Dr. Bermister passed through the tent and gave me great praise and the Maine Agency. The Commissioners also have been here about the voting list. One of them thought to get me to <u>sew</u> his ballots but finally did it himself.[24]

MONDAY OCT. 31ST 1864

A fine fix I am in truly! Dr Colic (I believe him well named) came round here this morning and, walking into the kitchen, he asked John who ordered him there. "Dr.

---

[23] HE expected her daughters to keep journals during their time away from her, so that she might read about their activities. It was not uncommon among nineteenth-century New Englanders to send journals to faraway relatives and friends as an epistolary form of communication. To my knowledge, none of these documents survived.

[24] Tuesday November 8, 1864 was a federal election day.

Bermister," he replied. "Well, do you go with my orderly," said he, so he took [him] right away and ordered him to the Front without even giving him a chance to get the dinner. He is a poor sick fellow and utterly unfit for duty. Here we are, I am cooking and washing the dishes for a doctor's mess. We have two strings to our bow now, Mrs. Linebeck and "Biddy the man." Mrs. Linebeck is sick, she is at the Mass. Agency, and Miss Dix has given orders that she shall return to Washington because, forsooth, there was a mistake about her pass. I want Mrs. Linebeck, but what matters it what I want! John's things are in a miserable dirty condition, but I do'nt think I shall clean up after him. What a time I had making a pudding to day, running about for a tent full of soldiers and trying to stir up a pudding. It was very good however and so was the fish. Captain Melcher called to day, also Capt. Thomas of the 2nd Battery who had his ambulance at the door and wanted me to spend the day with him. I should so like to have gone with him but could not leave. However, he says I may have their ambulance any time to go anywhere. Have finished a <u>letter to Miss Fox</u> to day.

TUESDAY NOV. 1ST 1864

I have <u>received a letter from Frank</u> to night which was mailed Saturday the 29th. How nice it seemed to hear so direct. Mrs. Linebeck has taken up her abode in the cook tent for the time being, uncertain whether or not she will be permitted to remain, that is for Dr. Dalton to say. She will at least take charge of the <u>diet kitchen</u> for a day or two. One of the Chris. Com. came (a Swede) and wanted me to go and see a Maine man who had his leg amputated. I got a man to wait in the tent while I went over to the 3rd Div. of the 2nd Corps. Poor man, so fine looking but so shattered for life, his lip quivered and I saw he found it hard to be reconciled, promised him a pillow for the leg.—Eight other Maine men in the ward. This is my work. Met Dr. [Abner O.] Shaw just coming from the tent. In the evening Chaplain Godfrey of the 20th, Dr. Shaw, and Dr. [Thomas C.] Barker spent the evening. How the Germans bother me for "de needle and de tred." I mean to send them all to the Chris. Com. tent.

WEDNESDAY NOV. 2ND 1864

We are busy with housekeeping accounts to day. Dr. Terhune is entering and he ca'nt square the reckoning. Capt. Plummer of the 20th called this morning. Had a very nice letter from Capt. Fogler this morning enclosing his photograph and requesting an exchange.—I am not going to be bashful about asking for photographs this time while I am here, for Mrs. F ca'nt dictate to me. Dr. S[haw] gave me an account of her visit to his family in Portland. Miss [Adelaide W.] S[mith] tells me some strange stories about some of the women on these grounds and

I do'nt wonder the surgeons get out of all patience. Last night Mrs. Linebeck gave me some nice stewed oysters, I ate a few but they were so delicious I had to keep them for Mr. Chick, the man with the amputated leg. One of his tent mates came in, and I warmed them and sent them to him. It rains so hard that I think the rest of the day will be pretty quiet. Rachel must get me some wood. Here I sit with the tent blowing open, fire all out.

THURSDAY NOV. 3RD 1864

Last evening I wrote a long letter to Perkins & Anna, a sheet and a half, and this afternoon I have carried it to the [Christian] Com. tent. The tent was perfectly crowded with the boys, who have left their cold quarters to read, write, and get warm. I asked one of our boys to stop here while I went to see Mr. Chick. He relished his oysters yesterday and to day I carried him some of Miss [Adelaide W.] Smith's tapioca pudding and this he relished too. Then I went to see Dr. Barker about W[illiam H.] Allen to see if I could get him transferred to a ward where it was warm. Dr. B's first remark was, I suppose there are 50 men just as badly off, however he promised to see him. I called a few moments on Miss Smith who is in a sad muddy condition while they are building her chimney. Mrs. Husband has been here to see me to day, she looks natural as life. Mrs. Mc Kay called last Tuesday morning before breakfast and we had a pleasant hour's chat.

FRIDAY NOV. 4TH 1864

To day I have preferred a request in due form to Dr. Dalton, Medical Director at City Point, praying most respectfully that Mrs. Linebeck be permitted to remain as cook at the Agency. I have also written to Mrs. Mayhew and Mrs. Rebecca S. Chick, East Thorndike Maine. Mr. Chick seemed to think it would do more good to have me write to comfort his wife than any one else. He said he told his nurse Mr. Bridge that he was going to give me a thousand dollars for his pillow, it had done his back so much good. Somehow I feel more uneasy about the children than usual. Oh Father, protect them and preserve them. Was happy to be the means of having Mr. Sumner Shaw and his brother-in-law Mr. Marble find each other to day.

SATURDAY NOV. 5TH 1864

Have had my hands full to day. The tent has been full. Mr. Hayes has come, but I have hardly spoken to him yet. Dr. O'Meagher is ordered away to the charge of a Brigade, as Medical Purveyor. He is very unwilling to go and I am sure I am sorry to have him. I do'nt know what will become of the mess. We had just laid in a stock of 20 lbs. butter, 1/2 barrel sweet potatoes, 1/2 barrel apples, and 1/2 barrel of turnips.—I feel very much disappointed this evening, I had hoped for a letter from my precious family and I do'nt get it. The colored bredren have noisy meetings, sometimes the singing is very peculiar. Mr. Hayes has at last arrived, but he says he has brought but very few stores. By him I have received a letter from Mrs. Mayhew and two from Miss Fox. Lieut. Stanwood is here, also Mr. Marble. Rachel found some "light wood" day before yesterday, with which we were much delighted, but we soon found ourselves enveloped in any thing but "<u>light</u>."[25] This evening I asked Lieut. S[tanwood] to put some wood in the stove, only not use the "light wood." In the honesty of his heart he sought for heavy wood and put it in and such a time as we had, part of us left the tent and part enduring the smoking process, opening wide the tent at ten o' clock at night. As a consequence I slept miserably cold, for now I am writing.

SABBATH MORNING NOV. 6TH 1864

I did want so much to go to meeting this morning, and so few have been in, I really think I might have left and I do'nt wish to go this afternoon. Yesterday they came to me to see what I could furnish them for communion service. I washed and ironed some napkins for their use and procured cups from Miss [Adelaide W.] S[mith] and Mrs. B[urmeister].—Since I commenced writing this, I have been quite charmed by the music that the little singing mice make. I have not been willing to believe they were mice. Miss S[mith] insisted they were birds, but just now, one came out and sitting on the board before me, twittered for a long time. Lieut. G[ould?] is here to day, and it seems like any thing but the Sabbath. Then too, they have brought that Mrs. Vanderslice in, and I do believe she will craze me. I have however snuck out a little time to go and see Mr. Chick and Lieut. Gibson of the 17th.

MONDAY NOV. 7TH 1864

A rainy day. Last evening I went to hear the colored sergeant again. "If any man &c. I will come in and sup with him &c." was the text. He was as interesting as ever. Returning from meeting I found letters for me from Frank, enclosing one from A[gnes], one from H[atty], and one from Sarah (Engles).[26] Did'nt she feel sour then when she wrote it. There was also a letter from Mattie and Sarah Caduc. The latter has been once more astonished by her erratic Aunt Harriet.—To day I have had a letter from Mrs. Bosworth that has contained intelligence that has filled my head to overflowing.[27] I know not how to restrain myself. Oh! that I may in faith be enabled to cast my burdened soul on my Heavenly Father. <u>Have written to Frank.</u>

[25] In other words, the wood created smoke instead of a blaze.
[26] Sarah Forsyth Engles (b.1839) was the eldest child of HE's niece, Octavia Augusta Bacon (b.1815), who herself was the eldest of Joseph Valentine Bacon's eight children. HE distinguishes Sarah Engles, her great niece, from her niece Sarah Caduc.
[27] Though the reference is cryptic, it may concern Frank Eaton or Irene Bosworth's son Fred who had died in late 1863 of a gunshot wound.

TUESDAY NOV. 8TH 1864

Another unpleasant day. The tent is full of mud from one end to the other. The polls are opened under our "fly" and I have no private quarters to day. Mrs. Vanderslice is here again & now she stays to dinner and supper. I ca'nt get rid of her. I have written a <u>letter for her to her daughter Maggie</u>, also <u>one to my dear Agnes, and one to Hatty</u>.—I am feeling intensely anxious for my dear children amid all this confusion.

WEDNESDAY NOV. 9TH 1864

Voting is over but we have Mr. Knowlton and Mr. Marble still here and the supervisors making up the poll lists.—Mrs. Vanderslice has a government steamer again to search for her son's body on Light House Point, but she will not find it. This time there are eight cavalry men, Miss [Adelaide W.] Smith and Mrs. Painter. Have <u>written to day to the little "Sprigs"</u>[28] and <u>Mrs. Doe</u> of Albion, with respect to her husband, who I fear will soon die. He belongs to the Sharpshooters and was wounded returning from picket, a very interesting man.

THURSDAY NOV. 10TH 1864

Letters from Agnes, Hatty, and Frank. Also a letter from Mrs. Coyle last evening. To day I have again been annoyed by Mrs. Vanderslice, but we think this will finish up her work, another government steamer this afternoon. Dr. Mann who was "born principally in Portland," here again and this is the third time. I should like to know who he is and what he wants. Mrs. Mc Kay came over from the Cavalry Hos. yesterday and wanted me to ride back with her, so I went. Had a very pleasant time. Miss Snyder, cousin of Miss Sharpless who goes as Hos. nurse on the transport *Connecticut* was there, a very lovely young lady. I attempted to walk back alone and just as I was gathering autumn leaves down in the valley, heard my name called and much to my displeasure there was Dr. Harnard, contract surgeon for the Corps, all out of breath, trying to catch me, and I lost my quiet walk.

FRIDAY NOV. 11TH 1864

To day I have supplied the 2nd Battery with stores, also walked over to the Cavalry Corps to find James Merritt, Mrs. Coyle's nephew. Glad was I to find him so comfortable. Mrs. Mc Kay had her ambulance at the door, so she brought me back and I had quite a ride round the country on my return. This evening I have written to

---

[28] Possibly a reference to Portland's Little Acorn Society, whose members were children. The Little Acorns donated the proceeds of a local sanitary fair to the MSRA in 1864.

By the time the great depot hospital at City Point was established in 1864, ambulances carried waiting soldiers from the Petersburg trenches to a rail line that brought them to City Point. Always at a premium, Eaton was charmed when an officer of the 2nd Maine Battery told her that she might use their ambulance "any time to go anywhere." FRANCIS TREVELYAN MILLER, THE PHOTOGRAPHIC HISTORY OF THE CIVIL WAR *(1911)*

Mrs. Coyle, Mrs. Sabrina Poor, Andover, and Mrs. Rebecca Chick, South Thorndike.[29] I would not be a nurse here at the Point for any thing. I never saw such a fuss as is made, one is not wanted and the other is not what she ought to be and then another.—Mrs. Vanderslice has gone home to day without her son's body.

SATURDAY NOV. 12TH 1864

Have received a letter from Mrs. Mayhew, and written a long curious letter to Miss Fox, also to Miss Sophia Doe, Boston.[30] I have spent the day at the Battery (the 2nd Maine) [with] Capt. Thomas, he is at Fort Porter and he took me all round the fort and explained the fortifications and entrenchments. He also showed me about the caissons and limbers, battery wagons and forge, then when I returned home, the ambulance driver took me round past the new line of breast works and six forts.

[29] HE's earlier correspondence identified the Chicks' home as East Thorndike, Maine.
[30] Sister of William Doe, a wounded soldier in the U.S. Sharpshooters, from Albion, Maine.

We have given to the 8th Maine who sent down by Mr. [John E. M.] Wright their chaplain, a large supply of Hos. stores, eight cans of beef, mutton, blackberries, meal, quilts, pillows, milk, corn starch, &c., &c.—This evening that I intended to have all to myself has had to be devoted to Col. Bowers, Major [William F.] Baker, and Dr. Weevil. I am weary, with this continual beau hunting, lady seeking, joking laughing community.

SUNDAY NOV. 13TH 1864

I determined this morning to have the day to myself if possible, so after Mr. Hayes and Mr. Marble went away, I tied up the tent and sat down quietly to read. Then I got ready to go to meeting at the Chris. Com. tent. The minister had any thing but agreeable manners, but he was a strong man and preached an excellent sermon to those who were accustomed to thoughtful inquiry. His text was "He that spared not his own Son &c. how shall he not with Him freely give us all things." I thought of Mr. Doe and in the afternoon I went to see him. Had a long and quiet conversation with him, read to him in the Bible and was deeply interested with his child like spirit.—When I entered the tent he exclaimed, "How glad I am to see you back again," for I did not get to see him the day before. I have promised to send him a chair to try to sit up. Have written to Mrs. Bosworth this evening. Poor Mr. Chick is having chills and fever, and my little lame boy, James William Brown has gone to General Hos. On the whole this is by far the best Sabbath I have spent since I came out.

MONDAY NOV. 14TH 1864

I have had a hard trial to write to day and this evening I am disappointed at not receiving letters. Dr. Baxter and Dr. Lowenthall called to day. Dr. Alexander dined with us. His resignation as surgeon of the 16th has just been accepted. He thinks Dr. Eaton will be commissioned rather than Dr. Baxter.[31] Dr. Mann called again this afternoon just when I wanted to write. Poor Mr. Doe and Mr. Chick are both very low to day. I carried them cocoa, milk, and pineapple preserves. Mrs. Dr. Bermister called, how sorry I am he has been relieved. Mrs. Mc Kay made a short call, said she was coming again to take me to the Point.[32] Surgeon Vogler [Vogeler], a very gentlemanly old man, called from the supply train, to see if he could get some quilts for himself and Capt. Barker. I gave him a real pretty one for himself and

---

[31] Joseph B. Baxter and William W. Eaton were both assistant surgeons of the 16th Maine at this time.

[32] HE is differentiating between the hospitals and the City Point depot itself—a port on the James and a railroad junction. Presumably the relief agencies and the 1st, 2nd, and 3rd division hospitals were some distance from the City Point landing and railroad terminus.

another for the Capt., also pillow cases too and a cap. Chaplain Patten of the 32nd was here and I gave him four quilts, one pillow, two doz. towels, and one dozen handkerchiefs.— <u>Asbury F. Haynes</u>, <u>Co. H. 17th Maine</u>, Passadunkeag [*sic*], came in this evening and I had a most interesting conversation with him, find he has experienced religion within a few days past. I gave him a secondhand blouse that came in one of the last boxes and a pair of drawers. Have <u>written this evening to my dear Agnes & Hatty, also Mrs. Griswold and Mr. Hayes</u>. John Chase of the wagon train has been here and informed me that they have orders to turn in their wagons and go to their corps, so I do'nt know what will become of the teams with which to draw the boards for our house. Have written to Mr. Hayes concerning the bricks for the chimneys. Dr. Weevil here this afternoon and wished Miss [Adelaide W.] Smith and myself to go to see their colored regiment on dress parade tomorrow, but I do'nt think I shall go.

TUESDAY NOV. 15TH 1864

Took the old stove all to pieces this morning and turned it on its side, determined to have a day without smoke if possible. Miss [Adelaide W.] Smith is over at "Jersey" to day.[33] Dr. Weevil just called & I told him I must be excused from going to his Regt. this afternoon & sent him to Miss S[mith] to Jersey. Since that, two boys came here, one a Maine boy, the other inquired for the New Jersey Agency and I sent him across the way. When he came back he remarked he saw a "lady with spectacles on, and two officers and they were having a high old time." Mr. Strout, Agent for Chris. Com. from Portland has just called, he says he saw a letter of mine in the Press about a week since. I'm sure I do'nt know what one they could have thought of publishing.—Miss S[mith] has been here to get me to go and says quite a large party are going and I tell her that is a reason why <u>I</u> would not go. Really, I do'nt know what some are thinking about or how much the private soldiers are being benefited by their presence in the Army.—I have this evening received three papers and two letters, one from Mrs. Mayhew and one from my dear Frank. Mrs. M[ayhew] writes that she do'nt see how she can return till the middle of December and Frank writes that he sha'nt spare me a day longer than the first agreement. I have <u>written to Mrs. Whittier and Mrs. Mayhew</u>. To the latter I have said that she must settle the dispute with the children as best she may. I am willing to remain if the rest are satisfied. On looking over the papers to night I was vexed and mortified to find that letter of mine printed there.—At least I think they might punctuate them for me when I am in such a hurry.

---

[33] New Jersey, along with Maine, Indiana, Ohio, and Pennsylvania, sponsored state relief services in individual tents at City Point. The Sanitary and Christian Commissions were also present in separate quarters.

WEDNESDAY NOV. 16TH 1864

This morning I hurried over to 3rd Div. thinking that Mr. Doe was dead, but instead I found he had been sent to General Hospital. Mr. Chick looks very feeble and I am afraid he is going to die. I saw that Miss Hart to day.—This afternoon a Mrs. Parker that Mrs. Painter had warned me against called, and I gave her the cold shoulder. Mr. [Joseph?] Myrick, a nurse from the Cav. Hos. called, he promised me some rings, but I am afraid he will forget it. Had a letter from Mr. Hayes to night. Mrs. Painter gone to W[ashington] again and Miss [Adelaide W.] S[mith] gone to Jersey to keep house. Lieut. Stanwood is here to night. Chaplain Godfrey called to day.

THURSDAY NOV. 17TH 1864

Hos. Steward of the 19th and a Lieut. from Penn. to breakfast this morn. Mr. Bridge came over, wishing me to hurry over to see Mr. Chick as he thought him dying, accordingly I hastened to the tent and after raising him he seemed to revive a good deal. I tried to talk with him, but poor man, though he is patient, he has no hope in Christ. I asked how he should feel if it became evident that the disease was wearing him out and he replied, "I suppose I should have to submit." Oh! that he could realize his situation. Capt. [Amos F.] Noyes of the 32nd here to dinner, that Regt. feels very bad about being consolidated with the 31st. Had a long talk with young Haynes this afternoon on the views of different denominations, his case interests me in a peculiar manner.—Letters this evening from each of my dear children, but they say nothing about my letters. After Mr. [J. S.] Houghton and Mr. [Benjamin] Williams[34] went out this evening I tied up the tent for the night, soon I heard a scratch at the door & invited them to walk round, when who should appear but Miss Nye and a young English lady, Miss Bane [Bain], who when in Glasgow heard that her brother was sick and crossed the ocean to see him, she has found him quite well and now intends to remain with our Army. I am exceedingly pleased with her. This afternoon Mrs. Mc Kay called for me to go to the Point with her. Once it might have been very pleasant but now—war, war, war! Saw Gen. Grant dashing along on his little horse. The gunboats seem to increase on the river and the monitors have come to the Point. But I must stop and write a letter to Mrs. Fidelia Mc Kay, Stoneham Mass. Mr. Chick's daughter called on Mrs. Bermister to day. Dr. O' Meagher sent down to [the Christian] Com. yesterday for six bed ticks and six pillows, they had neither, so I supplied him with pillows. Major [William F.] Baker had a pillow to day, and Capt. [Amos F.] Noyes of the 32nd also a bottle of currant wine.—A young man here this afternoon named Charles Dyer, I think Comp[any] D, 32nd. He has a bullet in his tongue that the surgeon dare not extract lest he bleed to death. It can

---

[34] Though HE refers to these men as "Mr.," both were assistant surgeons and probably had earned the title of "Dr."

be <u>seen</u> by pressing the tongue to one side. I tell him he shall have condensed milk as long as it lasts and crackers too, or any thing else.

FRIDAY NOV. 18TH 1864

Have opened the second cask of pickles. Capt. Thomas has kindly kept his promise and delivered a load of wood from the [2nd] Battery this morning, so I am well supplied. Dr. [Gideon S.] Palmer says he will keep the tent while I go to meeting this evening.— <u>Have written a letter to Mr. Hinds</u> for Benj. F. Fairbanks of the 19th with the hope that it will hasten either a furlough, a transfer or a discharge for him. He was <u>drafted</u> and never was fit to be in the Army. <u>Also, have written to Frank</u>, which makes <u>40</u> letters since I have been out this time. Had a solemn meeting this evening, some twelve or fifteen expressed themselves desirous of the prayers of Christians. Lieut. Stanley, 32nd, to tea.

SATURDAY NOV. 19TH 1864

A very severe storm to day. Have not been out of the tent. <u>Have written letters to Samuel & Elisabeth [Whitney] and sister Lavinia.</u>[35] This afternoon have had one more evidence of the blessedness of doing my duty. A young man of the 19th, cousin of Mr. Cyrus King, from Bowdoinham, came in, and I asked him into the inner tent to read by the fire. After a little conversation I was enabled to draw him out on the subject of religion, and oh! that he might resolve not to resist the evident strivings of the Spirit. His name Nathaniel P. Jaques. Just at night young Haynes came in and sat awhile and I enjoyed another precious conversation with him. He thinks he shall soon be ordered to the Front. I want to keep up a correspondence with him. Dr. Weevil came for a pillow, says Major [William F.] Baker has laid [*sic*] in bed ever since he got his, except he was obliged to go out and then he locked the pillow in his trunk. Mrs. Mallory came last evening and betted a shirt for a Penn. man, who is in a peculiarly critical state. This morning, there came another call for a shirt for a New York man, and as Dr. Terhune vouched for the necessity, I gave it. Next came Mrs. Husband for one. Uncle Richard came for a quilt for Dr. [Gideon S.] Palmer, the new Medical Director of the 2nd Corps. It was <u>policy</u> to give it, but Maine has got a great name for quilts.

SABBATH NOV. 20TH 1864

A stormy, quiet day. This morning I attended service at the Chris. Com. and heard a sermon from the words "They without ceasing." The preacher not very interesting. Few soldiers in the tent, to day I removed all secular reading from the table

---

[35] HE's only surviving sister was named Agnes. It stands to reason she was using the religious familiar form of "sister" in this reference, as she does about her neighbor "Brother [Byron] Greenough."

and placed instead that which I considered suitable for the Sabbath. Dr. Alexander called, he thinks Dr. [William] Eaton will get his commission.—He is going to take a contraband home to Chaplain Bullen.[36] Mr. Bridge has been in and tells me he thinks Mr. Chick cannot live but a few hours longer, how sad! I can get no evidence that he is a Christian, on my inquiry, how he should feel if he found the disease was wearing him out, he replied, "I suppose I should have to submit."—I have written a <u>letter to Mr. & Mrs. Greenough</u> to day. Mr. Hayes has arrived bringing the supplies, so tomorrow I expect to have quite a time arranging things in the tents. He also brought letters from Miss Fox and Mrs. [Ellen Usher] Bacon.

MONDAY NOV. 21ST 1864

The violent storm has continued during the day, no such thing as getting supplies. Poor Mr. Chick died last night at eight o' clock and <u>this evening</u> it has been my sad task <u>to write to his wife</u>. Oh! this dreadful war, she is poor and feeble. Mr. Bridge has brought over the things that were in his pocket and among them are some excellent letters. There is $20.75 in his port monnaie.[37] I have also <u>written a letter to my friend J[aques]</u>.—I am burdened in spirit for him.

TUESDAY NOV. 22ND 1864

To day <u>have written to Agnes</u>. Have received a letter from Mrs. Chick, oh dear, how little she realizes the sad news that awaits her.—Mr. Hayes (no thanks to the Hos. Department) has succeeded in getting teams to bring up our stores, and we have had a busy time packing away. No milk, no meal, and but few shirts, I am sorry but will be thankful for what has come, a nice lot of drawers and a good many stockings. Saw J[aques] to day and gave him his letter.

WEDNESDAY NOV. 23RD 1864

Chaplain Crawford staid with us last night, he is a good man, if there is one. Received letters for Mr. Doe from his wife and from his sister Miss Sophia Doe (No. 11 Edgerly Place, Boston) for myself. Have <u>written letters to Mrs. Doe & Miss Doe</u>, Mr. Hayes has been in a great taking [*sic*] to day to get up a Thanksgiving dinner for tomorrow. He has been to the Point and got his goose, also some raisins for a cracker pudding. Dr. Reynolds, a very gentlemanly surgeon of the "1st Maine Heavy" [Artillery] and

---

[36] White New Englanders affiliated with the Army of the Potomac were known to "adopt" former slaves with whom they came into contact in military camps. Such relationships were more likely an indentured servitude for the ex-slave than an emancipation. See Schultz, *Women at the Front*, 103.

[37] French term for change purse (*porte monnaie*).

the sutler of the Sharp Shooters, took tea with us, the joke was that they came in the afternoon and got sage for stuffing their goose and then they could'nt get the goose, so when they came back they said they'd take the sage and have <u>sage tea</u> for their dinner. Gave him some stores for his sick men, also a pillow and quilt for himself, though he seemed to think the pillow was too much of a luxury. This afternoon Miss Nye came to beg the liberty of rolling out a little pie crust in our kitchen, which has resulted in making fruit and meat pies and cake for 80 men. The work had to be continued till 'most eleven at night. An awful smoke in our tent drove me to "Jersey," but the trouble being discovered, I was most happy to return to my dear, cheerful home [in] time enough to pick over my raisins.—Carter's stockings have come.

THURSDAY NOV. 24TH 1864

Thanksgiving day! Young Haynes came first and I filled his haversack for the "Front." Then I thought to go to meeting, but the boys were so hungry that I felt it was more my duty to stay and take care of them. Oh! the multitude of my blessings, how full of thankfulness I ought to be!—Curtis came and was so delighted with his gift, that he started right for the Point and had his picture taken for Mrs. Griswold.—We had a grand dinner to day, every thing went off well. Major [Zemro A.] Smith of the "1st Maine Heavy" [Artillery] happened in just in time to dine with us. A letter for poor Mr. Chick from his daughter to night. How hard to write to her.

FRIDAY NOV. 25TH 1864

<u>Have written to Hatty, Lizzie, Mrs. [Ellen Usher] Bacon, also to Col. Hinds for Charles S. Dyer</u> of Chesterville, who has the bullet in his tongue. No letters to night. I am sick of having Rachel about and the sooner she goes the better. Mr. Hayes has been to the Batteries and engaged six teams to bring the logs for the stockade which the 1st Maine [Heavy Artillery] are cutting. I have written letters to day because I felt obliged to and not because I felt like it. Dr. Terhune has told me a sad story of Dr. Weevil and Dr. Taylor and others, glad I am [that] I have not been out walking with them. Surgeon Vogler of the supply train called again, he tells me he was a Baptist minister twenty years.

SATURDAY NOV. 26TH 1864

I am so out of patience with the want of sympathy that the doctors have with their sick men that I can hardly endure it. Mrs. Husband has just been in calling out, "another shirt, another shirt." Some nurse in her ward named Mc Cusick has'nt been treated well at the Maine Agency and she wants him to come and see what good people they have here now.—Chaplain [Alfred S.] Adams of the "1st Maine Heavy" dined here to day. He was formerly a private, has been recently commissioned. Ha!

Ha! Ha! did'nt that clerk come down from the Hos. with a rush to day, to find out where those teams came from with our stockade! We were perfectly independent of them and theirs, I am happy to say.—Have had a letter from Frank this evening and one from Mrs. [Ellen Usher] Bacon. The latter I have answered post haste and given them a piece of my mind about Nellie's coming out. If she comes now it wo'nt be because I have not done my duty.[38] Frank has done his best in his letter, to show his indignation at my prolonged stay and yet he thinks he must bear it. How hateful that they should have published that letter of mine. I gave them credit for a little common sense before. Young [Charles S.] Dyer was here and gave me a ring to day as a token of remembrance.

SUNDAY NOV. 27TH 1864

Attended service this morning but coughed so continuously that I could enjoy nothing. Feeling the same in the afternoon, I tied and pinned up all three tents, determined not to be disturbed with other callers, if I could not receive soldiers. Mr. Hayes called a few minutes with a Mr. Whitman, the Toby Candor of the Boston Journal. Then they went out and remained till evening. I wish the doctors would not make their calls on the Sabbath. Dr's. Baxter, Lowenthall, Lord, and Gladfelter have all been here this evening. Continual cannonading to day, nearby.

MONDAY NOV. 28TH 1864

Mr. Whitman still here. No letters from Agnes or Hatty. Have written to Mrs. Fidelia Mc Kay, Stoneham Mass., enclosing a lock of her father's hair, also to Mrs. Griswold, enclosing Mr. Curtis's picture. Continual firing to day and some thing this evening that sounded like an explosion.[39] Busy as a bee to day, the calls have been so frequent, but I have had to send any quantity of men away that did not belong to Maine. Had a call from Mrs. Hill, she wanted a quilt. Miss Hancock supplies all her bed linen from our stock, I wonder why she does not go to the Sanitary.—[Joseph?] Myrick from the Cavalry Corps here all day.—I do'nt like the way things are carried on here, I would soon make a change if it was to be my home, I mean with reference to the mess. This morning received a long letter from J[aques], he came into the inner tent and laid it down, he is looking very unwell, I gave him something to eat and had a long talk, oh! how gladly would I direct him aright. His frankness interests me most deeply.—

---

[38] A reference to Ellen Forbes Tolman of Norridgewock, Maine. It is possible that HE wished to discourage her from relief work at City Point because Tolman was a newlywed and because HE believed that too many relief workers were already assembled there.

[39] HE may have heard the explosion of the *Greyhound*, a steamer in the James River, blown up near Butler's headquarters on the previous evening.

TUESDAY NOV. 29TH 1864

No letters yet. We hear that 30 men are coming to go to work tomorrow. Capt. Thomas and Capt. [George H.] Abbot called and promised men to hew the timber. Have been <u>writing to J[aques]</u>. Help me, O God, in his behalf. My hand trembled as I wrote.

WEDNESDAY NOV. 30TH 1864

A busy day with us, although but four men came. We think the 1st Maine [Heavy Artillery] must have moved. The weather is warm as summer. No fires needed. Was disappointed this morning to see the tumbler on the table and think perhaps J[aques] was annoyed by my conversation and wished to shun me.[40] As I still had the letter, I felt constrained to <u>add another</u> to night.— Went to meeting this evening, 33 rose for prayers. I could wish they were a little more quiet, but God was evidently there.—Chaplain Patten here to day and took quite a supply of towels and handkerchiefs &c. for his men. Had a very beautiful present this morning from Levi D. Curtis 1st Maine Co. A. and [Frank] Drew 17th Co. [_____] of a frame which I shall value so much.[41]

THURSDAY DEC. 1ST 1864

Very warm again. Five men here at work to day. They have done nobly, but the 1st Maine [Heavy Artillery] have moved in connection with the movements of the Corps. Gen. Grant rode along by the tent to day. Have this evening had letters from Agnes, Augusta Hanna, Mr. & Mrs. Greenough, and Susan of Goffstown. Felt very anxious as to my duty in regard to J[aques] and at length decided to send the letter by the hand of a young man. Soon he came himself and after awhile came to the inner tent, where I had a deeply solemn conversation with him. How deep an experience I am permitted to have in his case. Capt. Fogler dined here to day.

FRIDAY DEC. 2ND 1864

Letters to day from Mrs. Chick, Sam and Ellis, Mr. Story, and Miss Fox. Eight men at work here to day.—I am in great distress for my friend, his state is critical, I cannot give him up. He has been with me a long time, says he ca'nt believe, have been to the Chris. Com. to get some little Tracts and have given him three of them and

---

[40] The implication is that Jaques has been drinking alcohol.
[41] As is her custom, HE leaves underlined blank spaces to later identify Frank Drew's Christian name and his company, which was B. I have supplied Drew's full name to clarify that he is not Joseph Drew, a man in the same regiment, who died in 1862.

marked them. Have also <u>written to my dear Agnes and Mr. Story</u>. The letter from Mr. S[tory] has been a source of great satisfaction to me as well as that from my dear child.

SATURDAY DEC. 3RD 1864

It seems as if my soul must burst this clayey tenement and soar away. My dear J[aques] has found Jesus. Last night my agony was so great, that I rose to pray for him. I felt that God alone could do the work and I gave it up to him just as much as I gave myself to him at my conversion. At noon he came in, while we were at dinner, and left me a letter. From the contents I knew the work was done, though he did not know it. He went to meeting and on his return, with tears rolling down his cheeks, he told me of his happiness. <u>I was just writing him a letter</u> which I gave him unfinished. Now the thought comes, "have I received him instead of my dear F[rank]?" Oh no, God is still holding out the same promises. The day has been one of utter confusion with 14 men at work. The tent in perfect uproar, two companies to dinner, for Mr. Whitman and Dr. Hersom were here besides our mess. An invitation to a dinner party at five o' clock which I was most thankful to decline, having good reason. Mrs. Linebeck came in and took tea with me. Dr. Palmer spent part of the evening and I gave him a quilt, then Mrs. L came in again, and I had a long talk with her, she is very serious. Oh! I have so much I want to write.

SUNDAY DEC. 4TH 1864

Just as we sat down to breakfast this morn., Mrs. L came to the tent and said they were assembling for a baptism. Such a lovely morning, I only stopped to put on my "sunset,"[42] and went immediately to the banks of the Appomattox, where three willing converts were buried in the likeness of their Lord beneath the wave.—So delightfully solemn was the scene. Mr. Strout administered the ordinance. Then I went to the morning service, Mr. S preached most beautifully, with such a tender spirit from the words, "Let your light to shine &c." In the afternoon, I wrote a letter to my dear son, telling him my last experience. Father of the fatherless, thou canst work and who shall hinder! After [a] while, my dear boy [Jaques] came to see me, happy in Jesus' love, and we talked over our experience. In the evening I had a letter from Mrs. Mayhew, she is happy and so am I, oh! how thankful I am and shall be to all eternity that I came here. I have been to meeting, the sermon I did not enjoy, or my seat, but I remained to the second service and my dear J[aques] rose and gave in his testimony. Truly, as he said, it was new business for him, but a heavenly light beamed in his countenance. Oh! that I may be kept <u>humble</u>.

---

[42] A type of bonnet with a large brim.

MONDAY DEC. 5TH 1864

Six men here to day at work. A call from J[aques] at breakfast time.—He has promised to gratify me in a request I have made him, provided I will, in turn, accede to his.—He says <u>now</u> he is ready to go to his Regt. at any time, only he would like to stay a week longer. He dreamed last night that he took an oath, and expressed his horror. Mailed my dear boy's letter this morning and had a talk with Mr. Hall about their promise to the 2nd Battery.—Mr. H did not see the Capt. [Melcher] but left things at the Battery. Had a letter from Mrs. [Ellen Usher] Bacon by the hand of Mr. Roberts of Westbrook. <u>Wrote to Sarah Caduc</u>.

TUESDAY DEC. 6TH 1864

Last night I got along very comfortably, notwithstanding my tent was open in all directions, so that I could see through it. Such a looking place was hardly ever seen. I found after riding over to the Point with Mrs. Mc Kay that <u>all</u> was confusion, beds and boxes all piled together, so with my dear J[aques] I took a walk over to the Cavalry Corps and we enjoyed sweet converse together of heavenly things.—To day we have had six men with us. Our tent to night is very comfortable and Dr. Terhune has provided a nice stove, which will save us from the dampness of the mud walls. Oh how much I have wanted to go to meeting to day. I <u>wrote a little note to Mr. Hull</u>. J[aques] is every thing I could wish, he spent an hour with me this morning. I love him as an own son. I am burdened for dear F[rank]. Received a letter to night from Mrs. [Ellen Usher] Bacon that I must try and answer soon. I wish these young ladies knew how to conduct [themselves], strange indeed that Miss Bane should have been so indiscreet as to come to the Army, her lover is here to day.[43] Had quite a talk with George [Whittier] this evening.

WEDNESDAY DEC. 7TH 1864

A rainy day, but our stockade is all plastered and we are very comfortable. <u>Wrote a little note</u> to send home by Mr. Roberts this morning. N[athaniel P. Jaques][44] was put on detail for the first time, but the rain prevented work, so he came to me and helped move my boxes and set things to rights, we talked and worked. Mr. Hayes works hard, he is determined in his efforts to have a nice house, but what would

---

[43] Annie Bain married Captain Robert C. Eden of the 37th Wisconsin Infantry in an Episcopal service at City Point in 1865. In November 1864, Bain, who was Scottish, had traveled to the Army of the Potomac from Glasgow under the pretext of looking after her wounded brother. Once it became clear to Adelaide Smith, Hettie Painter, HE, and others that Captain Eden was not a relative but a lover, a wedding was orchestrated.

[44] HE's switch to "N" in lieu of "J" indicates that they had agreed to call one another by their Christian names—a breach of convention.

people at home think of us without any doors! The rats carried away Mr. Hayes' stockings last night, he had better look out for them to night.⁴⁵ Had a letter from Mrs. Griswold. Had a solemn meeting this evening. Text from the words, "almost then persuadest me" &c. Young Wade promised me this afternoon that he would be there and I heard [sic] partly for him. Dear N spoke, and came home with me.

THURSDAY DEC. 8TH 1864

Our house progressing finely. Four sharp shooters, one of them a carpenter, here to day.—An invitation to go out to dinner to the [10th] Colored Regt. which I beg to decline. Young Wade came to see me again and oh it made me feel sad indeed, to hear him say "not now." Wrote a long letter to N[athaniel P. Jaques] to day with reference to his return to his Regt. This evening the rats made a raid on us, and in the "muss" the ink was spilled and candle put out. Had letters from Capt. Fogler, about George Stuart, also from Mrs. Chick and Mrs. Preble.—Wrote to Mrs. [Ellen Usher] Bacon and Hatty Belle.

[See Appendix letter 23. HE to Unknown, December 8, 1864.]

FRIDAY DEC. 9TH 1864

What a night I had of it. Our side of the top of the tent blew open and the rubber door blew open, so that all night old Boreas made a clean sweep of it. I covered my head and laid awake nearly all night, but I was very happy and not very cold. Sergeant Montgomery came in this morning and sewed the top together and Mr. Hayes fixed the door and I have great occasion to be thankful in this storm of snow and hail, that I am so comfortable. My dear N[athaniel P. Jaques] spent most of the day with me. The young man who asked for "novels" came in and I had a talk with him. Wrote a letter to W[ade] this evening.

SATURDAY DEC. 10TH 1864

An uncomfortable day, walking frightful. Dear N[athaniel P. Jaques] and Mr. Hayes changed the stove pipe this afternoon, so now I know it will burn well. Miss Nye took tea with me this evening.—Had a nice letter from N this morning, oh, how can I realize the happiness I am permitted to enjoy. I am surprised at the similarity of our views and at his own maturity of thought on these subjects. He has decided to give up a bad habit, partly because the habit is bad, and partly to please me.—I must stop now and write a letter to poor Mrs. Chick.

---

⁴⁵ In this case the malefactors are rodents and not "hospital rats," convalescing patients who faked symptoms to avoid being returned to combat units.

SUNDAY DEC. 11TH 1864

Attended service this morning but remained at home both afternoon and evening, not feeling very well. Sermon an excellent one from Dr. Lowry of Indiana, about Caleb, where God because his servant Caleb has served him he shall enter the land of Canaan. Dear N[athaniel P. Jaques] stopped here most of the day and I shall persuade him to remain to night. Mr. Hayes went to Washington this morning.

MONDAY DEC. 12TH 1864

Weather very cold and uncomfortable. Letters from Agnes, Hatty, and Mrs. Coyle. The weather too bad for the workmen to come. The army moving, oh how much suffering there must be.—Another letter of mine in the Press, well, let it bring things for the soldiers and I do'nt care for myself. Lots of newspapers mailed to the Agency now. Last night I had the privilege of hearing my dear N[athaniel P. Jaques]'s voice in prayer with me in our tent. Yesterday he had a talk with me in regard to my views on baptism. He began by saying, "Can you tell me where there is any authority for sprinkling in the Bible." On this, and the subject of <u>stillness</u> in the meetings, it has been delightful to me to see how his views coincide with mine.

TUESDAY DEC. 13TH 1864

Another happy day in the society of my dear son [Nathaniel P. Jaques], we cannot enjoy these seasons much longer, he feels his duty calls him to his Regt. Last evening the hours were most precious. Called on Mrs. Bermister yesterday, also on Dr. [Alexander] Parker but he was not in, to ask that a man might be sent to cut wood. Dr. Parker can remember to get quilts at the Agency, but he cannot remember to send a man to work. Mrs. Weeks from Portland of the 9th Maine[46] and Brigade Quartermaster [Howland] called to day.—Twitchell of the 7th Battery here again, and I went to the Chris. Com. and got some milk for him, also a can for N[athaniel P. Jaques]. My son will get me wood enough while he is here.

WEDNESDAY DEC. 14TH 1864

Oh what a sad day I have passed! My dear N[athaniel P. Jaques] was ordered to the Front this morning. He was willing to go to his Regt. but the circumstances that had transpired the evening previous, when Chaplain Patten and Lieut. [Charles F.] Burr spent the night here, had prevented us from an opportunity for that spiritual converse

---

[46] Mrs. Weeks was the mother of Charles Weeks, a soldier in the 9th Maine. Although HE and Isabella Fogg were not associated with their sons' regiments, it was common for women to seek such work at the regimental level.

we had expected. Dear N said he felt that he had been "robbed," and I felt the same. I tried to provide him things to make him comfortable as I could, but he did not think much about that. The Lord keep him as the apple of this eye, cover him in the day of battle, and enable him now to show his love for Jesus in his Regt.—We sat together at the meeting last evening and I heard his voice singing God's praise. All day the officers of the 32nd Maine have been going in and out, they feel very uncomfortable about the consolidation of the two Regts.[47] Lowell and [Howard] Gould of the 7th Bat[tery] called on me to day. Fine young men. Mr. Hayes has returned with lots of stores, as soon as we get them unpacked and acknowledged I shall be ready to go home. Letters from Miss Doe of Boston and Mrs. Barbour of Gorham this evening. Have written a long letter to my dear soldier son to day.[48] Have written to my dear Agnes to night.

THURSDAY DEC. 15TH 1864

I woke this morning after a quiet night's rest, something unusual for me. Mr. Hayes had a letter from Lt. Col. [Joseph W.] Spaulding of the 19th inquiring if there was any way his Regt. could get mittens. I shall remember that thoughtfulness in him. Dear N[athaniel P. Jaques] must have a pair, at some rate. Four men here to day, one bricklayer putting up the chimney, also a team, all from the 3rd Battery. Quartermaster Remick of the 17th here this morning.

FRIDAY DEC. 16TH 1864

Four men here to day, fire place done and floor laid. Hurry hurry all day. Chaplain [Alfred S.] Adams called this morning and seemed very glad to see me. Chaplain Crawford called and I had a long confidential conversation with him about the Chris. Com. He is sadly grieved with its present workings. Have sent a pair of gloves to dear [Nathaniel P.] J[aques] by mail. Have written letters this evening to my dear N, Augusta Hanna, and Miss Fox and if I am not tired I don't know who is. Had letters to night from all the children, Miss Fox, and Mrs. Coyle. Dr. Stevens of the Cavalry, now at dismounted camp, called to day. Jersey Agency as usual.

SATURDAY DEC. 17TH 1864

Have written to my boy. Attended meeting this evening, as[49] I had no candle to stay at home with. To day have had a long talk at my own request with Mr. [John A.]

---

[47] On December 12, 1864, the 32nd Maine was absorbed into the 31st, much to the consternation of those in the 32nd.

[48] It is unclear whether HE is referring to Nathaniel P. Jaques or Frank H. Eaton.

[49] HE has written in margin, "61st N York Comp B Sergeant Osborne Charles Montgomery."

Cole, head man of the Chris. Com. here. I have freed my mind and I feel better. He was very gentlemanly to me and with him I was much pleased. Capt. Twitchell of the 7th Battery called. Mrs. Mayhew has not come and I will commence another letter to my son, I fear I shall not enjoy the Sabbath tomorrow. I have a door.

SUNDAY DEC. 18TH 1864

This morning I woke feeling more in the right spirit than I had expected. Had some sweet thoughts about the obedience of Abraham in preparing to offer his son at God's command. May I claim the promise in any degree as made to Him?[50] Attended the morning service, heard a comforting sermon from Zach[ariah] 14: 6, 7 on the variability of the Christian's experience, which though often dim, would in the evening time be light. After I returned from meeting I was made indeed to rejoice by a call from Sergeant Montgomery, who clothed and sitting at Jesus' feet, came to tell me the wonderful change that had been wrought. He has been a pirate and a slaver, was born on board a pirate ship, is very intelligent. I warned him against tasting liquor in any way for any purpose, and he said God helping him, he never would touch it again.—In the afternoon, I wrote to N[athaniel P. Jaques] and waited to receive Mrs. Mayhew who came about four o' clock. Now my work here is about done, and my thoughts must turn homeward, but much as I want to see my precious children, it is hard to leave this place, this birth place of souls. This evening I have written to Haynes of the 17th and my N[athaniel P. Jaques]. Mr. Hayes will not hear of my going home, but I think he will have to. Mrs. M[ayhew] is looking remarkably well. This has been a precious day to me notwithstanding my fears.

MONDAY DEC. 19TH 1864

A busy day indeed. Steward Getchell and a Mr. Huntress of the Cavalry and Dr. Bussey and Steward [Charles H.] Dodge of the 19th dined with us to day, it was amusing to see what loads they were willing to take away with them for the sake of their sick men. Steward Dodge in particular took a bed sack filled at either end and hung over his shoulder, he also took a little package of goodies for my dear N[athaniel P. Jaques] and Charlie Sherwood Comp[any] I 36th Wisconsin carried the box down to the Point while Mr. Dodge very kindly said he would see to it that he had it. The men feel bad and so do I that I am going to leave. Poor Charlie could not help crying and I felt impressed to give him a good bye kiss. Mr. Weld thinks he wo'nt come to the tent any more, but he will I know. Mr. Hayes [has] gone to the Front.

[50] The implication is that HE compares herself to Abraham, having "offered" her "son" Nathaniel P. Jaques to God; in other words, spiritually releasing him to his fate as a soldier.

TUESDAY DEC. 20TH 1864

On board _____ at Fortress Monroe.⁵¹ A very comfortable passage thus far. 1/2 past three. The first thing this morning Charlie [Sherwood] brought me a beautiful letter and a ring. Then Mr. Weld came, but now it is all over, my dear, dear boys, shall I never see them again, till we meet in heaven?—George and Eliza were sadly grieved. I never can be thankful enough for the privilege I have enjoyed the last three months, eternity only can reveal the work. Mr. Hayes came down from the "Front" in time to take me to the boat. Passed first Light House Point, then Harrison's Landing, Harrison House, Fort Powell, Jamestown, wrecks of Florida and Cumberland,⁵² Newport News, Rip raps, &c., the rebel ram Atlanta,⁵³ formed a pleasing acquaintance with Mrs. E. L. Bishop, Norfolk.

WEDNESDAY DEC. 21ST 1864

Here we are in the Potomac at last. At two o'clock at night we ran on to a sandbar at Cedar Point by reason of the light boat being removed for the ice and we lay there six hours. It is storming most ferociously and no very nice prospect in W[ashington] for to day. <u>I have just written to both of my dear sons</u>. To one I am going, one I am leaving.⁵⁴ I have free transportation on the boat, thanks to Miss Dix's pass.

THURSDAY DEC. 22ND 1864

Rail Road Depot New York. Waiting for the cars which start at eight, we arriving at five. Arrived in W[ashington] yesterday noon. For some reason the clerk of the boat procured me a carriage and paid my fare. Found Mr. [Leonard W.] Watson and every thing at 273 F St. all safe. Went in all the slush to Armory Square Hos. to see Mr. Doe, he was quite affected at seeing me. Thence went to see Mrs. Gilmore who is good as ever and said she only wished I could stay at least a week. Better than all however I found the long wished for letter from my dear N[athaniel P. Jaques]

---

⁵¹ HE leaves an underlined blank space.

⁵² The 24-gun sloop U.S.S. *Cumberland* was sunk by the C.S.S. ironclad *Virginia* (also known as the Merrimack) in Hampton Roads on March 8, 1862. Both the Union and Confederacy had ships named *Florida*. The U.S.S. *Florida*, a blockade-running vessel, is undoubtedly the one HE saw in Hampton Roads on December 20, 1864.

⁵³ The C.S.S. ironclad *Atlanta*, also known as the *Fingal*, was disabled in a confrontation with the U.S.S. *Weehawken* at the confluence of the Wilmington River and the Wassaw Sound off the coast of Georgia on June 17, 1863. How the vessel was brought back to the James River is unclear. "Rip raps" might be a reference to the *Mary F. Rapley*, used by the Sanitary Commission during the peninsular campaign.

⁵⁴ The former, Frank Eaton, was still stationed in Washington in December 1864; the latter, Nathaniel P. Jaques, had gone back to the 19th Maine.

waiting for me at the Agency. I do hope there will be another waiting for me when I get home. Dear boy, how similar have been our feelings. May he have strength to meet all his trials. Took cars from W[ashington] at six and was happily disappointed in not being obliged to travel alone as Capt. [Amos F.] Noyes and several of the 31st officers are on the cars. Was very sorry to learn through Mrs. Gilmore that Hugh Fogg has lost his leg.[55] Mrs. F, she thinks, is in Baltimore. How I wish I had letter paper with me this morning.

FRIDAY DEC. 23RD 1864

Arrived at brother Joseph [Bacon]'s this evening about 1/2 past eight. Thermometer six degrees below zero. A very cold ride but a very pleasant conversation with <u>Senator Perham</u> to whom I was introduced by Capt. [Amos F.] Noyes. He seems an excellent man, temperate and patriotic. Drinking in the cars, before, behind, and at my right, by both men and women. Arrived in Boston two hours behind time and had a cold walk of it to bro. Joseph's.

SATURDAY DEC. 24TH 1864

Remained at Brookline till after dinner, then went into Boston, attended to some business, then found Mr. Hayward's store, and went with him to spend the night at Viola's. Had a very pleasant visit and in the morning took the cars for Spring St. Spring Hill, to visit the Kelly's &c. Took them quite by surprize [*sic*] and spent two hours delightfully with them, then left for Boston, hurried through with my business, took carriage for Maine Depot, where on arriving I called on the Superintendent and procured free transportation to Portland. I arrived at my own loved home to receive the greetings of my precious family in the evening. I never can express my gratitude for having been permitted this season with the Army. <u>Eternity</u> will reveal it all. <u>God bless the soldiers</u>.

[55] Isabella Fogg's son Hugh was shot in the left lower leg at the battle of Cedar Creek on October 19, 1864. The next day, in a field hospital in Winchester, Virginia, Hugh's leg was amputated. Several days later he was moved to Patterson Post Hospital in Baltimore. When Isabella learned the news, she made her way from her home in Calais, Maine, to Baltimore, where she stayed with Hugh into the first part of 1865.

NOTES

ABBREVIATIONS

ADAH	Alabama Department of Archives and History, Montgomery
AMA	American Medical Association
DCUCS	Josephine Dolan Collection, University of Connecticut, Storrs
DU	Manuscripts, Perkins Library, Duke University, Durham, North Carolina
EU	Manuscripts, Archives, and Rare Books, Emory University, Atlanta, Georgia
FSBC	Free Street Baptist Church, Portland
HE	Harriet Eaton
LC	Library of Congress Manuscript Division, Washington, D.C.
MCHA	Maine Camp Hospital Association
MHS	Maine Historical Society, Portland
MOLLUS	Military Order of the Loyal Legion of the United States
MSA	Maine State Archives, Augusta
MSH	*Medical and Surgical History of the War of the Rebellion*
MSRA	Maine State [Relief] Agency
NARA	National Archives and Records Administration, Washington, D.C.
NYHS	New-York Historical Society, New York City
ORR	*War of the Rebellion. Official Records of the Union and Confederate Armies*
SCDAH	South Carolina Department of Archives and History, Columbia
SHC	Southern Historical Collection, Wilson Library, University of North Carolina-Chapel Hill
UNC	University of North Carolina-Chapel Hill
USCC	United States Christian Commission
USSC	United States Sanitary Commission
WCRA	Women's Central Relief Association

INTRODUCTION

1. According to nurse Rebecca Usher, who followed them into the field later in the war, Eaton and Fogg were "the pioneers from the state in sanitary labor." They were not, however, the first women from Maine to care for soldiers. Nellie Forbes Tolman, niece

of U.S. Representative Sidney Perham, was in Washington when the war began and assisted hospitalized soldiers from July 1861 through February 1863; Mary E. Chamberlain (Perkins) was regimental nurse for the 11th Maine, beginning in November 1861; and Isabella Fogg, in the company of Ruth Mayhew, had cared for soldiers in Annapolis and Washington in the first fall and winter of the war. See Frank Moore, *Women of the War*, 453; and Sudlow, *A Vast Army of Women*, 77–78, 101–3, 92–100, 137–42.

2. See, for example, the testimony of "MMC" about her soldier son, written from St. John's College Hospital, Annapolis, December 10, 1864, where she was a nurse: "I trust some kind woman stood by him to minister to him when dying, as I am daily doing for brave men similarly situated." Quoted in Livermore, *My Story of the War* (Silber edition), 686. Even without sons in the service, female relief workers were honored to perform as surrogate mothers in a national culture that enshrined motherhood. Alice Fahs has argued that women—and mothers, in particular—were at the "emotive center of the nation," personalizing the war for men. See Fahs, "The Feminized Civil War," 1465–67.

3. This is Nina Silber's formulation in *Daughters of the Union*, 5–12. Barbara Cutter has defined this activist strain as the signal feature of "redemptive womanhood," a model based on the nineteenth-century belief that women were natural advocates for moral justice. See Cutter, *Domestic Devils, Battlefield Angels*, 7–17. On republican motherhood, see Kerber, *Women of the Republic*. On women in the public realm, see Ryan, *Women in Public*.

4. For discussions of the federal impetus of the USSC, see Fredrickson, *The Inner Civil War*; Silber, *Daughters of the Union*, 176; Attie, *Patriotic Toil*, 50–86; Giesberg, *Civil War Sisterhood*, 3–13; Richard, *Busy Hands*, 185–86; Leonard, *Yankee Women*, especially chapter 2; and Ross, "Arranging a Doll's House," 98.

5. Henry Burrage reports that by 1845, the year after Jeremiah Eaton assumed his pulpit in Portland, the Baptist Church in Maine alone had established 266 Sabbath schools, with 1,764 teachers and 11,663 students. See Burrage, *History of the Baptists in Maine*, 277. Philip Paludan notes that between 1855 and 1865, membership in the national church increased by 28%. See *"A People's Contest,"* 340; and Goen, *Broken Churches, Broken Nation*, 49–51.

6. See Paludan, "Religion and the American Civil War," 21, 28. See also Silber, *Daughters of the Union*, 35–36.

7. George M. Fredrickson observes competition among these professional "guardians" of the republic during the war, but also notes that "the crisis had reduced the capacity of the clergy to make critical or prophetic judgments on the conduct of public life." See "The Coming of the Lord," 112, 124.

8. James Moorhead has noted that New England's Baptist churches had been interested in abolition since the 1820s and that Baptists could come together on this issue in ways that Methodists and Presbyterians could not. See Moorhead, *American Apocalypse*, 86, 93. See also Goen, *Broken Churches, Broken Nation*.

9. For studies of slaves making the transition from bondage to freedom, see Frankel, *Freedom's Women*, especially chapter 2; Mohr, *On the Threshold of Freedom*, especially chapter 3; and Schwalm, *A Hard Fight for We*, 88–107.

10. See my "Seldom Thanked, Never Praised, and Scarcely Recognized," 228–30.

11. See Faust, *This Republic of Suffering*, 56, 61, 81–82, 137, 250–65.

12. See Woolsey, *A Century of Nursing*; Attie, *Patriotic Toil*, 271–72; and Giesberg, *Civil War Sisterhood*, chapter 7 especially. For the transition between the war and the professionalization of nursing, see Melosh, *The Physician's Hand*; Reverby, *Ordered to Care*; Gill, *Nightingales*, especially chapter 20; and D'Antonio, "Revisiting and Rethinking the Rewriting of Nursing History," 280–81.

13. See Schultz, *Women at the Front*, for a more detailed discussion of the variety of wartime medical narratives. I counted 347 narratives of relief work by including brief sketches in postwar commemoratives, but only sixty of these are full-length monographs. Since 2004, I have located several others.

14. Among those discovered and published later are Maria Lydig Daly, *Diary of a Union Lady* and Hannah Lide Coker, *A Story of the Civil War*.

15. The diaries were published between 1980 and 1994: Ropes, *Civil War Nurse*, edited by John Brumgardt, in 1980; Hawks, *A Woman Doctor's Civil War*, edited by Gerald Schwartz, in 1984; and Bacot, *A Confederate Nurse*, edited by Jean Berlin, in 1994.

16. See, for example, Taylor, *Reminiscences of My Life in Camp*; or the special act of Congress in the pension application of New Hampshire nurse Harriet Patience Dame, U.S. Bureau of Pensions, Department of the Interior, Record Group 15, NARA. The field work of regimental nurses has been under-represented because regimental workers were usually working-class women with little education and without the inclination or literacy to write about their services.

17. This is true of works written by commission historians, as well as the narratives of individuals. See Stillé, *History of the United States Sanitary Commission;* Moss, *Annals of the United States Christian Commission;* Bloor, *Letters from the Army of the Potomac;* and Wormeley, *The Other Side of War*.

18. See P. G. Bowman to Abby May, December 14, 1862, New England Women's Auxiliary Association Collection, referenced in Richard, *Busy Hands*, 207, 220 (n.59).

19. Esther Hill Hawks also edited her diary, but never published it during her life time. See Cumming, *A Journal of Hospital Life*, 5; and Cumming to "Nannie," April 18, 1866, Kate Cumming Collection, ADAH, in which she writes, "I have done little or anything else since the war closed, but get my book ready for the press."

20. See Schroeder-Lein for a description of the flying hospital, a precursor to the mobile army surgical hospital (MASH), in *Confederate Hospitals on the Move*; and Cumming, *A Journal of Hospital Life*, 189–99.

21. See Cumming, *Kate: The Journal of a Confederate Nurse*, 183 and 23. In another instance, Cumming directly addressed the "Women of the South": "Let us remember we have a foe as relentless as Tamerlane or Atilla, who, if we are to believe his own threats, has resolved to lay our towns in ashes, lay waste our fields, and make our fair land a blackened mass of ruins if we will not submit to his domination." See *Kate: The Journal of a Confederate Nurse*, 66.

22. Many scholars have observed religious similarities in the language and conduct of Northerners and Southerners during the war. See, for example, Wilson, "Religion and the American Civil War in Comparative Perspective," 396.

23. Bacot Diary, September 1, 1862, SCDAH.

24. Bacot, *A Confederate Nurse*, 9. Bacot's criticism of coworker Esse Habersham occurs in her diary entry of August 21, 1862.

25. Bacot married a second time within a year of leaving Virginia—a South Carolina soldier whom she met at the hospital. The soldier, Lieutenant Thomas A. Clarke, was the brother of Frances Jane Clarke, who had served with Bacot in Charlottesville. Jean Berlin suspects that they met when Thomas was a patient at Midway Hospital after Second Manassas. Sadly, a mere two months after their nuptials, Lieutenant Clarke was killed in action. See Bacot, *A Confederate Nurse*, 15, 181–82.

26. Hawks earned her medical degree in 1857. For Zakrzewska's career trajectory and her founding of the New England Hospital for Women and Children in 1862, see Tuchman, *Science Has No Sex*, 2–3, 156–76. Though, Hawks considered Zakrzewska a lifelong

friend according to Gerald Schwartz, there is no mention of the friendship in Tuchman's biography. See Hawks, *A Woman Doctor's Civil War*, 11.

27. See Milton Hawks's tenth-anniversary musings in Esther Hill Hawks Papers, LC.

28. Hawks credits her brother, Edward O. Hill, corporal and steward in the 4th New Hampshire Infantry, with her ability to practice. See Hawks, *A Woman Doctor's Civil War*, 49–50.

29. For example, Hawks substitutes a reminiscence of the period from October 1862 to February 1864 for actual diary entries. See *A Woman Doctor's Civil War*, 33–57.

30. Ropes's editor, John Brumgardt, believes that William Ropes left his wife and children sometime between 1847 and 1855, though he has been unable to document the exact year. No correspondence has led him to discover why Ropes abandoned his family, but he speculates that the move to Florida might have been for health reasons. In any case, the Ropeses never again lived as husband and wife. See Ropes, *Civil War Nurse*, 8–10.

31. Alcott chronicles her six-week stint at Union Hotel in the 1863 narrative that first brought her name before the public, *Hospital Sketches*.

32. I discuss these events in greater detail in *Women at the Front*, 134–36.

33. See Ropes, *Civil War Nurse*, 77, 117–19.

34. None of these veteran nurses wrote a monograph about the war, though each was well known from her letters, from pension proceedings, and from legend inscribed in postwar accounts. See the Mary Ann Ball Bickerdyke Papers, LC; the special act of Congress pensioning Mary Morris Husband, U.S. Bureau of Pensions, Department of the Interior, Record Group 15, NARA; the papers of Ellen Matilda Orbison Harris at the Pennsylvania State Archives, Harrisburg; and Anderson, *The Story of Aunt Lizzie Aiken*.

35. Maine's Rebecca Usher, sister of Eaton's correspondent Ellen Usher Bacon, noted in her pension application, "We kept no diary we had no time for that. We were doing what we could to make history and had no time or inclination to write it. All our letters home were sent round to friends all over the state and most of them were lost." See Rebecca Usher to Commissioner of Pensions William Lochren, February 16, 1894, Usher pension file #1,132,097, Department of the Interior, Record Group 15, NARA.

36. "No time for journalizing," she wrote. See Eaton Diary, December 1, 1862.

37. The Bacon family genealogy does not list a death date for Harriet's older sister Agnes (b. April 25, 1817). It is likely, since Harriet's parents gave her "Agnes" as a middle name and since she does not mention sister Agnes in the diary, that Agnes did not survive beyond childhood. See Baldwin, *Bacon Genealogy*, 220.

38. See Douglas, *The Feminization of American Culture*, 58–59; Flexner, *Century of Struggle*, chapter 11; and Horowitz, *Alma Mater*, 9–12.

39. The Newton Theological Institution merged with Andover Theological Seminary in 1965.

40. Jeremiah Sewall Eaton to HE, January 11, 1839, DCUCS.

41. Jeremiah Sewall Eaton to HE, September 13, 1839, DCUCS.

42. For a description of the Amistad episode, see Davis, *Inhuman Bondage*, 12–26.

43. No image of Eaton from the war years has survived, but an indistinct photograph of two women in a canal boat by Antietam Bridge shows a likeness of Eaton and coworker Isabella Fogg. The photo appears to have been taken during late 1862 or the spring of 1863, when Eaton and Fogg were in and around Sharpsburg and Frederick. Eaton's diary entry of November 2, 1862 reports her tour of the Antietam battlefield, and reference to canal boats on November 14 and in a letter to Hatty Belle on November 15 suggests that it was a common conveyance for the women during that period. More importantly, the woman on the right is almost certainly Fogg, making it a good bet that her companion in the boat is Eaton.

44. Henry Melville King delivered an address on the occasion of the FSBC's seventy-fifth anniversary, which noted that "the pastor of my earlier boyhood days, whose genial face and manly form I can still see, was Rev. Jeremiah S. Eaton, the third pastor of the church. He was a man of gracious and winning spirit, and his wife was like unto him. He may not have been as great a preacher as some of his successors, according to the human standard of judgment, but I am certain that no pastor has held a larger or more affectionate place in the hearts of the people. And God owned and blessed his labors, until failing health compelled him to relinquish his pastorate of the church. His resignation was soon followed by his release from all earthly labor, September 27, 1856." See King, "The Church of My Boyhood," 6.

45. According to Brian McCarthy, a descendent of Hannorah McCarthy, she was born in 1797 and emigrated around 1849 with her children, at least one of which died on the sea voyage. Upon her arrival in Portland, she learned that her husband Daniel, who had planned to join her, had died of cholera in Ireland. Hannorah McCarthy lived in Portland until her death in May 1862. The 1860 census indicates that she was no longer with the Eatons—in all likelihood because Harriet could not afford a servant after she was widowed in 1856. By 1860, Irish immigrants were two-thirds of Portland's foreign-born population and 11% of the city's entire population of 30,000. See Eagan, "Working Portland," 194. With gratitude for Brian McCarthy's e-mail message of August 26, 2008. See also Dudden, *Serving Women*, 62.

46. See Sudlow's study of Maine relief workers, entitled *A Vast Army of Women*.

47. See Brockett and Vaughan, *Woman's Work in the Civil War*, 464. I regret that I have been unable to find any of Eaton's correspondence from this period.

48. Linus P. Brockett to Clara Barton, August 4, 1877, box 65, Clara Barton Papers, LC.

49. See Eaton, "Annual Report for 1878/1879," DCUCS.

50. See Jane E. Thurston, "In Memoriam," *Eastern Argus*, June 17, 1884.

51. For secondary accounts of the medical war, see George W. Adams, *Doctors in Blue*; Steiner, *Disease in the Civil War*; Gillett, *The Army Medical Department*; and Humphreys, *Intensely Human*.

52. On the religious militancy that informed military service, see Moorhead, *American Apocalypse*; Woodworth, *While God Is Marching On*, 93–116; and Fredrickson, "The Coming of the Lord," 118–19.

53. See Goen, *Broken Churches, Broken Nation*, especially chapter 4; and Shattuck, *A Shield and Hiding Place*, 16–20.

54. See Brekus, Marty, Gilpin, and Stout, "Religion and Violence in American Culture," 12–15.

55. See, for example, Stout, *Upon the Altar of the Nation*. Barbara Cutter notes that several years before the war, even conservative ministers were already exhorting women to play a more active role in national affairs, in the hope that they could stem the tide of unchecked male violence and dissipation. See Cutter, *Domestic Devils, Battlefield Angels*, 126–27.

56. Philip Paludan supports the notion that claims about conversion may have been inflated. See *"A People's Contest,"* 349.

57. See Blackett, *Running a Thousand Miles for Freedom*, 49.

58. See Reilly, *The Diaries of Sarah Jane and Emma Ann Foster*, li.

59. See Venet, *Neither Ballots nor Bullets*, 46; Moorhead, *American Apocalypse*, 39; and Reilly, *The Diaries of Sarah Jane and Emma Ann Foster*, 8–9.

60. See *Portland Daily Press*, April 1, 1864. Half the proceeds of Douglass's lecture were promised to the MCHA.

61. See *Portland Daily Press*, October 24, 1864.

62. See Judd, Churchill, and Eastman, *Maine, the Pine Tree State*, chapter 15.

63. Kelsey, "Maine's War Governor," 244; and Calhoun, "Longfellow's Portland," 85.

64. See, for example, Ring, *Maine in the Making of the Nation*, 396; and Kelsey, "Maine's War Governor," 246–47.

65. Quoted in Shain and Shain, *The Maine Reader*, 169. Travel from Portland to Virginia took several days and necessitated stops in Boston or New York, Philadelphia, and Baltimore, depending on the mode of conveyance. Benevolent workers in Philadelphia established the Cooper Shop saloon on Otsego Street in 1861 as a feeding and medical station for troops heading south, and later, for those heading north again. On June 3, 1861, 770 men from the 1st Maine dined there, while the 16th, 17th, and 19th Maine infantries all stopped there in August 1862 on their way to Virginia and the battle of Antietam. Cooper Shop volunteers fed 475, 520, and 500 soldiers, respectively, from these units during a three-day period. The 450 men of the 10th Maine took their ease there in April 1863 when, having been mustered out and ordered back to Maine to regroup, they broke their journey in Philadelphia. See Whitman and True, *Maine in the War for the Union*, 252; and John Moore, *History of the Cooper Shop Volunteer Refreshment Saloon*, 129, 155.

66. See *Portland Daily Press*, March 19, 1863.

67. See Frank Moore, *Women of the War*, 489.

68. See *Portland Daily Press*, January 24, 1863.

69. Charles W. Oleson to Charles Thurston, March 23, 1863, Thurston Papers, EU.

70. Frances Clarke has written extensively about the familial foundations of martial honor in *War Stories*.

71. Scontras, *Collective Efforts among Maine Workers*, 165–66.

72. Scontras, *Collective Efforts among Maine Workers*, 167; and Paludan, "A People's Contest," 189–95.

73. Scontras, *Collective Efforts among Maine Workers*, 173–74.

74. Ellen Usher Bacon to Rebecca Usher, April 12, 1865, Usher Family Papers, MHS. Ellen Usher Bacon was no relation to Harriet Bacon Eaton.

75. See Haley, *The Rebel Yell and the Yankee Hurrah*, 282.

76. See Savage, *Standing Soldiers, Kneeling Slaves*.

77. See, for example, Sudlow, *A Vast Army of Women*; MacCaskill and Novak, *Ladies on the Field*; Leonard, "Rebecca Usher of Maine"; and Conforti, *Creating Portland*.

78. The MCHA drafted a resolution on May 20, 1863, giving Eaton permission to return home. The language of the resolution declared that Eaton had "been compelled, on account of domestic considerations," to end her first tour of duty; that she had performed "disinterested, faithful, and arduous services...even amidst the deadly missiles of the enemy"; and that she had acted "as a ministering angel of mercy for the preservation of the lives of many, who, but for her aid, could not have survived their injuries." It is likely that Eaton begged permission to see her children after an eight-month absence, and she was ill as well. See resolution from the Office of the MCHA, Portland, May 20, 1863, DCUCS.

79. The WCRA would soon be subsumed under the umbrella of the USSC. See Boyd, *The Excellent Doctor Blackwell*, 184; Giesberg, *Civil War Sisterhood*, 31–34; and Attie, *Patriotic Toil*, 82–86.

80. Eaton Diary, October 27, 1864.

81. Jeanie Attie has written that "the Sanitary scheme called not only for relinquishing gendered control over benevolent work but foregoing allegiances to regional and state entities as well." See *Patriotic Toil*, 108; and Coon, "The Sisters of Charity in Nineteenth-Century America," 97.

82. Eaton Diary, October 11, 1862; and December 2 and 14, 1862. For more on Gilson and Fay, see Miller, "Angel of Light."

83. See, for example, Wittenmyer, *Under the Guns*; or Hoge, *The Boys in Blue*.

84. See, for example, Eaton Diary entries of January 5, 7, 15, 16, and 28, 1863; and February 14, 1863.

85. A steward charged with reporting to the Governor of Maine on the condition of relief services in the Army of the Potomac had this to say: "I find that the sanitary condition of the sick in Quarters and in field hospitals is much more neglected than that of those in hospitals about the cities. Many of the men have a sort of dread to [sic] going into hospitals and consequently suffer considerable [sic] rather than do so, and they are not so readily reached by the sanitary agents generally as others." See Steward Dill to Gov. Samuel Cony, February 2, 1864, Relief Agencies Collection, MSA.

86. Eaton Diary, May 10, 1863.

87. Eaton Diary, May 11, 1863.

88. Eaton Diary, May 12, 1863.

89. HE to Frank Moore, April 11, 1866, Frank Moore Papers, DU.

90. Philip Paludan, and more recently Drew Faust, has observed that death was a social process with as much emphasis on the witness as on the person dying—"a dialogue," in Paludan's words, "in which loved ones comforted the dying person and...that person could teach others how to give up the world and move toward the Lord." See Paludan, "*A People's Contest*," 365; and Faust, *This Republic of Suffering*, 137–70.

91. For information on Chamberlain's career with the 20th, see Pullen, *The Twentieth Maine*; Desjardins, *Stand Firm Ye Boys from Maine*; and Chamberlain, *The Passing of the Armies*.

92. For casualty statistics at Gettysburg, see Jordan, *Red Diamond Regiment*. These losses were not as significant as those of the 19th Maine, which lost 376 men, the 16th Maine, which lost 440, or the 1st Maine Heavy Artillery, which lost an astounding 683 men—more than 400 in battle and the rest to disease. See the Civil War Soldiers and Sailors System, a National Park Service website, for statistics at [http://www.itd.nps.gov/cwss/soldiers]. These numbers must be understood in the context of Maine's having sent a larger proportion of her available adult male population to war than any other Union state, nearly 60 percent by the end of the war. See Kelsey, "Maine's War Governor," 244.

93. Because Eaton's diary covered only the first and second tours of duty, we have no evidence of how she thought about her final tour in 1865.

94. Eaton Diary, November 5, 1862.

95. On a November evening in 1862, Eaton has a conversation with John M. Gould, Chaplain George Knox, and Charles Tibbets—all of the 10th Maine. Gould was from Portland, Knox from Brunswick, and Tibbets from Cape Elizabeth. See Eaton Diary, November 5, 1862.

96. Historian and diplomat Henry Adams had once described Washburn as "ugly as the very devil" but "good-humored" and "kindhearted." Quoted in Kelsey, "Maine's War Governor," 237. During the war's first winter (1861–62), illness ravaged under-supplied troops encamped in Augusta, waiting for orders to move to Washington. See Ring, *Maine in the Making of the Nation*, 394.

97. Eaton noted on her first day in Washington that "nearly all the states have men and women at work here for their own men, while we of Maine are quite behindhand [sic]." See HE to Agnes Eaton, October 8, 1862, DCUCS. A surgeon in the same regiment, Horatio N. Howard, also persuaded officials that a state organization could do much good: "There is a want in Regimental Hospitals which neither the Medical dept. of the army, nor the Sant Com can reach, and that want, the Relief Society, if its original plans be carried out energetically and in good faith, is destined to relieve. In order to accomplish its whole work its Agents must take the field, and there learn by personal observation the

deprivations and sufferings of the soldiers in camp, and bring them relief directly." For Howard and Knox letters, see MCHA minutes of November 17, 1862, MCHA Collection, MHS.

98. Hayes also became a wound dresser after the battle of Gettysburg, where he changed bandages for more than a hundred soldiers on one day alone. See Charles C. Hayes to Gov. Abner Coburn, July 8, 1863, Relief Agencies Collection, MSA.

99. See, for example, the *Portland Daily Press* of December 22, 1862, March 19, 1863, and June 1, 1863.

100. Eaton Diary, October 14, 16, and 24, 1862.

101. See, for example, J. W. Hathaway to Gov. Israel Washburn, December 3, 1862, Relief Agencies Collection, MSA. Hathaway came in time to praise the women's work.

102. See, for example, Maxwell, *Lincoln's Fifth Wheel*; Hawk, "An Ambulating Hospital," 197–219; and Garrison, *With Courage and Delicacy*. The primary source on the USSC, Charles Stillé, *History of the United States Sanitary Commission* also outlines these procedures, but without enough historical distance to evaluate their wartime efficacy.

103. See Oates, *A Woman of Valor*, 152–53; Pryor, *Clara Barton, Professional Angel*, 111–13; and Schultz, "Between Scylla and Charybdis," 58.

104. Rebecca Usher noted that despite all of the groups assembled to help soldiers at City Point, there were still those falling through the institutional cracks. She was shocked that the USCC had denied the men's request for shelter "on the ground of precedent." See Usher Diary, February 1, 1865, Usher Family Papers, MHS.

105. Adelaide W. Smith reported that during wet seasons, the roads became "a problem to try men's souls and women's soles too." See, Smith, *Reminiscences of an Army Nurse during the Civil War*, 80, 96; and Christie, "Performing My Plain Duty," 214.

106. Transports also carried soldiers to Baltimore and Philadelphia when Washington hospitals were filled to capacity. See, for example, George W. Adams, *Doctors in Blue*, 151; and Gillett, *The Army Medical Department*, 181, 186, 195, 214.

107. In the aftermath of the battle of Totopotomoy Creek (Virginia), the *New York Tribune* published a dispatch from an anonymous soldier on May 31, 1864 called "What a Woman Can Do—An Incident of the Late Battle," in which he lauded Quaker nurse Cornelia Hancock. He also noted that some relief workers were of "solid worth," while others of "tinsel" were capable only of a "desultory and fitful labor," which "is not what wounded men want." Hancock reported that "the piece in the paper has made a great stir and gained me many enemies." See Cornelia Hancock to her mother, June 24, 1864, Cornelia Hancock Papers, William L. Clements Library, University of Michigan, Ann Arbor.

108. Eaton Diary, October 23, 1864. For dissension between the commissions and state agencies, see also Cannon, "The United States Christian Commission," 61–80; and Bloor, *Letters from the Army of the Potomac*.

109. See Palmer, *The Story of Aunt Becky's Army Life*, quoted in Christie, "Performing My Plain Duty," 222.

110. See Hawk, "An Ambulating Hospital," 214.

111. Dr. Frederick Burmeister to Dr. Charles Crane, June 30, 1864; and Dr. E. B. Dalton to Dr. Frederick Burmeister, Record Group 112, Union Surgeon General's Office, NARA.

112. Eaton Diary, October 17, 1864.

113. See Thomas J. Brown's discussion of this matter in *Dorothea Dix, New England Reformer*, 312–15. Five weeks after Surgeon General Barnes was appointed, he made it possible for any U.S. surgeon to appoint any hospital worker, thus rendering Dix's selection standards inconsequential. See also Schultz, *Women at the Front*, 115.

114. Eaton Diary, October 18, 1864. By this time, Dix was widely known to reject youthful and good-looking petitioners from relief service. Eaton drolly considered that Dix's delight in her might not be "complimentary."

115. See Brown, *Dorothea Dix*, 298–300. See also Attie, *Patriotic Toil*, 190–93; and Giesberg, *Civil War Sisterhood*, 46–49, 108–9.

116. Eaton Diary, October 18, 1864. Eaton's experience resembled that of Louisa May Alcott, who described a similar set of roadblocks on her way to Union Hotel Hospital in *Hospital Sketches*.

117. Quoted in Alice Fahs' edition of Alcott's *Hospital Sketches*, 27.

118. Frances Clarke has demonstrated the authenticity of nostalgia as a psychological and physical affliction in "So Lonesome I Could Die."

119. Nina Bennett Smith argues that medical rivalries caused surgeons to perceive female nurses as additional threats. See Smith, "Men and Authority," 32.

120. Eaton Diary, March 27 and 31, 1863.

121. See Mattocks, *Unspoiled Heart*, 30. Mattocks would later be promoted to colonel of the 17th Maine.

122. The soldier in question, Private John West Haley, recorded this view in his diary entry of August 5, 1863. See Haley, *The Rebel Yell and the Yankee Hurrah*, 86.

123. See Pullen, *The Twentieth Maine*. Other regiments, like the 10th Maine, fared somewhat better by quarantining sick men before the disease spread. See Kallgren and Crouthamel, *"Dear Friend Anna"*, 52.

124. Eaton Diary, October 24, 1862. Dr. Wixom also reports having unintentionally killed a patient. See Eaton Diary, February 15, 1863.

125. Eaton Diary, January 11, 1863. On April 23, 1863, Eaton recorded her disgust at Wixom's fate: "Dismissed from the service in disgrace, forfeit his back pay and fined $150.00 in all amounting to $1590.00. So much for spending about $3000.00 and raising three companies, besides statistics proving him to be one of the most official surgeons in the army. A fitting reward! Oh my country."

126. Eaton Diary, May 6, 1863. An historian of the 17th Maine reported this account of Eaton's and Fogg's service at Chancellorsville: "Among those tending the enormous number of wounded were Mrs. Harriet Eaton and Mrs. Isabella Fogg of the Maine Camp Hospital Association. They were both in attendance at a field hospital in an old house near U.S. Ford. Despite the fact that the hospital was frequently struck by solid shot and shells, the two nurses did not leave until the wounded were evacuated Tuesday, May 5. While there they prepared huge quantities of beef stew and coffee which they ladled out to the famished troops. When the wounded were transferred to Washington hospitals, those valiant ladies accompanied them. Late in May, they were back in Portland preparing shipments of supplies for the sick and wounded they had so recently left." See Jordan, *Red Diamond Regiment*, 57.

127. Eaton Diary, May 4, 1863.

128. See Schultz, *Women at the Front*, 102–104; and "Seldom Thanked, Never Praised, and Scarcely Recognized," 220–36. On October 9, 1862, three days after Eaton's arrival, she visited George Whittier in camp and "looked...into the whites of the eyes of his piece of 'animated ebony'." See also Adelaide Smith, *Reminiscences of an Army Nurse*, 234–38.

129. See, for example, Eaton Diary, November 20, 1864.

130. Eaton Diary, October 22 and 29, 1864.

131. See, for example, Davis, *Inhuman Bondage*; and Patterson, *Slavery and Social Death*. The Unionist Kentuckian Frances Peter similarly observed willful disregard among the "servants" in her father's household: In 1862, they were willing to go to any lengths to help prepare food and supplies for hospitalized Union soldiers. But by early 1863, "they seem to think it is doing you a favor for them to consent and seem to have lost all interest in it." See Peter, *A Union Woman in Civil War Kentucky*, 118.

132. Eaton Diary, October 27 and November 25, 1864.

133. See, for example, Burrage, *History of the Baptists in Maine*, chapter 20.

134. See Scontras, *Collective Efforts among Maine Workers*, 168; Shain and Shain, *The Maine Reader*, 152; and Kelsey, "Maine's War Governor," 242.

135. See Charles W. Oleson to Charles Thurston, January 13 and April 5, 1863, Thurston Papers, EU. In the April letter, Oleson complained of abolitionist cowardice, "Not with the knapsack and cartridge box but rather skulking at home denouncing patriots and patriotic deeds and obstructing the wheels of government if they do not cry Nigger!! Nigger!!" He also mentioned that he and the other stewards at Eckington Hospital had formed a "negro minstrel club" called the Eckington Echoes.

136. See Benjamin Buxton to Julia Buxton, Donovan, *Civil War Surgeon, 5th Maine Volunteers*, 110.

137. See Lee, "'What They Lack in Numbers'," 219.

138. Eaton Diary, February 26, 1863.

139. Eaton Diary, December 28, 1862.

140. Eaton Diary, October 23 and November 5, 1864.

141. Eaton Diary, November 14 and 15, 1864 and December 8, 1864.

142. See, for example, Katharine Prescott Wormeley's account of her "sister" workers during the peninsular campaign, who were "efficient, wise, active as cats, merry, light hearted, [and] thoroughbred" in *The Other Side of War with the Army of the Potomac*, 44.

143. Aside from the commemorative works of Moore and Brockett, other narratives that convey a rosy picture of female cooperation include Dunlap, *Notes of Hospital Life from November 1861 to August 1863*; and Holstein, *Three Years in Field Hospitals of the Army of the Potomac*.

144. See Fogg's pension file (#129830), U.S. Bureau of Pensions, Department of the Interior, Record Group 15, NARA.

145. Eaton Diary, November 14, 1862.

146. The Adjutant General's Office of Maine lists Franklin Henry Eaton as a private in company A of the 25th Maine, a nine-month infantry regiment mustered out in July 1863; and in December 1863, as a private in company G of the 29th Maine. Frank left the service as a sergeant-major, having been promoted at some point during his sojourn with the 29th, but not likely during Eaton's first or second tour of duty, since she does not mention it in her diary. See *Annual Report of the Adjutant General of the State of Maine*. The friends who joined Frank in company A were Charlie Shaw, Bernard Hobbs, George Abbot, Lewis Robinson, Charles Cole, Alfred Whitmore, Frank L. Jones, and Hanson Hart—all of whom were from Portland.

147. Charley Oleson noted that Frank "steams it rather hard" and was fond of playing billiards at Swasey's in Portland before his enlistment. The implication is that Frank was a drinker. See Charles W. Oleson to Charles Thurston, April 29, 1862, Thurston Papers, EU.

148. For accounts of Hugh and Isabella Fogg's travails, see Sudlow, *A Vast Army of Women*, 92–100; MacCaskill and Novak, *Ladies on the Field*; Frank Moore, *Women of the War*, 113–26; Brockett and Vaughan, *Woman's Work in the Civil War*, 504–10; and Mundy, *No Rich Men's Sons*.

149. Eaton Diary, October 21 and November 14 and 15, 1862. The bickering resulted in HE's refusal to accompany Fogg on a trip to the regiments the following day.

150. See, for example, Eaton Diary, December 9, 1862 and March 12, 1863. On the growing rift, see Eaton Diary, December 12, 18, and 19, 1862.

151. Charles C. Hayes to J. W. Hathaway, December 22, 1862, Relief Agencies Collection, MSA.

152. Eaton Diary, January 12, 1863.

153. Eaton Diary, January 21, 1863.

154. See Isabella Fogg to Geroge W. Dyer, February 26, 1863, Relief Agencies Collection, MSA. For a discussion of trouble with Quartermaster Litchfield, see Sudlow, *A Vast Army of Women*, 97; and MacCaskill and Novak, *Ladies on the Field*, 28–31. MacCaskill and Novak hypothesize that Eaton was acting only as secretary to Fogg, taking down her letter, but the turns of phrase are so much like Eaton's that I believe Eaton composed the letter and simply declined to sign it.

155. Eaton Diary, March 15, 1863. Fogg's reasons for calling upon Dr. Hezless to treat her are unknown.

156. Eaton Diary, March 17, 1863.

157. Dr. John Moore from Bloomington, Indiana, was one of the Army of the Potomac's medical directors when he saw Fogg in March 1863. A man of vast medical and military experience known for his pleasant demeanor, he served as U.S. Surgeon General from 1886 to 1890. Charles D. Gilmore, the man HE referred to as "Major," was a soldier in the 20th, but he spent little time in action after he was wounded at Lee's Mills in April 1862. On detached service in Washington, Gilmore befriended Eaton and defended her when Fogg went on the attack.

158. Quoted in Denney, *Civil War Medicine*, 227. Thanks to Lyn Sudlow for bringing this passage to my attention.

159. See minutes of the MCHA, November 30, 1863, MCHA Collection, MHS.

160. Eaton Diary, October 22, 1864 and December 22, 1864.

161. Though "the lady with the lamp" was first used to describe Florence Nightingale's work in the Crimea, it came to characterize any nurse engaged in hospital work during the Civil War. "A woman of valor" plays both on the Biblical proverb (*Proverbs* 31:10) and the title of Stephen Oates's biography of Clara Barton.

162. Eaton Diary, October 12, 1862.

163. Eaton Diary, October 26, 1862; November 2, 1862; and December 21 and 28, 1862. John Haley of the 17th Maine wrote, "Here the observance of [Sunday] is generally of the most farcical character. We now and then go through the forms of service, but Sunday is no different from any other day, except that the inspections are more rigid than on secular days." See entry of October 16, 1864 in Haley, *The Rebel Yell and the Yankee Hurrah*, 209.

164. Eaton Diary, October 18, 1862.

165. On the other hand, some soldiers believed that the deathbed was no place for proselytizing. A Bangor man was critical of what he believed were pious do-gooders: "Is it possible that any Christian men in attendance upon dying men will torture them with inquisitions on controversial questions of theology? If so, they should be driven from camp." Doubts of this order did little to lessen the zeal of those who were certain that such interventions were always in the soldier's best interests. See Godfrey, *The Journals of John Edwards Godfrey*, 84.

166. Harry Stout has noted that moral and religious imperatives paved the way for a rationalization of war-making in both sections. The conduct of women called to serve Jesus in serving the nation was part of the larger schematic that Stout describes. See *Upon the Altar of the Nation*. For a discussion of the blurring of the physical and psychological dimensions of nostalgia, see Clarke, "So Lonesome I Could Die," 253–82.

167. Franny Nudelman emphasizes this point in *John Brown's Body*, where the pain of families at losing their kinfolk in battle was exacerbated without a body to bury. To forestall this fate, Elizabeth Ring reports that women in Limington with sons in the service instructed them to write home with all the details of their comrades' illnesses and deaths. See Ring, *Maine in the Making of the Nation*, 391.

168. My reference is to Drew Faust, "The Civil War Soldier and the Art of Dying," 3–38. Though Faust makes primarily southern sources the meat of her study, she implies that the

religiously enacted conventions of dying transcended section. Alice Fahs has noted that "it was a cultural affront that wartime death occurred outside of the framework of sentimental norms that emphasized a tender, emotive parting from family and friends." See her introduction to *Hospital Sketches*, 39. For further evidence of the consternation caused by the prospect of unprepared military souls passing into eternity, see Janney, *The Civil War Journals of Paulena Stevens Janney*, January 24 and February 12 and 19, 1862.

169. See Woodworth, *While God Is Marching On*, 207–8, and chapter 11 more generally; and Faust, "Christian Soldiers," 63–90. Even though Faust's focus is on Rebel soldiers, revivalism was common in both sections.

170. Small, *The 16th Maine Regiment in the War of the Rebellion*, 125. Woodworth notes that this elaborate worship space was not completed until 1864. See *While God Is Marching On*, 229.

171. Eaton Diary, November 7 and 9, 1862; and January 25, 1863.

172. Eaton Diary, February 22, 1863. For views about the efficacy of one-on-one conversions in which Adams placed the greatest confidence, see *Memorial and Letters of Rev. John R. Adams*; and Brandegee, *The Bugle Call*.

173. Though understandable, Eaton's worry was needless. The 25th was involved in no action during its nine-month period of service. Frank's friend Charley Oleson, who had managed to get himself out of foot soldiering with the 16th Maine into a plum position as a hospital steward in Washington, noted that the 25th, stationed at Long Bridge in February 1863, were "having a very easy time of it indeed," billeted in an old hotel. "It is holiday soldiering with them, none of the marches, the wet camping grounds, the turbid-sickening water and poor and insufficient rations which were my lot last summer in Virginia." Two months later, Frank's regiment had been ordered to picket duty at Fairfax Court House, but still no action. Oleson reported that "the boys say they should be ashamed to go home and say that they had never seen a rebel and be dubbed like the 1st Maine as 'the guardians of farm-houses and hencoops'." See Charles W. Oleson to Charles Thurston, February 19 and April 5, 1863, Thurston Papers, EU.

174. Eaton Diary, April 15, 1863.

175. Eaton Diary, November 21, 1864.

176. Eaton Diary, November 29 and December 1, 1864.

177. Eaton Diary, December 3 and 4, 1864.

178. Eaton Diary, December 6 and 10, 1864.

179. In HE's last journal entry, she writes, "I never can express my gratitude for having been permitted this season with the Army." See Eaton Diary, December 24, 1864.

180. See U.S. censes for 1870, 1890, and 1910 for "Nathaniel P. Jaques." For full histories of postwar veterans' homes, see Kelley, *Creating a National Home*; and Rosenburg, *Living Monuments*.

181. See A. M. Childes to HE, February 24, 1868, DCUCS, for information about Frank Eaton's marriage.

182. See Cumming, *Kate: The Journal of a Confederate Nurse*, 39, 40, 61–65.

183. Eaton Diary, April 28, 1854.

184. Eaton Diary, May 10, 1854.

185. See Jeremiah Eaton's account books, DCUCS; and Harriet Eaton's supply lists, Eaton Diary, SHC.

Appendixes

LETTERS, NEWSPAPER ACCOUNTS, AND OFFICIAL CORRESPONDENCE CONCERNING HARRIET EATON

1. HE to Agnes Eaton, October 8, 1862, DCUCS.

Washington, Oct. 8th 1862

My darling Agnes,

You see by the date that I have started on my mission.—I left P[ortland] in company with Mrs. Fogg (a lady who has been with the army a year) on Monday morning and traveling day and night arrived here on Tuesday evening 7 o' clock.—Hatty Belle went to Gorham with Mrs. Whittier on Sabbath afternoon after meeting. She seemed very happy about going to the very last. Frank came in town Saturday night and staid till Monday morning not being very well, but was better or I should have delayed my journey. There was some prospect that their regiment would be ordered off tomorrow. As yet no definite plan has been arranged, for we have not yet seen the Maine agent. Yesterday we first called on Mrs. Mc Intyre, who you know resides here (Abby Hart). Then we went to the Post Office and Patent Office departments to see the agents of the Mass. and Michigan Relief Associations and learn from them their plan of operations.—Nearly all the states have men and women at work here for their own men, while we of Maine are quite behindhand. Then we visited the Armory and Douglas Hospitals and talked with our poor sick men of their homes and tried to comfort them.—Oh if you could have seen how they <u>cried</u> for joy to see some one from their own state.—It is a sad, sad sight to see so many maimed for life but the [*sic*] most of them were cheerful. One poor fellow had <u>both eyes</u> shot out and yet he seemed in good spirits. Another one with a shattered arm was leading him about. Edward Whittier came to see us yesterday, and to day he came with an ambulance to take us out to their camp about 2 miles from here.—It is situated in a most lovely grove and there I saw George Whittier too, and we went into their little tents, each one has his own tent not large enough to stretch in, but still comfortable because the place is so beautiful. Near them is Aikington [Eckington] Hospital, formerly the splendid residence of a secesh whose property is confiscated. Here poor Charley Oleson is sick.—He is sadly emaciated so that I should hardly have known him, but his mother came to see me Sunday and begged me to find him.—Poor fellow, he did not know I was coming and he kissed me again and again.—He is getting better they think, but has no appetite and is very low spirited.—The Hospitals we have visited are among the very best in the vicinity of Washington and everything looks very nice, still there is not much variety in the food to tempt the taste of a poor invalid and if this is the case here, how the poor sick ones in the camps, where we want to go, must suffer.—George Whittier had a letter from his mother yesterday in which she told him to tell me Hatty Belle had just been helping to get in a load of potatoes and was perfectly contented. It seems as if I could hardly wait till I can get to work in some way for these sick, suffering men. There seems to be great uncertainty whether there is to be another battle soon or not. The weather is intensely hot. We sleep with both windows open, and can scarcely bear any covering on the bed. I shall be glad when it is cooler, I can do more. Nothing is known or thought of here but the war. Oh you can have no idea of it.—The city is one vast assemblage of troops, army wagons and Hospitals and the streets, avenues of choking dust.—Mrs. Fogg has gone to the War department to make inquiries in regard to the situation of our regiments while I have remained at our boarding house to meet our agent if he should call.—I am anxious to receive word from you about receiving your trunk &c. but I suppose I must wait several days first.—I cannot tell yet where to have you direct your letters, perhaps before I seal this I may know. I have not yet taken my trunk from the depot. Friday morn, I have got my trunk, nothing new to tell you yet though rumor says the 25th, Frank's regiment, is ordered to Baltimore. Love to Aunt and Uncle and all friends and always do what your conscience tells you to be right.

Your affectionate mother

2. HE to Mrs. B[osworth], October 14, 1862, Semi-Annual Report of the MCHA, 1863, MHS.

Washington, Oct. 14th 1862

My Dear Mrs. B.:

No doubt you have wondered at our long silence, but we have been rather compelled to it, as you will learn from this. I think in the hurried note I pencilled to you on our arrival, I mentioned we were to have an interview with Mr. Hathaway that day.

*** On Friday he came to us in great haste, requesting us immediately to go to the Georgetown Seminary Hospital for officers to look after the wants of a very sick man. Capt. Rand, Co. D, 16th Me., as well as several others who were sick there. We found him dangerously ill and lacking suitable attendance. I went again next day and sat with him during the afternoon. His expression of feeling that a lack of sympathy had been manifest in our own State with reference to the sick, as compared with other States, was in unison with the statements of all our sick in hospitals. It is evident a great work is to be done here, to meet such wants, but outside of these we cannot forget the suffering ones, who are wholly destitute of care. I could fill my letter with incidents of interest concerning the Maine men in hospitals. The tears often roll down their cheeks as they give expression to their joy, at last, seeing a face from Maine. * * * We are just going to start for Frederic[k] and Harpers Ferry, and I shall not be able to finish this till we get there.

"Relay House," quarter to one. Here we have to remain till five, for the cars for Frederic[k] and Harpers Ferry. Mrs. Fogg was very successful in her efforts to obtain supplies for regiments from the Commission this morning. Mr. Knapp was very cordial, and gave orders for anything we wished of such things as they had. Mrs. Fogg has been writing to Mr. Jewett, and she mentions, perhaps, about the same things as myself among them a letter received from Mr. Hathaway, as a certificate of good character, &c., recommending us to the kind attentions of all we meet.

Yours truly, H. Eaton

3. HE to Mrs. B[osworth], October 23, 1862, Semi-Annual Report of the MCHA, 1863, MHS, Reprinted in the *Portland Daily Press*, October 30, 1862.

Letter to the Army

The following communication is from Mrs. H. A. Eaton, widow of the late Rev. J. S. Eaton of this city. Mrs. Eaton, in company with Mrs. Fogg of Calais, left Portland some four weeks since with the purpose of laboring for the sick and wounded connected with the Maine regiments in the Army of the Potomac. It is believed that many soldiers when first attacked by disease, who feel unwilling to be sent to the hospitals, might, by suitable and timely care, be saved from a fit of sickness, and perhaps from death. It is evident also that the <u>regimental</u> hospitals suffer exceedingly for want of that <u>special, extra</u> care which now render the hospitals in and near Washington "<u>comparatively</u>" comfortable. A few individuals in this vicinity have felt that great good and a much needed service could be rendered our Maine regiments, by sending a few <u>valuable nurses</u> who should <u>visit</u> them—<u>not abide with them</u>—and minister to the necessities of the sick, the wounded, and the needy.—Other communications are expected; and if they shall favor the enterprise, it is proposed to organize a committee which shall look after the support of such as may be employed in this mission, and the supply of materials for their benevolent operations.

Washington, Oct. 23rd 1862

My Dear Mrs. B.:

On leaving the Relay House, where our last letters were mailed, I was somewhat dismayed at the prospect of reaching Frederick in the evening without positive accommodations for the night. When shall I learn to trust? A gentleman in the cars kindly offered to secure us rooms, and we had no trouble. You must know every place there is filled with sick and wounded men. Every church but one, and the basement of that, every school house, every hotel but two, as well as private houses.

In the morning Col. [Samuel] Allen of the Maine Cavalry, went out with us to their encampment.—We visited their hospital, ministered to their wants, also to those of the sick in their quarters. The hospital seemed very well cared for, and looked quite neat; two or three were very sick. Col. Allen expressed a wish that we should visit another hospital of about 700 patients, at Comp. A, about a mile distant.—For this purpose he sent an ambulance, and Lieut. Coleman attended us. Here we saw sights to make the heart ache. In some of the wards the stench and filth was almost intolerable. On one bed lay one of our Maine boys with no shirt, and only a linen coat to cover him. We gladly supplied him with a nice flannel shirt. On the opposite cot lay a poor fellow who had been shot in the lungs; he was almost black with flies, had been vomiting without being able to move, and had had no attendance for some time. In one ward were five Maine men, mostly from Saco and Biddeford, who said they were almost starved—had only five loaves of bread dealt out for seventeen men. This hospital is cared for by male nurses, entirely. We reported its state to Col. Allen, who said it was just the corroboration of his own opinion that he wanted, and he would report the case to the Medical Director for that post.

Stopped at a farm house for the night, where one of the captains and the quartermaster of the regiment were boarding. They entered into our plans with much enthusiasm, the quartermaster expressing the utmost confidence in the good that would result, only fearing that we might be overworked or taken prisoners! Col. Allen and other officers gave us "God speed" with great warmth.

Next morning started for Harpers Ferry, and had a delightful ride on the banks of the Monocacy, the railroad pursuing the winding course of the river for many a mile. "Point of Rocks" is indeed rightly named; now we see encampments in all directions, soldiers at every turn, and nothing seen or thought of but war, war, war! Never, however, did I see desolation till we reached Harpers Ferry. One of the most lovely spots in nature covered with evidences of the ravages of war. At the cars, as we were stepping out, we were met by Lieut. Coleman again, who informed us that he had been summoned there, after leaving us the day before, to see his brother, of the Maine 19th, who was very sick of typhoid fever. On our offering to go to see him, he seemed much gratified, and procured a conveyance for us to Bolivar, that regiment being camped on the Heights. Finding the young captain very sick, I decided to remain with him, while Mrs. Fogg proceeded to headquarters to learn what she could with reference to our mission, the possibility of securing an ambulance for our work, and last, though not least, to find the Maine 6th and visit her son. * * * She hastened back to the Ferry Sabbath afternoon, but not till she had fully detailed our plans to many commanding officers and medical directors, who, without a dissenting voice, approved our work. In the mean time, I stood by the bedside of that noble young captain, prepared his nourishment (I wish you could have seen the gruel made before I came), bathed his head, and tried to point him to Jesus. His brother, in an agony of grief, tried to get from him some message for his mother; then he would step aside and beg me to gain from him some assurance that he was prepared to die, but in his delirium he would only exclaim, "March on my men, march on." I could only keep repeating in his ear passages from the Bible or a stanza from some appropriate hymn, leaving the case with Him who judgeth righteously. His brother and myself were alone with him when he passed away, and as I closed those glazed eyes, those speechless lips, I thanked my Heavenly Father I had been permitted to perform those last sad offices in place of those dear ones with whom he was almost an idol. He died on Saturday morning and in company with his brother, I went to the Ferry with his remains, he deciding to take them immediately home to Lincolnville, Maine.

Sabbath morning, I walked over to Bolivar Heights to the encampment of the Maine 19th to attend the service. Was received very courteously by Col. Sewall and other officers. * * * After service, in company with the surgeon, I visited the hospital; it was very neat, but the poor men have nothing but cotton shirts, and it is very cold. Found also they have no stimulants, for want of which some of the men are dying, no farina, &c. The surgeon begged us to get these things for their use immediately. Next morning we visited the General Hospital; the young doctor there felt all sufficient, and said his wants were all supplied. Whether the men thought so or not, is another question. * * *

I went over to the Regimental Hospital of the 19th Massachusetts at the earnest request of one of the male nurses.—Here I found the men in a sad condition. They had the shelter of a house to be sure, but it was an empty one indeed, no beds, not even straw, part of them no blankets, no pillows, their knapsacks under their heads. Two of them, I think, will live but a short time; one, I think, from Lynn, has a wife and two children, sick with chronic diarrhea and rheumatism; it is with difficulty he can move, he lays near the door, wind blowing on him; says he thinks he may stand it a month longer. Oh! how it makes my heart ache to look at them. We returned to Washington on Monday. All we have seen and heard during our absence confirms us in the opinion that the great work now left undone, is in our regiments. The city hospitals are comparatively well cared for.—But to do this work money must be had and supplies furnished, as we cannot live on air. I do not think a large outlay would be called for.

Yours truly, H. Eaton

4. HE to Mrs. B[osworth], November 5, 1862, Semi-Annual Report of the MCHA, 1863, MHS, Reprinted in the *Portland Daily Press*, November 15, 1862.

Berlin, Nov. 5th 1862

My Dear Mrs. B.:

One month to-morrow has elapsed since we left Portland; it seems nearer six months, so much has transpired since I saw you. Writing is almost out of the question. We go from ambulance to hospital and from hospital to ambulance. Sometimes we find a corner to lie down in a parlor, sometimes in a common dining hall we throw ourselves on the floor for the night, and think how much better off we are than our poor suffering soldiers. I am now writing in a room where there are ten or twelve eating dinner and two sick men. We have been visiting hospitals and hovels where the poor fellows who have fallen back or been sent back from the main army, are lying on the floor without the first thing necessary for comfort, no beds, no pillows, no surgeon even, and only hard bread and pork to eat. In one miserable hovel, without door or windows we found seven men, one of whom I thought looked very suspicious as a case of small pox. We searched round, found a doctor, had the case examined, found our suspicions correct, reported the case to Col. Fillebrown of the Maine 10th, received his earnest thanks, while he sent the officer of the day with us to point out the hut.

Now about our movements since I last wrote you or Mrs. Jewett. We were then at Frederic[k]. We remained there, partly waiting for a box of supplies which they had neglected to send us, but not without plenty of work to do, until Saturday morning. Sometimes the Sanitary Commission aids us, and sometimes it baffles us. In one case, we were refused a flannel shirt where a young man needed it immediately, who had had the measles. We were determined he should have it, and I went to a store and bought one myself. Afterwards they apologized, said it was a blunder of theirs. Then some of the poor fellows wanted a little cracker toast. At that time they had no crackers in the "Commission," so we bought those, made the toast, and carried them lemons the same way. These things were for the Regimental Hospital of our Maine Cavalry. Part of their sick men were on straw on the ground; but before we left F. we gave ourselves no rest till we saw them all on cots with their hospital tents floored. We left Frederic[k] on Saturday morning, in an ambulance for Sharpsburg, accompanied by Mr. Hayes. Stopped first at Middletown, visited a hospital in which were two Maine men. Here we found the sick comfortably provided for by the kind ladies in the place. We crossed two battlefields and saw all over the ground the sad evidences of those fearful days. At Kedarsville [Keedysville] we visited four hospitals in which were many Maine men in a most miserable condition. They had been there but a few days, were without medicine and hospital stores; and as yet we were without supplies. We hope to visit them again very soon.

Instead of going to Sharpsburg that night we decided to turn aside to Smoketown Hospital. <u>Smoketown</u> indeed! We found the air stifling, both from smoke and the effluvia from soiled clothes and all kinds of filth all around the camp. Here were about 700 men, some thirty from our own State, and here, to their shame I say it, were five ladies with hospital tents, abundance of stores, cook stoves, and with all other appurtenances; to their shame, I say, because they had not taken measures to see that the filth was removed that was producing malarious diseases to add to their other sufferings. Sick men were lying here who begged, as we were passing, for clothing to put on that they might rise from their beds and walk about a little. They had not even drawers. Oh if we had only had some comforts for these poor fellows. The tears started for joy, even for a friendly shake of the hand and a kind word.

We stopped at a farm house near the hospital, and next morning continued our journey. On the way found in a school-house at Bakersville twenty-three men of the Maine 5th. They had been left behind as their regiment moved on, and by some mistake were left without any supplies. They seemed to have a very excellent hospital steward, and were trying to make the best of it. We promised to see that things were provided for them by the Commission at Sharpsburg, if they could send there; and they tho't [*sic*] they should be able to do this through the kindness of a good Union man in the neighborhood. Arriving at Sharpsburg in the morning, crossed the pontoon bridge for Harpers Ferry. We had already kept our ambulance a day longer than it had been detailed for us, although Capt. Boothby, of the Cavalry, told us the driver was to take us where we might wish to go. Gen. Slocum detailed an ambulance to take us to the convalescent camp at Loudon Valley, which we visited especially at his request.

We now had a load of supplies in our ambulance procured not without a <u>vast amount</u> of grumbling from the Sanitary Commission, who in every way, show their hatred to State organizations. However, by little and little, we succeeded in gathering quite a stock to start with. At the convalescent camp, the poor men had just arrived; their tents and supplies were on the way, while they were hungry and suffering. We made gruel and hot coffee for the <u>worst cases, about fifty in number, did what we could for them for a few hours, then returned over the Shenandoah and Potomac and proceeded to Berlin. Our Maine 10th are here. We are taking our meals at one house and sleeping at another</u>. When at Bolivar, we visited the hospital of the Maine 19th, left there on the advance of the regiment. They were almost destitute of hospital supplies, had 51 men in charge, some very sick, a good physician, Dr. [John Q. A.] Hawes, son of Rev. Mr. Hawes, of Maine. It was a source of great satisfaction to us to inform them that through a requisition we had made at Frederic[k], a box of supplies was then ready for them at the Ferry. It was immediately sent for, and gladdened many hearts, as well as healed their bodies. Here at Berlin the Maine 10th have a hospital in the negro church, of some eighteen or twenty men. Dr. [Horatio] Howard seems interested in his men, and doing all he can for them. They have beds, pillows, and blankets. We have made gruel and milk punch for those who required it, and one man who was <u>very low</u> seems really to be rallying from the effects of a little extra care, and change of diet. It is one vast hospital. I cannot picture it; my heart is sick. The great army must be attended to; but the thousands and tens of thousands who have fallen by the wayside, how few care for such!

Truly yours, H. Eaton

5. Isabella Fogg [HE] to Col. John W. Hathaway, November 10, 1862, Relief Agencies Collection, MSA.

Berlin, Nov. 10th 1862

Mr. Hathaway,
Dear Sir,

I suppose Mr. W[atson] has given you some information in regard to how we were occupying our time in Frederic[k], so I will give you some account of our movements since. We left Frederic[k] on Saturday, the 1st in company with Mr. Hayes, stopped at Middletown, and found them very comfortable, men happy, said the ladies were very kind, went on to Kedarsville [Keedysville], but what a painful contrast! there we found several Maine men in a church and three other buildings occupied as Hospitals, lying on the bare floor with their coats for pillows. Their stores consisted of hard bread, beef, and coffee, as we had no supplies with us, of course we could not relieve, they promised to apply to the Commission on the day following. We then went up to Smoketown Hospital, here we found 30 Maine men. This place is in a most miserable condition, the men complain very much although Mrs. Harris and several Penn. ladies, with a great quantity of supplies were there. The effluvia arising from the condition of these grounds is intolerable, quite enough to make a man in perfect health sick, and how men can recover in such a place is a mystery to me. We then went to Bakersville, saw there 25 of the 5th Maine, left in a school house in care of the steward, without supplies; found him making every effort to keep them comfortable, we inquired why he did not call on the Commission, he replied, he had always found so many difficulties in obtaining them from this source he preferred purchasing himself. We told him, we would go to the Commission; and have what he required put up for him, here we opened your box of jelly. We then came to Sharpsburg, the Maine troops had crossed the river, only five Maine men were left here, also Capt. [Lysander] Hill of the 20th in a private house. We did what we could for his comfort and then proceeded to Harpers Ferry. Here the sick are in a fearful condition, in every old house and church and hundreds on the ground. You no doubt think your ladies in Washington are doing a great work, but I can assure you, if they were here, they would find the <u>stern reality of want, privation, and extreme suffering</u>. We visited the sick of the 19th in care of Dr. [John Q. A.] Hawes asst. surgeon, he has upwards of 50, does all in his power for their comfort. At Gen. Slocum's request we went over to Loudon Valley to learn the condition of several hundreds who had been sent the day previous without any preparation. We found them lying about on the ground, in all directions, many convalescent, but a great many <u>very low</u>. At this time no surgeons, nurses, or cooks were on the ground and hard bread their only food. Fortunately, we had that morning obtained a <u>few supplies</u> from the Commission, after much pleading, for they actually appeared as if they were contributing out of their own pocket and for <u>our</u> personal wants, however, we went to work to administer to the wants of the sick, Mrs. E[aton] to wash and clean them, which they stood greatly in need of, while I prepared food for them. Mr. Hayes went in search of Maine men, but I found none, we however found famishing soldiers. After feeding every one who could not help themselves we left for Berlin, and here the misery and suffering beggars all description, the heart sickens at the sight. We visited the Hospital of the 10th Maine, found them more comfortable than many others, but yet very much can be <u>added</u> to <u>their</u> comfort. Taking a stroll through the town, we searched every old school house, log cabin, &c. for the poor men who had been left behind, as our army moved on. In an old hut destitute of doors or windows and minus a part of the roof, we found 7 men, who having slept in the woods the night before, had crept in there, for the miserable shelter the place afforded.—Our inquiries were for Maine men, and although these were not from our State, they claimed our sympathy.—Conversing with one of them, he told us he was sick, thought he had the measles, on this point our opinion did not coincide with his, we supposing it to be a case of small pox, which of course required immediate attention. With no little difficulty we at least succeeded in finding the surgeon of the district, who corroborated our opinion, our next step was to report to Col. [James S.] Fillebrown who expressed earnest thanks for our attention to the case.—In a dilapidated school house, without fire place, we found a man sick and old, who had enlisted in the Maine 12th. He was now 57 years old, had been left, injured in the spine at Fortress Munroe [sic], then knocked about from one Hospital to another, thrust into a New York Regiment, till at last all discouraged, he knew not what to do. Measures have now been set on foot [sic] by Mr. Hayes for his discharge.—Learning there were men left from Franklin's Corps in a very destitute condition at Hagerstown, and feeling anxious to furnish some supplies for those we had seen the week previous at Kedarsville, we here separated, Mrs. E[aton] to attend to duties here, while I, in company with Mr. Hayes who was anxious to find more of our men who were scattered all along the way, took an ambulance en route for Hagerstown.—While at Harpers Ferry, we had stated the suffering condition of those at Kedarsville to Dr. [John] McNulty, Medical Director in charge at Harpers Ferry, who expressed great surprize [sic] to learn that there were any there, he having had them all removed from that place a short time since, (but of our sick and wounded men it may be said their name is Legion and almost as fast as an old ruined building is emptied, it is filled by other stragglers) however, through the information received from us, he had again caused their removal and we were spared from again witnessing that scene of want and hunger.—Next visited the Russell Springs Hospital, found them comparatively comfortable with only three Maine men.—Again we went to Smoketown, hoping to find them in a more comfortable condition than when we were last there, but how sadly were we disappointed.—How I wish I could introduce you, and the Washington Com. to Smoketown Hos. in the midst of this driving snow storm! You would have seen the poor fellows huddled together, with their pallets of straw on the ground, their tents connected by flys [sic], the same as erected in the heat of summer, many without walls and no stoves.—Those who were able to creep out of their tents were crouched over fires, built in the woods, their heads covered with snow. And all, I may say, almost without exception with their muslin shirts on.—The exposure has been such that diphtheria has broken out among them, and in nearly every case proves fatal. One of our poor Maine boys who had been very diligent in looking up for us those belonging to Maine, at our last visit had been seized suddenly with diphtheria, caused by exposure, and lived but two or three hours.—Distributing what few articles we had received from the Commission among them, we moved on, deeply regretting we had no winter clothing, as many of them were destitute of stockings. I cannot describe what my feelings were that I had no articles of clothing to distribute especially as the chaplain told us, there were plenty to take their names but few to relieve their wants. Next, we proceeded to the school house at Bakersville, where so many of the 5th Maine had been left without supplies. Imagine our indignation to find that the requisition we had left for them with the Commission at Sharpsburg had been cut off fully one half on every article. They probably were not expecting we should be on the track again.—We found the industrious steward, William Noyes of Saco, grating corn on a grater he had made from an old canteen, to furnish meal wherewith to make gruel for his sick men. This is only a sample of his expedience for his men, give his name a place in your reports for he is worthy. At Hagerstown we found several Maine men, but in a more comfortable condition than we had expected. The citizens deserve great credit for their efforts in providing for the wants of the sick soldiers as there are nearly a thousand in that vicinity. But we found very many of our Maine men with muslin shirts on and some without any.— Here we found three boxes for Maine Regiments, one of them not much account, containing mostly old pillow cases, another chiefly muslin shirts but the third, to our great joy, contained upwards of a hundred flannel shirts, with some other useful articles. Imagine now, with what pleasure we retraced our steps, to Bakersville and Smoketown! Could you have seen the happy faces and heard the thankful expressions of gratitude you would have felt that too much could not be done for their comfort.—We then came on to Burketsville, found many Maine men there and they likewise were without woolen shirts. We were able also to supply them and arrived home about 7 o' clock, after the tedious labor and hard exposure of three days. I should have written before but I suppose Mr. Hayes and Mr. Watson kept you informed of our movements. You may [be] assured however we have not spent much idle time. It will not be necessary to reply to this, as we expect soon to report to you at Washington unless ordered otherwise by you.

Yours with very great respect,
I[sabella] Fogg

6. HE to Hatty Belle Eaton, November 15, 1862, DCUCS.

Berlin Maryland, Saturday evening
Nov. 15th 1862

My precious little daughter,

I was made very happy last Sunday night by receiving your nice long letter. It was printed so plain that I could read it very easy. I am glad you thought so much of dear mother as to send such a long letter. It makes me very happy that you are getting along so well, also that Aunty says you are such a good girl. I do not think you would like to be here, for there is nothing pretty about the place, the houses are very old and the streets are so bad, so full of rocks and holes, that you cannot ride in them. They are very dirty too, and the pigs are running all about. There is an old cat that likes to come into the room where we stop, and there are some little mice that run round all night, so if we have anything to eat, we must put it on the mantel piece.—I am tired to night for I have been making gruel almost all day for the sick men. We are going to Washington next week in a canal boat drawn by a horse, and when I get to W[ashington] I hope I shall see Frank, dear Frank. I am very glad that he was able to go out to Gorham and see you, and I do hope this war will be over soon, and we can <u>all</u> be happy at home again. I was very much pleased with the pretty flowers you sent me and I shall keep them in the letter. It is so warm here to day, that I have gone to the Hospital without any thing on over my calico morning dress and my scarf tied over my head, but last Saturday night it was a thick snow storm. I have had one letter from dear Agnes.—Now dear Hatty, be a very good obedient girl and give them <u>all</u> kisses for me.

Your own dear mother

7. HE to Mrs. B[osworth], December 11, 1862, Semi-Annual Report of the MCHA, 1863, MHS, reprinted in the *Portland Daily Press*, December 30, 1862.

Stoneman's Station
Dec. 11th 1862

Dear Mrs. B.:

I must seize a few moments to write you this evening, though I must acknowledge I do not feel much like writing after the day's anxieties. It is a new thing to me to listen to the cannon's roar from early dawn till evening. I cannot describe my feelings; first, for about half an hour, it seemed, I could not endure it, but soon I became more calm, and at length so accustomed to the sound that I could pursue the duties of the day. We understand, to-night, that Fredericksburg has been burned; indeed, we could see the smoke distinctly; but you will have learned all the particulars.

We left W[ashington] for Aquia Creek on Tuesday, Dec. 2nd. Arriving there safely in the evening, we found to our surprise that the place had been so thoroughly destroyed when last burned, that there was not even a place of shelter for us. We lodged on the floor of the cabin of the boat and next day proceeded to Falmouth Station, where we found ourselves in the same condition, no house there. A colonel of a Maryland regiment camped there politely took our baggage in charge, and sent "the officer of the day" with us to Gen. Sumner's headquarters. There an ambulance was furnished for Gen. Burnsides' headquarters. There Dr. Letterman, Medical Director of the Army of the Potomac, with whom Mrs. Fogg was previously acquainted, ordered another ambulance for Gen. Hooker's headquarters. It was now evening, and a house was found for our accommodation. I wish you could have seen it. On the floor lay a large hog that had been slaughtered that day, and could not be trusted out of sight when the soldiers were around. Up stairs, where we slept, it was not difficult to tell whether the stars were shining, though the room was destitute of a window. But I forebear, I merely mention it as one day's experience.

Next morning we called on Gen. Hooker, who received us in a most affable and gentlemanly manner, approved our work, and gave us an ambulance to visit the Maine Regiments in that vicinity. Since that time we have spent some time with the Maine 20th, also the 17th, as you have doubtless heard ere this. We find many sick among them. In the 20th about seventy-five are receiving medical treatment, though they have had but few in hospital, not having a suitable hospital tent. In the 17th they had over a hundred on the sick list, about eighteen in hospital. I can assure you our visits are most gratefully received by those for whom we labor, and if I may judge from appearances, favorably appreciated by officers.

Mrs. F[ogg] went in company with me to the 17th, and then left to visit the 6th with Mr. Hayes, expecting to call for me and return to our usual lodgings for the night. But the roads were bad, and the mules not being in good condition gave out, and they were obliged to stop on the road, but providentially the detention occurred in the vicinity of an Illinois regiment, with whose officers Mrs. Fogg was well acquainted. On their return yesterday, they overtook the Maine 16th and the 5th Battery; as wearied with marching, they camped for the night. Many of them were sick, and most grateful were they to receive a part of the supplies that had been intended for the 6th, which regiment they had failed to find, as they had moved forward. Apples, crackers spread with butter, and marmalade were dealt out to the sick and weary boys, and oh, how cheering it must have been as they march forward, all uncertain of what the morrow would bring forth, to feel thus assured that friends at home were caring for them, while others came to their relief.

Sabbath evening [Dec. 16th]—Mrs. Fogg is just going to Washington for more supplies. We have been yesterday and to-day tending the wounded and dying. Yesterday we were within half a mile of the battle, at the Lacey [Lacy] House, but on this side of the river. Two shells struck the house we were in; oh, it was an awful scene, but my nerves I find strong enough to bear it all. We are well. You will know more of the particulars than we, until we are permitted to cross the river. Oh! pray that this awful strife may end. Send supplies.

Yours, &c., H. Eaton

8. HE to Mrs. B[osworth], December 22, 1862, Semi-Annual report of the MCHA, 1863, MHS, reprinted in the *Portland Daily Press*, December 31, 1862.

...I had, perhaps, better make at this point, some statement with reference to the use of the $100 committed to our charge. Before leaving W[ashington] I purchased from this fund half a gallon of alcohol with a can, half dozen canned chicken, two dozen concentrated milk, and four lbs. candles, amounting to $13.80. These articles were absolutely necessary in the prosecution of our work, and were purchased at Mr. Hathaway's suggestion. After the battle we found our supplies of many articles far too limited, and a week ago Mrs. Fogg went to W[ashington], and besides collecting a quantity of quilts, pillows, &c., she purchased from the fund, one dozen canned chicken, half dozen pickled oysters, one and a half dozen condensed milk, five packages nutmegs, seventeen farina, half gallon whiskey with demijohn, and tin ware, all amounting to $22.56.

Saturday, that day of slaughter, we were as near the dreadful scene as was permitted, near enough to have shells strike the house we were in, tearing off splinters, one of which fell not far from the spot where Mrs. Fogg was standing. But at such a time, who would think of fear, when the dying and the dead were lying all around! On that day and the Sabbath, my time was spent in washing wounds and assisting to dress them, and Mrs. Fogg's either in the same manner or in preparing food. On Monday Mrs. F went to W[ashington], returning Wednesday night, as the state of things here makes it necessary that a responsible individual should accompany the supplies, and but few can obtain passes. On Monday and Tuesday I remained with the sick of the 20th Maine, and at one of the Division Hospitals where the 2nd Maine were left. Here I saw again the deficiency of every comfort where the sick are left behind. Who cares for the helpless when the <u>great army</u> moves! Here I found necessity for the use of our condensed milk for the low diet cases.

On Wednesday and Thursday I went to the Thrashley House and Tent Hospital, where there were about four hundred sick and wounded men. Oh what a vast amount of suffering was congregated here. Amputations were constantly going on, and deaths occurring. I had but little time for personal conversation with the men, being almost incessantly occupied in the preparation of food. The first day I prepared about four gallons of chicken broth, between two and three of broma, besides gruel, also spread crackers with marmalade. The little time that elapsed between getting dinner and supper, I went through the tents where there were Maine men, and was astonished at the patience manifested in such intense suffering. Oh 'tis sad to see so many of our brave men crippled for life by this horrid war. Not the body alone is crippled, but the mind too, in many cases is but a wreck. The dog kennels of the North are better than the miserable shelter tents where our noble men <u>endure</u> their privations when our army is in its best condition, to say nothing of their sufferings as they march, or on the battle-field. But I did not intend to allude to this, I was writing of the hospitals. The sick and wounded of the Maine 3rd, 4th, and a part of the 17th were at the hospital of which I was visiting. The 4th Maine went into battle with about 228, and came out with 111. On Thursday it was decided to move about 200 to hospitals in the vicinity of W, and I prepared chicken broth for them before they started. I had two large camp kettles and an enormous iron pot, all filled with broth and cooked over a camp fire. So you see the canned chicken came into requisition. On Friday morning we were storing our supplies, which Mrs. Fogg had brought from the Creek the day before, and in the afternoon [we were] working in the hospital of the 20th. On Saturday morning we started off in [an] ambulance, very happy, and why? because we had our team literally loaded with hospital supplies. The arrangement was to leave me at the 19th Regiment, while Mrs. Fogg and Mr. Hayes proceeded to the 16th. They found the sick and wounded of this regiment at one of the Division hospitals, also the 2nd Maine Battery, similar to the one where I had spent Wednesday and Thursday previous. There they remained two days; their services were greatly needed and warmly appreciated. They found surgeons, stewards, and nurses all actively engaged in using every effort for the comfort of those under their care, and I desire to bear the same testimony for the Regimental Hospital of the 19th Maine.* * *

Do not relax your efforts, for the wants of our men are ever increasing; <u>self-denial there must be in the home work,</u> as well as with our brave soldiers; the latter sacrifice everything, home and <u>every</u> comfort. At the 19th I found a great demand for woolen clothing; I distributed one dozen shirts, one dozen pair of drawers, and about thirty pairs socks. Many of the men had just been out forty-eight hours on picket duty, and had no stockings. The destitution of clothing will increase rather than diminish, during the winter months. I have no excuses to make for my letters, no time to correct them, they must go as they are, or not at all.

Truly yours, H. Eaton

9. HE to Mrs. B[osworth], January 8, 1863, Semi-Annual Report of the MCHA, 1863, MHS.

Bellair, Stafford County, Jan. 8th 1863

My Dear Mrs. B.:

I suppose you may have been expecting a letter from me for several days. I had intended to write last Saturday, on the reception of the box of chicken, but we have been away on one of our long trips, and at such times it is impossible for me to write. I did not want to send a letter until we had tried the chicken, for you know you expressed special anxiety about the "biddles." I have now to tell you that on Monday morning we started for the region of Belle Plains [sic], Mrs. F having some business to transact with the 16th, with reference to the remains of Capt. Hutchins of that regiment, who was killed in battle and buried in Fredericksburg. While in Washington she met with some of his relations, who were making the second attempt to procure the body, and found it difficult to procure a pass from W. Mrs. F offered to make the attempt, and in connection with communications between "Headquarters" and Col. Tilden, of the 16th, we went to that regiment. As it is some nine or ten miles from this place, we loaded the ambulance, and arriving there, stopped at their hospital and left supplies, she returning to Gen. Burnside's camp, also Sumner's, thence to the place we call "home" for the night, while I proceeded to the Maine Cavalry. We had not visited the latter since we had been with the army in its present position. I found them in a healthy state, in comparison with many of our regiments, having only fourteen sick in hospital, and not many more in "quarters." Here I had that can opened, and, to our great joy, found it as sweet and nice as when first prepared. Oh! it would have paid you for your labor to see how the sick men enjoyed their dinner of chicken broth and a soft cracker. To the sick men in quarters I carried some tea, a cracker, and an apple. Left the sick half a dozen shirts, as many pairs of drawers and stockings. One man was then lying without any shirt, he having taken off the only one he had that it might be washed. I also gave them some condensed milk, farina, sago, black and red pepper, ginger, shrub, and jelly, also handkerchiefs and towels. This was Tuesday, I having stopped on Monday all night at a real secesh house in the neighborhood. As soon as the men had their dinner, the quartermaster sent me with his team to the hospital of the 16th. Here there were forty-eight men sick in the hospital. I asked the doctor if the chicken broth was suitable for their supper. "By all means," said he, "if they could have it;" so the camp kettle went on, but the rain came down, and I had to leave the preparation to the cook, with the exception of an occasional run out of the tent to give directions. The men assured me it was eaten with relish, such as could only be given by "Maine chickens." Just at night Mrs. F returned from the effort she had been making, through Gen. Burnside and Gen. Sumner, for a flag of truce, the matter still remaining in a state of uncertainty. We again stopped for the night with "secesh," and in the morning took the homeward route, taking in Gen. Sumner's headquarters on the way. No reply had been received from Gen. Lee, and the impression was that he did not intend to grant the request. As the 17th was but a short distance from the road, we took the track over the stumps to their encampment. They have recently had a number of cases of typhoid fever, and had that day buried two of their men, having one now, very low. A "requisition" was again made on that can of chickens, and enough left for their supper last night and to-day's dinner. * * * To-day, while Mrs. F again went to learn the result of the flag of truce, I went with her as far as the 4th Maine, and thence walked to the 3rd, camped near them, that they might have their share in the good dinner from the State of Maine. I also visited the sick in quarters, carrying them tea, apples, and crackers. Bro. G[reenough]'s apples (by the way) have come to hand, many of them decayed, partly frost bitten; still, what is left of them is a real luxury to the men, and received with many thanks. Then, that salt fish, we strip it into little bits, and give each sick man a taste about half as big as your finger, with a little cracker, and oh! what happy faces it makes. I wish we had a large quantity of it; that, with broma and butter, seems to be our greatest want just now. * * * We live mostly on tea and hard bread, usually going without dinner; butter we make use of as our only luxury, when we have it. To-day we found Mrs. J. Dyer's card under a roll of butter, and tell her for us that both the sick soldiers and ourselves thank her for it; one of them to-day would not have tasted breakfast had it not been for soft crackers and butter, prepared in toast; also one of Mr. Greenough's apples roasted. To-morrow we are going to give the 20th a dinner.

Friday—Early this morning we were aroused by a dispatch from Gen. Longstreet's headquarters, that the long looked for permission had been granted, for the removal of the remains of Capt. Hutchins. And Mrs. F, to her great satisfaction, was permitted to telegraph this communication to the friends anxiously waiting in Washington. To-day the 20th in hospital and sick in quarters have had their chicken broth, also in five companies the sick have been supplied with dried apples, and Mrs. F will now supply the rest. I cannot convey to you an idea of the pleasure of that haggard looking company of men as I dealt out their dinner to them in their tin dippers. You may send as much more of it as you please, and mutton, too, but I should think it would be preferable to put it in smaller cans, that we may keep it longer. <u>Butter, butter, butter.</u> I must send this to mail.

Love to all, from all, Yours, H. E.

10. HE to Lewis Smith, January 15, 1863, MCHA Collection, MHS.

Stafford County, [Va.], Jan. 15th 1863

Dear Sir,

Your letter of the 9th came to hand day before yesterday. As I was at the Hospital of the 16th last week and they are camped some eight or ten miles from this place, I thought probably I should not see them for a few days. Mr. Hayes, however, had business that called him there yesterday, and I, through him, made the inquiries you desired. He learned that Mr. William F. Lombard of Comp. D had quite recovered from his wounds, and was doing duty with his Regiment. He did not see him, as he was absent from camp about a mile, where he had gone to visit a friend. With much love to your wife and family and all dear Portland friends, I remain.

Yours in the good cause, H. Eaton.

11. HE to Harriet Fox, January 28, 1863, reprinted in the *Portland Daily Press*, February 13, 1863, and in the *Portland Transcript*, February 14, 1863.

Near Falmouth Va., Jan. 28th 1863

Miss Fox,

Some two or three weeks since a letter was received from you, giving information that a barrel of Hospital supplies had been forwarded to us through you, as Secretary of the Maine C. H. Association. A reply to it was delayed until its reception by us, at this place. It is now about a week since its contents were unpacked, and it gives me pleasure to inform you that the articles were in excellent condition, nothing broken or injured.

The contents were just such articles as we needed, and I have no doubt they will prove a blessing to many a poor soldier. You may think me dilatory in my reply, and I acknowledge that more time has elapsed than seems desirable, but with us, time is exceedingly precious, every moment is occupied; we had some ten boxes and four barrels that arrived at the same time, and a large number of letters have been required, acknowledging their reception. Just now, we do not even have our evenings, as an officer of the Maine 20th is here, and occupies the room where we have our fire. He is very sick, and in the evening other officers of the Regiment call to see him; but I know you understand my position and will excuse the delay, without feeling that it arises from any lack of interest in the supplies received.

You inquire what articles are most needed for the relief of the sick and wounded soldiers. We have felt thus far the supply most lacking has been butter; we have also been unfortunate in losing nearly all the pickles that have been sent, by the breaking of the glass bottles in which they were sent. It would be better to pack them in stone jars. Soft crackers, we can never be too largely supplied with, also canned chicken. Send us tea in small packages, suitable to give to the men in their tents, as we carry it to them when we visit the "quarters." Black pepper, cayenne and ginger, farina, maizena, &c., barley, dried apples, bottled cider, cranberry preserves with other preserves or jellies, handkerchiefs always needed in large quantities, made from old dresses, better colored than white, towels, stockings, woolen under clothing. This perhaps will do for a list, at present, but in this cause, no apology is needed; I <u>love</u> to beg for our suffering men who give up everything for our country. The number of sick is constantly increasing, as must necessarily be the case after such fatiguing marches as have recently been made.—With other writing pressing on my immediate attention, I must close this very hastily written letter. Continue earnest in the work. The daily blessing of the soldier rests upon the daughters of Maine, who with her sons, aid in this glorious cause.

Yours sincerely, Harriet Eaton

12. HE to Hatty Belle Eaton, January 30, 1863, DCUCS.
You must always write to me when you can. Your letters do me a great deal of good. I see you sometimes <u>write</u> words quite nicely. When you write, tell me if Agnes has answered your long letter yet.

January 30th 1863

My own little Hatty,

You don't know how much I want to see you this morning, but then if I could see you, I could not be taking care of the sick soldiers. This morning I am making barley broth for a dinner for the Hospital sick, and when it is ready, I carry it to them.—Well Hatty, as I was walking over to the camp with my broth I met Mr. Hayes and he gave me a package of letters one from you and Aunty, one from Frank, one from Mrs. Bosworth, and some others on business. I am feeling very sad that dear Aunty has been so sick, I hope she is better now, and I hope too, that you are a very quiet little girl when she is ill, and very attentive to her. I know you are very kind when I have the head ache, I don't have it very often now, and I don't take cold, though I sleep on the floor every night.—Frank writes me that he saw Agnes and she is looking, as he says, "prettier than ever," but better than that, he says she is very well and a famous skater. He says he likes his camp very much, that the log houses are better than they had at Camp Lincoln, and they have soft white bread every day. And now, about that nice present you sent to me, that dear picture of your own darling self. You could not have sent me any thing that I should have liked better, especially as I had not a single picture with me. I only brought my little black valise with me, so that if the "rebels" came where I was, they could not get much, if they took me, I am not at all afraid that they would keep me long. I take it out of my pocket, and kiss it, and sometimes, I show it to the sick men and tell them it is my "baby." I think Gen. Scott makes quite a fine appearance at your feet, wouldn't he dance for joy if he could see his master? Tell Aunty I shall go to see the boys just as soon as the roads get so that I can travel. There is quite a lot of snow on the ground to-day, but it is all mixed with mud and does not look pretty.—They have three cats and two little pigs here that run all about the house. Now you must give a great deal of love to Uncle, and all the rest for me. I am very glad you like your sled. God bless you my darling.

Your own dear mother

13. HE to Col. John W. Hathaway, January 30, 1863, Relief Agencies Collection, MSA.

Stoneman's Station near Falmouth, Jan. 30th 1863

Mr. Hathaway, Sir,

I have just received a letter from you relating to boxes, also requesting one of us, to go to Windmill Point Hospital. You will probably have heard through Mr. H[ayes] before this reaches you, that I was there last week.—After my last communication to you, orders soon came for the army to move and this prevented visits to Regts. that we feel very desirous to see. There was however, enough to be done near at hand, as the 20th left about one hundred and forty sick in quarters, besides about thirty who were sent to a large Division Hos. established within a few steps of this Hos. To these, we gave them most of our attention, and indeed, they needed all the aid we had to bestow, left, as they were, without comforts of any kind. Besides these, Major Gilmore, who went out the day the army moved, returned sick, and his tent having been removed, he came here, and has since that time been very sick requiring watchful attention. As <u>one</u> could do this service better than two, Mrs. F has devoted her energies untiringly to meet his wants.—On Saturday, I went to Aquia Creek, thence to Windmill Point, carrying some supplies, not however expecting to find so many of our Maine men there. Mr. Hayes has probably given you the number from the Maine Regts. who have been removed to this place, numbering in all, I think, nearly 140. I saw and conversed with each one of them, and found they were ready to express themselves satisfied with the kindness of the Hos. attendants, feeling they were willing if they had the <u>means</u>, but, as usual, in these newly established Hos. the <u>means</u> were lacking. The tents are well arranged on sandy soil, well trenched, iron frame cots, mattresses and pillows, so far well, but when I add, that they had <u>nothing</u> but hard bread and pork until that day, and <u>no</u> cooking utensils, except each man's cup, nor any wash basins, you will see the dark side of the picture. I have no doubt several men have died there from this cause, because they <u>could not</u> eat such rations. On Saturday, they issued tea and rice, and as they aimed to make it a model Hospital I have no doubt by this time they have other articles of diet, and means for cooking it. We shall make an effort to visit them again soon. On Monday I went to the 17th. They have a few sick in the quarters but none in Regimental Hos., they having been removed to a Division Hos. near by. I left with them a few articles, and went to where the sick had been carried. It was their expectation to be removed to Windmill Point in a few days, but I left with them, some articles of clothing, also farinaceous food, dried apples, &c. On Tuesday I went to the 19th.—Last Sabbath they sent all their sickest men to the Point, they have now 14 in Hos. and about 40 in quarters, none dangerously ill. Regt. seems in very good condition.—Since that time we have had a severe storm rendering the roads almost impassable. We desire to go to the more distant Regiments as soon as the traveling shall make it practicable, though I can assure you, we need not spend idle time here, as we think there is no Regiment, if we except the 16th that suffers so much from sickness.—Major Gilmore is a little better we hope, though still requiring constant care, he has applied for a furlough, and if he gets it and is sufficiently strong, will leave for W[ashington] next week.—With reference to our boxes Mrs. F who knows far more than I do about it, thinks it would not be safe to send them even from W[ashington] to the Creek without an attendant.—I cannot write anything more definite than this at the present with reference to them except that though there may to you, seem to be a great many, still our field is so large we find ample room to dispense and yet not half meet the demand.

Yours respectfully, H. Eaton

14. Isabella Fogg [HE] to George W. Dyer, February 26, 1863, Relief Agencies Collection, MSA.

Rooms of Maine Camp Relief Association
Stoneman's Station, near Falmouth, February 26th 1863

Mr. G. W. Dyer, Sir,

Situated as we are near the encampment of the 20th Maine and knowing that there exists a certain degree of anxiety in your vicinity, in regard to this Regiment and also having every opportunity for obtaining information concerning its Sanitary conditions, as well as a thorough acquaintance with the officers in command also, certain circumstances having come under my observation recently, which clearly indicate to me that it is very imperative duty to communicate with you in regard to the matter, although I must request to have it confidential, as far as my name is concerned. I am aware that many would say that it is no part of the duty of a lady to interfere in these matters, but if I know my duty, I think it is to look after the interests of our sick men and when I know them to be maltreated and abused I feel it a duty to make it known, more especially as I learn there are steps being taken to give this miscreant a situation in some other of our Maine Regiments, solely for the purpose of getting rid of an Officer so utterly void of all good principles. Of this I was informed by a commissioned officer who had placed his name to the paper recommending him to the favorable notice of the authorities of Maine, he added, however, that he did not read it. I comment lest his conscience might prevent his signing it, and further said that he regretted very much now that he had done so, having learned so much more of this conduct recently. This officer is none other than the Quartermaster. A more wicked profane cruel unprincipled man I think could not be found in the State of Maine. You are aware that there have been three movements made this winter by the Army of the Potomac, first the battle of Fredericksburg, second a reconnaissance in force, third, the last great failure to cross the river.[1] Each time very many sick were left on the ground, and all the other officers being needed with the Regiment, as a matter of course this man was left in charge of the camp ground. <u>Words</u> would be tame to describe the abuses these poor sufferers received at his hand, the heart sickens at the thought. Poor sick men scarcely

---

1. Reference to Burnside's failure to cross the Rappahannock during the Mud March of late January 1863.

able to walk were dragged from their little shelter tents in a drenching rain to stand guard over an old lame horse, because, <u>forsooth</u>, it was the private property of the surgeon, as if the loss of a horse was to be compared with the life of one of the brave sons of Maine. It was painful, truly painful, to be compelled to witness such abuse. I could name very many more, such as driving out these helpless victims to bury one of their comrades, telling them with horrid oaths, that if they were not expeditious in hustling him into the ground, he would cause a hole to be dug in which to inter them. The <u>haste commanded</u> was the more painful, as the spirit had but just departed and the body was not yet cold. I am aware that many have censured their young, but gallant and brave colonel [Ames], but this, as far as my knowledge extends, is unjust, I have never yet observed anything that would lead me to think that these charges were correct. On the contrary, he has acted on every suggestion we have given for the comfort of his men, especially the sick & he has given us every facility in his power to carry out our plans for their relief. But this Quartermaster has never failed to tell the men, even in my hearing, that all these outrages were ordered by the Colonel himself (which I have every reason to believe was wholly untrue) and hence the discontent there has existed in regard to their commanding officer. Being well assured that you will not deem an apology necessary for calling your attention to these facts,

I remain very respectfully yours,
Isabella Fogg

15. IF. to Col. John W. Hathaway, March 8th, 1863, Relief Agencies Collection, MSA.

Stoneman's Station, Near Falmouth, 8th March 1863

Mr. Hathaway,

It is about time that we should report our doings to you again. Since my last communication the state of the roads has been such as to impede the progress of our work to some extent. We have however visited the 2nd, 3rd, 4th, 5th, 6th, 16th, 17th Regiments of Infantry, the 2nd & 5th Batteries, & the Maine Cavalry.—We also sent some fruit to the sick of the 7th Maine, and hope to visit that Regiment soon.—We find an improvement in the general condition & health of the Regiments, which has no doubt been promoted by the favorable change in the rations, giving them much greater variety, also various sanitary movements, such as company cooks, &c.—Some of the hospitals too have been much improved in the internal arrangements.—We have thought it might be well to give a statement of the amount distributed since my last report. We have aimed to make a fair division of these supplies, so that each Regiment should receive its true proportions & we keep a list of all the articles distributed with the date of distribution which can be referred to at any time. Since the 7th of Feb'y comprising a period of one month (nearly one week of which we were in Washington) we have carried, & as far as possible, placed in the hands of the sick men, given them information that they would receive it, or given to the Hospitals the following articles:

12 shirts
10 pr drawers
165 pr socks
68 pr mittens
24 doz. handkerchiefs
36 quilts
30 pillows
70 towels
1 ½ doz. hos. caps
8 pr slippers
1 doz. nutmegs
2 nutmeg graters
5 bottles brandy
10 doz. combs
14 jars jelly
9 jars marmalade
4 bottles currant wine
3 bottles elderberry wine
2 bottles port wine
1 box herring
3 quarts sago
3 quarts tapioca
20 pounds stripped fish
5 lbs. butter
1 box guava jelly
10 lbs. tea

6 dressing gowns
13 cases meat
22 cans con. milk
44 papers farina & cornstarch
30 papers broma and cocoa
35 doz. lemons
10 doz. oranges
1 barrel dried apples
2 barrels green apples
1 barrel crackers
2 bottles hackberry brandy
1 bottle hackberry syrup
1 bottle cherry rum
4 bottles raspberry vinegar
2 bottles ketchup
1 jar pickles
1 jar strawberry
1 jar cranberry
2 bottles tamarinds
4 bottles cologne
6 dozen figs
4 ½ doz. eggs
4 lbs. soap
black pepper
cayenne pepper
candy, lozenges & pepper

Other articles have been distributed such as second hand clothing for discharged men, also as we are situated near the 20th, we prepare many articles of diet & carry to them.—In many Regiments we have found the [recipients] required the articles that we had it in our power to bestow, and in every case we have met with a healthy reception, and are more than ever convinced of the importance of the Camp Relief Association.

Yours respectfully—
H. Eaton
I. Fogg

The report of my work, varies but little from that of last year, except the increase of the number of those whose burden of care and trouble have claimed a larger amount of Christian sympathy than ever before. More of my time has been devoted to this work thru out [sic] any previous year since I have been with you, consequently there are many whose names are on our church list and whom I have become accustomed to visit at least once a year that I have necessarily passed by.—Three have been admitted to our Hos. One was a patient there about four months, and I have visited them often and can bear decided testimony to the kind attention and careful nursing they received while there. Several of those to whom it has been my privilege to minister from week to week as earthly strength failed have given evidence even at the eleventh hour that God heard prayer in their behalf. It has been less my object to see how many calls I could make in a day or a week but rather to listen to the out bursts of the burdened heart, mingle my tears with theirs and manifest my special interest [in] them, trying to point them to the dear Savior, the Burden bearer, even though hours might be spent with one individual. I find in referring to my Journal which is quite imperfect, partly from trouble with my eyes which prevented writing sometimes for two or three weeks, that I have made 700 calls, distributed more than 400 articles of clothing, given in money or groceries or medicines, &c. for the sick $247.17 receiving from the Church Treasury and other sources to which I have applied $250.42 cts leaving a balance on hand of $3.23.

16. HE To Hatty Belle Eaton, March 15, 1863, DCUCS.

Same old log house
March 15th 1863

Dear Hatty Belle,
How does my little pet lamb do to night, I wonder? I hope she is very well and very happy and very good. So you are beginning to read my letters yourself. I am very much pleased with the improvement in your writing and as for the sewing, I hardly know what to say, I am so glad you are learning to use your needle enough to make yourself useful. As long as you live you will remember the pleasant winter you spent with Aunty and Uncle Whittier and Hatty and Davie, yes and Hannah too. When we get home again, how much you will have to tell me, and I shall have a great deal to tell you too, you and Agnes have had such fine times sled[d]ing and skating, while I have waded in mud. You would laugh if you should see our room, from where I sit I can see 34 boxes & 5 baskets with supplies in them, for the sick and one large table, two boxes, a bureau, and a mantel piece, completely filled with bottles and jars. Then, in front of the house, we have a large tent and a soldier who lives in it, for a guard and that is full of boxes and barrels.—I expect you would like to run in and out of the tent, there is a funny little "knapsack stove" in it, to keep it warm and for the guard to cook by. There are lemons and oranges and apples there, for sick soldiers, and lots of quilts and pillows and shirts and drawers and stockings and many other things. Sometimes I work there all day unpacking boxes and barrels. There is a sick man in the Hospital who has made a little bone ring, which the soldiers call a "ration ring." And the other day he gave it to me to give to you, so when I come home you will have it. I have three or four that my boys have given me for keepsakes. When I went into the Hospital last night they called out, "How do you do, mother."—But my

paper is full. You may kiss them all round for me for I had <u>two</u> good kisses from Ned and George when I saw them.

Has Frank sent you a letter yet? You must write to him. Give my love to Hannah with the rest. Now my darling, be a good girl and mother hopes to see you before long.

Your own dear mother

17. Frank Eaton to HE, March 23, 1863, Veteran's Pension, NARA.

Camp Tom Casey
March 23rd 1863

My dear Mother,

We have just received marching orders and shall break camp tonight or tomorrow with shelter tents—I have no time or I would write more, but thought I would inform you of our movements—The report is that we are to go to Centreville or Chanc[elors]ville—under Heintzleman—Am quite well, all but the cough, and I will write again as soon as I get a chance—

Your aff[ectionate] son,
F H Eaton

18. HE to Mrs. Bosworth, April 25, 1863, NYHS; excerpted in the *Portland Daily Press*, May 13, 1863.

Rooms Maine Camp Relief Association
Stoneman's Station, April 25th 1863

Dear Sister,

I find your last letter was dated April 6th, had no idea it was so long since I received it, but at the time had an impression that you were going to journey and I would not write till your return. Now I suppose you are home again, and feel recruited by the change, also Mr. B. Freddie was here to see me last Sabbath and read portions of letters he had received from you since you left. How you will miss Sarah, and I shall miss her too, do you know you never have mentioned one word about her, till your last since I came away.

So you saw Mr. Foster, and had an opportunity to inquire into the little minutiae that one cannot write about, but I am sorry he discouraged you about sending the box, as although of some articles we had a good supply, of others, we were nearly destitute, such as jellies, preserves, wines, salt fish, butter, eggs, Indian meal, &c. If we do not wish to, we need not receive them from the Rooms at Washington, but in case of battle <u>large</u> supplies are needed, the want that is felt then is almost overwhelming. What strange times we live in, last week a powerful army appeared to have risen up and buckled on their armor, all ready to push forward immediately. The roads were filled with Cavalry who had already started on their onward movement. This week, there are no indications of a <u>speedy</u> advance. True, this may be but the calm before the storm, Gen. Hooker <u>wisely</u> keeps his own counsel, and if they will only let him alone, I trust he will lead on to victory, but if the rumors now current should prove true, to me, it seems the effect would be most disastrous.—Can it be that he will be superseded by Fremont? Have you anything rebellious to say if another change should be made in the command of the Army of the Potomac? But, hush, we must not even <u>write</u> after the sort. Oh for a calm and quiet mind that can rise above the management of earthly potentates, and see an Almighty arm wielding the sword of omnipotence and ordering all things after the counsel of his own will.—<u>Sometimes</u>, I reach that point but too often I feel myself gaining by it no adv[antage].

<u>Thursday May 7th</u>. Shall I finish this? I have no better paper, all has been wet on the "<u>retreat</u>" for it is a retreat, one more retreat! <u>I cannot write about it</u>.—We are pretty well, considering what we have been through, have not had our clothes off till last night, since last Thursday. Freddie [Bosworth] has no doubt written to you that he met us, but dear boy, he did not tell you how much help he was to us while we were preparing food for the poor wounded fellows.—I cannot describe my feelings to day, neither can I describe the painful, agonizing scenes through which we have passed. I trust we have been permitted to save many lives, by providing nourishment for those who were being carried so many miles to the General Hospital.—Day before yesterday we were ordered to leave the Hospital at Unites States Ford, and I left with our team, and Mrs. F waited for an ambulance train, for whom she would prepare supper, a terrific storm of hail and rain, thunder and lightning, put the roads in such a condition that I was obliged to stop on the road, we turned up to a house and found it filled in every corner with wounded men. The top of our ambulance was not proof against such a storm and I was completely drenched (yes, to my skin as they say). It was about twelve o'clock, I went into the house, and the surgeon gave me a blanket in which I rolled myself and laid down in one corner of a little attic, with the wounded, at five o'clock I rose, and had the satisfaction, through this providential detention, of preparing breakfast of coffee soft crackers and beef soup, for 150, almost starving wounded men, for whom they had no other means of procuring a single mouthful.—I arrived home about ten, and Mrs. F came on about an hour after, so here we were at our old quarters again. Edward Whittier has just called, both himself and George were spared, even a wound, Edward (he came to see us at the "Ford"), both his captain and two lieutenants were sadly wounded, the captain lost a leg.—We were shelled out of our Hospital, and obliged to leave it in hot haste about five o'clock in the morning, with the fearful things screeching over our heads.—Two men were killed close by us, others wounded.—I felt perfectly calm, still I prefer to be out of reach of their missiles.—As things look at present, the whole army returning to their old camping ground, I shall hope soon to see

you and tell what I cannot write.—I am glad I decided to remain this long.—You must excuse this letter for mind and body are both affected, <u>quiet</u> is producing some reaction, after the week's intense excitement. I do not know how soon I shall be home. If my dear Frank is anywhere accessible, I shall try and see him first. Mrs. Fogg has borne the fatigue wonderfully considering how sick she has been. Love to all.

Yours truly, H. Eaton

Gov. Coburn called on us last Thursday and after satisfying himself that we had been under the sanction of the State, he paid us $113.33, towards the amount then due. I don't think he approves of its being a <u>State</u> affair.

19. HE to Mrs. G[reenough], May 8, 1863, Semi-Annual Report of the MCHA, 1863, MHS.

Stoneman's Station, May 8th 1863

My Dear Mrs. G.:

I must find time to drop you a few lines to-night with reference to our recent movements, though the aspect of affairs seems so discouraging that I would gladly blot out the last week from my remembrance. But the Lord reigns, he has wise purposes in view, in all this, though by the fulfillment of that purpose we may be humbled and brought very low. * * * We left here last Friday under the protection of the first train of ambulances that went to the "front" to gather the wounded. As vehicles were not allowed to cross the river, we took possession of a small house, nearest United States Ford, and unloaded our supplies; next we sent word to one of the Medical Directors that we were located there. Soon there came a note from him, requesting us to have food in readiness for about fifty wounded men whom he was about sending to General Hospital, distant some fourteen miles. By a large fire, built in the field, we soon had a good supper of beef, chicken and oyster soup, hot coffee, and crackers ready for them. The ambulances drew up, and our suffering, wounded boys were strengthened for their tedious ride. This was one part of our work, which was followed up all the time we were there. By Sabbath afternoon the lower part of the house where we stopped, and all the ground around it, was covered with the wounded, many of whom had managed to creep thus far, and seeing us, made sure their wants would be met. Sabbath night, in the moonlight, we worked, feeding the famishing, till one o' clock. Then I laid myself down on the bare floor, but the groans of the wounded down stairs, with other circumstances, forbade much rest. During the night the rebels planted a battery, and succeeded in getting the range of our hospital; the shells began to fly over us in altogether too close proximity to our quarters to be agreeable. I felt very calm, had time to think, felt that I was in the path of duty, and that I should be preserved if it was for the best. Then I heard for the first time, one of those almost unearthly yells made by the rebels, for there were about 700 prisoners on the ground close by us, and they shrieked as they were marched off, by their guard, at double quick. We put on our bonnets and sacks and walked away, in company with the vast multitude of wounded, ambulance drivers, teamsters with their horses and mules, to seek a place of greater safety. Two men were killed and several wounded, but the firing soon ceased, and we immediately returned to our work, and remained there, till orders came the next day to fall back. At our first stopping place word reached us that wounded, to the number of a hundred, were on the way, and depending on us for food. We were only too happy that we were able to meet these demands. A terrific storm detained me all night on the road. About midnight I stopped at a house for shelter, Mrs. F. having stopped behind to come on in an ambulance train. At this house I found a large number of the wounded, who, like myself, had been obliged to seek shelter, for the bridges had been carried away, and my ambulance leaked like a sieve, and I was completely drenched. One of the surgeons gave me a dry blanket, and showed me a corner of an old attic, where there was room for me to roll myself up, in the dark, with a lot of our poor wounded boys. Early in the morning I set the ambulance drivers to work helping me, with wood and water, and about seven o'clock a good, hot breakfast was ready for 150 men. How kindly Providence ordered it, that I should be there with supplies, as there was no other means of providing anything for them. But I weary you; I am very thankful I remained thus long.

Yours in great haste, Harriet Eaton

20. **Resolution of May 20, 1863, Minutes of the MCHA, MCHA Collection, MHS.**
Whereas, Mrs. Harriet Eaton after more than seven months valuable services in the Camp Hospital of the Army of the Potomac has been compelled on account of domestic considerations to return home, it is voted, that the thanks of the Association be, and they are hereby most cordially tendered to her, for her disinterested, faithfull [sic], and arduous services to our sick and wounded soldiers; a service that even amidst all the exposures and privations of camp life, and even amidst the deadly missiles of the Enemy, has been faithfully and unremittingly performed; and which through the blessings of a kind Providence has enabled her to act as a ministering angel of Mercy for the preservation of the lives of many, who but for her aid, would not have survived their injuries.

21. **HE to Hatty Belle Eaton, October 24, 1864, DCUCS.**

Banks of the Appomattox, Oct. 24th 1864

My dear Hatty Belle,

If you are a pretty good scholar in Geography I hardly think you will be able to find the river named at the head of this letter, it is a branch of the James River and I can see both rivers from the door of the tent I sleep in. Agnes will show you where I am on my map, which I am very sorry I forgot to take with me. Your letter was very nice and did me a great deal of good and now I want another very much. I could tell from it just how you were getting along.—But the Dew Drops must hurry up and send the "comfort bags" along, we want them very much, they keep [asking?] all the time for "the little bags with needle and thread" and then they say, "Please find one that has a <u>letter</u> in it, if you can."—Last night I went to meeting in the colored Hospital and I wish you could have seen what a funny place it was, all crowded with our black soldiers. They had one of their Sergeants to preach for them, he was very black but he preached a very nice sermon, and the people kept saying "That's so," "I believe it," and all such things.—I think from your letter you will learn a great deal before I come back but I am sorry you have had such a cough and think Lizzie was very kind to let you stay at home from school. There are four sick men sitting talking to me right now, and two or three have just gone out. Will you go and see Aunty White and give my love to her and let me know how she is when you write again? Be sure and write soon. Give my love to Ella and all the rest.

Your loving mother

22. HE to Hatty Belle Eaton, October 28, 1864, DCUCS.

City Point, Oct. 28th [1864] Friday

My dear Hatty,

I have written Agnes how happy I was to receive the letters from both of you. If you were here this afternoon I believe you would run out doors for the wind blows so hard it seems as if my house would come right down about my ears.—I have a floor to my tent, and before the stove a piece of carpet like the one in Frank's room. It was a piece I sent to Mrs. Mayhew in one of the boxes that was packed at our house and it looks very natural. I enjoy it very much, when I sent it out how little I thought I should ever see it again. Two or three evenings ago I was sitting all alone writing and I was sure I heard somebody moving about, I thought they were going to steal some of our things, so I got up very softly and took my candle and went to catch them when what should it be but a <u>great white cat</u>! I thought it was very funny to see a cat out here where there is nothing but tents. Last night I saw something that was not quite so pretty as a cat.—Just before 9 o'clock, I happened to look in the corner where my bed was and what should be there but a great spider that as he walked along covered a space as large as the top of a cup in the tea set you play with.—Now since I began to write that last sentence I have killed another as large.—If you have made your comfort bags, I want you little Dew Drops to fill them and send them along as fast as you can, for they ask me for them at all hours in the day. I was very glad to hear that you got a card at school, for I know it is not very <u>easy</u> for you to get it and that makes it so much the better. I suppose you have seen Mrs. Mayhew by this time and she will tell you many things that I can't stop to write about.

Be a good girl and do just as Lizzie wants you to. Remember me to "Goodness" if you please. Don't forget to write in the Journal every day. Good night and God bless you.

Your affectionate mother

23. HE to Unknown, December 8, 1864, quoted in Frank Moore,
Women of the War, 459–60.

City Point, Dec. 8th 1864

For a week we have been very busy. The first Maine heavy artillery detailed men to cut our timber for the stockade. The second and third batteries sent teams to haul it; the second battery and first battalion of Maine sharpshooters have sent their men to put it up. We are under great obligations to them for their kindness, as it is against military regulations to detail men from these grounds for such a purpose.

Our stockade is now all up and chinked, but we have no door or fireplace. Our roof is of canvas, and we use rubber blankets, quilts, and bed-sacks for doors. A nice little army stove was given me for our use on yesterday. To-morrow we expect to build the chimney; and all this is being done while we live within. You may imagine the confusion, with our pile of stores in the centre, to give room to set up the logs, and a long procession of our boys continually coming for what is frequently at the bottom of the pile. The stockade is forty feet by fifteen, and contains three apartments: at the entrance is a reading-room, which we mean to make literally a "Soldier's Home," then our own dormitory and store-room, and in the rear the cook-house. We wish to keep our reading-room supplied with late Maine papers, and with stationery, that the boys may have facilities for writing here. Sacks, boxes, and barrels are piled six feet high on every side.

24. Resolution of July 8, 1865, MCHA Collection, MHS.

Whereas Mrs. J. S. Eaton has been connected with this Association from its organization till now when it disbands with the disbanding of the Army of the Potomac, having acted as its agent with the Army some seven months in 1862–3, and some three months in 1864 and during the intervening periods cooperating with its managers in procuring and forwarding supplies to the front, therefore, Resolved that we hereby express to Mrs. Eaton our sense of her devotion to the interests of our common country and to the welfare of our heroic and suffering soldiers in voluntarily leaving her family and the comforts of home, and without hope of compensation enduring the privations and hardships inevitable to a lady who follows and abides with the Army in such a service. Resolved that as an Association we owe to Mrs. Eaton an expression of our grateful appreciation of her valuable and self-denying services at "the front," and cooperation at home, which have contributed largely to our great success in attempting to relieve the distress and to supply the necessities of our sick and wounded soldiers. Her kindness, her discretion, her fortitude, her indefatigable exertions, her self-forgetfulness, and her unassuming Christian dignity, as well as her fidelity to the Government and to the Army of its brave defenders, has sustained the high esteem which she has ever been held in at home, and won for her an enviable reputation and grateful memories from all who have known her on the battle-field, in the Camp, and in the Hospital. She bears with her from these connections, the best wishes of the Association for her future welfare and happiness.

25. HE to Frank Moore, April 11, 1866, Frank Moore Collection, DU.

Portland, April 11th 1866

Mr. Moore, Sir,

Yours of March 31st has been received and I reply at my earliest opportunity. With reference to your request for a communication from me, concerning the <u>particular</u> character of the work in which I was engaged, during eleven months of our country's struggle, also incidents relating thereto, I shall be obliged simply to refer you to a small pamphlet, forwarded to you by Mrs. Preble. My engagements are such that <u>time</u> is wanting, for such a purpose. As the work in which we were engaged differed materially from that of a <u>nurse</u> in the Army, and was entered into with great zeal, by those cognizant of the facts, in our own state, I feel that in a work such as I am led to suppose yours is designed to be, it is very desirable that history should record, to some extent, the peculiar work of the Maine Camp Hospital Association. I should be glad if Mrs. Mayhew could be induced to prepare something for the book.

Respectfully yours,
Mrs. J. S. Eaton

P.S. It just occurs to me that the name signed to this (being the initials of my husband's name), differs from the signature (H. Eaton) in the book.

26. Mrs. William P. Preble to Frank Moore, April 9, 1866, Frank Moore Collection, DU.

Portland, April 9th [1866]

Mr. F. Moore,
Sir,

I forward another package of several pages, giving a slight sketch of the labors of our ladies in the field, and hope you find something <u>valuable</u>, as well as interesting to read. I have endeavored in the various packages to have the dates also, that, as you will see, Mrs. Eaton went very <u>early</u> to the Front <u>before</u> prejudice yielded to humanity and when there was much opposition to a <u>lady</u>'s ministering upon the field. Mrs. Mayhew joined her, and after Mrs. Eaton's return home to her children, Miss Rebecca Usher of Hollis, Maine went to assist Mrs. Mayhew, and they remained until there was no more work to be done for our brave men there. My friend Miss Usher has kindly at my request made the accompanying extracts from letters written home and I think they convey a fairly good idea of the kind of labor and the variety connected with the intervals between the battles, although Mrs. Mayhew & Mrs. Eaton went through terrible scenes of suffering upon the battle grounds, more than these letters relate. Mrs. Eaton is the widow of a Baptist minister, and I think Mrs. Mayhew is the widow of a clergyman of the same denomination, both of them are agreeable, lady like and Christian women—and held dear not only to the hearts of the soldiers, but to us few ladies, who, unable to go ourselves, collected and sent supplies which they so nobly, faithfully, and wisely distributed.

Whatever papers you think superfluous will [you] be kind enough to return, I should like to have sent to me again. I trust I have not encroached too much upon your time by the bulk of the packages I have sent, but I thought I would send them for you to extract from as you wish.

Respectfully,
Mrs. William P. Preble

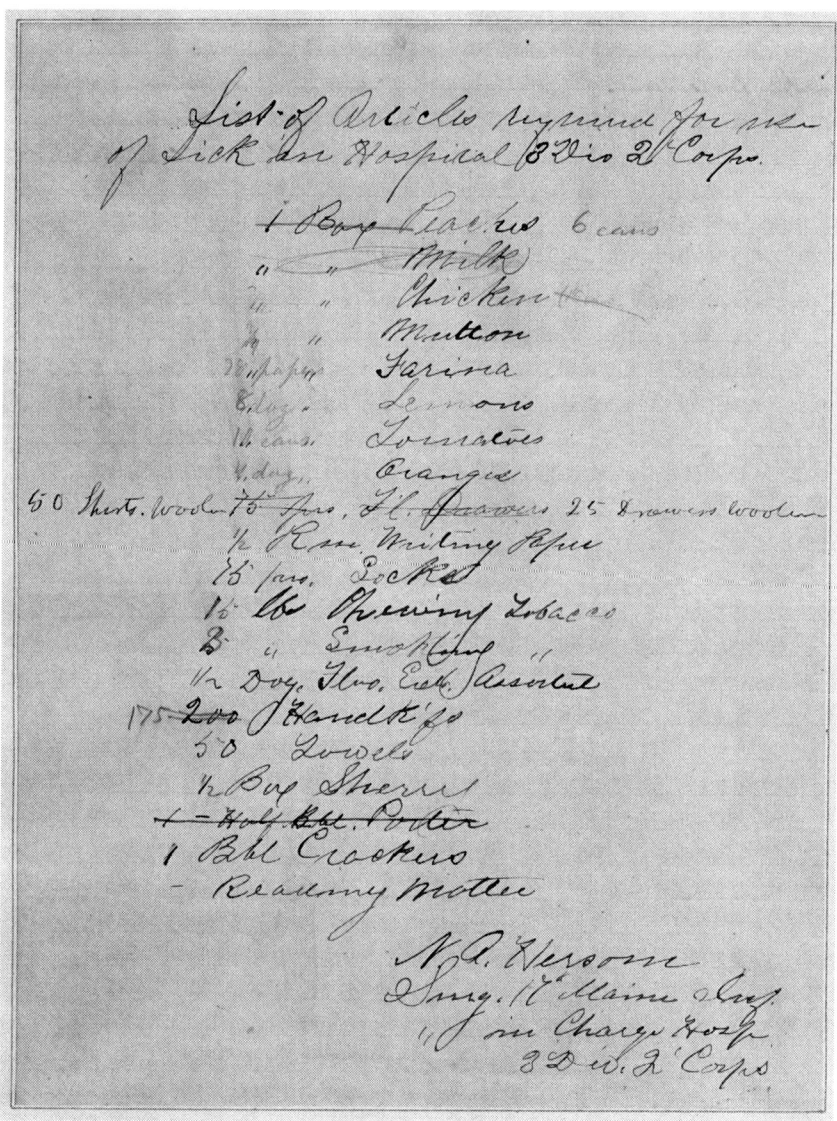

List of sanitary supplies signed by surgeon Nahum Hersom, including tomatoes, sherry, and both chewing and smoking tobacco. COLLECTION OF THE NEW-YORK HISTORICAL SOCIETY, NEGATIVE NO. 82575D

BIOGRAPHICAL DICTIONARY

The full biographical dictionary can be accessed at www.janeschultz.org. An abbreviated version follows.

John Ripley Adams (1802–66)
Fifty-nine-year-old chaplain of the 5th Maine, from Gorham, mustered in with the regiment in June 1861. In addition to offering daily prayer services and hymn singing with his unit, Adams offered a lecture series on temperance. He discouraged soldiers from using profanity by singling out the user of such language and mentioning, "I hope God will not hear that prayer of yours" (quoted in Armstrong, 50). Adams contracted malaria during the peninsular campaign of 1862, but he served the 5th until it was mustered out in June 1864. The next month he was back serving the men of the 121st New York. A eulogy written after Adams's death on April 15, 1866 found him "earnest, true, sympathetic, [and] unobtrusive" (Armstrong, 62).

Dr. Zabdiel Boylston Adams (1829–1902)
Harvard- and Bowdoin-trained surgeon of the 7th and later the 32nd Massachusetts, from Boston, a military Jack-of-all-trades. Known as "Zab" by his peers, he was just thirty-three years old when HE met him in April 1863, having already had an MD from Harvard for a decade. Before the war, Adams sought further medical education in Paris and practiced at the Boston Dispensary. Adams would distinguish himself at Gettysburg on July 2, 1863 by setting up a roving field dressing station only a hundred yards from the line of battle. After attending to wounded men for three nights and two days without a break, he collapsed from exhaustion and was honorably discharged from the service. However, he was back at the front as a line officer by early 1864. At the Wilderness he sustained a leg wound, but convinced his Confederate captors not to amputate. He ended up at Libby Prison, but was paroled in the autumn of 1864. After making a full recovery, he rejoined Union troops early in 1865 and was in the trenches at Petersburg until he left the service in July. Adams was known for holding

forth to younger colleagues about his strangest cases. The *MSH* reports his operation on a soldier suffering from a hatchet wound to the left knee in October 1862.

Samuel Henderson Allen (1826–1905)
Thirty-five-year-old officer of the 1st Maine Cavalry, from Thomaston, mustered in as major on October 21, 1861 and promoted to colonel in March 1862. Allen saw action at 2nd Bull Run and Cedar Mountain, before being discharged for disability at the beginning of 1863. Still perceived as a valuable military servant, he was named military governor of Frederick, Maryland—a town full of citizens with Confederate sympathies. Allen was plagued by kin and friends of imprisoned rebel soldiers who wanted to bring them food, money, and clothing; his unwillingness to make exceptions made him unpopular with the locals. In 1888, he became warden of the state penitentiary at Thomaston—a post he held for at least twelve years.

Adelbert Ames (1835–1933)
Twenty-six-year-old colonel of the 20th Maine, an ambitious 1861 graduate of West Point. A tough-as-steel soldier and disciplinarian, Ames was wounded in the thigh at 1st Bull Run where he continued in command of the regiment until he passed out. He was awarded the Congressional Medal of Honor for this performance. Because of his leadership at Fredericksburg and Chancellorsville, Ames was promoted to brigadier on May 20, 1863, leaving Joshua Chamberlain in command of the 20th. Elizabeth Blair Lee, who saw Ames late in 1863 noted that he looked "thin and sick" (328). After the war, Ames had a long political career as provisional governor of Mississippi and U.S. senator.

Ellen Usher Bacon (1817–1902)
A founding member of the MCHA, Ellen Usher was the eldest of four daughters of a wealthy and well-connected lumberman from Hollis. She moved to Portland in the 1850s after marrying dentist Elbridge Bacon. Bacon's sister Rebecca Usher, also known as Bess, nursed soldiers at Chester, Pennsylvania, from November 1862 to May 1863, and again at City Point after HE's departure in December 1864. The sisters who remained in Hollis gathered local supplies and sent them to Ellen at 70 Park Street in Portland; once there, they were distributed by the MCHA to Mainers in the field and later to men in the Army of the Potomac recuperating at City Point.

William F. Baker (1836–1917)
Twenty-eight-year-old major of the 10th U.S. Colored Infantry, from Bingham. Baker was so thrilled with a pillow that HE provided him at City Point in November 1864, that he took to locking it in his trunk to prevent its disappearance. In April 1865, he bore the news of Abraham Lincoln's death to nurse Adelaide Smith of New York. By 1870, he was a lumberman with four children in Skowhegan.

Clara Barton (1821–1912)
Educator and self-appointed nurse from North Oxford, Massachusetts, Barton was working in the U.S. Patent Office as a copyist when the war began. She provided relief to men wounded at Antietam and Fredericksburg by stockpiling supplies in her Washington flat and convincing Quartermaster Montgomery Meigs to "lend" her teamsters and wagons to get the supplies to men in the field with dispatch. Barton believed that her solo work was timelier and thus more effective than that of slower-moving bureaucratic agencies like the Sanitary Commission. At war's end, she established a clearing house for the families of missing soldiers. She also traveled to the Confederate Andersonville Prison in Georgia to recover the names of the Union soldiers who perished there. A postwar speaking tour and friendships with several well-placed Congressmen raised Barton to the mythic status of America's Nurse—a sobriquet that paved the way for her founding of the American Red Cross in 1878.

Mary A. Blackmar (Bruson) (1842–1916)
Originally from Hillsdale, Michigan, Blackmar was in her twenties attending the Women's Medical College of Pennsylvania when she interrupted her studies to travel to City Point, where she served as nurse for ten months. Regarded as a skillful wound dresser, nurse Sarah Palmer noted that "she has no fear of spoiling white hands, nor shrinks from dirty uniforms, as the poor fellows come in" (168). Blackmar described an incident where, in a round-the-clock effort to save a hemorrhaging soldier, she slept so soundly that she failed to realize that a hot brick used as a bed warmer had burned through her mattress ticking. In 1866, Blackmar earned her medical degree and practiced at Emily and Elizabeth Blackwell's New York Infirmary for women and children. After marrying in the 1870s, she moved to Florida and practiced medicine for four more decades.

Stephen Boothby (1834–64)
First lieutenant in company F of the 1st Maine Cavalry, a twenty-seven-year-old attorney from Portland, mustered in on October 19, 1861. Boothby was promoted to captain in May 1862, to major in March 1863, and to lieutenant colonel by June of that year. One of fifty-seven casualties sustained by the 1st at Gettysburg, he was shot in the arm but recovered. Regimental lore has it that once in the winter of 1863–64 when halting the regiment for the night, he told his men to build fires using the nearby fence, which turned out to be made of stone. Shot in the arm again at Beaver Dam Station, Virginia, in May 1864, he died of pyemia a month later. Chaplain Samuel Merrill called him a man of "genial spirit, quick sympathies, agreeable manners, native modesty, and a ready perception [who] gave early promise of a brilliant future.... He was a model man" (quoted in Tobie, 454–55).

Frederic W. Bosworth (1843–63)

Nineteen-year-old sergeant in company A of the 17th Maine, from Portland, the eldest child of George and Irene. Bosworth was hospitalized in early 1863 and wounded in July of that year—a wound from which he ultimately died. Major Charles Mattocks of the 17th noted in his diary entry of July 23 that Bosworth took "an unexploded six pounder" to the thigh and was not expected to live (*"Unspoiled Heart,"* 59). Lieutenant Colonel Charles B. Merrill referred to Bosworth as a "boy hero" who died too soon, though men in the ranks disagreed with this assessment. John W. Haley of company I considered Bosworth "posthumous taffy": "What he ever did to merit any special notice is beyond my knowledge.... Bosworth died from a wound received at Wapping Heights, but I never knew of any special display of heroism on his part" (*Rebel Yell*, 212).

John Marshall Brown (1838–1907)

Twenty-four-year-old lieutenant in company E and adjutant of the 20th Maine, from Portland, mustered in on September 1, 1862. Schooled in Bethel and Andover, Brown was a stand-out at Bowdoin College when he graduated in 1860. In the field at Antietam, Fredericksburg, and Chancellorsville and commended by Adelbert Ames, he was promoted to captain and assistant adjutant general of U. S. Volunteers on June 23, 1863. He left the adjutant general's employ in March 1864 when he became lieutenant colonel of the 32nd Maine and returned to fighting at Totopotomoy and Cold Harbor. A month later he was wounded at Petersburg and discharged for disability. When the Portland soldiers and sailors monument was dedicated in 1889, General Brown, known for his oratorical skill, gave the address. He also held leadership positions in the Maine Agricultural Society, the Maine Historical Society, the Episcopal church, and Bowdoin College for twenty-five years—truly a man for all seasons.

Dr. Frederick F. Burmeister (1823–81)

Prussian-born assistant surgeon of the 73rd Pennsylvania, from Philadelphia. In December 1862, Burmeister was promoted to surgeon of the 69th Pennsylvania. By 1864, he was on duty at City Point. Nurses Cornelia Hancock and Sophronia Bucklin spoke disparagingly of Dr. Burmeister, under whom patients and staff suffered when he headed one of the hospitals there. Bucklin complained of wormy crackers and an inferior diet during his tenure, which righted itself after his departure (in what Bucklin implies was a demotion). Hancock too regarded Burmeister's replacement as "such an improvement" (Hancock, 172). Burmeister, whose wife Margaret (*c.*1830–?) HE befriended at City Point, was also a pension examiner. [HE misspells as "Bermister."]

Dr. Benjamin F. Buxton (1810–76)

Forty-one-year-old surgeon of the 5th Maine, from Warren, mustered in June 24, 1861. Buxton was apprenticed to his physician-father before he attended medical school at Bowdoin College. After his graduation in 1839, he established a flourishing practice due to his willingness, as one source put it, to walk ten miles in snow shoes to see a patient. In 1849, he sought his fortune in the California gold rush by supplying goods to miners. His business collapsed when his ship foundered off the coast of Mexico, but Buxton survived the wreck and built a hospital in Acapulco that catered to sailors. In 1853, he fell ill in Panama, probably with malaria, and returned to Maine. Less than a month after mustering, he was captured by Confederate forces but treated leniently by General Pierre G. T. Beauregard, a former business associate, in exchange for his medical services to Union troops imprisoned near Richmond. Following several months in prison hospitals, Buxton was finally paroled and rejoined his regiment in mid-1862. On hand for both Antietam and Fredericksburg, he resigned his commission by mid-January 1863 when the tropical illnesses he had contracted in the 1850s reemerged.

Sarah Hopkins Bacon Caduc (1821–1905)
HE's niece (daughter of her half brother, Joseph Valentine Bacon) who lived in London during the war. Only three years younger than HE, Caduc had married in 1846 and was widowed six years later.

Joshua Lawrence Chamberlain (1828–1914)
Lieutenant colonel of the 20th Maine, commissioned on August 8, 1862 and Governor of Maine from 1867–71. An 1852 graduate of Bowdoin and Bangor Theological Seminary in 1855, Chamberlain planned a career as a missionary but instead was hired as a professor of rhetoric at Bowdoin. In 1862, he left the college to join the army and, despite his slight stature and sensitive features, he made a name for himself as a warrior, fighting at Antietam, Fredericksburg, Chancellorsville, Gettysburg, Spotsylvania, Cold Harbor, and Petersburg. At Gettysburg, Chamberlain and his troops held off the rebel offensive at Little Round Top, which sealed his fate as a war hero in Maine. Wounded at Fredericksburg in the cheek and Gettysburg in the foot, Chamberlain sustained what looked like a mortal wound at Petersburg when a ball entered his hip, breaking his pelvis and piercing his bladder. Despite the seriousness of his condition and the prevalence of infection, he survived. During his convalescence he was brevetted a brigadier general (June 1864), and later received the Congressional Medal of Honor for war valor. Despite any obligation to do so, Chamberlain returned to the Army of the Potomac in February 1865 as it began its final engagements with Lee's Army of Northern Virginia. At Five Forks, he was credited with stopping a Union retreat (and another bullet) and was on hand to receive the Confederate infantry surrender at Appomattox in the spring. He left the army as a major general who had taken six bullets. After serving as governor, Chamberlain returned to Bowdoin as its president, from 1871 to 1883. In the 1880s, he became a railroad businessman, wrote his memoirs, and remained active in the Maine State Militia. He finally

succumbed to an infection in the wound sustained at Petersburg fifty years earlier, when he was eighty-five years old.

Dr. Edward B. Dalton (1834–72)

Chief medical officer at City Point. After serving the 36th New York earlier in the war, Dalton was appointed as a medical inspector in the Army of the Potomac in 1864. In that capacity, he oversaw the construction of the depot field hospital and the creation of an ambulance service at City Point. Before the war, he had been a staff surgeon at New York's Bellvue Hospital—to which he returned after the war, but as sanitary superintendent for New York City and environs. Based on Jonathan Letterman's field ambulance model, Dalton instituted the service at Bellvue, making it the first American medical institution to have one.

Bridget Divers

Irish-born nurse and camp follower known fondly by soldiers and relief workers as "Irish Biddy" and "Biddy the Man," who accompanied her husband to the front with the 1st Michigan Cavalry in 1861 along with her young son. Divers (also called "Devens" and "Deavers" by contemporary sources) participated in battles, performed picket duty, and carried wounded men from battlefields while under fire. Mary Morris Husband praised her endurance and determination to return wounded soldiers abandoned on the field to their units and spoke of her skill in horsemanship. Rebecca Usher and Charlotte McKay observed her at City Point, the latter commenting that she was "fearless of shell or bullet" and "ma[de] her home in the saddle or the shelter tent; often sleeping in the open without a tent" (*Michigan Women in the Civil War*, 30). After the war, Divers joined the Regular Army in Colorado.

Dorothea Dix (1802–87)

Superintendent of U.S. Army Nurses, from Hampden. Appointed in April 1861, Dix cut her teeth in the 1840s in work with the mentally ill. Her Office of Army Nurses in Washington at 505 Twelfth Street between E and F became a way station for nurses moving to and from assignments in general hospitals and the field. Early in the war, Dix appointed all nurses, but her authority was circumvented by Surgeon General Hammond's Order 351 in October 1863, which made it possible for surgeons to appoint female staff as needed. Famous for her requirement that volunteers should wear no hoopskirts, bows, or curls and should be of mature age, Dix would later explain that her service to the Union was not the work for which she wanted to be remembered. Mary Livermore later commented, not without irony, that "in her youth [Dix] must have possessed considerable beauty, much as she deprecated its possession by her nurses" (*My Story of the War*, 247). Abby Hopper Gibbons, a Quaker nurse from New York, sized up Dix more critically: "If she loved power less, humility more, and was possessed of a little tact she might accomplish her work in a far more acceptable way" (quoted in Bacon, 92).

Agnes Ramsey Eaton (1849–87)
Harriet's daughter and second child, staying with her aunt and uncle, the Bacons, in Massachusetts during her mother's wartime absences.

Franklin Henry Eaton (1843–86)
Harriet's son and eldest child, born in Hartford, a private in company A of the 25th Maine, mustered in on September 29, 1862 and out on July 10, 1863. Before the war, Frank was working as a clerk in a Portland furniture store. In December 1863, he joined company G of the 29th Maine as a private and was promoted to sergeant major. Frank became a U.S. commissioner during Reconstruction and married a South Carolinian after the war; they raised three daughters and lived in Columbia.

Harriet I. "Hatty Belle" Eaton (1855–1942)
The youngest of HE's three children, who lived at the Whittiers' in Gorham, Maine, during her mother's wartime absences. Hatty Belle significantly outlived her mother, brother, and sister, all of whom died in a three-year period in the 1880s.

Franklin Brigham Fay (1821–1904)
Mayor of Chelsea, Massachusetts, like his father before him, Frank Fay found his calling as a relief agent when he encountered the wounded of the Chelsea Light Infantry in hospital after First Bull Run. By mid-war, Fay worked closely with Helen Gilson, a twenty-six-year-old, whom Fay had employed as a governess. Fay and Gilson devoted their efforts to the USSC. In May 1864, Fay established an auxiliary relief corps designed to provide around-the-clock care to wounded pouring in from the Wilderness. The corps was also at Spotsylvania, Cold Harbor, and Petersburg to transfer incapacitated soldiers from field hospitals to general hospitals in the North. A gifted negotiator and self-proclaimed pacifist, Fay's ease of manner worked as an open-sesame with military authorities. William Howell Reed dedicated his *Hospital Life in the Army of the Potomac* to Fay in 1866, and edited Fay's privately published war papers in 1911. Of Fay, Reed wrote, "His sober gray dress, his tall spare form, his rather long hair, his kindly face, his generous plans for service, made him so marked a personality that the way was opened for him where civilians were not generally allowed to go" (*War Papers*, vi).

Hugh M. Fogg (1844–80)
Eighteen-year-old private in company D of the 6th Maine, a laborer from Calais, mustered in on December 1, 1861. The son of Eaton's coworker Isabella Fogg, Hugh was born in New Brunswick, Canada, and was slight of build in contrast to the large lumbermen of Calais who filled out the 6th. During the war, he contracted both malaria and syphilis. Fogg's left leg was amputated two inches above the knee, following a severe wound at the battle of Cedar Creek on October 19, 1864. Isabella was with him when he was transferred to Patterson Hospital in Baltimore, interceding with army officials to move him to Christian Street Hospital in

Chester, Pennsylvania, where she believed that occupational therapists would better rehabilitate him. When released on June 8, 1865, Fogg married a girl from Portland and was hired to superintend Union cemeteries in Fort Leavenworth, Kansas, and later, in Louisville. He was only thirty-six when he died there of tuberculosis.

Isabella Morrison Fogg (1823–73)
HE's coworker during both her tours of duty. Scottish by birth, Fogg grew up in New Brunswick, married, and started a family there before moving to Calais. Widowed well before the Civil War, Fogg referred to herself as a "tailoress." When son Hugh enlisted in the 6th Maine in 1861, Fogg headed with supplies for the hospitals in Annapolis. By 1862, the USSC had dispatched her to the *Elm City*, one of its fleet of steamers, during the peninsular campaign. She continued to provide relief services to soldiers in the Army of the Potomac in the aftermath of the Seven Days battles until she returned to Maine in the late summer. Her report of the miserable conditions facing hospitalized soldiers prompted the state of Maine to appoint Colonel John W. Hathaway to organize relief efforts at the state level. By October 1862, the FSBC pledged to contribute aid and asked HE to join Fogg in her work with Maine soldiers in Maryland and Virginia. Worn down after caring for the wounded at Fredericksburg, Fogg contracted pneumonia in March 1863, but recovered enough by early May to assist Maine regiments at Chancellorsville. Though Fogg continued to serve through the Gettysburg campaign, she was back in Maine in early 1864 when the MCHA dismissed her without explanation. Determined to return to her work, she gathered endorsements from Joshua Lawrence Chamberlain and Charles D. Gilmore and was reinstated with the Army of the Potomac for the summer campaigns of 1864. When Hugh's leg was amputated in the fall of 1864, Fogg joined him to nurse him back to health. By November, she sought work in the western theater and joined the USCC's fleet on the Ohio. Two months later, she fell through a hatch on the *Jacob Strader*, sustaining a back injury from which she never fully recovered. Unable to earn a living through active labor, Fogg turned to writing but had little success. Better at lobbying for pension increases, she died in relative poverty at the age of fifty.

Harriet Lewis Fox (c.1824–1901)
Corresponding secretary of the MCHA, Fox was the administrative go-between for supplies sent by Maine households to soldiers in the field. Fox collected boxes at 49 Danforth Street, the home she shared with her mother and siblings in Portland, and forwarded them from 1862 to 1865 to regiments stationed in Washington, D.C., Virginia, and Maryland.

Charles Davis Gilmore (1819–84)
Forty-year-old captain in company C of the 7th Maine, mustered in on August 22, 1861, from Bangor. Gilmore was promoted to major of the 20th Maine on August

8, 1862, to lieutenant colonel on May 20, 1863, and to colonel on June 15, 1864. Wounded by a shell at Lee's Mills in April 1862, Gilmore missed most of the major action of the 20th because he was on detached service in Washington, hearing court-martials. Before the war, he served as deputy sheriff of Penobscot County, and after the war, having taken up permanent residence in the nation's capital, he opened a pension assistance office and purchased significant land in the West.

Helen Louise Gilson (1835–68)
A special diet cook and nurse in her twenties, Gilson worked as governess for the children of Frank Fay, mayor of Chelsea, Massachusetts, for two years before the war began. In 1861, she organized a local soldier's aid society, but got her big break in April 1862 when Dorothea Dix—uninformed about Gilson's youth—placed her as a nurse in Columbian College Hospital in Washington. Gilson soon moved to more active employment on the peninsula through the aegis of Mayor Fay and his USSC connections. She worked at White House Landing on the Pamunkey River through the summer of 1862, joining USSC workers on hospital steamers. Here she contracted malaria from which she never fully recovered. Gilson was present with supplies after Antietam, Fredericksburg, Chancellorsville, and Gettysburg. She continued working alongside Fay as a member of the USSC's auxiliary relief corps, and ended her service, like many others, at City Point, where she was on duty during the Wilderness, Cold Harbor, and the siege of Petersburg. She spearheaded the building of huts for contraband workers at City Point and worked after the war in a Richmond orphanage for black children (herself orphaned as a teenager). Known to veterans for her fetching looks and sweet singing voice, she married and died in childbirth less than a year and a half later, at the age of thirty-two.

Byron (1798–?) and Mary (1802–?) Greenough
The Greenoughs were the Eatons' next door neighbors in Portland. Byron, a hat, cap, and fur dealer, was a deacon in the FSBC. He served as president of the Sunday school society from 1836 to 1837 and again from 1854 to 1855. Mary was central in church activities and became one of HE's regular correspondents.

Maria M. C. Hall (1836–1912)
Hall was a seasoned battlefield nurse when she met Harriet Eaton in 1864. A resident of Washington, D.C., Hall nursed soldiers at the Patent Office Hospital after 1st Bull Run. By 1862, she had joined the medical crew of the *Daniel Webster* on the Pamunkey and James Rivers, caring for men wounded during the peninsular campaign. After the Seven Days and Fair Oaks battles, Hall helped move eleven thousand men to Washington hospitals. She is best known for her service at Smoketown Hospital, established in a grove of oak and walnut trees after the battle of Antietam. When the hospital disbanded in May 1863, Surgeon Bernard Vanderkieft asked her to work with him in the naval academy hospital at Annapolis, where she continued

on staff through the battles of Gettysburg and the Wilderness, the release of Union soldiers from Confederate prisons, and the siege of Petersburg, until the hospital closed in the summer of 1865.

Cornelia Hancock (1840–1927)
Twenty-three-year-old New Jersey Quaker who installed herself as a nurse after the battle of Gettysburg when she joined her brother-in-law, Surgeon Henry T. Child, at the front, despite Dorothea Dix's refusal to enlist her aid. Three weeks later, she wrote, "It seems to me as if all my past life was a myth, and as if I had been away from home for seventeen years" (July 26, 1863). In the fall of 1863, she was caring for contrabands in Washington, including five unattached children stricken with smallpox. By the winter, she was a field nurse with the 3rd division's 2nd corps at Brandy Station, Virginia, able to come and go as she saw fit. Funded by Philadelphia Quakers, Hancock helped move five hundred soldiers on a steamer to general hospitals in Washington after the battle of the Wilderness in May 1864. By June, she had landed at City Point and remained until war's end. Boasting about her privileges there, she noted that Edward P. Dalton, head of medical services, was so pleased with the order of her supply tent that he remarked, "If any one in this Army was deserving of good quarters, it was Miss Hancock" (Nov. 14, 1864). After the war, she established the Laing School for African American children in Mount Pleasant, South Carolina, serving as principal for ten years and building a student body of more than two hundred. Active in postwar nursing organizations and GAR reunions, Hancock was eighty-seven when she died.

Mrs. Hanson (Caroline R.) Hart (1820–?)
Member of the MCHA and superintendent of the FSBC Sunday school. Caroline's husband, Hanson Hart, Senior, was a Portland wool dealer. Her son, Hanson (Junior), was in Frank Eaton's company.

James W. Hathaway (1835–?)
Twenty-seven-year-old captain in company A of the 19th Maine, from Mercer, mustered in on August 25, 1862. Hathaway was a soldier for fewer than three months when he fell ill at Frederick and was discharged for disability on November 5.

John W. Hathaway (1813–?)
Head of the Maine State [Relief] Agency, referred to as "Colonel" or "Mr." Hathaway, a lumberman from Penobscot County.

Charles C. Hayes (1809–?)
Clerk and agent of the MSRA, whose immediate superior was J. W. Hathaway. During his three years of service, Hayes made weekly trips from Portland to Washington and environs. Described as "indefatigable" in his labors (*Portland*

Daily Press, February 6, 1865), Hayes was responsible for making sure that packages sent to Washington reached Maine soldiers in the surrounding countryside. He continued to make his home in Portland after the war, where he worked as a grocery clerk.

Dr. Nahum A. Hersom (1835–81)
Twenty-seven-year-old surgeon of the 17th Maine, from Lebanon, Hersom was appointed surgeon in late 1862 over Dr. William Wescott [see listing below]. Soldiers wrote a letter of protest when Hersom, who had begun his service as assistant surgeon of the 20th Maine, was appointed, but he and Wescott ultimately worked together in the 17th. Charles Mattocks notes that both surgeons lost their horses at Chancellorsville (*"Unspoiled Heart,"* 24). Hersom's medical degrees were from Bowdoin College and the University of Pennsylvania. After the war, he practiced medicine in Portland.

Dr. William B. Hezless (1832–84)
Surgeon of the 3rd Pennsylvania Cavalry from August 1861 to August 1864, and of the 6th Pennsylvania Heavy Artillery until the end of the war. Hezless, who was from Allegheny, was an 1854 graduate of Philadelphia's Jefferson Medical College. Court-martialed for inebriation in February 1864, coworkers testified that he had been drinking during a skirmish; one even alluded to a botched amputation. However, when others noted that his drinking had not affected the outcome of the surgery, the court-martial found him not guilty and he returned to duty. An 1885 pension request from his indigent widow suggested that the proceeds of his practice supported what was likely alcoholism.

Oliver Otis Howard (1830–1909)
Major general from Leeds, Maine, educated at Bowdoin College and West Point. A father of seven, Howard began service as colonel of the 3rd Maine and was promoted to brigadier general after he distinguished himself at 1st Bull Run. Because of his conversion experience in the late 1850s, Howard was known in the ranks for his piety. Two wounds at Fair Oaks in 1862 led to an amputation of his arm above the elbow. Promoted to major general that fall, he went on to lead the 11th corps at Chancellorsville and Gettysburg. Envied by officers who were jealous of his promotions in light of what they believed was a lackluster combat record, Howard found himself at odds with the likes of Hooker and Winfield Scott Hancock, though Sherman's postwar memoir praises him. After the war, he headed the Bureau of Refugees and Freedmen and helped found Howard University, which was named for him. In 1893, he was awarded a Congressional Medal of Honor for his service thirty-one years earlier at Fair Oaks. Retiring to Vermont in the 1890s, Howard continued to promote educational reform and was a darling of the lecture circuit.

Mary Morris Husband (1820–94)
Wife of a Philadelphia lawyer and grand-daughter of Revolutionary War hero, General Robert Morris, Mary Husband began visiting local hospitals after sending two sons off to war in 1861. When one son was wounded during the peninsular campaign, she located him and spent several months nursing men transferred from the peninsula to Washington hospitals. After Dorothea Dix appointed her to the Camden Street Hospital in Baltimore, Husband occupied herself, along with Maria Hall and Ellen Orbison Harris, at Smoketown Hospital near the Antietam battlefield. At Chancellorsville, she and HE dressed wounds in a private residence and the 3rd and 11th corps hospitals. By July she moved to Camp Letterman at Gettysburg, where she fell ill for three weeks. After her recovery, she served at Camp Parole in Annapolis, where the USSC installed her as its agent. With the spring and summer campaigns, the army base moved from Port Royal to White House Landing, and finally to City Point, and Husband served the hospitals at each location. Known for a capacious apron with many pockets, Husband helped soldiers reclaim back pay and pensions, accompanied the ill back to their homes in the East, and interceded on behalf of those unfairly sentenced. On her return to Philadelphia after the war, her home became a meeting place for the thousands of men she had attended during four years of war.

Nathaniel P. Jaques (1837–1918)
Twenty-five-year-old private in company F of the 19th Maine, a tinsmith from Bowdoinham, mustered in on August 25, 1862. Though promoted to corporal and later sergeant, Jaques' illness kept him from the field. In 1870, Jaques was recorded by two census takers as a resident of Tioga County, New York, where he was living in a boarding house with HE, and of Newton, Massachusetts, HE's hometown, where he lived with his wife Charlotte and their nine-month-old son Claude. In 1880, the Jaqueses were residents of Reno, Nevada. By 1900, Jaques had been widowed and was living in a boarding house in Vancouver, Washington. His last address was the National Home for Disabled Volunteer Soldiers in Malibu, California, where he died in 1918.

Frank L. Jones (c.1829–?)
Captain in company A of the 25th Maine, a telegraphist from Portland, commissioned on September 29, 1862. Jones resigned on March 7, 1863, but reenlisted as captain in company I of the 30th Maine on January 8, 1864. He was mustered out on August 20, 1865.

William P. Jordan (1830–1906)
Thirty-one-year-old captain in company C of the 1st, 10th, and 29th Maine, from Portland, commissioned on October 5, 1861. Jordan saw significant action at Antietam and the battle of Cedar Mountain in August 1862.

Samuel T. Keene (1833–64)
Twenty-nine-year-old captain in company F of the 20th Maine, a lawyer from Rockland, mustered in on August 29, 1862. Keene sustained a shot to his sword belt at Gettysburg and was shot again by a sniper at Petersburg on June 22, 1864 and instantly killed.

George Knox (1816–64)
Baptist chaplain of the 1st, 10th, and 29th Maine, from Brunswick, commissioned on May 2, 1861. Born in Saco, Knox held undergraduate and graduate degrees from Waterville College (1840 and 1845) and attended Newton Theological Seminary from 1840 to 1841. The rank and file knew him as "our beloved chaplain," "a noble man," and "a true Christian" (Kallgren and Crouthamel, 22, 49). Knox died on October 31, 1864 after a freak accident at Cedar Creek, Virginia: On his way to a troop review, his horse threw him and fell on him, breaking his neck; he died within hours, leaving four young children and a wife who outlived him by more than forty years.

Dr. John M. Kollock (1837–89)
Assistant surgeon of the 118th Pennsylvania, promoted to surgeon of the 50th Pennsylvania in September 1864, from Virginia. This was HE's "Dr. Colic," a man she averred was well named. After the war, Kollock married and moved to Alabama.

Alden Litchfield (1831–?)
Thirty-one-year-old quartermaster of the 20th Maine, a clerk from Rockland, mustered in on November 20, 1862. HE and Isabella Fogg so despised Litchfield for his cruelty to the men that they wrote to Maine advocate George W. Dyer in February 1863, requesting his removal but to no avail; Litchfield was not mustered out until June 4, 1865. In 1870, he was serving time in a Belfast (Maine) jail.

William C. Manning
Known variously as Willy and Billy, Manning, from Portland, was sergeant major of the 1st Massachusetts Infantry when he sustained wounds in the left arm and hip at the Seven Days battles in 1862. Discharged for disability in February 1863, he regularly contributed articles to the Portland *Transcript*. Later that year, he was appointed lieutenant of the 2nd Massachusetts Cavalry. Some time in 1864, Manning was imprisoned at Salisbury, North Carolina, but made it back to his unit and was appointed a major before leaving the service.

Ruth Swett Mayhew (1822–74)
Relief agent with the MCHA. The widow of a Rockland minister, Mayhew moved to Portland in 1856 and was working as a public school teacher when the war began.

In 1861, she offered her services to the 4th Maine but was barred from joining the regiment (Dalton, 16). That winter, Mayhew traveled to Washington to attend sick soldiers with Isabella Fogg. The MCHA authorized her to go to Gettysburg on July 9, 1863, where she and Sarah Sampson [see listing below] remained for several weeks. By mid-1864, she joined others at the depot field hospital at City Point. There she noted that she rose at 6:30 a.m. and "work[ed] without intermission until eleven or twelve at night" (Mayhew to Harriet Fox, February 26, 1865, Relief Agencies Collection, MSA). While at City Point, Mayhew took a month's furlough to care for Agnes and Hatty Belle Eaton. Like HE, she corresponded with the *Portland Daily Press*, enjoining citizens to supply Maine's soldiers with comforts and assuring them that their largesse would not be squandered. After the war, Mayhew spent three years teaching at an Indian school in Ottawa, Kansas, but returned to Maine in 1868 to become matron in the soldiers' orphans' home in Bath.

Charlotte McKay (1818–1894)
Spurred into service by the deaths of her husband and son before war, the Maine-born nurse also lost a brother at Chancellorsville, where she searched in vain to find his body. On hand also at Antietam, Fredericksburg, Gettysburg, the Wilderness, and Spotsylvania, she served at the Cavalry Corps hospital at City Point, where she sometimes mistook the vocalizations of mules to be those of human despair. Like HE, she spent evenings writing in a journal, which she published in 1876 as a series of sketches entitled *Stories of Hospital and Camp*.

Charles H. Mero (1843–1921)
Nineteen-year-old private in company E of the 20th Maine, a farm laborer from Waldoboro, mustered in on August 29, 1862 and out on June 15, 1864. Mero was the ladies' guard at Falmouth. After the war, he farmed in Wisconsin and Minnesota.

Charles B. Merrill (1827–91)
Thirty-five-year-old lieutenant colonel of the 17th Maine, a lawyer from Portland, who enlisted on July 15, 1862. Merrill was edged out of the running for colonel by Thomas A. Roberts [see listing below], which created bad blood between them forever. Though Merrill did become colonel in June 1863 when Roberts was discharged for disability, Private John Haley reported that he was "as tender-hearted as a woman" and "too tender-hearted for a warrior" (*The Rebel Yell*, 183, 138).

Dr. Nahum P. Monroe (1808–73)
Surgeon of the 20th Maine, from Belfast (Maine). Born in Surry, New Hampshire, the youngest of eight children, Monroe graduated from Albany Medical College in 1839 and set up a surgical practice in Belfast. In April 1863, Monroe reported that he had eighty-four soldiers with smallpox and asked that the 20th be quarantined—a request that was granted. HE's coworker C. C. Hayes complained about Surgeon

Monroe's skill and believed that the unusual amount of illness in the regiment was due to his sanitary negligence. Monroe himself developed erysipelas after a year of service and resigned his commission. However, by 1865, Governor Samuel Cony appointed him surgeon general of the state of Maine. When he died of tuberculosis in 1873, he was a member of the AMA and a trustee of the Maine insane asylum. [HE misspells as "Munroe."]

Dr. John Moore (1826–1907)
A surgeon, medical director, and later U.S. surgeon general with wide responsibility during the war, from Bloomington, Indiana. Moore received an undergraduate degree from Indiana State University in Terre Haute in 1845 before seeking medical training at the University of Louisville. He attended the University of the City of New York in 1849 and received his MD in 1850. Before entering the service in 1853, Moore interned at Bellvue Hospital and the New York Dispensary. By June 1862, he had been promoted to medical director of the Army of the Potomac's central grand division, and served at 2nd Bull Run, Antietam, Fredericksburg, and Chancellorsville. He was in charge of medical services at the battles of Chickamauga and Lookout Mountain, and joined Sherman for the March to the Sea. During the two decades until he was appointed surgeon general, he served in New York City; Texas; Richmond, Virginia; Fort Vancouver in Washington Territory; and in San Francisco. His term of service as surgeon general (1886–90) was notable for sanitary improvements at military posts.

Frances M. Nye (1836–?)
While studying homeopathy, she met her future husband, the unlikely named Francis M. Nye of Indiana, and the two married in 1861. Inspired by her service at City Point, Frances Nye went to medical school in her home state of New York after the war and became a physician. The couple established a joint medical practice in New York City, which they maintained through the end of the century.

Charles Wilmot Oleson (1842–1906)
Twenty-year-old private in the 5th Maine Battery, a druggist-clerk from Portland, mustered in on August 28, 1862. Oleson was promoted to hospital steward of U.S. Regulars on June 15, 1863 and served at Eckington Hospital in Washington, which later merged with Finley Hospital. A blue-eyed young man with light hair, Oleson counted Frank Eaton, Fred Bosworth, and Will Manning among his friends [see listings above].

Dr. William O'Meagher (c.1831–96)
Originally with the 37th (Irish Rifles) and 69th New York, the Irish-born O'Meagher was surgeon in charge of the 1st division 2nd corps hospital at City Point. He served as assistant surgeon under John McNulty for four months, before Surgeon McNulty left the post and O'Meagher was named surgeon on October 10,

1861. Before the war, he was coroner of New York City. Nurse Cornelia Hancock referred to him as "a smart little Irish man who knows what is what" (Hancock, 159 [Sept. 16, 1864]).

Dr. Hettie Kersey Painter (1821–89)
A physician who served as a state relief agent for New Jersey. Born in Philadelphia and orphaned as a young child, Painter was raised by an aunt and uncle. Known for her culinary skill and elegant manners, Painter was a close friend of Adelaide Smith. She was said to be small, of the "old time Quaker stamp," wearing "a little white cap" and "a short gown and petticoat" (Maxwell, 259). After the war, she practiced medicine in Washington, Richmond, and Lincoln, Nebraska.

Rebecca Rosaignol Holliday Pomroy (1817–84)
Forty-three-year-old widow from Chelsea, Massachusetts, known to her familiars as "Auntie Pomroy," who went to Washington in 1861 to find work in hospitals after reading an ad in a local paper. Pomroy served briefly at a Georgetown hospital before joining the staff of Columbian College Hospital in September 1861. In 1862, Dorothea Dix asked her to accept a special assignment as nurse to the First Family and she became a valued servant, moving back and forth between the White House and Columbian. After the war, Pomroy became matron of a girls' reformatory in Newton, Massachusetts (HE's hometown), and held that post for more than twenty years. She published her memoirs in 1884, *Echoes from Hospital and White House*.

Sarah Jane Prentiss (1823–77)
Matron of Trinity Church Hospital in Washington, and later at Finley Hospital, where she tended the erysipelas and gangrene wards, from Paris (Maine). HE saw Prentiss on her way to Maine camps in Virginia in 1862. In her late thirties, a dedicated abolitionist and spinster, Prentiss was a talented writer and landscape painter. She published several small sketches about wartime nursing, including one about her coworker Almira Fales. Like many who worked in southern latitudes, she contracted malaria and eventually left the service to convalesce. [HE misspells as "Prentice."]

Almira F. Quinby (1828–1909)
Thirty-two-year-old daughter of an elite family from Stroudwater, living in Biddeford in 1862 when she began to nurse under the auspices of Dorothea Dix. Quinby's first assignment was at Chester Hospital near Philadelphia. In the summer of 1863, she and other Mainers were caring for soldiers wounded at Gettysburg in the naval academy hospital at Annapolis. This hospital also received Union soldiers imprisoned at Andersonville, Libby, Salisbury, and Florence. After the war, Quinby settled in Portland with her cousin Louisa Titcomb, who had worked with her in Annapolis.

Rachel
Contraband woman who served in the Maine relief tents at City Point.

Dorcas M. Rea (c.1809–73)
Widowed secretary of the ladies' committee of relief workers, from Portland, working closely with the MCHA.

Thomas A. Roberts (1817–?)
Commissioned as colonel of the 17th Maine on July 15, 1862, a housepainter and wallpaper hanger from Portland. At Chancellorsville, Roberts was wounded in the leg; surgeons could not save it. Lieutenant Colonel Charles B. Merrill [see listing above], also from Portland, was promoted to colonel in June 1863 when Roberts was discharged for disability. After the war, Roberts continued in the painting business with two of his sons, George and Thomas F., and was still alive in 1880.

Sarah Smith Sampson (1832–1907)
Thirty-year-old Maine state relief agent, from Bath. In June 1861, Sampson followed her husband's regiment to Washington and was hooked. Charles Sampson, employed as a ship's carver during Maine's whaling heyday, was captain of company D in the 3rd Maine, commanded by Oliver O. Howard [see listing above]. Sarah Sampson nursed the sick soldiers of the 2nd, 3rd, 4th, and 5th Maine regiments encamped around the Union capital during the war's first year, but did not realize the extent of medical need until she witnessed the battle of Fair Oaks, where forty-five hundred men were wounded. It was here that General Howard lost his right arm and Sampson took care of him. She and Charles returned to Bath briefly in the summer of 1862 to regroup: he had resigned his commission for having been critical of commanders' strategy during the Seven Days battles; she had lost her supplies and personal effects on the peninsula. In October—the same month HE embarked on her first tour of duty for the MCHA—Sampson worked her way back to Washington under the aegis of the Bath ladies' aid society and soon was named agent for the newly formed MSRA at a salary of $40 per month. Oddly, Sampson's and HE's paths crossed only once during the war—at Fredericksburg. Well connected with the military medical establishment, she did not hesitate to appeal to powerful friends when rule-followers impeded her. Leonard Watson of the MSRA praised her effectiveness: "Mrs. Sampson is much better than the average of women who undertake to assist in work of this kind.—excellent" (July 20, 1863, Relief Agencies Collection, MSA). After the war, she founded a home for soldiers' orphans in Bath, which remained the state children's home for more than a hundred years. Widowed in 1881, Sampson secured work at the U.S. Pension Bureau and moved to Washington, where she lived for twenty-three years—a relocation that she always regretted since it kept her from her native state. She received a pension by special act of Congress in 1885 based on her published account of the MSRA's wartime activities

and testimonials from former Vice President Hannibal Hamlin and Dr. Gideon S. Palmer.

Adelaide W. Smith (1831–1914)
Union nurse and spinster from Brooklyn, New York, who entered service at Long Island College Hospital in July 1862 and worked at hospitals on Bedloe's and David's Islands. In 1863, Smith was assigned, along with Clara Barton, to the division hospital of Butler's Department of the James at Point of Rocks, Virginia. She was transferred to City Point in 1864 and began working with Ruth Mayhew and HE for the MSRA. Later she assisted at the tents of the New Jersey and Pennsylvania relief associations as well. When HE met her at City Point in October 1864, she noted that Smith was "a bright sparkling lady full of wit and quick repartee" (Eaton Diary, October 22, 1864). After the war, Smith returned to Brooklyn and helped distribute the USSC's surplus supplies to the needy of New York City. By 1867, she had accepted the position of Superintendent of Colored Schools in Norfolk, Virginia.

Lewis B. Smith (1825–?)
Corresponding secretary of the MCHA and prominent Portland citizen who had been city council president and a local custom-house official. Smith was chief engineer of Portland's fire department in 1860 and deputy collector of the port in 1870.

Ellis Spear (1834–1917)
Twenty-seven-year-old captain in company G and later major and colonel of the 20th Maine, a schoolmaster from Wicasset, mustered in on August 29, 1862 and out on July 16, 1865. He was brevetted a brigadier general in April 1865. Spear was a mild-mannered, terse, and witty warrior who drolly speculated that the army required men to have a strong set of teeth, not to bite off the end of cartridges but for chewing and swallowing hardtack (Pullen, 92).

Byron Sunderland (1819–1901)
Abolitionist and legendary minister of Washington's First Presbyterian Church from 1853 to 1898. In 1857, as he encouraged female parishioners to use their morality for the good of the nation, he also helped found Gallaudet University for the deaf. President Lincoln appointed Sunderland chaplain of the Senate during the war, and he was frequently present in camps of the Army of the Potomac. Sunderland invited Frederick Douglass to address his congregation in 1866, a step not ventured by any of his ministerial colleagues, and over the years a variety of other distinguished citizens spoke there, including statesmen Henry Clay and Daniel Webster and theologians Henry Ward Beecher and DeWitt Talmage. In 1885, he delivered U. S. Grant's funeral oration, and in 1886, officiated at President Grover Cleveland's wedding to Frances Folsom. Sunderland's church stood on Capitol Hill from 1811 to 1930, when ground was broken for the U.S. House of Representatives' Rayburn office building.

Charles William Tilden (1832–1914)

First lieutenant in company B of the 2nd Maine, a merchant from Castine, appointed on May 28, 1861 and promoted to captain in July 1861. A year later, he became lieutenant colonel of the 16th Maine and by January 1863, its colonel. Tilden was slightly wounded at Hanover Courthouse during the peninsular campaign and taken prisoner at Gettysburg on July 1, 1863. Seven months later, he escaped from Richmond's Libby Prison through a tunnel and managed to rejoin his command only six weeks later. After another capture and escape in 1864, this lithe soldier was made a commander of the 3rd brigade and at the end of the war, brevetted a brigadier general. [HE mistakenly refers to him as "Lieutenant Tilton."]

Ellen Sarah Forbes Tolman (1837–1908)

Nurse and relief agent from Norridgewock, known by the nickname of "Nellie." Forbes worked in Washington hospitals from 1861 until February 1863, when she was diagnosed with typhus, a relatively rare affliction during the Civil War. Like HE, she conveyed hospital supplies from individuals and aid societies to men in the field. Despite Dorothea Dix's best efforts to curb the romantic enthusiasm of hospital nurses, Forbes married Eleazer Tolman, a soldier-patient in the 2nd Maine in April 1864. Though she did not return to the field after her marriage, she helped disabled soldiers secure pensions and became an advocate for the Army Nurses' Pension Act of 1892. Her own monthly pension of $25 was granted in 1886 by a special act of Congress; it had been endorsed by several prominent veterans and former Vice President Hannibal Hamlin.

George Varney (1834–1911)

A well-to-do merchant from Bangor, known as "a brick" by the soldiers of the 2nd Maine, the twenty-seven-year-old Varney rose swiftly through the ranks. He entered the service as a major on May 28, 1861, was promoted to lieutenant colonel three months later, and became the regiment's colonel in January 1863 when Charles W. Roberts resigned. At Gaines Mill in June 1862, he was captured and thrown into Libby Prison, but was exchanged by August. A veteran of thirteen battles, a bullet grazed Varney's head at Fredericksburg, from which he never fully recovered. Two years after it had been mustered in, the 2nd marched home with only a quarter of its original thousand members. Unable to return to the front, Varney served in the state legislature in 1863. After the war, he became a director of the Maine Central Railroad and sat on bank boards.

Leonard W. Watson (1824–?)

MSRA agent in Washington, a cabinet maker from Wilton, keeping stores at 273 F Street, to be carried to soldiers in the field. One of his colleagues described him as "a man of Descression [sic], energy & admirable working qualities, [who] devote[d] his whole time to the cause & whose heart is in the work" (C. R. Vaughan to Governor Israel Washburn, August 22, 1862, Relief Agencies Collection, MSA).

Dr. William W. Wescott (1818–77)
Forty-four-year-old assistant surgeon of the 14th and later the 17th Maine, from Standish, commissioned on July 29, 1862 and dismissed for inefficiency on December 5, 1862, despite the support of the regiment.

William Edward Seaver Whitman (1832–1901)
Known as "Toby Candor" in the world of journalism, the Boston-born Whitman was Maine's correspondent for the *Boston Globe*, *Herald*, and *Journal* during the Civil War. Whitman scooped all other northern newspapers with the first account of the firing on Fort Sumter. He interrupted his journalistic career just once, to seek his fortune in gold mining in California, but returned to Gardiner, Maine, before the war. In 1865, he coauthored with Charles True *Maine in the War for the Union*.

Samuel M. (1825–?) and Mary Elisabeth Whitney (1823–?)
Samuel Whitney was a clergyman who befriended Sewall Eaton at Newton Theological Institute. Massachusetts-born, he and his wife Elisabeth moved to Windsor, Vermont, and in 1870 were hosting Agnes and Hatty Belle Eaton, while their mother was running a hardware store in Tioga County, New York.

Edward Newton Whittier (1840–1902)
Twenty-one-year-old sergeant in the 5th Maine Light Artillery, from Gorham, mustered in on December 21, 1861. Though promoted to 2nd and 1st lieutenant in 1862 and 1863 and brevetted a captain on March 13, 1865, Whittier's most honored service was as acting assistant adjutant general of the 6th corps—a laurel earned after he commanded the battery on the second day of fighting at Gettysburg. Also known by the nickname of Ned, he was brother to George and son of Mary Webster Whittier [see listings below].

George Williams Whittier (1842–72)
Nineteen-year-old private in the 5th Maine Light Artillery, from Gorham, mustered in on August 28, 1862. By June 1863, Whittier had been appointed clerk to the chief of the 2nd artillery division of the Army of the Potomac. The brother of Edward and son of Mrs. Whittier, HE's close friend.

Mary Webster Whittier (1817–80)
Friend of HE's from Gorham, who cared for Hatty Belle in her absence. The mother of Edward and George Whittier and the wife of Samuel A. Whittier, a merchant.

Georgiana Willets (1840–1912)
Twenty-four-year-old nurse from Jersey City, New Jersey. Willets went to Washington in the spring of 1864 and joined relief efforts in Fredericksburg after the battle

of the Wilderness, just before Grant ordered the evacuation of the town and the removal of eight hundred patients. Willets volunteered to minister to a thousand men still lying on the field; four days later she helped move them by steamer to White House Landing. By mid-June, the Army of the Potomac advanced to City Point and Willets was assigned to the 2nd division hospital of the 2nd corps, where she remained, notwithstanding one trip by transport to Washington, for the rest of the war. In 1868, Willets married James M. Stradling, the quartermaster sergeant of the 1st New Jersey Cavalry. By 1870, they were living in Bucks County, Pennsylvania working at the Soldiers' Orphans' Home for Colored Children, caring for over fifty children. Willets received a pension for her hospital work and was buried at Arlington National Cemetery.

Dr. Isaac Wixom (1803–80)

New York–born surgeon of the 16th Michigan, from Genesee County, Michigan. Longtime physician and a father of six children, Wixom was fifty-eight and a state legislator when he began service with the 16th in 1861. A local newspaper lionized him in August 1861 as the "most heroic of surgeons, a man of large experience." However, the 16th's lieutenant colonel, Norval Welch, accused Wixom of mismanaging food and medicinal liquor in camps near Sharpsburg and Falmouth, and he was court-martialed on March 28, 1863 in a tent near 1st division headquarters. It appears that Wixom drew rations in the field for convenience instead of hiring out his own mess as military regulations required him to do; he also liberally shared hospital liquor among the unit's officers. The panel of officers sitting on the case, which included Maine's Joshua L. Chamberlain, found Wixom guilty on all charges. He was sentenced to pay $150 restitution and to forfeit all further pay. An appeal the following year was unsuccessful, and Wixom was dishonorably discharged. Despite these proceedings, Wixom was never disgraced publicly. The Michigan papers that had praised him for years refused to report the court-martial, and the good doctor returned to Fenton, where he lived until his death.

BIBLIOGRAPHY

PRIMARY SOURCES

Manuscripts and Manuscript Collections

Ann Arbor, Mich.
    Clements Library
        Cornelia Hancock Papers
Atlanta, Ga.
    Emory University Special Collections, Woodruff Library
        Charles Brown Thurston Papers
Augusta, Me.
    Maine State Archives
    MOLLUS Collection, Maine Commandery
        Maine Relief Agencies Collection
            "The Battle of Aldie" by William O. Howe, *c.*1896
Boston, Mass.
    Massachusetts Historical Society
        New England Women's Auxiliary Association Collection
Chapel Hill, N.C.
    Southern Historical Collection, Wilson Library, University of North Carolina
        Harriet H. A. Eaton Journals
Columbia, S. C.
    South Carolina Department of Archives and History
        Ada Bacot Diary
Durham, N.C.
    Manuscripts, Perkins Library, Duke University
        Amy Morris Bradley Diary and Letterbook, 1861–65
        Frank Moore Papers
        Walter M. Howland Papers
Hartford, Conn.
    Connecticut Historical Society

Madison, Wis.
   University of Wisconsin Special Collections
      State of Wisconsin Collection, Cordelia A. P. Harvey Papers
   Wisconsin Historical Society
      Cordelia Adelaide Harvey Papers
Montgomery, Ala.
   Alabama Department of Archives and History, Manuscripts
      Kate Cumming Collection
New York, N.Y.
   New-York Historical Society
Portland, Me.
   Maine Historical Society
      Forbes-Pottle-Tolman Papers
      Maine Camp Hospital Association Papers
      Usher Family Papers
Storrs, Conn.
   Thomas J. Dodd Research Center, Archives and Special Collections
      Josephine A. Dolan Collection of Nursing History, Harriet Eaton Papers
Washington, D. C.
   Library of Congress Manuscript Division
      Clara Barton Papers
      Mary Ann Ball Bickerdyke Papers
      Esther Hill Hawks Papers
Waterville, Me.
   Colby College Archives
      John B. Foster Papers

Documents at the National Archives and Records Administration, Washington, D.C.

Army Nurse Corps Historical Data File, 1898–1947. Entry 103. Union Surgeon General's Office. Record Group 112.

Card Index for Female Contract Nurses, 1861–65. Adjutant General's Office. Record Group 94.

Carded Service Records of Hospital Attendants, Matrons, and Nurses, 1861–65. Entry 535. Adjutant General's Office. Record Group 94.

Classified Schedule of Female Hospital Employes [sic]. Record and Pension Division, War Department. Record Group 94.

Colored Contract Nurses, July 16, 1863–June 14, 1864. Medical Department Register. Record Group 94.

Letters Received, 1818–70. Entry 12. Boxes 10, 11, 12, 13, 14, 26, 27, 28. Union Surgeon General's Office. Record Group 112.

Office of Female Nurses, Hospital Papers 1–430. Adjutant General's Office. Record Group 94.

Organization Index to Pension Files, Film Series T289. Pension Files Relating to 2,448 Army Nurses. Veterans Administration. Record Group 15.

Pensions of Rebecca Usher, Isabella Fogg, Harriet Patience Dame. Veterans Administration. Record Group 15.

Reports and Correspondence Regarding Contracts for Nurses, 1861–65. #1–1198. Adjutant General's Office. Record Group 94.

Published Narratives (Memoirs, Diaries, Letters, Collections)

Adams, Rev. John R., D.D. *Memorial and Letters of Rev. John R. Adams, D.D.* Privately printed, 1890.
Alcott, Louisa May. *Hospital Sketches.* Edited by Alice Fahs. Boston: Bedford/ St. Martin's, 2004.
Anderson, Mary E. Roberts. *The Story of Aunt Lizzie Aiken.* Chicago: Jansen, McClurg, 1880.
Bacot, Ada. *A Confederate Nurse: The Diary of Ada W. Bacot, 1860–1863.* Edited by Jean V. Berlin. Columbia: University of South Carolina Press, 1994.
Barnes, Francis, ed. *Autobiographical Sketch of Rev. Royal C. Spaulding.* Houlton: Smith, 1891.
Blackett, R. J. M., ed. *Running a Thousand Miles for Freedom: The Escape of William and Ellen Craft from Slavery.* Baton Rouge: Louisiana State University Press, 1999.
Bloor, Alfred J. *Letters from the Army of the Potomac, Written during the Month of May, 1864, to Several of the Supply Correspondents of the U.S. Sanitary Commission.* Washington: McGill and Witherow, 1864.
Brandegee, Mrs. S. K. *The Bugle Call; or, a Summons to Work in Christ's Army, by a Volunteer Nurse.* New York: American Tract Society, 1871.
Brockett, Linus P. and Mary C. Vaughan. *Woman's Work in the Civil War: A Record of Heroism, Patriotism, and Patience.* Philadelphia: Zeigler, McCurdy, 1867.
Bucklin, Sophronia E. *In Hospital and Camp.* Philadelphia: John E. Potter, 1869.
Chamberlain, Joshua Lawrence. *The Passing of the Armies: An Account of the Final Campaign of the Army of the Potomac.* New York: G. P. Putnam's Sons, 1915.
Coker, Hannah Lide. *A Story of the Civil War.* Edited by Nathaniel C. Browder. Raleigh: n.p., 1984.
Collis, Septima Levy. *A Woman's War Record, 1861–65.* New York: G. P. Putnam's Sons, 1889.
Cumming, Kate. *A Journal of Hospital Life in the Confederate Army of Tennessee from the Battle of Shiloh to the End of the War.* Louisville: John P. Morton, 1866.
―――. *Kate: The Journal of a Confederate Nurse.* Edited by Richard Barksdale Harwell. Baton Rouge: Louisiana State University Press, 1959; revised edition, 1987.
Daly, Maria Lydig. *Diary of a Union Lady, 1861–1865.* Edited by Harold Earl Hammond. New York: Funk and Wagnalls, 1962. Reprint, Lincoln: University of Nebraska Press, 2000.
Dunlap, Julia. *Notes of Hospital Life.* Philadelphia: J. B. Lippincott, 1864.
Fay, Frank B. *War Papers of Frank B. Fay.* Edited by William Howell Reed. N.p., 1911.
Gibbons, Abby Hopper. *Life of Abby Hopper Gibbons. Told Chiefly Through Her Correspondence.* Edited by Sarah Hopper Emerson. New York: Putnam's, 1896–97.
Godfrey, John Edwards. *The Journals of John Edwards Godfrey, Bangor, Maine, 1863–1869.* Edited by James B. Vickery. Rockland: Courier-Gazette, 1979.
Grant, Ulysses S. *Personal Memoirs of Ulysses S. Grant.* 2 Vols. New York: Charles L. Webster, 1885–86.
Greenleaf, Charles R. *A Manual for the Medical Officers of the United States Army.* Philadelphia, 1864. Reprint San Francisco: Norman Publishing, 1992.
Haley, John West. *The Rebel Yell and the Yankee Hurrah: The Civil War Journal of a Maine Volunteer.* Edited by Ruth L. Silliker. Camden: Down East Books, 1985.
Hancock, Cornelia. *South After Gettysburg; Letters of Cornelia Hancock, 1863–68.* Edited by Henrietta Stratton Jaquette. New York: Thomas Y. Crowell, 1937.

Hawks, Esther Hill. *A Woman Doctor's Civil War: Esther Hill Hawks's Diary.* Edited by Gerald Schwartz. Columbia: University of South Carolina Press, 1984.

Hoge, Jane. *The Boys in Blue; or, Heroes of the "Rank and File."* New York: E. B. Treat, 1867.

Holland, Mary Gardner. *Our Army Nurses.* Boston: B. Wilkins, 1895.

Holstein, Anna Morris. *Three Years in Field Hospitals of the Army of the Potomac.* Philadelphia: J. B. Lippincott, 1867.

Janney, Paulena Stevens. *The Civil War Journals of Paulena Stevens Janney.* Edited by Christie A. Russell. Baltimore: Gateway Press, 2007.

Kallgren, Beverly H. and James L. Crouthamel, eds. *"Dear Friend Anna": The Civil War Letters of a Common Soldier from Maine.* Orono: University Press of Maine, 1992.

King, Henry Melville. "The Church of My Boyhood" [pamphlet]. Providence, R.I.: F. H. Townsend, 1912.

Lawrence, Catherine S. *Autobiography.* Albany: Amasa J. Parker, 1893.

Lee, Elizabeth Blair. *Wartime Washington: The Civil War Letters of Elizabeth Blair Lee.* Edited by Virginia J. Laas. Urbana: University of Illinois Press, 1991.

Letterman, Jonathan. *Medical Recollections of the Army of the Potomac.* New York: D. Appleton, 1866.

Livermore, Mary A. *My Story of the War: A Woman's Narrative of Four Years Personal Experience.* Hartford: Worthington, 1889.

———. *My Story of the War: The Civil War Memoirs of the Famous Nurse, Relief Organizer, and Suffragette.* Edited by Nina Silber. New York: Da Capo Press, 1995.

Mattocks, Charles. *"Unspoiled Heart": The Journal of Charles Mattocks of the 17th Maine.* Edited by Philip N. Racine. Knoxville, Tenn.: University of Tennessee Press, 1994.

McElligott, Mary Ellen, ed. "'A Monotony Full of Sadness': The Diary of Nadine Turchin, May 1863–April 1864." *Journal of the Illinois State Historical Society* 70, No. 1 (February 1977): 27–89.

McKay, Charlotte. *Stories of Hospital and Camp.* Philadelphia: Claxton, Remsen, and Haffelfinger, 1876.

Moore, Frank, ed. *Women of the War; Their Heroism and Self-Sacrifice.* Hartford: S. S. Scranton, 1866.

Newcomb, Mary A. *Four Years of Personal Reminiscences of the War.* Chicago: H. S. Mills, 1893.

Palmer, Sarah A. *The Story of Aunt Becky's Army Life.* New York: John F. Trow, 1867.

Peter, Frances. *A Union Woman in Civil War Kentucky: The Diary of Frances Peter.* Edited by John David Smith and William Cooper, Jr. Lexington: University Press of Kentucky, 2000.

Reed, William Howell. *Hospital Life in the Army of the Potomac.* Boston: William V. Spencer, 1866.

Reilly, Wayne E., ed. *The Diaries of Sarah Jane and Emma Ann Foster: A Year in Maine during the Civil War.* Rockport: Picton Press, 2002.

Ropes, Hannah. *Civil War Nurse: The Diary and Letters of Hannah Ropes.* Edited by John R. Brumgardt. Knoxville: University of Tennessee Press, 1980.

Sawtelle, Daniel W. *All's for the Best: The Civil War Reminiscences and Letters of Daniel W. Sawtelle.* Edited by Peter H. Buckingham. Knoxville: University of Tennessee Press, 2001.

Scott, Kate M. *In Honor of the National Association of Army Nurses.* Atlantic City: n.p., 1910.

Small, Abner R. *The Road to Richmond: The Civil War Memoirs of Major Abner R. Small of the 16th Maine Volunteers; with His Diary as a Prisoner of War.* Edited by Harold Adams Small. Berkeley: University of California Press, 1959.

Smith, Adelaide W. *Reminiscences of an Army Nurse during the Civil War.* New York: Greaves Publishing, 1911.

Stevens, George T. *Three Years in the Sixth Corps: A Concise Narrative of Events in the Army of the Potomac from 1861 to the Close of the Rebellion, April 1865.* Albany: S. R. Gray, 1866.

Stevens, Greenlief T. *Letter to the Members of the 5th Maine Battery Association.* Augusta: Charles E. Nash, 1890.

Taylor, Susie King. *Reminiscences of My Life in Camp.* Boston: n.p., 1902. Edited by Anthony G. Barthelemy. Reprint, New York: Oxford University Press, 1998.

Third, Fourth, and Fifth Semi-Annual Reports of the Ladies Aid Society of Philadelphia. Philadelphia: C. Sherman and Sons, 1862–63.

Von Olnhausen, Mary Phinney. *Adventures of an Army Nurse in Two Wars: Edited from the Diary and Correspondence of Mary Phinney, Baroness von Olnhausen.* Edited by James Phinney Munroe. Boston: Little, Brown, 1904.

Wheelock, Julia S. *The Boys in White; The Experience of a Hospital Agent in and Around Washington.* New York: Lange and Hillman, 1870.

Whitman, Walt. *Specimen Days and Collect. Complete Poetry and Prose of Walt Whitman.* Edited by Malcolm Cowley. Garden City: Garden City Books, 1954.

Wilder, Burt G. *Practicing Medicine in a Black Regiment: The Ciivl War Diary of Burt G. Wilder, 55th Massachusetts.* Edited by Richard M. Reid. Amherst: University of Massachusetts Press, 2010.

Wittenmyer, Annie Turner. *Under the Guns; A Woman's Reminiscences of the Civil War.* Boston: E. B. Stillings, 1895.

Wormeley, Katharine Prescott. *The Other Side of War with the Army of the Potomac.* Boston: Ticknor, 1889.

Newspapers and Periodicals

Boston Daily Globe, September 29, 1901
Bangor Daily Whig and Courier, November 14, 1876
East Saginaw Courier [Michigan], August 17, 1861
Eastern Argus, June 17, 1884
Fitchburg Daily Sentinel [Massachusetts], February 15, 1884
Hartford Daily Times, June 11, 1885
Kennebec Journal, October 28, 1864
New York Times, November 27, 1864
New York Tribune, May 31, 1864
Portland Daily Advertiser, 1856, 1885
Portland Daily Press, 1862–64, 1885
Portland Sunday Times, 1885
Portland Transcript, 1863, 1885
Wisconsin Daily State Journal, 1862

Websites

Family History http://www.ancestry.com

Biographical Directory of the U.S. Congress, 1774–Present http://bioguide.congress.gov/scripts/biodisplay

Maine Civil War Regimental Records of the Maine State Archives http://www.maine.gov/sos/arc/archives/military/civilwar/reghis.htm

National Park Service Civil War Soldiers and Sailors System http://www.itd.nps.gov/cwss/soldiers.htm

New York State Military Museum and Veterans Research Center http://www.dmna.state.ny.us/historic/reghist/civil/infantry/5thInf/5thInfCWN.htm

State of Wisconsin Collection—Cordelia A. P. Harvey Papers http://digital.library.wisc.edu

Virtual American Biographies http://www.virtualology.com

SECONDARY SOURCES

Reference Works

Annual Report of the Adjutant General of the State of Maine, for the Year Ending December 31, 1866. Augusta: Stevens and Sayward, 1867.

Atkinson, W. M. B., ed. *The Physicians and Surgeons of the United States.* Philadelphia: Charles Robson, 1878.

Baldwin, Thomas W. *Bacon Genealogy: Michael Bacon of Dedham, 1640, and His Descendants.* Cambridge: N. P., 1915.

Beckett, S. B. *Portland Directory and Reference Book for 1852–53.* Portland: Brown Thurston, 1852.

Biographical Directory of the Governors of the United States, 1789–1978. Westport: Meckler Books, 1978. 4 Vols. (online)

Biographical Directory of the U.S. Congress, 1774–Present. (online)

Boatner, Mark M., III. *Civil War Dictionary.* New York: David McKay, 1959.

Butler, Samuel W., ed. *The Medical Register and Directory of the United States.* 2nd Ed. Washington: Office of the Medical and Surgical Reporter, 1874–77.

Clayton, W. W. *History of Cumberland County, Maine, with Illustrations of and Biographical Sketches of Its Prominent Men and Pioneers.* Philadelphia: Everts and Peck, 1880.

Dictionary of American Biography. New York: Scribner's, 1928–36.

Directory of Deceased American Physicians, 1804–1929: A Genealogical Guide to Over 149,000 Medical Practitioners, Providing Brief Biographical Sketches Drawn from the American Medical Association's Deceased Physician Master File. 2 Vols. Chicago: American Medical Association, 1993.

Dornbusch, C. E. *Regimental Publications and Personal Narratives of the Civil War: A Checklist.* Vol. 1. Part III: New England States. New York: The New York Public Library, 1961.

Faust, Patricia L. *Historical Times Illustrated Encyclopedia of the Civil War.* New York: Harper and Row, 1986.

General Catalogue of Bowdoin College and the Medical School of Maine: A Biographical Record of Alumni and Officers, 1794–1950. Brunswick: Bowdoin College, 1950.

Harper, Judith E. *Women during the Civil War: An Encyclopedia.* New York: Routledge, 2004.

Heidler, David S. and Jeanne T. Heidler, eds. *Encyclopedia of the American Civil War: A Political, Social, and Military History.* 5 Vols. Santa Barbara: ABC-Clio, 2000.

Henry, Guy V. *Military Record of Army and Civilian Appointments in the United States Army.* Vol. 1. New York: Van Nostrand, 1873.

Hubbell, John T. and James W. Geary, eds. *Biographical Dictionary of the Union: Northern Leaders of the Civil War.* Westport: Greenwood Press, 1995.

James, Edward T., ed. *Notable American Women.* 3 Vols. Cambridge: Harvard University Press, 1971.

Long, Everette B. and Barbara Long. *The Civil War Day by Day: An Almanac, 1861–1865.* New York: Da Capo, 1971.

Phalen, James. "Chiefs of the Medical Department, U.S. Army, 1775–1940. Biographical Sketches." *Army Medical Bulletin* 52 (April 1940).

Polk's Medical Register and Directory of the United States and Canada. 1886, 1890, 1896.

Portland Soldiers and Sailors: A Brief Sketch of the Part They Took in the War of the Rebellion. Portland: B. Thurston, 1884.

Roster of Regimental Surgeons and Assistant Surgeons in the U.S. Army Medical Department during the Civil War. Gaithersburg: Old Soldier Books, n.d.

Schroeder-Lein, Glenna R. *The Encyclopedia of Civil War Medicine.* Armonk: M. E. Sharpe, 2008.

Scott, Robert N., ed. *The War of the Rebellion: A Compilation of the Official Records of the Union and Confederate Armies.* Series I. Vol. 12. Washington: U.S. Government Printing Office, 1885.

Sifakis, Stewart. *Who Was Who in the Civil War.* New York: Facts on File, 1988.

Spencer, James, ed. *Civil War Generals: Categorical Listings and Biographical Directory.* Westport: Greenwood Press, 1986.

Transactions. Portland: Maine Medical Association, 1871–73, 1874–76, 1877, 1881, 1889.

Wagner, Margaret E., Gary W. Gallagher, and Paul Finkelman, eds. *The Library of Congress Civil War Reference.* New York: Simon and Schuster, 2002.

War of the Rebellion. Official Records of the Union and Confederate Armies. 128 vols. Washington, 1880–1901.

Watson, Irving A., ed. *Physicians and Surgeons of America: A Collection of Biographical Sketches of the Regular Medical Profession.* Concord: Republican Press, 1896.

Books and Monographs

Adams, George Worthington. *Doctors in Blue; the Medical History of the Union Army in the Civil War.* New York: Henry Schuman, Inc., 1952.

Adams, John G. B. *Reminiscences of the 19th Massachusetts Regiment.* Boston: Wright and Potter, 1899.

Armstrong, Warren B. *For Courageous Fighting and Confident Dying: Union Chaplains in the Civil War.* Lawrence: University Press of Kansas, 1998.

Attie, Jeanie. *Patriotic Toil: Northern Women and the American Civil War.* Ithaca: Cornell University Press, 1998.

Bacon, Margaret Hope. *Abby Hopper Gibbons, Prison Reformer and Social Activist.* Albany: State University of New York Press, 2000.

Beedy, Helen Coffin. *Mothers of Maine.* Portland: Thurston, 1895.

Bicknell, George W. *History of the Fifth Regiment Maine Volunteers.* Portland: Hall L. Davis, 1871.

Bingham, Stephen D. *Early History of Michigan, with Biographies of State Officers, Members of Congress, Judges, and Legislators.* Lansing: Thorp and Godfrey, 1888.

Blair, William. *Cities of the Dead: Contesting the Memory of the Civil War in the South, 1865–1914.* Chapel Hill: University of North Carolina Press, 2004.

Blight, David W. *Race and Reunion: The Civil War in American Memory.* Cambridge: Belknap Press of Harvard University Press, 2001.

Blustein, Bonnie Ellen. *Preserve Your Love for Science: Life of William A. Hammond, American Neurologist.* New York: Cambridge University Press, 1991.

Bollet, Alfred J. *Civil War Medicine: Challenges and Triumphs.* Tucson: Galen Press, 2002.

Boyd, Julia. *The Excellent Doctor Blackwell: The Life of the First Woman Physician.* Stroud: Sutton Publishing, 2005.

Brown, Thomas J. *Dorothea Dix, New England Reformer*. Cambridge: Harvard University Press, 1998.

Burrage, Henry S. *The History of the Baptists in Maine*. Portland: Marks Printing House, 1904.

Chase, Henry, ed. *Representative Men of Maine: A Collection of Portraits with Biographical Sketches of Residents of the State*. Portland: Lakeside Press, 1893.

Clarke, Frances. *War Stories: Suffering and Sacrifice in the Civil War North*. Chicago: University of Chicago Press, 2011.

Cleaveland, Nehemiah and Alpheus Spring Packard. *History of Bowdoin College with Biographical Sketches of Its Graduates from 1806 to 1879 Inclusive*. Boston: James R. Osgood, 1897.

Conforti, Joseph A., ed. *Creating Portland: History and Place in Northern New England*. Durham: University of New Hampshire Press, 2005.

Conklin, Eileen F. *Women at Gettysburg, 1863*. Gettysburg: Thomas Publications, 1993.

Coon, Katherine E. "The Sisters of Charity in Nineteenth-Century America: Civil War Nurses and Philanthropic Pioneers." M.A. thesis, Indiana University-Purdue University-Indianapolis, 2009.

Cordeau, Mary Ann Urban. "Acts of Caring: A History of the Lived Experience of Nurse-Caring by Northern Women during the American Civil War." Ph.D. dissertation, University of Connecticut, 2004.

Crawford, Kim. *The 16th Michigan Infantry*. Dayton: Morningside House, 2002.

Creighton, Margaret S. *The Colors of Courage: Gettysburg's Forgotten History: Immigrants, Women, and African Americans in the Civil War's Defining Battle*. New York: Basic Books, 2005.

Culpepper, Marilyn Mayer. *Trials and Triumphs: The Women of the American Civil War*. East Lansing: Michigan State University Press, 1991.

Cutter, Barbara. *Domestic Devils, Battlefield Angels: The Radicalism of American Womanhood, 1830–1865*. Dekalb: Northern Illinois University Press, 2003.

Dalton, Peter P. *With Our Faces to the Foe: A History of the 4th Maine Infantry in the War of the Rebellion*. Union: Union Publishing Co., 1998.

Dannett, Sylvia G. L. *Noble Women of the North*. New York: Thomas Yoseloff, 1959.

Davis, David Brion. *Inhuman Bondage: The Rise and Fall of Slavery in the New World*. New York: Oxford University Press, 2006.

Dawes, James. *The Language of War: Literature and Culture in the U. S. from the Civil War to World War II*. Cambridge: Harvard University Press, 2002.

Denney, Robert E. *Civil War Medicine: Care and Comfort of the Wounded*. New York: Sterling Publishers, 1994.

Desjardin, Thomas A. *Stand Firm Ye Boys from Maine: The 20th Maine and the Gettysburg Campaign*. New York: Oxford University Press, 1995.

Donovan, John J. *Civil War Surgeon, 5th Maine Volunteers*. N.p., 2002.

Douglas, Ann. *The Feminization of American Culture*. New York: Knopf, 1977.

Dudden, Faye. *Serving Women: Household Service in Nineteenth-Century America*. Middletown: Wesleyan University Press, 1983.

Fahs, Alice. *The Imagined Civil War: Popular Literature of the North & South, 1861–1865*. Chapel Hill: University of North Carolina Press, 2001.

Fahs, Alice and Joan Waugh, eds. *The Memory of the Civil War in American Culture*. Chapel Hill: University of North Carolina Press, 2004.

Faust, Drew Gilpin. *This Republic of Suffering: Death and the American Civil War*. New York: Knopf, 2008.

Fellman, Michael, Lesley J. Gordon, and Daniel Sutherland. *This Terrible War: The Civil War and Its Aftermath*. New York: Longman, 2003.

Flexner, Eleanor. *Century of Struggle: The Women's Rights Movement in the United States*. Cambridge: The Belknap Press of Harvard University, 1959.

Frankel, Noralee. *Freedom's Women: Black Women and Families in Civil War-Era Mississippi*. Bloomington: Indiana University Press, 1999.

Fredrickson, George. *The Inner Civil War: Northern Intellectuals and the Crisis of the Union*. New York: Harper and Row, 1968.

Garrison, Nancy Scripture. *With Courage and Delicacy: Civil War on the Peninsula: Women and the U.S. Sanitary Commission*. Mason City: Savas Publishing, 1999.

Giesberg, Judith. *Civil War Sisterhood: The U.S. Sanitary Commission and Women's Politics in Transition*. Boston: Northeastern University Press, 2000.

Gill, Gillian. *Nightingales: The Extraordinary Upbringing and Curious Life of Miss Florence Nightingale*. New York: Ballantine Books, 2004.

Gillett, Mary C. *The Army Medical Department, 1818–1865*. Washington: Center of Military History, 1987.

Ginzberg, Lori D. *Women and the Work of Benevolence: Morality, Politics and Class in the Nineteenth-Century United States*. New Haven: Yale University Press, 1990.

Goen, C. C. *Broken Churches, Broken Nation: Denominational Schisms and the Coming of the Civil War*. Macon: Mercer University Press, 1985.

Henshaw, Sarah E. *Our Branch and Its Tributaries; Being a History of the Work of the Northwestern Sanitary Commission*. Chicago: Alfred L. Sewell, 1868.

Hilde, Libra R. "Worth a Dozen Men: Women, Nursing, and Medical Care during the American Civil War." Ph.D. dissertation, Harvard University, 2003.

Hoffert, Sylvia. *Jane Grey Swisshelm: An Unconventional Life, 1815–1884*. Chapel Hill: University of North Carolina Press, 2004.

Horowitz, Helen Lefkowitz. *Alma Mater: Design and Experience in the Women's Colleges from Their Nineteenth-Century Beginnings to the 1930s*. New York: Knopf, 1984.

Houghton, Edwin B. *The Campaigns of the Seventeenth Maine*. Portland: Short and Loring, 1866.

Houston, Henry C. *The 32nd Maine Regiment of Infantry Volunteers, an Historical Sketch*. Portland: Southworth Brothers, 1903.

Humphreys, Margaret. *Intensely Human: The Health of Black Soldiers in the American Civil War*. Baltimore: Johns Hopkins University Press, 2008.

Jordan, William B., Jr. *Red Diamond Regiment: The 17th Maine Infantry, 1862–65*. Shippensburg: White Mane Publishing, 1996.

Judd, Richard W., Edwin A. Churchill, and Joel W. Eastman, eds. *Maine, the Pine Tree State, from Prehistory to the Present*. Orono: Univ. of Maine Press, 1995.

Kelley, Patrick J. *Creating a National Home: Building the Veterans' Welfare State*. Cambridge: Harvard University Press, 1997.

Kerber, Linda K. *Women of the Republic: Intellect and Ideology in Revolutionary America*. Chapel Hill: University of North Carolina Press, 1980.

Kernek, Clyde B. *Field Surgeon at Gettysburg: A Memorial Account of the Medical Unit of the 32nd Massachusetts Regiment*. Indianapolis: Guild Press, 1993.

Laas, Virginia J., ed. *Wartime Washington: The Civil War Letters of Elizabeth Blair Lee*. Urbana: University of Illinois Press, 1991.

Lapham, William B. and Silas P. Maxim. *History of Paris, Maine*. Paris, 1884.
Lawson, Melinda. *Patriot Fires: Forging a New American Nationalism in the Civil War North*. Lawrence: University Press of Kansas, 2002.
Leech, Margaret. *Reveille in Washington, 1860–1865*. New York: Harper and Brothers, 1941.
Leonard, Elizabeth D. *Yankee Women: Gender Battles in the Civil War*. New York: Norton, 1994.
———. *All the Daring of the Soldier: Women of the Civil War Armies*. New York: Norton, 1999.
Lowry, Thomas P. and Jack Welsh. *Tarnished Scalpels: The Court-Martials of Fifty Union Surgeons*. Mechanicsburg: Stackpole Books, 2000.
MacCaskill, Libby and David Novak. *Ladies on the Field: Two Civil War Nurses from Maine on the Battlefields of Virginia*. Livermore: Signal Tree Publications, 1996.
Marshall, John A. *American Bastille: A History of the Illegal Arrests and Imprisonment of American Citizens during the Late Civil War*. New York: Da Capo, 1970.
Maryniak, Benedict and John Brinsfield. *The Spirit Divided: Memoirs of Civil War Chaplains: The Union*. Macon: Mercer University Press, 2007.
Massey, Mary Elizabeth. *Bonnet Brigades*. New York: Alfred A. Knopf, 1966.
Maxwell, William Quentin. *Lincoln's Fifth Wheel: The Political History of the United States Sanitary Commission*. New York: Longman's, Green, and Company, 1956.
McPherson, James. *Battle Cry of Freedom: The Civil War Era*. New York: Ballantine, 1988.
Medical and Surgical History of the Civil War. 12 Vols. Philadelphia: Broadfoot, 1990–92.
Melosh, Barbara. *The Physician's Hand: Work, Culture, and Conflict in American Nursing*. Philadelphia: Temple University Press, 1982.
Miller, Randall M., Harry S. Stout, and Charles Reagan Wilson, eds. *Religion and the American Civil War*. New York: Oxford University Press, 1998.
Mohr, Clarence. *On the Threshold of Freedom: Masters and Slaves in Civil War Georgia*. Athens: University of Georgia Press, 1986.
Moore, James. *History of the Cooper Shop Volunteer Refreshment Saloon*. Philadelphia: James B. Rodgers, 1866.
Moorhead, James H. *American Apocalypse: Yankee Protestants and the Civil War, 1860–1869*. New Haven: Yale University Press, 1978.
Moss, Lemuel. *Annals of the United States Christian Commission*. Philadelphia: J. B. Lippincott, 1868.
Mundy, James H. *Second to None: The Story of the 2nd Maine Volunteers, the Bangor Regiment*. Scarborough: Harp Publications, 1992.
———. *No Rich Men's Sons: The 6th Maine Volunteer Infantry*. Cape Elizabeth: Harp Publications, 1994.
Nudelman, Franny. *John Brown's Body: Slavery, Violence, and the Culture of War*. Chapel Hill: University of North Carolina Press, 2004.
Oates, Stephen B. *A Woman of Valor: Clara Barton and the Civil War*. New York: Free Press, 1994.
O'Leary, Cecelia E. *To Die For: The Paradox of American Patriotism*. Princeton: Princeton University Press, 1999.
Packard, Alpheus Spring. *Bowdoin in the War*. Brunswick: n.p., 1867.
Paludan, Phillip Shaw. *"A People's Contest": The Union and Civil War, 1861–1865*. New York: Harper and Row, 1988.
Patterson, Orlando. *Slavery and Social Death: A Comparative Study*. Cambridge: Harvard University Press, 1982.

Peabody, Charles Newton. *Zab: Brevet Major Zabdiel Boylston Adams, 1929–1902, Physician of Boston and Framingham.* Boston: Francis A. Countaway Library of Medicine, 1984.

Pryor, Elizabeth Brown. *Clara Barton, Professional Angel.* Philadelphia: University of Pennsylvania Press, 1987.

Pullen, John J. *The Twentieth Maine: A Volunteer Regiment in the Civil War.* Philadelphia: Lippincott, 1957.

Randall, James G. and David Donald. *Civil War and Reconstruction.* Boston: Heath, 1961.

Reed, William Howell. *Hospital Life in the Army of the Potomac.* Boston: W. V. Spencer, 1866.

Reverby, Susan M. *Ordered to Care: The Dilemma of American Nursing, 1850–1945.* London: Cambridge University Press, 1987.

Richard, Patricia L. *Busy Hands: Images of the Family in the Northern Civil War Effort.* New York: Fordham University Press, 2003.

Ring, Elizabeth. *Maine in the Making of the Nation, 1783–1870.* Camden: Picton Press, 1996.

Rosenburg, R. B. *Living Monuments: Confederate Soldiers' Homes in the New South.* Chapel Hill: University of North Carolina Press, 1993.

Ross, Kristie R. "'Women Are Needed Here': Northern Protestant Women as Nurses during the Civil War, 1861–1865." Ph.D. dissertation, Columbia University, 1993.

Rowe, William Hutchinson. *Ancient North Yarmouth and Yarmouth, Maine.* Somersworth: New England History Press, 1980.

Rutkow, Ira M. *Bleeding Blue and Gray: Civil War Surgery and the Evolution of American Medicine.* New York: Random House, 2005.

Ryan, Mary P. *Women in Public: Between Banners and Ballots, 1825–1880.* Baltimore: Johns Hopkins University Press, 1990.

Samuels, Shirley. *Facing America: Iconography and the Civil War.* New York: Oxford University Press, 2004.

Savage, Kirk. *Standing Soldiers, Kneeling Slaves: Race, War, and Monument in Nineteenth-Century America.* Princeton: Princeton University Press, 1997.

Schroeder-Lein, Glenna R. *Confederate Hospitals on the Move: Samuel H. Stout and the Army of Tennessee.* Columbia: University of South Carolina Press, 1994.

Schultz, Jane E. *Women at the Front: Hospital Workers in Civil War America.* Chapel Hill: University of North Carolina Press, 2004.

Schwalm, Leslie. *A Hard Fight for We: Women's Transition from Slavery to Freedom in South Carolina.* Urbana: University of Illinois Press, 1997.

Scontras, Charles A. *Collective Efforts among Maine Workers: Beginnings and Foundations, 1820–1880.* Orono: University of Maine Press, 1994.

Shattuck, Gardiner H. *A Shield and a Hiding Place: The Religious Life of the Civil War Armies.* Macon: Mercer University Press, 1987.

Silber, Nina. *Yankee Correspondence: Civil War Letters between New England Soldiers and the Home Front.* Charlottesville: University Press of Virginia, 1996.

———. *Daughters of the Union: Northern Women Fight the Civil War.* Cambridge: Harvard University Press, 2005.

Sizer, Lyde Cullen. *The Political Work of Northern Women Writers and the Civil War, 1850–1872.* Chapel Hill: University of North Carolina Press, 2001.

Small, Abner R. *The 16th Maine Regiment in the War of the Rebellion, 1861–1865.* Portland: B. Thurston & Co., 1886.

Smith, John Day. *The History of the 19th Regiment of Maine Volunteer Infantry, 1862–1865*. Minneapolis: Great Western Printing Company, 1909.

Smith, Nina Bennett. "The Women Who Went to the War: The Union Army Nurse in the Civil War." Ph.D. dissertation, Northwestern University, 1981.

South, John F. *Household Surgery, or Hints on Emergencies*. Philadelphia: Henry Carey Baird, 1850.

Sprenger, George F. *Concise History of the Camp and Field Life of the 122nd Regiment Pennsylvania Infantry*. Lancaster: New Era, 1885.

Steiner, Paul E. *Disease in the Civil War: Natural Biological Warfare in 1861–1865*. Springfield: Charles C. Thomas, 1968.

Stillé, Charles J. *History of the United States Sanitary Commission*. New York: Hurd and Houghton, 1868.

Stout, Harry S. *Upon the Altar of the Nation: A Moral History of the Civil War*. New York: Viking, 2006.

Straubing, Harold Elk. *In Hospital and Camp: The Civil War through the Eyes of Its Doctors and Nurses*. Harrisburg: Stackpole Books, 1993.

Sudlow, Lynda L. *A Vast Army of Women: Maine's Uncounted Forces in the American Civil War*. Gettysburg: Thomas Publications, 2000.

Third Annual Report. Lansing: Michigan Soldiers' Relief Association, 1864.

Tobie, Edward P. *History of the First Maine Cavalry, 1861–1865*. Boston: Emery and Hughes, 1887.

Tuchman, Arleen M. *Science Has No Sex: The Life of Marie Zakrzewska, M.D.* Chapel Hill: University of North Carolina Press, 2006.

Venet, Wendy Hammand. *Neither Ballots nor Bullets: Women Abolitionists and the Civil War*. Charlottesville: University Press of Virginia, 1991.

Washburn, Israel. *Notes, Historical, Descriptive, and Personal of Livermore, in Androscoggin (Formerly in Oxford) County, Maine*. Portland: Bailey and Noyes, 1874.

Weigley, Russell F. *A Great Civil War: A Military and Political History, 1861–1865*. Bloomington: Indiana University Press, 2000.

Whitman, William E. S. and Charles H. True. *Maine in the War for the Union: A History of the Part Borne by Maine Troops in the Suppression of the American Rebellion*. Lewiston: Nelson Dingley, Jr., 1865.

Whittier, Kathryn, ed. *The Church at Walnut Hill: A History of the First Congregational Church, United Church of Christ, North Yarmouth, Maine*. Portland: J. Weston Walch [sic] Publishing, 2006.

Wiley, Bell I. *The Life of Billy Yank: The Common Soldier of the Union*. Baton Rouge: Louisiana State University Press, 1994.

Woman's Central Association of Relief. *Manual of Directions Prepared for the Use of the Nurses in the Army Hospitals by a Committee of Hospital Physicians of the City of New York*. New York: Baker and Godwin, 1861.

Woodworth, Steven E. *While God Is Marching On: The Religious World of Civil War Soldiers*. Lawrence: University Press of Kansas, 2001.

Woolsey, Abby Howland. *A Century of Nursing*. New York: Putnam's, 1876.

Young, Agnes Brooks [Agatha Young, pseud.]. *The Women and the Crisis; Women of the North in the Civil War*. New York: McDowell, Obolensky, 1959.

Young, Elizabeth. *Disarming the Nation: Women's Writing and the American Civil War*. Chicago: University of Chicago Press, 1999.

ARTICLES

Attie, Jeanie. "Warwork and the Crisis of Domesticity in the North." In *Divided Houses: Gender and the Civil War*. Edited by Catherine Clinton and Nina Silber, 247–59. New York: Oxford University Press, 1993.

Blustein, Bonnie Ellen. "'To Increase the Efficiency of the Medical Department': A New Approach to U.S. Civil War Medicine." *Civil War History* 33.1 (March 1987): 22–41.

Boston Medical and Surgical Journal 120 (28 February 1889): 228 [Horace Stevens obituary].

Brekus, Catherine A., Martin E. Marty, W. Clark Gilpin, and Harry S. Stout. "Religion and Violence in American Culture: A Discussion of Harry Stout's *Upon the Altar of the Nation: A Moral History of the Civil War*." *Criterion* (2007): 1–24.

Brucken, Carolyn. "In the Public Eye: Women at the American Luxury Hotel." *Winterthur Portfolio* 31.4 (Winter 1996): 203–20.

Calhoun, Charles. "Longfellow's Portland." In *Creating Portland: History and Place in Northern New England*. Edited by Joseph A Conforti, 72–89. Durham: University of New Hampshire Press, 2005.

Cannon, M. Hamlin. "The United States Christian Commission." *Mississippi Valley Historical Review* [*Journal of American History*] 38.1 (June 1951): 61–80.

Christie, Jeanne Marie. "'Performing My Plain Duty': Women of the North at City Point, 1864–1865." *Virginia Cavalcade* 47.2 (Summer 1997): 214–24.

Clarke, Frances. "'Honorable Scars': Northern Amputees and the Meaning of Civil War Injuries." In *Union Soldiers and the Northern Home Front: Wartime Experiences and Postwar Adjustments*. Edited by Paul A. Cimbala and Randall M. Miller, 361–94. New York: Fordham University Press, 2002.

———. "'Let All Nations See': Civil War Nationalism and the Memorialization of Wartime Voluntarism." *Civil War History* 52.1 (March 2006): 66–93.

———. "So Lonesome I Could Die: Nostalgia and Debates over Emotional Control in the Civil War North." *Journal of Social History* 41.2 (Winter 2007): 253–82.

Culpepper, Marilyn Mayer and Pauline Gordon Adams. "Nursing in the Civil War." *American Journal of Nursing* 88.7 (July 1988): 981–84.

Dalton, John Call. "Memorial of Edward B. Dalton, MD." New York: n.p., 1872.

D'Antonio, Patricia. "Revisiting and Rethinking the Rewriting of Nursing History." *Bulletin of the History of Medicine* 73.2 (Summer 1999): 268–90.

Desjardins, Tom. "Self-Imposed Work of Mercy: Civil War Women of the Maine Camp and Hospital Association, 1861–1865." Unpublished manuscript, MSA.

Douglas, Ann. "The War within a War: Women Nurses in the Union Army." *Civil War History* 18.3 (September 1972): 197–212.

Eagan, Eileen. "Working Portland: Women, Class, and Ethnicity in the Nineteenth Century" In *Creating Portland: History and Place in Northern New England*. Edited by Joseph A Conforti, 193–217. Durham: University of New Hampshire Press, 2005.

Endres, Kathleen L. "The Women's Press in the Civil War: A Portrait of Patriotism, Propaganda, and Prodding." *Civil War History* 30.1 (March 1984): 31–53.

Fahs, Alice. "The Feminized Civil War: Gender, Northern Popular Literature, and the Memory of the War, 1861–1900." *Journal of American History* 85.4 (March 1999): 1461–94.

———, ed. Introduction to *Hospital Sketches* by Louisa May Alcott, 1–49. Boston: Bedford/St. Martin's, 2004.

Faust, Drew Gilpin. "Christian Soldiers: The Meaning of Revivalism in the Confederate Army." *Journal of Southern History* 53.1 (February 1987): 63–90.

———. "'Ours as Well as that of the Men': Women and Gender in the Civil War." In *Writing the Civil War: The Quest to Understand*. Edited by James McPherson and William J. Cooper, 228–40. Columbia: University of South Carolina Press, 1998.

———. "The Civil War Soldier and the Art of Dying." *Journal of Southern History* 67.1 (February 2001): 3–38.

Fredrickson, George M. "The Coming of the Lord: The Northern Protestant Clergy and the Civil War Crisis." In *Religion and the American Civil War*. Edited by Randall M. Miller, Harry S. Stout, and Charles Reagan Wilson, 110–30. New York: Oxford University Press, 1998.

Garvey, Ellen Gruber. "Anonymity, Authorship, and Recirculation: A Civil War Episode." *Book History* 9 (2006): 159–78.

Goldfarb, Walter B. "History of Surgery in Maine." *Archives of Surgery* 136 (April 2001): 448–52.

———. "William Warren Greene, 1831–1881: Pioneering Maine Surgeon." *Archives of Surgery* 138 (2003): 331–35.

Greenwood, John T. "Hammond and Letterman: A Tale of Two Men Who Changed Army Medicine." *Journal of Civil War Medicine* 10.4 (October, November, and December 2006): 131–34.

Haller, John S. "The Glass Leech: Wet and Dry Cupping Practices in the Nineteenth Century." *New York State Journal of Medicine* 15 (February 1973): 583–92.

Harvey, Paul. "'Yankee Faith' and Southern Redemption: White Southern Baptist Ministers, 1850–1890." In *Religion and the American Civil War*. Edited by Randall M. Miller, Harry S. Stout, and Charles Reagan Wilson, 167–86. New York: Oxford University Press, 1998.

Hawk, Alan. "An Ambulating Hospital: or, How the Hospital Train Transformed Army Medicine." *Civil War History* 48.4 (December 2002): 197–219.

Holmes, Oliver Wendell. "Doings of the Sunbeam." *Atlantic Monthly* 12 (July 1863): 11–12.

Journal of the American Medical Association. 18 (1892): 29; 34 (1900): 957 [miscellaneous obituaries].

Kalisch, Philip A. and Beatrice J. Kalisch. "Untrained but Undaunted: The Women Nurses of the Blue and the Gray." *Nursing Forum* 15.1 (1976): 4–33.

Kalisch, Philip A. and Margaret Scobey. "Female Nurses in American Wars: Helplessness Suspended for the Duration." *Armed Forces and Society* 9.2 (Winter 1983): 215–44.

Kebler, Geneva. "A Cool Hand for the Fever'd Brow." In *Michigan Women in the Civil War*, 85–112. Lansing: Michigan Civil War Centennial Observance Commission, 1963.

Kelsey, Kerck. "Maine's War Governor: Israel Washburn, Jr. and the Race to Save the Union." *Maine History* 42.4 (July 2006): 235–57.

Kramer, Howard D. "The Effect of the Civil War on the Public Health Movement." *Mississippi Valley Historical Review* [*Journal of American History*] 35.3 (December 1948): 449–62.

Lee, Maureen Elgersman. "'What They Lack in Numbers': Locating Black Portland, 1870–1930." In *Creating Portland: History and Place in Northern New England*. Edited by Joseph A. Conforti, 218–46. Durham: University of New Hampshire Press, 2005.

Leonard, Elizabeth D. "Civil War Nurse, Civil War Nursing: Rebecca Usher of Maine." *Civil War History* 41.3 (September 1995): 190–207.

Lowry, Thomas P. "An Epidemic of Geezers." *Journal of Civil War Medicine* (July 2004): 81.

McTeer, Frances Davis. "In Bonnet and Shawl." In *Michigan Women in the Civil War*, 64–84. Lansing: Michigan Civil War Centennial Observance Commission, 1963.

Melosh, Barbara. "Every Woman Is a Nurse; Work and Gender in the Emergence of Nursing." In *"Send Us a Lady Physician": Women Doctors in America, 1835–1920*. Edited by Ruth J. Abram, 121–28. New York and London: W. W. Norton, 1985.

Millbrook, Minnie Dubbs. "Michigan Women Who Went to War." In *Michigan Women in the Civil War*, 12–34. Lansing: Michigan Civil War Centennial Observance Commission, 1963.

Miller, Edward A. "Angel of Light: Helen L. Gilson, Army Nurse." *Civil War History* 43.1 (1997): 17–37.

Nelson, Michael C. "Writing during Wartime: Gender and Literacy in the American Civil War." *Journal of American Studies* 31.1 (1997): 43–68.

Newman, Kathy. "Wounds and Wounding in the American Civil War: A (Visual) History." *Yale Journal of Criticism* 6.2 (1993): 63–86.

Paludan, Philip Shaw. "Religion and the American Civil War." In *Religion and the American Civil War*. Edited by Randall M. Miller, Harry S. Stout, and Charles Reagan Wilson, 21–40. New York: Oxford University Press, 1998.

Phalen, James M. "Chiefs of the Medical Department, U.S. Army, 1775–1940: Biographical Sketches." *Army Medical Bulletin* 52 (April 1940): 52–54.

Rosenberg, Charles E. "Florence Nightingale on Contagion: The Hospital as Moral Universe." In *Healing and History*. Edited by Charles E. Rosenberg, 116–36. New York: Science History Publications, 1979.

Ross, Kristie R. "Arranging a Doll's House: Refined Women as Union Nurses." In *Divided Houses: Gender and the Civil War*. Edited by Catherine Clinton and Nina Silber, 97–113. New York: Oxford University Press, 1993.

Schultz, Jane E. "The Inhospitable Hospital: Gender and Professionalism in Civil War Medicine." *Signs* 17.2 (Winter 1992): 363–92.

———. "Between Scylla and Charybdis: Clara Barton's Wartime Odyssey," *Minerva Quarterly* 14.3–4 (Fall/Winter 1996): 45–68.

———. "Healing the Nation: Condolence and Correspondence in Civil War Hospitals." *Proteus: A Journal of Ideas* 17.2 (Fall 2000): 33–41.

———. "Seldom Thanked, Never Praised, and Scarcely Recognized: Gender and Racism in Civil War Hospitals." *Civil War History* 48.3 (September 2002): 220–36.

Shain, Charles and Samuella Shain. "Maine and the Civil War." In *The Maine Reader: The Down East Experience from 1614 to the Present*. Edited by Charles Shain and Samuella Shain, 149–91. Boston: David R. Godine, 1991.

Smith, Nina Bennett. "Men and Authority: The Union Army Nurse and the Problem of Power." *Minerva Quarterly* 6.4 (December 1988): 25–42.

Stimson, Julia C. and Ethel C. S. Thompson. "Women Nurses with the Union Forces during the Civil War." *Military Surgeon* 62.1 (1928): 208–30.

Tierney, Roberta. "The Beneficent Revolution: Hospital Nursing during the Civil War." In *Florence Nightingale and Her Era: A Collection of New Scholarship*. Edited by Vern Bullough, Bonnie Bullough, and Marietta Stanton, 138–51. New York: Garland, 1990.

Tock, Annie. "An Inadequate Ideology: Republican Motherhood and the Civil War." *Historia* 14 (2005): 77–92.

Townsend, Luther Tracy. "History of the Sixteenth Regiment, New Hampshire Volunteers." *The Granite Monthly* 22.3 (March 1897): 135–53.

Varney, George Jones. "History of Thomaston, Maine." Boston: B. B. Russell, 1886.
Venet, Wendy Hammand. "The Emergence of a Suffragist: Mary Livermore, Civil War Activism, and the Moral Power of Women." *Civil War History* 48.2 (June 2002): 143–64.
Wilson, Charles Reagan. "Religion and the American Civil War in Comparative Perspective." In *Religion and the American Civil War*. Edited by Randall M. Miller, Harry S. Stout, and Charles Reagan Wilson, 385–407. New York: Oxford University Press, 1998.

INDEX

Abbott, George H., 116, 176, 194n146
Abolitionism, 3, 8, 11, 16, 17, 33, 120, 186n8, 194n135
Adams, Alfred S., 174, 181
Adams, Rev. John Ripley, 41, 98, 119, 120, 123, 124, 135, 229
Adams, Dr. Zabdiel Boylston, 138, 229
African Americans, 121, 159
  "Aunt Betsy," 161
  "Barker," 118, 121, 125n, 138
  "Charlotte," 34, 99
  in Portland, 34
  interactions with whites, 33, 193n131
  and labor, 32–33
  "Lucy," 34, 121
  as objects of medical interest, 5, 8
  "Rachel," 33–34, 156n, 158, 162–63, 165–66, 245
  "Uncle Richard," 159, 161, 172
  and racist perspectives, 3, 16, 34, 58, 165–66
  and religious practices, 3, 4, 16, 34, 159, 165–66
  See also slavery and religion
Alcott, Louisa May, 9, 188n31, 193n116
Alexander, Charles, 100, 104, 123, 169, 173
Alger, Horatio, 152
Allen, Samuel Henderson, 61, 70, 202, 230
Alvord, Rev. John Watson, 131, 139

Ames, Adelbert, 87–88, 95, 102, 107, 113, 118, 123, 128, 130, 135, 137, 218, 230
Amistad episode, 10–11
amputations. *See* medical procedures
Aquia Creek, 37, 86, 87, 88, 91, 94, 106, 108, 110, 111, 117, 142, 209, 216
Army Medical Department, 14, 28, 30, 57n
Army of the Potomac, 3, 14, 16, 23–27, 30, 32, 32, 41, 47, 57n, 102n, 111n, 139, 140n, 143n, 145n, 173n, 178, 191n85, 210, 209, 217, 221, 224, 226
Ayres, Lieut., 93, 120, 131n, 139, 145

Bacon, Ellen Usher, 21, 39, 154, 173, 174–75, 177, 179, 188n35, 190n74, 230
Bacon family
  Agnes Ramsay Hope (mother), 9–10
  Joseph Valentine (brother), 166n, 184
  Joshua Butters (brother), 138n
  Josiah (father), 9–10
Bacot, Ada, 6–7, 187n23–25
Bain, Annie, 171, 178n
Baker, Gen. Lafayette Curry, 158n
Baker, William F., 160, 169, 171, 172, 232
Baltimore, Md., 26, 36, 47, 56, 58, 80, 152, 184, 190n65, 192n106, 200, 236, 240,
Baptist church. *See* religion
Barbour, Mary L., 85, 181

Barbour, Miss Lucy E., 89
Barker, Thomas C., 158, 163–65
Barnes, James, 144, 155
Barnes, Dr. Joseph K., 22, 29, 154, 161, 192n113
Barton, Clara, 13, 26, 86n, 92n, 189n48, 195n161, 231
Bassford, Levi L., 124, 140, 148
Bates, Alvah Jones and Martha M., 121–25, 138, 144
Bates, John A., 115
Battlefields
    Antietam [Sharpsburg], 1, 24–26, 36, 62n, 63n, 70, 71n, 72, 74, 99n
    Cedar Creek, 36
    Chancellorsville, 23–24, 31, 32, 36, 41–42, 47, 132n, 140n, 141n, 143n, 145n, 146, 148n, 153n, 156n
    Cold Harbor, 24, 42
    Fredericksburg, 24, 26, 36–37, 41–42, 47, 89, 91n, 92n, 93n, 94, 96, 98n, 102n, 103, 106n, 123, 143n, 148, 156n, 217
    Gettysburg, 24, 42, 47
    Petersburg, 24, 42, 47
    Shiloh, 6
    Spotsylvania, 24, 42
    Totopotomoy, 24, 192n107
    Wilderness, 24, 42
Baxter, A. J., 59n, 124, 158, 163, 169, 175
Baxter, Dr. Joseph B., 99, 169n
Bennett, Dr. Siroella, 125
Benson, Andrew M., 128, 130
Bigelow, Rebecca M., 65, 83, 117
Billings, Dr. Adoniram Judson, 63, 95, 112, 127
Birney, Gen. David Bell, 104
Blackmar (Bruson), Mary A., 159, 160, 161, 231
Blackwell, Dr. Elizabeth, 22, 235
Bliss, Dr. D. W., 56n
blistering. *See* medical procedures
Blossom, Dr. Alden, 98, 124
Boller family, 87, 89, 92, 94, 109, 112, 133
Booth, John Wilkes, 17

Boothby, Stephen, 70, 205, 231
Boston, Mass., 1, 7, 9, 17, 36, 50, 55, 85, 138, 151, 175, 184, 190n65, 229–30, 248
Bosworth, Frederic W., 20, 88, 115, 118–19, 132, 142, 146, 166n, 221, 232
Bosworth, Rev. George W., 12, 20, 83, 85, 95, 102, 105–6, 122, 127, 137–38
Bosworth, Irene Frances, 19, 20, 58, 60–1, 65, 76, 90, 93n, 100, 104, 113–14, 120, 122, 125, 127, 132, 138, 148, 158, 166, 169, 200–201, 203, 209–10, 212, 215, 221
Bowers, Theodore Shelton, 169
Bradley, Amy Morris, 19, 57n
Bridge, Mr., 114, 165, 171, 173
Brown, John Marshall, 87, 93, 97, 102, 232
Buck, Dr. William, 124, 140
Bullen, Rev. George, 104, 173
burial, 13, 71, 74, 79, 80, 81, 87, 88, 97, 100, 104, 109, 113n, 128, 138, 195n167, 218, 212, 213
Burmeister, Dr. Frederick F., 28, 50, 156, 158, 161, 164, 192.111, 232
Burmeister, Margaret, 159.161, 163, 166, 169, 171, 180
Burnham, Hiram, 141–42, 148
Burnside, Gen. Ambrose, 86, 91n, 98, 102n, 108, 110n, 113, 143n, 209, 212, 217
Burr, Charles Frederick, 180
Burr, Dr. George, 160
Bussey, Dr. Benjamin, Jr., 182
Butler, Gen. Benjamin, 156n, 175n
Butterfield, Gen. Daniel, 142
Buxton, Dr. Benjamin F., 33, 98–99, 232–33

Caduc, Sarah Hopkins Bacon (niece), 65, 82–83, 108–109, 117, 122, 125, 135, 160, 166, 178, 233
Carr, Joseph Bradford, 121
Carr, Dr. Josiah, 66
Carver, Lorenzo D., 93
Cary, William R., 57, 135
Chamberlain, Frances Caroline Adams, 90, 121–23, 128

Chamberlain, Gen. Joshua Lawrence, 22, 24, 87, 89–90, 93, 95, 97, 102, 107–8, 112–13, 115, 121, 123, 130, 133, 137–38, 147, 153n, 191n91, 233–34
Chase, Benjamin, A., 130–31
Chick, Elias and Rebecca, 165–66, 168, 169, 171, 174, 176, 179
Christian Commission. *See* United States Christian Commission
churches
    Episcopal Church of South Carolina, 7
    First Baptist Church, Hartford, 11, 13
    Free Street Baptist Church, Portland, 1, 3, 11–12, 16, 19–20, 66, 70, 82, 129, 189n44
    negro church, 75
    New England Baptist Church, 2
    White Oak Church, Virginia, 98, 98n, 124, 125, 130, 136
City Point, Va.
    African Americans in, 16, 34–36, 50, 159, 165–66, 170, 172
    description of, 15, 26–28, 156n, 225
    military and medical administration of, 5 28–30, 47, 174
    Nathaniel Jaques in, 14, 44–47, 172, 175–84
    obstacles to gaining entry, 28–31, 154–55
    religious services in, 16, 36, 158, 165–66, 169, 172, 175, 176, 177, 179, 180, 181, 182
    society in, 24, 26–28, 29–30, 42–44, 167, 169–70, 175n
    staffing, 13, 21, 23, 24, 28, 165, 168
    voting and elections, 163, 167
    work of the Sanitary and Christian commissions in, 29, 158–59, 170, 192n104
clergy, 3
Clark, Atherton, W., 142, 146
Clark, Daniel C., 99, 119
Clark, Orson B., 131, 149
Cobb, Dr. Albion, 131
Coburn, Gov. Abner, 144–45, 222

Coffin, Charles Carleton, 55
Colby, Dr. George W., 67n, 69–70, 102, 125
Cole, Charles O., 116, 194n146
Cole, John A., 181–82
Coleman, William P. and Lindley M., 61–62, 69, 83, 202
Collins, Dr. James, 161
Confederate Army of Tennessee, 4, 46
Confederate civilians, 34, 57, 62, 98–99, 102, 104, 117, 200, 212–13
Connor, Selden, 153, 154
copperheads, 18, 152
costs and expenses, 56, 57, 60, 61, 64, 67, 70, 71, 74, 79, 81, 97, 152, 155, 210
Couch, Gen. Darius N., 145n
Coventry, Dr. Walter B., 123
Cowan, Louis O., 61, 67n, 86
Coyle, Mrs., 167–68, 180–81
Craft, William and Ellen, 17
Crane, Dr. Charles Henry, 29, 154, 192n111,
Crawford, George C., 163, 173, 181
Cumming, Kate, 4–6, 46, 187n19–20, 196n182
Cumpston, Mary J. and Martha, 77
cupping. *See* medical procedures
Curtin, Gov. Andrew Gregg, 132
Curtis, Levi D., 174, 176

Dalton, Dr. Edward B., 28–29, 154, 161, 164–65, 192n111, 234
Davis, George R., 25, 93, 100, 113–14, 117, 122, 127, 136, 141
Davis, Gorham, 115
Dickinson, Anna Elizabeth, 17
disease and illness
    cholera and cholera morbus, 76, 189n45
    diarrhea and dysentery, 76n, 203
    diphtheria, 77, 77n, 207
    among Maine troops, 36, 61
    malaria, 31, 36, 73, 204, 229, 233, 235, 237, 244
    measles, 14, 67, 68, 73, 73n
    pneumonia, 77, 129, 132

disease and illness (*continued*)
  smallpox and varioloid,, 14, 31, 76, 133n, 136, 136n, 137, 139, 140, 141, 142, 142n, 144, 204, 207, 238, 242
  syphilis, 36, 235
  tuberculosis, 1, 13, 46, 122, 236, 243
  typhoid, 8, 38, 101, 113, 128, 202, 213
  typhus, 247
Divers, Bridget, 164, 234
Dix, Dorothea, 4, 8, 22, 29, 59, 65, 155, 161, 163–64, 183, 192n114, 193n115, 234
Doe, Sophia, 168, 173, 181
Doe, Mrs., 167, 173
Doe, William D., 168n, 169, 171, 173, 187
Doolittle, Dr. Frank W., 146
Douglass, Frederick, 18
Douty, Calvin Sanger, 67n
Dow, Joseph B., 104, 136
Dyer, Charles S., 171, 174
Dyer, George W. and Mrs, 116, 121, 141, 195n154, 213, 217

Eaton, Agnes (daughter), 11, 13, 45–46, 58–59, 69–70, 80, 82, 90, 102, 105, 107, 116, 118, 130, 137, 144, 148, 154, 159, 163, 166, 167, 170, 173, 175–77, 180–81, 199, 209, 215, 220, 224, 235
Eaton, Franklin Henry (son), 1, 11, 13, 20, 23–24, 33, 36, 41, 43, 45–47, 51, 58, 64, 66, 69, 82, 85, 93, 100, 105–7, 113, 116–8, 121, 125, 127–28, 130, 132, 135, 139–40, 143, 148–50, 51, 152–53, 158, 163–64, 166–67, 170, 172, 175, 177, 183n, 194.146, 196n173, 199–200, 209, 215, 221–22, 224, 235
Eaton, Harriet Hope Agnes,
  as able accountant, 47, 50
  anxiety regarding publicity, 16, 50, 97, 105, 107, 170, 175, 180
  changes in housekeeping, 11–12
  conflict with Isabella Fogg, 34–40, 80, 94, 111, 135, 149
  desire for privacy, 77, 78, 96, 167, 175

  disillusionment, 78, 80, 114, 132, 140, 162–63, 168
  family context, 9–14, 43, 44–45, 112–13, 185
  homesickness, 94, 97, 112–113, 143–44, 190n78
  illness and indisposition, 23, 47, 64, 71, 76–77, 85, 106, 112, 122, 139, 144, 145, 149, 175
  letter and journal writing, 16–17, 37, 39, 43, 48–50, 64–65, 80, 86, 107, 125, 174, 176, 177
  mission work in Hartford, 11, 13
  motives for service, 1–3, 6, 12, 15, 66
  relationship with Nathaniel Jaques, 42–45
  religious expression, 2, 13, 37, 40, 41–42, 45, 66, 73, 81, 84, 222–23
  self-assertion and resistance to authority, 26, 30, 133, 150, 154, 158–59, 164
  status as a nurse, 22–24, 150, 161, 168, 226
  terms of service, 22, 25, 156
  widowhood, 1, 2, 22, 45, 58, 177
Eaton, Harriet I. "Hatty Belle" (daughter), 5, 11, 13, 46, 50, 58, 64, 81–82, 89, 94, 100, 105–7, 113, 117, 127–28, 136–37, 141, 148, 154, 159, 163, 166–67, 170, 174–75, 179, 180, 199–200, 215, 220, 224, 235
Eaton, Rev. Jeremiah Sewell (husband), 1, 10–13, 38, 46–47, 186n5, 188n40, 189n44, 196n185, 201
Eaton, Dr. William W., 104, 123, 163, 169n, 173
Eclectic Medical College, 7
Eddy, Dr. William, 144
Edwards, Clark S., 119, 148
Emancipation, 33
Estes, Llewellyn Garrish, 84
Etheridge, Annie, 31

Fabyan, Charles F. and Mrs., 114, 119n, 120
Fay, Franklin Brigham, 22, 59, 86, 92, 235
Fillebrown, James Sullivan, 76, 78, 204, 207

Fitch, Joseph B., 100–101, 105, 133
Flint, Charles M., 98, 140
Fogg, Hugh M., 36–37, 39, 139, 141, 148, 184, 194n148, 202, 235–36
Fogg, Isabella Morrison, 3, 17, 19, 25–26, 34–40, 50, 55, 58, 61–65, 68–71, 76–83, 86, 88–102, 104–12, 115–25, 127–33, 135n, 136, 138–42, 144–5, 147–50, 158, 164, 180n, 184, 185n1, 193n126, 194n144, 194n148, 195n154, 199–202, 205, 208–13, 215, 217, 223, 236
Fogler, William Henry, 159, 164, 176
Forbes, Darius, 50, 58
Foster, John Barton, 125, 143
Fox, Harriet Lewis, 25, 106, 112, 114, 118, 122, 127–28, 135, 137, 141, 143–44, 166, 168, 173, 176, 181, 214, 236
Franklin, Gen. William Buel, 104
Free Street Baptist Church, 1, 3, 11–12, 16, 19–20, 66, 70, 82, 129, 189n44
Furlong, Reuel W., 98, 140, 141, 148

Garrison, William Lloyd, 18
Getchell, Emory T., 158, 182
Gilmore, Charles Davis, 29, 39, 110n, 111–15, 118, 121, 125, 128, 135, 138–43, 145, 147, 153–54, 195n157, 216, 236–37
Gilmore, Mary Jane Whitney, 141n, 153, 155, 183–84
Gilson, Helen, Louise, 22, 59, 86n, 92, 145, 237
Glatfelter, Dr. Noah M., 162, 175
Goddard, Abba, 19
Godfrey, Alfred C., 164, 171
Gould, Howard, 166, 181
Gould, John Mead, 76, 191n95
Grant, Gen. Ulysses Simpson, 21–22, 156, 171, 176,
Greenough, Byron, 57, 79, 82, 143, 173, 176, 213, 237
Greenough, Mary, 85, 94, 106–107, 173, 176, 222, 237
Greeley, Horace, 152
Griffin, Andrew, 67, 70, 79, 83, 102
Griffin, Roscoe T., 71

Grinnell, James A., 102, 110
Griswold, Caroline, 85, 111, 114–15, 129, 170, 174–75, 179

Haley, John West, 19, 21, 88n, 121n, 193n122, 195n163
Hall, Charles Badger, 20, 107, 151
Hall, James Abram, 124, 136, 178
Hall, Maria M. C., 70–73, 237–38
Hall, Theron Edmund, 86
Hammond, Dr. Fletcher M., 159
Hammond, Dr. William H., 9
Hancock, Cornelia, 10n, 161, 175, 192n107, 238
Harris, Benjamin F., 141–43
Harris, Ellen Orbison, 64, 70–71, 121–3, 206
Hart, Mrs. Hanson (Caroline R.), 68, 82, 102, 117, 142, 238
Hart, Hanson M., 116, 194n146
Hart, Miss, 171, 199
Hartford, Conn., 5, 10, 13, 17, 36, 45, 46, 47, 251, 256, 261
Hathaway, James W., 67, 93, 141, 192n101, 194n1, 238
Hathaway, John W., 3, 25–26, 37, 58–60, 65–66, 69–70, 76, 82, 83, 85–67, 89, 94, 96, 16, 113, 115–16, 125, 142n, 144, 201, 205, 120, 216, 218, 238
Hathaway, Sarah, 86, 145
Hawes, Dr. John Q. A., 74, 135, 162, 205–206
Hawes, Rev. Dr., 127, 151, 205
Hawks, Dr. Esther Hill and John Milton, 4, 6–8, 187n19, 26, 188n27
Haycock, Joel A., 98, 125, 140–41, 146
Hayes, Charles C., 23, 25–26, 29, 37–38, 50, 70, 74, 76–77, 82, 88, 94, 96, 99, 102, 106–10, 113–14, 120–21, 130, 132, 135, 138–39, 141, 143, 149, 150–54, 159, 165–66, 169–71, 173–75, 178–83, 192n98, 194n151, 204–8, 210–11, 214, 216, 238–39
Haynes, Asbury F., 170–72, 174, 182
Hawthorne, Nathaniel, 116

Henries, Henry Clay, 83
Hersey, Harvey, 88n
Hersey, Samuel F., 128
Hersom, Dr. Nahum A., 30–31, 38, 88, 94, 105, 112, 125–26, 129–30, 131n, 132–33, 135, 141, 162, 177, 239
Hezless, Dr. William B., 38, 128, 130, 132, 135, 147–48, 195n155, 239
Hildreth, Dr. Thaddeus, 96, 132
Hill, Lysander, 73, 206
Hinds, Benjamin H., 154, 174
Hobbs, Joshua "Bernard," 116, 194n146
Hodgkins, 96, 102, 106, 110–13, 115
Hodgman, Osgood A., 122, 132, 142
Holmes, Dr. Freeland Salmon, 98, 124, 140–41
Holmes, Oliver Wendell, 74n
Holstein, Anna Morris, 160n
Hooker, Gen. Joseph, 23, 41, 86–87, 89, 92, 109, 113, 135, 137n, 141n, 143, 221
Hooper, Otis, T., 128, 149
Hopkins, Pauline, 17
hospital ships, 14, 24, 26, 29, 36, 86, 94, 149, 150, 154–56, 158, 167, 175, 183, 192n106
hospitals, 61, 71, 76
  Arlington Hospital, 57
  Armory Square, 19, 56n, 183, 199
  Barracks Hospital, 69
  Campbell Hospital, 152
  Carver Hospital, 65n
  Casparis Hospital, 82n
  Cavalry Hospital, 167, 171
  Chesapeake Hospital, 156
  College Green Hospital (St. John's College Hospital), 84n, 85, 186n2
  Colored Hospital, 159, 224
  Columbian College Hospital, 59n, 65n
  convalescent camp in Loudon Valley, 75, 205
  Convalescent Camp, Washington, D.C., "Camp Misery," "Camp Convulsion," "Rendezvous of Distribution," 19, 56, 57n
  Douglas Hospital, 56n, 57, 153–54, 199
  Eckington Hospital, 20, 66n, 194n135, 200
  Fairfax Seminary Hospital, 31, 64n, 66
  Finley Hospital, 58n
  General Hospital, 169, 171, 203, 222–23
  German Reformed Church Hospital, 79–80n
  Judiciary Square Hospital, 60n
  Lincoln Hospital, 154
  Midway Hospital, 187n25
  Monticello Hospital, 7
  Mount Pleasant Hospital, 65n
  Navy Yard Hospital, 84
  New England Hospital for Women and Children, 187n26
  Patterson Post Hospital, 184n
  Pavilion Hospital, 80
  poor conditions in field hospitals, 14, 61, 191n85, 203–4
  regimental hospitals, 69, 75, 79, 116, 136, 201, 203–4, 211, 216
  Russell Springs Hospital, 77, 207
  St. Elizabeth's Insane Asylum, 29, 155
  second division hospital (Falmouth), 5
  Seminary Hospital, 58, 63, 200
  Smoketown Hospital, 70–73, 77n, 83, 204, 206, 207
  Trinity Church Hospital, 59n
  Union Hotel Hospital, 8, 193n116
  Windmill Point Hospital, 111, 114, 117–18, 131, 216
  See also City Point, Va.
Houghton, Edwin B., 130
Houghton, J. S., 171
Howard, Dr. Horatio N., 75, 138, 144, 191n97, 203
Howard, Gen. Oliver Otis, 57, 78, 96n, 139, 145n, 239
Howe, Julia Ward, "The Battle Hymn of the Republic," 15, 18
Howland, Walter M., 88, 180
Hunkins, Dr. Seth Chellis, 110
Hunt, Charles Oliver, 124
Hunter, Warren, 104
Huntress, Henry Orin, 182

INDEX | 273

Husband, Mary Morris, 70–71, 147–49, 165, 172, 174, 240
Hutchins, Charles K., 102, 212, 213

Immigrants and nativism, 11, 78, 84, 189n45
Ingalls, Joshua, 108
Irish, Nathan F., 80n

Jackson, Gen. Stonewall, 62n, 74, 78, 148
Jaques, Charlotte and Claude, 44
Jaques, Nathaniel P., 16, 42–45, 50, 172–73, 175–83, 196n180, 240
Jennison, William H., 120, 127
Jewett, Jedediah, 61, 67, 106, 110, 201
Jewett, William Henry, 132
Jones, Frank L., 71, 116, 117n, 160, 194n146, 240
Jordan, Mrs., 75–76, 78
Jordan, William P., 76n, 240
Judson, O. A., 65n

Keene, Samuel T., 107, 241
Knox, George, 25, 41, 76–77, 80–81, 138, 191n95, 241
Kollock, Dr. John M., 163, 241

Lacy House, 91, 91n, 92n, 106, 210
Lancy, Emeline, 70, 106, 117, 125, 135, 137
Leavitt, Archibald "Arch" D., 123
Lee, Gen. Robert E., 21, 23, 57, 62n, 140n, 213
Lee, Samuel Perry, 132
Letterman, Jonathan, 28, 86, 209
Levensaler, Henry C., 96n, 127
Lewis, Addison, Wesley, 119, 131, 144
Lewis, Mrs. 131, 133, 137, 143–44
Lincoln, Abraham, 6, 17–18, 21–22, 65, 136
Lincoln, Joseph W., 133, 137
Lincoln, Mary Todd, 137, 142
Lincoln, Willard, 114
Linebeck, Mrs., 164–65, 177

Litchfield, Alden, 37–38, 109, 115, 118, 122, 125, 139, 195n154, 174, 241
Lombard, William F., 107, 214
Longfellow, William Wadsworth, 17, 18
Longstreet, Gen. James, 213
Lord, John, 175
Loring, Mr., 114, 116, 122
Lowell, James S., 181
Lowenthal, Dr. Herman, 158, 169, 175

Maine Camp Hospital Association (MCHA), 1, 3–4, 24–26, 36–37, 39, 47, 50, 93n, 118, 142, 189n60, 190n78, 191n97, 193n126, 195n159, 201, 210, 212, 214, 219, 222, 224, 226
Maine State Relief Agency (MSRA), 3–4, 25, 29, 37, 85n, 138, 153–55, 156n, 157n, 163, 167, 174, 180, 184
Malibu (California) Soldiers' Home, 44, 241
Manning, William C. "Willy," 64, 89, 119, 241
Marble, Mr., 165–67, 169
Marsh, A. J., 60
Martin, George W., 88, 96, 104, 115, 131
Martin, Dr. George W., 137, 140
Mattocks, Charles, 31, 193n121
May, Abby, 6
Mayhew, Ruth Swett, 12, 19, 154, 156–59, 162, 165–66, 168, 170, 177, 182, 186n1, 225–27, 241–42
McCarthy, Hannorah Cronin, 11, 189n45
McClellan, Gen. George B., 74, 113
McIntyre Family, 50, 56, 58–60, 64–66, 69, 82, 85, 116–17, 199
McKay, Charlotte, 112, 131–32, 137, 142, 145, 147, 165, 167, 169, 171, 178, 242
McNulty, Dr. John D., 74–75, 207
Meade, Gen. George Gordon, 137 143n, 145
medical authority, 9
medical procedures and medicines
    amputations, 32, 36, 39, 56, 60, 93n, 147, 164–65, 184, 211
    blistering, 38, 128
    bone-setting and traction, 153

medical procedures and medicines (*continued*)
cathartics, 129
cupping, 128
dosing and stimulants, 32, 60, 105, 203
evacuation of wounded, 26, 28
poultices and powders, 34, 38–39, 67, 95, 124, 129, 148, 154
surgery, 67, 101, 116, 171
vaccination, 125, 133
Melcher, Holman Staples, 164, 178
Mero, Charles H., 118, 120–21, 123, 125, 159, 242
Merrill, Charles B., 87, 129n, 242
Merrill, Samuel Hill, 158, 162–63
Miles, Dixon S., 62n
military authority 3, 14, 23, 29, 31, 211
Monroe, Dr. Nahum P., 30, 88, 97, 113, 116, 128–29, 132–34, 137, 139n, 140–41, 242–43
Montgomery, Osborne Charles, 179, 181n, 182
Moore, Frank, 24, 225–26
Moore, Dr. John, 30, 39, 131–33, 135, 137–40, 142–44, 146, 148, 195n157, 243
Morse, Henry Bagg, 92
motherhood and domesticity, 1–3, 8, 15, 36, 50, 82, 85, 106, 165, 167, 170, 186n2, 286n3, 220
Myers, Frederick, 140

National Freedman's Relief Association, 8
New England Female Medical College, 7
New England Soldiers' Relief Association, 6
New York City, 4, 29, 30, 47, 76n, 151n, 155, 183, 190n65, 234, 243, 244, 246
  Bellvue Hospital, 234, 243
  draft riots, 21
  New York Dispensary, 243
Newton, Mass., 9, 10, 44, 139, 188n39, 240, 241, 244, 248
Nightingale, Florence, 31
Noyes, Amos F., 171, 184
Noyes, William S., 98, 119, 208
nurses and nursing

changes in antebellum perceptions, 3, 22, 186n12
conflict between civil and military authority, 14, 190n81, 204–5
diaries, 4–9, 34, 40, 46, 188n35
field work, 5, 15, 24–28, 32, 47, 148, 187n16, 193n126, 206, 211
hardening process, 14, 26, 84, 203
and impropriety, 7, 28, 42, 45, 165, 178
last rites, 41, 62, 168, 191n90, 195–96, 195n165, 195n168, 196n172, 202–3
as moral arbiters, 15, 40
nurse/patient relations, 22, 25, 28, 40, 47, 56, 58, 89, 114, 127, 164, 182–83
nurse/surgeon relations, 6, 7, 8–9, 30, 32, 39, 64, 67, 88, 95, 96, 108, 123, 127, 131, 147, 162, 164–65, 205
professional development and nursing education, 3
relations among co-workers, 7, 14, 17, 26, 30, 34–38, 84, 161, 168, 192n107
"roving" nursing, 5, 14, 23, 187n20, 192n102, 204
training and duties, 16, 22, 24, 210–11
See also relief work and workers
Nye, Frances M., 160n, 171, 174, 179, 243

Oleson, Charles Wilmot, 20, 33, 57, 66, 190n69, 194n147, 196n173, 200, 243
O'Meagher, Dr. William, 156, 160–62, 165, 171, 243–44

Painter, Dr. Hettie Kersey, 158, 160, 167, 171, 178n, 244
Palmer, Rev. Edwin Beaman, 63, 74, 95
Palmer, Sarah, 28
Parton, Sara Payson Willis (Fanny Fern), 17
Patrick, Gen. Marsena Rudolph, 146n
patriotism, 1, 2, 6, 15, 19–20
Patten, William Aaron, 159, 170, 176, 180
Pelouze, Louis Henry, 29, 155
Pendleton, Lewis W., 87, 89, 105
Perham, Sidney, 184, 186n1
Perry, Dr. Daniel Owen, 60

Philadelphia, Penn., 26, 29, 47, 152n, 190n65, 192n106, 232, 238, 239, 240, 244
Phillips, Wendell, 18
physicians and surgeons
  alcohol and alcoholism, 32, 239
  court-martial of Isaac Wixom, 32, 249
  criticism of, 30–31, 58, 133–34, 137, 174, 217–18
  female physicians, 7–8, 158, 160, 167, 171, 187, 188, 243, 244
  graft and immorality, 89
  medicinal supplies and practices, 31, 96, 105, 124
  neglect and incompetence, 30–31, 32, 66, 114, 118
  professional conflict, 31, 125, 132, 140, 169
  See also individual physicians
Piggert Family, 60, 117
Plummer, Rufus B., 159, 164
Pomroy, Rebecca Rosaignol Holliday, 65, 244
Portland, Me
  aid work, 16, 18–19, 130, 193n126, 214
  benevolent organizations, 20, 167n, 12
  citizens of, 56, 116
  Confederate breach of harbor, 18
  Free Street Baptist Church, 1, 3, 11–12, 16, 19–20, 66, 70, 82, 129, 189n44
  great fire of 1866, 12
  hospitality to troops, 18–19, 21
  labor strife and working-class concerns, 20–21
  local regiments, 24, 116
  newspapers, 18, 19, 25, 50
  soldiers and sailors monument, 21–22
  urbanization and culture, 17–18
  war-end celebration, 21
  war fervor in, 17–18
Putnam, Black Hawk, 67n, 104

Quinby, Almira F., 84, 244

Rand, Moses W., 58–59, 200
Randall, Richard, 34, 99, 102, 104, 125, 136
Rea, Dorcas M., 85, 94–95, 245

Reconstruction, 13
refugees, 75
relief work and workers
  accidents, 69, 98, 139, 241
  accommodations and food, 59, 63, 65, 71, 74–75, 82, 89, 98, 158, 161–62, 174, 190n65, 209
  dangerous conditions, 32, 36, 74, 92, 147, 206, 210, 222
  exploitation of African American workers, 32–33, 158, 162–63, 165–66, 173, 174
  graft and theft, 85, 160n, 225
  lack of cooperation, 86, 92, 158–59
  local vs. national organization of, 2, 3–4, 5, 7, 22, 28, 175, 204–5
  religious inspiration for, 1, 2, 14
  state-sponsored relief, 5–6, 22, 27, 190n81, 191n97, 200–201, 222
  supply and distribution, 19, 23, 25–26, 37, 47, 56, 68–69, 79–80, 83, 85, 88, 92–94, 107, 117, 130, 158, 172–73, 207, 211–15, 219
  women's influence on, 2
  See also nurses and nursing
religion
  African American practices, 4, 16, 34, 75, 159, 165–66
  baptism, 42–43, 44, 177, 180
  Baptist church, 2, 11, 13, 149n, 186n5, 186n8
  Baptist ministers and chaplains, 10–12, 59, 174, 227, 241
  Christian militancy and redemption, 15, 40–41, 189n52, 195n166
  conversions, 15–16, 40–45, 62, 77, 120, 171, 177, 182, 191n90, 222
  last rites, 41, 62, 191n90, 195n165, 195n168, 196n172, 202–3
  as mandate for wartime benevolence, 2, 6, 14, 15
  military neglect of Sabbath, 40, 67, 83, 166, 195n163
  proselytizing, 78, 108, 120, 169, 172, 195n165, 220

religion (*continued*)
  resistance to, 41, 77, 111
  revivalism and religious services in camp, 40, 41, 43, 59–60, 78, 85, 98, 149, 159, 169, 172, 175–82
  schisms over slavery, 3, 186n8
  seminaries, 10, 11, 188n39, 233, 241
  submission and Christian deportment, 11, 40, 84, 191n90
Reynolds, Dr. Henry A., 173
Ricketts, Gen. James Brewerton, 78
Ripley, Thomas Baldwin, 104
Roberts, Albert D., 125, 133, 141, 144–45
Roberts, Charles Winslow, 87–88, 130
Roberts, Thomas A., 87–88, 93, 116, 133, 245
Robinson, Dr. William Chaffee, 56–57, 85
Ropes, Hannah Chandler, 4, 6, 8

Sampson, Sarah Smith, 19, 23, 149, 245–46
Sanitary Commission. *See* United States Sanitary Commission
Saxton, Gen. Rufus, 8
Scott, Sir Walter (Waverly novels), 93n, 215
Sedgwick, Gen. John, 146
Sewall, Frederick Dummer, 63, 69, 203
sexual vulnerability of women, 28, 43–45
Sharpless, Hattie R., 83, 112, 167
Shaw, Dr. Abner O., 164
Shaw, "Mother" Jane, 82, 109
Shaw, Sarah, 109, 117
Sherwood, Charles A., 182, 183
Shurtleff, Mrs., 116, 154
Sickles, Gen. Daniel Edgar, 121, 137
Skillins, Alfred, 102, 104–5
slavery, 3, 10–11, 46
  contraband community, 16, 34, 99, 173n
  controversy in Maine, 33
  escape of William and Ellen Craft, 17
  as morally and socially debilitating, 46–47
Slocum, Gen. Henry Warner, 75, 205–6
Smith, Adelaide W., 158–59, 160n, 161, 163–67, 170–71, 178n, 192n105, 246
Smith, Lewis B., 15, 106–7, 214, 246

Smith, Gen. William Farrar "Baldy," 104
Smith, Zemro A., 61, 174
Smithsonian Institution, 117
Snow, Edward A., 61, 67, 69, 110n
soldiers and soldier life, 19, 33
  and alcohol, 43, 55, 66, 77, 81, 88n, 176n, 179, 182, 184
  carpentry skills, 102, 165, 181
  casualties, 24–25, 81, 91–93, 146–47, 191n92, 211, 222
  conditions in camp and field, 14, 25, 26, 84, 199–200, 215
  disability discharges, 30, 75, 86, 108, 114, 115, 119, 123, 127, 129–34, 137, 172, 207, 219
  exposure and hunger, 61, 63, 67–68, 71, 75, 85, 96, 110–11, 148, 202, 206–8, 216
  honor, 20, 22
  kinfolk in camp, 70, 77, 113, 115, 158–59, 160, 166–68
  morale and morality, 20–21, 41, 42, 160
  recruitment and conscription, 18, 20, 76n
  temptations and vices, 15, 20, 43, 160
Spaulding, Miss, 129, 131–32, 135–37
Spaulding, Joseph Whitman, 43, 129, 133, 137, 147, 181
Spear, Ellis, 142, 246
Stanton, Edwin, 9
Stanwood, James H., 166, 171
Stearns, Amanda Akin, 56
Steiner, Dr. Lewis Henry, 68
Stevens, Greenlief T., 61, 124, 136, 147
stewards and quartermasters, 37, 43, 80, 88, 98–99, 109–10, 121–23, 137, 182, 191n85, 196n173, 202, 204, 206, 208
Stoneman, Gen. George, 137
Stout, Dr. Samuel, 6, 177
Strout, Mr., 170
Stuart, Gen. J. E. B., 63n
Sumner, Gen. Edwin Vose, 37, 86, 104, 106, 132, 209, 212–13
Sunderland, Rev. Byron, 59, 246
sutlers, 27, 61, 74–76, 152, 174

Tennyson, Alfred Lord, 140n
Terhune, Dr. Gilliam C., 156, 162, 164, 174, 177
Thomas, Albert F., 164, 168, 172, 176
Thompson, Emily, 84
Thurston, Charlie, 20, 190n69, 194n147, 196n173
Tibbets, Charles A. and Ira Franklin, 76, 84, 191n95
Tilden, Charles William, 99n, 102, 123, 212, 247
Tolman, Ellen Sarah Forbes, 65n, 175n, 185n1, 247
travel and transience, 5, 12, 14, 25
  ambulances, 26, 28, 56, 62, 70, 86–87, 94, 98, 115, 119, 130, 145, 164, 167, 209
  to City Point, 29, 151–53
  Eatons' trip to the South, 11, 46
  relief worker transport to/from relief locations, 7, 8, 23–24, 37–38, 55, 62–63, 67, 71, 74, 75, 81, 83, 86, 89, 104, 110–11, 123, 131, 137, 139, 141, 183–84, 190n65, 205
  See also nurses and nursing
Tripler, Dr. Charles, 28
Truell, Mr., 98–99, 106, 109, 124, 130–31
Twitchell, Adelbert Birge, 158, 180, 182, 303
Twitchell, William F., 39, 99, 124, 136, 147, 158

United States Christian Commission (USCC), 5, 7, 27, 36, 39, 41, 139, 158–59, 161, 164–65, 169, 170n, 171, 176, 181–2, 187n17
United States Sanitary Commission (USSC), 1, 4–7, 18, 22, 25–28, 68–69, 73, 79, 86n, 97, 112, 121, 158, 170n, 175, 183n, 187n17, 190n79, 191n97, 192n102, 201, 204–6, 208, 231
Usher, Rebecca, 21, 156n, 185n1, 188n35, 190n74, 192n104, 227

Vanderkieft, Dr. Bernard, 70
Vanderslice, Mrs., 160, 166–68
Varney, George, 91–91, 102–3, 106, 247
Vogeler, Dr. Edward, 169, 174

Waite, Henry H., 100, 102, 140–41, 304
Walker, Adeline, 84
Walker, Charles (of Yarmouth), 70, 97
Walker, Charles (of Portland), 97, 105
Warren, Dr. Francis G., 119, 130
Washburn, Gov. Israel, 21, 25, 191n96, 192n101
Washington, George, gravesite, 47
Waterhouse, Dr. Ai [*sic*] J., 135, 305
Watson, Leonard W., 66, 68–70, 85, 138, 183, 205, 208, 247
Welch, Norval E., 109n, 143n
Wescott, Dr. William W., 31, 88, 133, 248
Wevill, Dr. Richard Henry, 160, 169, 172, 174
White, John S., 88, 96–97
White, Mary J., 83, 102, 109
Whiting, Elizabeth, 82, 138
Whitman, William Edward Seaver, 175, 177, 248
Whitney, Mary Elizabeth and Samuel M., 44, 67, 82, 108, 160, 172, 248
Whittier, Edward Newton and George Williams, 12, 57–58, 89, 99, 124n, 125, 136, 139, 147–48, 178, 193n128, 199–200, 220, 222, 248
Whittier, Mary Webster, 12, 58, 64, 81–82, 87, 94, 100, 105, 106, 113, 117, 127–28, 137, 141, 148, 170, 199, 220, 248
Wiggin, Dr. Henry Love Keog, 31, 101
Wiley, Belle I., 120
Willets, Georgiana, 155n, 248–49
Wittenmyer, Annie Turner, 23
Wixom, Dr. Isaac, 31–32, 38–39, 105, 107–9, 111–12, 118, 120–21, 125, 127–32, 142–44, 149–50, 193n124, 249

Women's Central Relief Association (WCRA), 22, 190n79
Wood, Dr. R. C., 4
Woolsey, Georgeanna, 30
wounds and wounding, 47, 67–68, 69–70, 91–93, 146, 147, 154, 162–63, 171, 193n126, 199, 210, 211, 214, 221–23

Yonson, Mrs., 67–68, 71, 104

Zakrzewska, Dr. Marie, 7, 187n26

CPSIA information can be obtained at www.ICGtesting.com
Printed in the USA
BVOW020528231012

303710BV00002B/16/P

9 780199 899548